"Strong and Brave Fellows"

"Strong and Brave Fellows"

New Hampshire's Black Soldiers and Sailors of the American Revolution, 1775–1784

GLENN A. KNOBLOCK

McFarland & Company, Inc., Publishers
Jefferson, North Carolina, and London

LIBRARY OF CONGRESS CATALOGUING-IN-PUBLICATION DATA

Knoblock, Glenn A.
  "Strong and brave fellows" : New Hampshire's black soldiers and sailors of the American Revolution, 1775–1784 / Glenn A. Knoblock.
    p.   cm.
  Includes bibliographical references and index.

  ISBN-13: 978-0-7864-1548-9
  (softcover : 50# alkaline paper) ∞

  1. United States—History—Revolution, 1775–1783—Participation, African American.   2. New Hampshire—History—Revolution, 1775–1783—Participation, African American.   3. African American soldiers—New Hampshire—History—18th century.   4. African American sailors—New Hampshire—History—18th century.
  5. United States—History—Revolution, 1775–1783—Campaigns.
  6. United States—History—Revolution, 1775–1783—Registers.
  7. New Hampshire—History—Revolution, 1775–1783—Registers.
  8. African Americans—New Hampshire—Genealogy.   9. New Hampshire—Genealogy.   10. African Americans—New Hampshire—History—18th century.   I. Title.
  E269.N3K57   2003
  973.3'442'08996073—dc21   2003009936

British Library cataloguing data are available

©2003 Glenn A. Knoblock. All rights reserved

No part of this book may be reproduced or transmitted in any form or by any means, electronic or mechanical, including photocopying or recording, or by any information storage and retrieval system, without permission in writing from the publisher.

Cover illustration ©2002 Art Today

Manufactured in the United States of America

McFarland & Company, Inc., Publishers
  Box 611, Jefferson, North Carolina 28640
  www.mcfarlandpub.com

For Terry—
Simply the Best

Acknowledgments

Perhaps it was best stated in 1925 by Revolutionary War historian Allen French, when he wrote "no historian writes his book alone." This book fully demonstrates the accuracy of that statement.

First and foremost, I wish to thank my wife, Terry, for all her support and encouragement. Without it, this book could never have been completed. I also wish to thank my children, John and Anna, for their support, patience and understanding while their dad was at work.

No less encouraging were other members of my family. My father, William Knoblock, read portions of the manuscript and offered some helpful criticism, while my mother, Ceceilia Knoblock, was a willing companion during my attempts to locate the graves of several of New Hampshire's black soldiers. She also located and photographed the final resting place of soldier Cuff Chambers. My brothers-in-law also gave valuable assistance. David Wemmer provided expert computer assistance when it was sorely needed, and David Minnick was instrumental in organizing the book into manuscript form.

I would also like to thank my good friends, Ed Doherty and Kevin Roddy, for their help and encouragement. For their assistance in finding the final resting place of soldier Charles Bowles in Constable, New York, I am grateful. Ed also read the work as it was being written, and offered helpful criticism.

Not to be outdone, many local historians, both amateur and professional, rendered valuable assistance. Chief among them is Professor Emeritus Robert Dishman. Now retired from the University of New Hampshire, Bob is recognized in New Hampshire as an expert on slavery and slaveowners during the state's colonial period. He, too, has had an interest in New Hampshire's black soldiers of the Revolution, and did much research in the area. During my own research on the subject, I was given his name as a contact. We met periodically over several years, sharing information and ideas. We intended to one day write a book on the subject together. However, time and circumstances prevented us from doing so. Despite this, Bob willingly shared the results of his research, much of which is incorporated into this work. His pioneer work in identifying black soldiers by researching and identifying slave holders of northern New England, as well as his thorough research in state and county court records for information on black soldiers, has been invaluable.

Another historian who kindly shared his work was George Quintal, Jr., of Gardiner, Maine. His report for the National Park Service, *Patriots of Color*, helped identify several black soldiers from Massachusetts with ties to New Hampshire who are included in this work. George's work in identifying black soldiers who served at Lexington and Concord and at the Battle of Bunker Hill is exhaustive and will be available in book form in the near future.

For going above and beyond the duties of any town librarian, I am grateful to Tony Pikramenos of the Reading, Vermont, Public Library. He was most helpful in tracking down information on Silas Burdoo and his descendants. In a most timely and enthusiastic manner he also visited their final resting places and provided photographs that appear in these pages.

In addition to those listed above, the following individuals have given their kind assistance in one way or another, often unknowingly: Marjorie Carr, Valerie Cunningham, Daniel Daily, Captain Jeff Durell, Sergeant Clayton Emery, Laura Griggs, Bob Haas, Mary Hardy, Patricia Hoffman, Paul Hughes, Joan Knight, Tracy Martin, Nancy Merrill, Joyce Motchsman, T.J. Rand, Jane Rice, Marjorie Swain, Matthew Thomas, Don Wickman, Madeline Williamson, Professor Louis Wilson, and Virginia Wolfe.

The following institutions and their staffs have been most helpful: the Dover Public Library, the Portsmouth Public Library, the Exeter Public Library, Dimond Library at the University of New Hampshire (Durham), Rauner Library at Dartmouth College (Hanover), the Tuck Library at the New Hampshire Historical Society Museum (Concord), the Reading (VT) Public Library, the Woodstock (VT) Historical Society, the New Hampshire Division of Records Management and Archives (Concord), the Massachusetts Historical Society (Boston), the Museum of Fine Arts (Boston), and the Metropolitan Museum of Art (New York).

Finally, one of the great thrills I experienced during the writing of this work was my "term of service" in the 1st Newmarket Militia, 2nd New Hampshire Regiment, an excellent group devoted to reenacting the battles and encampments of the Revolutionary War. I learned and experienced history firsthand while working with its officers and NCOs. While ranging the grounds and ramparts of such legendary locales in American history as Fort Ticonderoga and the battlefield at Saratoga, I was able to understand, if only for a brief moment, what it meant to be a soldier in the war. Indeed, walking the grounds of Fort Ticonderoga late one moonlit night, I chanced to pass near the location of mass graves for American soldiers who died there. A palpable feeling that the spirits of these men, dead for over 225 years, were still on guard came to me and remains to this day. It may be that the biographies of some of these men are found within these very pages.

Glenn A. Knoblock
Dover, New Hampshire
Spring 2003

Contents

Acknowledgments	vii
Preface	1
Source Abbreviations	3
Introduction	5

I. Black Life in New Hampshire Before, During and After the Revolution

Pre-war Slavery in New Hampshire	7
Black Soldiers and the Continental Congress	11
Black Enlistment in New Hampshire	13
Service as Free Men	15
Service for Freedom	17
Service with No Freedom	18
Status as Soldiers	19
Service as Sailors	23
The Black Veteran and Pensioner	25
Blacks as Pioneer Settlers	29
Religion and the Black Veteran	30
Death and the Black Veteran	31
Descendants of Black Veterans	33
The Black Soldier as a Patriotic Symbol	35

II. Campaigns and Engagements

Introduction	41
The Battle of Lexington and Concord, April 19, 1775	41

The Battle of Bunker Hill, June 17, 1775	42
The Invasion of Canada, September 1775 to June 1776	43
New York City Campaign, September 15 to October 28, 1776	44
The Frigate *Raleigh*, May 1776 to September 1778	45
The Battle of Trenton, December 26, 1776	45
Fort Ticonderoga and the Battle of Hubbardton, July 1777	47
The Battle of Bennington, August 16, 1777	48
Victory at Saratoga, September 19 to October 17, 1777	49
Winter at Valley Forge, December 1777 to June 1778	51
The Sloop of War *Ranger*, May 1777 to May 1780	53
The Battle of Monmouth, June 1778	53
Continental Service, July 1778 to May 1779	55
The Battle of Rhode Island, August 29, 1778	56
Sullivan's Campaign Against the Six Nations, June to October 1779	57
Militia Service, 1779	58
Continental and Militia Service, 1780	59
New York City and the Siege of Yorktown, 1781	60
Additional Continental and Militia Service, 1781	62
Final Continental Service, 1782 to 1784	64

III. The Men

Introduction	67
New Hampshire Soldiers	74
Soldiers with Service to New Hampshire and Other Colonies	193
Soldiers from New Hampshire Who Served for Other Colonies	243
Appendix 1: Black Soldiers Who Died During the War	311
Appendix 2: Breakdown by Regiment of Black Soldiers Who Served for New Hampshire	312
Appendix 3: Black Soldiers Before the Revolution	313
Appendix 4: Black Place Names and Locales in New Hampshire	315
Bibliography	317
Index	327

Preface

Just as the fighting in the American Revolution lasted seven long years, so, too, did the writing of this book. My sole focus has been a thorough search of New Hampshire records and related works for information on her black soldiers. The work before you is the result of this effort. I have made no such search of other states' records. Thus, it may be that the full stories of the men, and their extended families, whose biographies are contained herein, have yet to be told. Although this work will undoubtedly be classified as a work of genealogy, this is only a beneficial sidelight of my real intent: to give a full and personal account of the role black soldiers played in serving New Hampshire during the American Revolution. By learning how some of these men lived both before and after the war we can gain a better understanding of what it meant to be a black man in New Hampshire during a critical phase of American history. In addition, the stories contained in these pages for such men as Robert Randall, Jude Hall, and a host of others make for exciting reading and help give further flesh to that mythic American figure known as "a soldier of the Revolution."

Albert Annett and Alice Lehtinen, historians of Jaffrey, New Hampshire, describing that town's black population, once wrote that "the earth closed over them like the waters over one lost at sea." And so it has been, seemingly, with New Hampshire's black soldiers of the American Revolution. It is my hope that this book helps to part these waters and reveal the true depth of these soldiers' contribution to America's fight for independence.

Source Abbreviations

A list of sources follows each biographical entry in this book. The source listings generally include abbreviations keying specific sources to specific entries in the bibliography. A few frequently cited sources, such as the New Hampshire Revolutionary War Rolls, are also abbreviated in the source listings. Abbreviations are as follows:

CEN	Federal Census Records
CH	County Histories of New Hampshire
GSP	Genealogical and Societal Publications
MSS	Published rolls of Massachusetts Soldiers and Sailors of the Revolution
NA	National Archives Materials
NEHGR	New England Historical and Genealogical Record
NEW	Period Newspapers
NHGR	New Hampshire Genealogical Record
NHRWR . . .	Published New Hampshire Revolutionary War Rolls
NHSP	New Hampshire State Papers
NSDAR	National Society, Daughters of the American Revolution
OPS	Other Published Sources
PEN	United States Pension Records
PSR	Published State Records
RCR	Rockingham County, New Hampshire Records
TH	Town Histories
TR	Town Records
US	Unpublished Sources

Introduction

New Hampshire, despite her small size, played a sizable role in the American Revolution. The deeds of New Hampshire men, soldiers and statesmen, on and off the field, have been well documented. However, one aspect of New Hampshire's Revolutionary War history has yet to be examined in full. This is the contribution of her black soldiers, and the role they played in manning New Hampshire regiments. Although several books have been written on the black soldier during the American Revolution, none focuses on New Hampshire. Benjamin Quarles's *The Negro in the American Revolution*, originally published in 1961, is still the definitive work on the subject, but gives New Hampshire's blacks only brief mention. Rhode Island, the center of the slave trade in New England, organized an all black regiment, the 1st Rhode Island, in early 1778, and Connecticut and Massachusetts both had regiments that formed all black companies toward the end of the war. The 2nd Company of the 4th Connecticut regiment was established in 1781, while Massachusetts had "the black company" (GSP-NSDAR-Mass., pg. 2) commanded by Capt. Matthew Chambers in the 6th Massachusetts regiment. Though New Hampshire never formed such a unit, a surprising number of black soldiers served the state throughout the entire course of the war. Their contributions and successes were substantial and are well worthy of study.

There are several reasons why the story of New Hampshire's black soldiers should be told. Most significantly, it is an interesting and enlightening one. Their length of service and achievements varied greatly, but many blacks were accomplished soldiers who served long terms and participated in rigorous campaigns. Some black soldiers, like their white counterparts, served valiantly during the entire course of the war from 1775 to 1783. In doing so they helped insure a successful outcome for American independence, even while their own personal liberty was not so assured. Slavery in the North was effectively dead after the Revolution, but it would take another 80 years, and hard fighting by a later generation of black soldiers, until the issue of slavery was settled once and for all.

The second reason for telling the story of New Hampshire's black soldiers during the Revolution was best expressed by black historian William C. Nell, who wrote, in 1855, that it "may rescue many gallant names from oblivion" (OPS-Nell, pg. 9). This is, perhaps, the best reason of all. The largest and most important part of this work is the service records of all known black soldiers with ties to New Hampshire. It includes the records of 139 men who served in New Hampshire forces, 34 who served in both New Hampshire's and another state's forces, and 51 men who served in the forces of other colonies but lived in New Hampshire at some point in their lives. Preceding this is material regarding official policies on black enlistment and the varying circumstances under which black soldiers served, as well as an account of the campaigns and battles in which New Hampshire's forces were involved. Although the contribution of New Hampshire's soldiers to the war effort has been recognized in an overall fashion, there has been little knowledge, or recognition, of the role black soldiers played in manning her state regiments. The recognition they deserve is overdue, and it seems especially fitting to remember these men, whose great desire to fight for a homeland they were, at least in the beginning, forced to call their own, resulted in a share of the glory of newfound freedom.

I. Black Life in New Hampshire Before, During and After the Revolution

Pre-war Slavery in New Hampshire

Although slavery was not widely practiced in New Hampshire, the fact that it existed at all must be recognized to its full extent. The widely held notion, perpetuated by many town historians and still somewhat prevalent today, that slavery in the small New England states, such as New Hampshire, was a kinder, more benevolent (acceptable?) version than what existed in the South, is patently false. Because slavery in New Hampshire was not based on large-scale agricultural production, fewer slaves were brought here than in the Southern states. Because slaves in New Hampshire were often owned by prominent citizens, such as town ministers, they were often well-fed and educated. However, the act of enslaving an individual, no matter where one was located, produced harsh conditions and life-altering consequences. Despite the assertion by one historian that "Fortunately, Portsmouth had no part in the slave trade" (OPS-Shipton, vol. 12, pg. 384), both that town, and the state as a whole, were engaged in the buying, selling, and leasing of slaves on a regular basis. This is amply demonstrated by advertisements that appeared regularly in local newspapers.

There is no accurate count of the number of slaves held in New Hampshire during the entire Colonial period. However, at any given time it was probably under 1,000 individuals. By the time the war began in 1775, there were fewer than 700 statewide.

> *This* **DAY**
> TO BE SOLD,
> At Public Vendue,
> At the House of Capt. James Stoodly Innholder in Portsmouth, at Two o'Clock Afternoon, ONE Negro MAN about 20 Years of Age, has been with the English about Two Years; One Negro Girl about 17 Years Old: About Ten Tun of Lignumvitia, in Lotts of one Tun each: One Piece of new 9 Inch Cable, about 30 Fathom; one Piece of 8 Inch Dit. about 15 Fathom; and a Parcel of Cordage which has been Cutt: A few Hogsheads of West-India Rum: Likewise some Mucovado Sugar in Hogsheads, and a few Baggs of Cotton Wool.——Conditions of Sale to be seen at Time and Place of Sale.

Advertisement for the sale of a "Negro Man" and a "Negro Girl." Slaves were regularly bought and sold on the New Hampshire Seacoast, despite statements to the contrary by some historians. Here, several slaves are sold, along with other goods, at the house of Captain James Stoodly. *New Hampshire Gazette,* May 1, 1767. Courtesy Portsmouth Public Library.

One way a slave could express his displeasure with his overall condition or treatment was to run away from his master. Surprisingly, this happened quite frequently in New Hampshire in the years preceding the American Revolution. Among the black soldiers during the war who ran away when they were slaves were Jude Hall (1775), Primas Coffin (1768), Oliver French, Peter Long, and Cato Moulton (all 1775). Undeterred, masters anxious to recover their property often advertised their runaway slaves in the newspaper, offering a reward for their return and paying the expenses involved in their capture. Even after the American Revolution began, some slaves were denied their freedom and went to war with their masters. While some slaves, like Prince Whipple (Portsmouth), saw active duty and were later freed for their service, others, like Cato Dearing (Portsmouth), saw it as an opportunity to run away, and did just that.

The reasons for slaves running away were numerous and varied. Their overall position in life as slaves may have been one reason, but others with more immediate import also existed. Corporal punishment was likely one such reason. Though little documented, slaves in New Hampshire did suffer beatings, whippings, branding, and were even killed by their masters. Such events were not condoned, or even the norm, but isolated occurrences have been recorded. One example is that of Asa Porter of Haverhill. A wealthy man in town who served as a court judge and a militia officer, he once decided to punish one of his slaves, a Negro girl, by whipping her. In order to keep her from running away and in reach of his whip, he tied a rope around her body and secured it to his own. When he started to flog

> RANAWAY from FORT WASHINGTON, Cato Dearing, a Negro Man, belonging to Capt. Dealing of Portsmouth; he was about Forty Years old, about five Feet Six Inches tall, thick set; had on a gray Jacket, and Leather Breeches, blue Yarn Stockings. Whoever will take up said Negro Man, and return him to Capt. TITUS SALTER shall receive Thirty Shillings Lawful Money, and all necessary Charges paid by me
> July &c. 1777   TITUS SALTER, Capt.

Runaway slave ad for Cato Dearing. This ad is unusual in that it is one of only a few such ads found for slaves who ran away while their masters were in the service. All that is known about Cato is detailed in this brief ad. *New Hampshire Gazette*, July 26, 1777. Courtesy Portsmouth Public Library.

the girl, however, she ran straight toward the Connecticut River, dragging her master with her. Porter is said to have later remarked, "I imagined the creature would drown me" (TH-Bittinger, pg. 84). This story seems humorous at first glance, but it seems likely that Porter probably followed through with his serious intention to administer a whipping to his slave girl. It is much to New Hampshire's credit that it was the only New England colony to enact a law forbidding cruel treatment of slaves. Passed on May 13, 1718, it provided that "any master convicted of maiming or otherwise cruelly treating his servant was not only required to free him, but also to compensate him as the court might adjudge" (OPS-Greene, pgs. 233–34). Section two of this law also provided the death penalty for any person "who shall willfully kill his ... negro servant" (Greene, pg. 234). Despite this advanced legislation, which may have acted as a deterrent for such behavior, there are no records indicating its strict enforcement.

Another reason that slaves often ran away was the instability that existed in their life. It is possible that some slaves may have been content if they were owned by families who treated them well and regarded them, almost, as a member of their families. However, those slaves who were continually bought and sold, or hired out to perform work for others, often led very unhappy lives. Not only were they challenged by the demands of various masters, but they had the added disadvantage of no stable home and living area, and the frequent separation from friends and family, both within the slave community and their masters' families. When Tom, the Negro servant of Portsmouth merchant John Wendell, ran away in May 1772, he headed toward Boston and was later captured there. Wendell's uncle, Edmund Quincy, talked to Tom during his confinement in the "gaol at Boston," and explained that Tom "means honestly to return home if you

> RAN AWAY on the evening of the 29th inft. a NEGRO MAN, named Seneca, about five feet eight inches high, 47 years of age ; a ftout thick fett fellow, talks good Englifh ; he carried with him two coats, one red the other blue ; one blue pea Jacket ; one brown lappell'd, and one ftrip'd homefpun dit. 2 pair leather breeches ; 2 pair worfted, and 2 pair yarn ftockings ; 2 pair fhoes ; a mill'd cap turn'd up with fur,&c. Whoever will return faid Negro, or confine him fo that his mafter may have him again, fhall have FOUR DOLLARS reward, and all neceffary charges paid by SAMUEL HALL.
> Portfmouth, May 31ft.   2—4

Runaway slave ad, *New Hampshire Gazette*, June 1, 1776. A typical period ad of this type. Seneca Hall was eventually returned to bondage, since he was one of 20 Portsmouth slaves to petition the New Hampshire government for their freedom in 1779. Courtesy Portsmouth Public Library.

have altered your mind touching his changing masters ... he says he suddenly left you thinking some person here (Boston) might be likely to buy him, and here chose to be if parted from you." Quincy gave further advice about Tom and Wendell's options, commenting that slavery "begins to be more and more disagreeable to the people of this continent, particularly to the Northward, where Liberty, in its most genuine and proper idea, runs so high" (*Proceedings of the American Antiquarian Society*, vol. XXXV, pg. 249).

The era of the American Revolution helped to hasten the end of slavery in the North, even though it was never officially abolished in New Hampshire. Although black soldiers were accepted with some reservations when the war first began, practical considerations soon came to the front and, ultimately, their service became commonplace and beneficial to all concerned. It is rather ironic that many slaves gained their freedom by enlisting with the local muster-master, while those slaves who tried to gain freedom through the political process were ignored. Twenty Portsmouth slaves petitioned the state legislature on November 12, 1779, asking to be freed in a most eloquent address, stating, in part, "That the God of nature gave them life and freedom, upon the terms of most perfect equality with other men" (OPS-Upton, pg. 215). Among the signers of this petition were black soldier Prince Whipple, and a former runaway slave named Seneca Hall. A hearing on this petition was granted by the House of Representatives on June 9, 1780, but was tabled without further discussion on the question of emancipation. Thus, it was on the field of battle that New Hampshire's black soldiers, many of whom were slaves, were able to make their case for freedom and respect.

Black Soldiers and the Continental Congress

When the war began in April of 1775 at Lexington and Concord, many men, black and white, answered the call to arms, and soon the beginnings of what was to be the Continental Army, commanded by Gen. George Washington, was formed. The army initially consisted of New England troops, with regiments being recruited and organized on a state-by-state basis. At this time, there was no policy, official or otherwise, on the enlistment of blacks as soldiers, whether free or slave. As a result, many blacks were accepted into service to participate in the Siege of Boston. It was not until June 14, 1775, just days before the Battle of Bunker Hill, that the Continental Congress, at the urging of the New England states, created a national force by adopting "the American continental army" (OPS-Wright, pg. 23). In addition to accepting responsibility for the New England troops, Congress also authorized the raising of 10 companies of riflemen, requested for protection of key points in New York, and appointed a committee to draft rules and regulations for the new army. The following day, June 15th, Congress unanimously chose George Washington of Virginia as commander of the Continental Army. With the addition of rifle companies from Virginia, Maryland, and Pennsylvania, many of them composed of unruly frontiersmen, and the advent of control over the army, still largely New Englanders, by the Continental Congress, problems soon arose for black soldiers. As early as July 10, 1775, Adj. Gen. Horatio Gates issued orders to recruiting officers not to enlist, among others, "any deserter from the Ministerial Army, nor any stroller, negro, or vagabond" (OPS-Quarles, pg. 15).

Reaction to blacks in the service was decidedly prejudiced. John Adams, Massachusetts' own delegate to Congress, wrote "in alarm" from Philadelphia in October of 1775, stating that many of the soldiers were reported to be "boys, old men, and negroes" (OPS-Quarles, pg. 16). He also wondered how their numbers compared to that of New Hampshire and the other New England states. The service of blacks was especially troublesome and offensive to soldiers from outside New England. Alexander Graydon, a white officer from Philadelphia, commented favorably on Col. John Glover's Marblehead, Massachusetts, regiment, but also noted the number of blacks in its ranks. He further commented that the mixing of black and white soldiers had "a disagreeable, degrading effect" on "persons unaccustomed to such associations" (OPS-Quarles, pg. 72). Southern states, especially, were unwilling to consider the option of arming blacks to reinforce the military. Although they had a fear of a mass uprising of slaves against their masters should they be armed, it is interesting to note that this never happened with slaves and free blacks in the North, admittedly a much smaller number than in the South, that served in the military. In fact, there is only a hint of one trouble of this kind that occurred in the North during the war. The Marquis de Lafayette alludes to a plot in a letter he wrote, dated March 11, 1778, from Albany, New York, to Henry Laurens, the prominent South Carolina patriot who was then the president of the Continental Congress. He states that he had received an anonymous letter detailing a plot by slaves and soldiers to burn the city of Albany and "that many officers and gentlemen were to be assassinated by their own nigroes" (OPS-Aptheker, *American Negro Slave Revolts*, pgs. 205–6). Whether the letter to Lafayette was a hoax or not is unknown, but no such plot was ever carried out. Even as the war progressed and the need for soldiers continued unabated, officers outside New England were less than enthusiastic about the use of blacks. In early 1777, with the threat of a British invasion looming large, the commander at Fort Ticonderoga, Gen. Anthony Wayne of Pennsylvania, gloomily reported that "at least one third of the Troops now on the Ground are composed of Negroes, Indians, and Children," and stated that it was a "melancholy Reflection that we should be necessitated to Retain Indians and Negroes in our Ranks" (OPS-Ketchum, pg. 44). Indeed, continued statements like this "galled" New England leaders and it didn't help cooperation between the states when Gen. Philip Schuyler, the commander of the Northern Army, echoed Wayne's sentiments by describing New England soldiers as "old men, Boys, & negroes ... unfit for garrison duty" (OPS-Ketchum, pg. 253).

In the first year of the war, Congress continued to deal with the issue of black troops in a halting manner. On September 26, 1775, it rejected a resolution by Edward Rutledge of South Carolina requiring the discharge of all Negroes in the army, both free and slave. Several weeks later, on October 8, a council of war at Cambridge, Massachusetts, held by eight generals regarding the Siege of Boston, agreed to exclude from enlisting both free blacks and slaves. On October 31, the quartermaster general was directed to supply clothes to all who would re-enlist, "negroes excepted, which the Congress do not incline to list again" (OPS-Quarles, pg. 15).

Despite the mixed messages from Congress regarding black troops, Washington ordered his recruiting officers to enlist free blacks in an order dated December 30, 1775. This was a result not only of discontent among black troops, who Washington, writing to John Hancock, pointed out were "dissatisfied at being discarded" (OPS-Quarles, pg. 16), but was also due to a critical shortage of troops to man the siege lines around Boston. Many of these men planned to depart for home on January 1, 1776, unwilling to serve any further. On January 16, 1776, reacting to a letter by Washington,

Congress recommended that free blacks who had already served be reenlisted, but none other. The exclusion of slave enlistment was reaffirmed by a military order dated February 21, 1776 (*ibid.*).

Black Enlistment in New Hampshire

When the war began in 1775, blacks in New Hampshire responded in similar fashion to whites and answered the call to arms. At the time, there were 626 slaves in New Hampshire, 533 of whom resided in the Seacoast in Rockingham and Strafford counties. While New Hampshire had a law on the books, dating from 1719, prohibiting the service of blacks in the state militia, it appears not to have been strictly enforced. Throughout New Hampshire, reaction to black enlistment was mixed. Although Aaron Oliver and Ezra Fuller, both free black men of New Ipswich, were accepted into Capt. Ezra Towne's company of soldiers without hesitation during the Lexington alarm in April 1775, the same could not be said for Robert Miller, a free black of Kensington. When he attempted to enlist in Capt. Winthrop Rowe's company, it was contingent on whether or "if the committee will accept him" (PSR-NHRWR, vol. 1, pg. 111). Miller was ultimately accepted for service, but similar reservations to their enlistment were experienced by other blacks. Despite this, during the first year of the war, many New Hampshire blacks enlisted and did good service, both during the Siege of Boston, and the Battle of Bunker Hill.

On January 16, 1776, a congressional resolution approved Gen. Washington's action regarding the enlistment of free blacks, stating that "The free negroes who have served faithfully in the Army at Cambridge may be re-enlisted, but no others" (GSP-NSDAR-Massachusetts, pg. 2). New Hampshire, however, apparently contradicted this when, on April 12, 1776, the Committee of Safety requested that all males above the age of 21 sign a declaration, known as the Association Test, pledging themselves to oppose British hostilities with arms, "lunatics, idiots, and Negroes" (OPS-Quarles, pg. 17) being excepted. Despite this prohibition, a revival of the old 1719 law in part, some blacks were allowed to sign the Association Test by their communities, including George Blanchard (Wilton) and Wentworth Cheswill (Newmarket). Six months later, the state legislature barred Indians and Negroes from serving in the state forces. This law was never enforced when it became apparent that the war was to be a long and hard fought affair, and that it would be difficult to raise an all volunteer force. Laws in New Hampshire and other New England states may have prohibited the enrollment of blacks but, in many cases, on the local level "muster masters calmly ignored the law" (OPS-Quarles, pg. 52). In 1777, with the passage of the Eighty-Eight Battalion Resolve by Congress, each state, New Hampshire included, had a troop quota to fill. At this time that the use of blacks as soldiers gained many supporters, and many towns appointed committees to hire men, both black and white, to enlist. In the end, the enlistment of black soldiers in New Hampshire caused little controversy or concern, mainly because "slavery was never a widely prevalent institution in the state" (OPS-Upton, pg. 214). This was in direct contrast to the situations in Massachusetts and Connecticut, where Negro recruitment became a public issue. New Hampshire passed its first draft law on January 18, 1777, which provided that whenever voluntary enlistments failed to fill the state's quota, the colonels of each militia district were empowered to draft men from towns in their district to complete the quota. Many of the men who were so drafted legally avoided military service by hiring substitutes. Caesar Lear, a black slave of Tobias Lear of Portsmouth, was hired out by his master for naval service. However, three blacks, George Blanchard (Wilton), Anthony Boston (Boscawen), and Jonathan Miller (Hampton Falls), are also known to have hired out substitutes to serve in their places. While Blanchard and Miller hired white men as substitutes, Boston is the only black soldier known to have found another black soldier to serve in his place.

Black enlistees in New Hampshire, whether slave or free, received the same bounty, or pay, as whites. However, according to the Reverend Jeremiah Belknap, often the bounty paid to slaves "their masters received as the price of their liberty, and then delivered up their bills of sale, and gave them a certificate of manumission. Several of these bills and certificates were deposited in my hands; and those who survived the three years' service were free" (OPS-Nell, pg. 121). Two such soldiers who enlisted and were freed in this manner were Cato Baker and Gloster Watson. While the amount varied by town, the average bounty was around £10 per enlistment. This was supplemented by a state bounty of £10 upon enlistment, 18 shillings paid annually, and 20 shillings paid semi-annually. In addition to these town and state bounties, the Continental Congress offered a bounty of $20, 100 acres of land, and a suit of clothes. Despite these seemingly high rewards, raising troops became more difficult as the war dragged on and the currency depreciated.

The terms of service for New Hampshire troops, black and white, varied greatly. Militia service might run anywhere from mere days to a period of several months, or more. Continental service was generally for the term of three years or "during the war." The later phrase was ambiguous and often a source of later contention between enlisted men, who took it

> Dover June 4th 1777
>
> This may certify all Persons that I Thomas Watson as administrator to the Estate of my Father Dudley Watson deceased do hereby give the within named Ned Glouster his freedom & discharge him from the Service of the heirs of said Estate forever
>
> Witness Jeremy Belknap
>
> Thos. Watson

Manumission document for Gloster Watson. Watson, a soldier in the war, was freed by his late master's son on June 4, 1777, likely due to the influence of the Reverend Jeremy Belknap of Dover. After his military service, Gloster Watson returned to Dover where he lived the rest of his life. Jeremy Belknap Papers, 161.D.95. Courtesy Massachusetts Historical Society.

to mean three years, and their officers, who often took the phrase "during war" quite literally. As a result, many disputes in this area arose for all soldiers, sometimes resulting in unwarranted charges of desertion. Those soldiers who did serve shorter terms often re-enlisted almost immediately, usually in the same regiment and company without an interruption in service. This enabled them to collect another bounty payment for continued service. Later in the war, when men were harder to recruit, the terms of enlistment fell, in 1777-78 to eight and nine-month periods, and by 1780-81 many enlistments were for six-month terms. Despite these varying terms, many blacks in New Hampshire served consecutive terms of enlistment which, for some, meant serving for nearly the entire war. Jude Hall (Kensington) served during the entire war from 1775 to 1783, as did Reuben Roberts (Newmarket). An examination of the available records shows that black soldiers, regarding pay and terms of service, received the same treatment as white soldiers in the same situation. Black enlistment truly was a non-issue in New Hampshire.

Service as Free Men

Records are usually vague as to whether or not a black soldier was free at the time of his enlistment. Of the 221 black soldiers associated with New Hampshire, only a small number can be readily identified in the surviving records as free men. The actual number of free men who enlisted, however, is probably much higher. Those men who can be identified as

> *This paper belongs to Cato, late servant to Otis Baker — but now Free*
>
> *Rec'd June 4th 1777*

Manumission document for Cato Baker. Baker was freed by his master on June 4, 1777, under the influence of prominent Dover clergyman Jeremy Belknap. Soon after, Cato joined the army, corresponding with both Belknap and his former master. Jeremy Belknap Papers, 161.D.92. Courtesy Massachusetts Historical society.

free men before their service, and the towns they came from, are as follows; George Blanchard (Wilton), Peter Brown (Temple), Scipio Brown (Kingston), Wentworth Cheswill (Newmarket), Castor Dickinson (Dunstable), Ezra Fuller (Temple), Elisha Hubbard (New Ipswich), Scippio Martin (Durham), Robert Miller (Kensington), Jonathan Miller (Hampton Falls), Aaron Oliver (Temple), Asa Perham (New Ipswich), Reuben Roberts (Newmarket), Isaac Tatten and Isaac Tatten, Jr. (Lempster), and Ichabod Twilight (Sandown).

Equally difficult to ascertain is whether or not a slave was freed specifically to serve in the war. One such example is that of Peter Stearns of Epping. It is said that his master, the Reverend Josiah Stearns, "felt the inconsistency of holding a fellow being in legal bondage while thus struggling for national independence, and pronounced him henceforth free, whereupon Peter, in company with his master's sons, shouldered his musket and did good service in the common cause as a freeman" (CH-Hurd, Rockingham, pg. 229).

Another example of a slave freed so he could enlist is that of Cato Baker of Dover, who was freed by his master, Col. Otis Baker, in June 1777. Soon after, Cato enlisted in the 2nd New Hampshire regiment for a term of three years. Other examples of blacks given their freedom just prior to enlisting include Seco Barnard (Hopkinton), Corydon Chesley (Dover), Tobias Cutler (Rindge), Cato Fiske (Epping), Richard Hunking (Barrington), Dan Martin (Durham), and Gloster Watson (Dover). It is interesting to note that three of these men were from Dover and were freed, no doubt, by the influence of the Reverend Jeremy Belknap and his strong anti-slavery sentiment. In a sermon preached at Dover in July 1774, he declared that "would it not be astonishing to hear that a people who are contending so earnestly for liberty are not willing to allow liberty to others? Is it not astonishing to think that, at this day, there are in the several colonies upon this continent some thousands of men, women, and children in bondage and slavery for no other reason than that their skin is of a darker color than our own? Such is the inconsistency of our conduct" (OPS-Upton, pg. 214–5). The impact of Belknap's preaching was a slow, but steady, erosion of the institution of slavery in Dover. In 1767 the town had 28 slaves, 19 male and 9 female, out of a total population of 1,614. In 1775, this number was down to 26 "slaves for life," out of a population of 1,666. The number of 26 slaves was further reduced in 1777 with the manumission of Baker, Watson, and Chesley.

Service for Freedom

In addition to those slaves who were freed in order to serve in the military, a number of men gained their freedom after they had enlisted and served out their terms. Once again, while it is impossible to ascertain the true number of slaves who gained their freedom in this manner, at least 12 can be identified as doing so. This freedom was gained in several different ways. Some slaves enlisted to serve in their owners' places as substitutes. Salem Colby (Concord) was freed for doing "good service" (TH-Bouton, pg. 252), while Sampson Moore (Canterbury) enlisted with the promise that, if he did "good fighting" (OPS-Potter, pg. 335n), he would be freed. His owner, Col. Archelaus Moore, kept his promise, giving Sampson, in addition, 100 acres of land. Other men, like Prince Whipple (Portsmouth), the slave of Gen. William Whipple, Oxford Tash (Newmarket), the slave of Col. Thomas Tash, and Paul and Prince Jenness (Rye), slaves of Job Jenness, enlisted to serve alongside their masters and gained their freedom afterwards. In such cases as this, their master likely received the bounty money due them for enlisting, possibly with the promise that it would be given to them at war's end. Several men, including Ezra Fuller (Temple) and Peter Stearns (Epping), enlisted along with their masters' sons, no doubt with the intent not only to serve, but to protect as well.

Finally, some men bought their freedom with the bounty money they received for enlisting. Although the records are generally silent on this matter, a few men are identifiable as receiving their freedom in this way. Records involving disputes between slave owners and towns over the payment of bounty money are most interesting in this regard. The town of Somersworth "treated" with "Madame" Wallingford "respecting her Negro man," resulting in a decision to pay Cato Wallingford the town bounty of 15 pounds (TR-Somersworth, vol. 1, pgs. 463, 655). It is likely that "Madame" Wallingford received or retained the Continental and state bounties due for Cato's enlistment.

Service with No Freedom

Although many slaves gained their freedom as a result of the Revolutionary War, both due to matters of conscience and because of military service, some fought in the war without gaining their freedom. The number of slaves who fall into this category is hard to determine. The number of slaves listed in the Federal Census for New Hampshire in 1790 is quite small in comparison to the number of free non-whites listed, which may lead one to conclude that most minorities who were previously slaves (blacks and "Indians") were now free. However, this may be misleading. The accuracy of the 1790 Federal Census regarding slaves may be called into question. One anecdote about the taking of the census in Massachusetts relates that when a census taker inquired about slaves, most people answered that they had none — if any said that they did, the official would tell them that no one else had reported having slaves, and did they mean to be "singular," whereupon they changed their answers, listing their slaves, presumably, as "free non-white" people instead (OPS-Belknap, pg. 165). It is impossible to determine how widespread such falsification was, but there can be no doubt that such political correctness was not unusual. After all, the war had just ended in the not too distant past, and the incongruity of holding slaves, while living in a newly established, free republic could not have been lost on the minds of New England slave holders.

An interesting take on slavery in New Hampshire, and the nation as a whole, in the decade or so after the war ended is offered in the pamphlet *Tyrannical Libertymen — A Discourse Upon Negro-Slavery in the United States*. The work, which was composed in New Hampshire and published at Hanover in 1795, is a scathing indictment of the institution of slavery. In referring to the small number of slaves found in New Hampshire at the 1790 Census, the author declares that "They might indeed be free.... But to our disgrace, they are and ought to be considered slaves, till government shall take effectual measures, as their guardians, to see, that they are in fact free; and till, for the sake of example, their freedom shall be made known to the world" (OPS-Fisk, pg. 4). The author goes on to refute the various arguments of the day in support of slavery, and even supports the establishment of a Negro state in "our new territories" and advocates that they "in due time, have a voice in Congress" (OPS-Fisk, pg. 10). In closing his argument, one of the author's final appeals asks, "When will Americans show, that they are, what they affect to be thought, friends to the cause of humanity at large, reverers of the rights of their fellow creatures?" (OPS-Fisk, pg. 15).

Despite the fact that slavery was on the decline in New Hampshire, there are several examples of slaves who served during the war, yet did not gain their freedom. One of these was Thomas Dunkin, a slave of John Dunkin of Grantham. Thomas Dunkin enlisted in 1777 for a term of three years in the 1st New Hampshire Regiment. Despite his service, he is still listed as a slave as late as 1798. Another example is that of Caesar Wood, of Stratham. He was the slave of Capt. George March, a Tory. He enlisted for three years in 1781, in the Second New Hampshire Regiment, and served until 1784. He died shortly after his service ended, in 1785. Perhaps the most striking example of a case where freedom was denied for a black soldier was that of Peter Bartlett, the slave of Josiah Bartlett of Kingston. Bartlett, one of New Hampshire's signers of the Declaration of Independence, was still a slave holder in 1800. Although many slaves did not gain their freedom, their reasons for serving in the war were much the same as those of the white soldier. Patriotism, a desire to defend hearth and home, and a chance for adventure were all compelling reasons to serve. As one historian states, "As an American soldier, the Negro proved to be much like his fellows. His morale was likely to be above average. Military service was a step up in life for him, and active campaigning was often no more arduous, and certainly more exciting" (OPS-Quarles, pg. 198).

Status as Soldiers

Once they were enlisted in the army, what was the role of the black soldier? The common perception that blacks served mainly in such subordinate positions as waiters or servants to officers who were often their masters, or as wagon drivers, is inaccurate. Some blacks did serve in such capacities, but the majority served as regular soldiers, on the same footing as their white counterparts. Jack Diamond (Epping), and William Small, Jr. (Amherst) both served as waiters to officers, but it is also important to note that there are examples of white men who filled such positions. Black soldiers saw service in all areas of the army and, as far as is known, performed the same tasks as white soldiers. Cato Tufts (Londonderry) served as a matross (gunner) in the artillery, while London Dow (Hanover), Primas Chandler (Amherst), Stephen Lovewell (Litchfield), and Prime Wheeler (New Ipswich), among others, served as rangers. Other men served as fifers and drummers. Among those identified as fifers are Peter Abbott (Kingston), William Davison (Portsmouth), Cato Fisk (Epping), Cato Moulton (Hampton), and Barzillai Lew (Hollis). Cato Fisk also did duty as a drummer. Musical positions like these were very important ones. Their lively music not only kept the men in rhythm and step during marches and military maneuvers, but it also kept morale high and helped develop an esprit de corps. Once again, white soldiers also filled these positions. Finally, one man, the afore-mentioned Barzillai Lew, was important in that he may have been leader of a small partisan group during the war, conducting guerrilla raids, and John Cook (Pembroke) served for a short time as a hospital attendant, or orderly, helping to tend sick soldiers at Valley Forge.

As might be expected, no blacks served as commissioned officers. However, there are records of two men, both from New Ipswich, who served as non-commissioned officers. Elisha Hubbard served as a sergeant, while Nathan Weston served as a corporal. Men who held such ranks would have had the respect of both the officers they served under, and the men they commanded. Traditional then as it is now, non-commissioned officers are the backbone of any army and are the men who make sure that orders from above get carried out. In addition to acting as non-commissioned officers, at least one man, Prince Whipple (Portsmouth), served as an aide, of sorts, to an officer. Prince was the slave of Gen. William Whipple. Although he served as a servant to his master, Prince was very much trusted by Gen. Whipple and no doubt served in other capacities, including as an aide and as a bodyguard.

Due to the fairly small number of black soldiers, New Hampshire never had an all-black unit. The closest unit of this type was probably the 5th company of the 2nd New Hampshire regiment, commanded by Capt. John Drew of Barrington. Of the 37 men in his company, five of them, about 14 percent of the total, are known to have been blacks. These men were Cato Baker, Corydon Chesley, and Gloster Watson, all of Dover, and Richard Hunking and Zach Kelsey, both of Barrington. Captain Drew himself was a former slave owner. As to the question of discrimination, and how black soldiers were treated by their white counterparts, the records are generally silent. On one hand, one would like to think that black soldiers were treated like comrades in arms and shared the unique bond that all soldiers experience in combat situations. The prospect of facing death on a daily basis is often a great equalizer and cuts across racial lines, often resulting in strong friendships that last a lifetime. One example of this is found in military pension records, where there are many instances of white soldiers who attest to the service of their fellow soldiers who were black in an effort to help them get the pensions they deserved.

Unfortunately, despite their service, black soldiers still experienced a degree of prejudice. While mostly anecdotal, and written well after the war was over, there are several examples that show that black soldiers were viewed by some as less important than their white counterparts.

I. Black Life in New Hampshire

Thomas Bellows, a resident of Walpole, in speaking of that town's 12 men who went to Saratoga, said that he "never was able to recall to mind the name of the 12th one," and after some hesitation, would say "no matter, twas a black man anyway" (TH-Aldrich, pg. 47). The man to whom he was referring was Cato Marcy, who died in the course of his service. Another example of disregard for the black soldier is the following account of an unknown black soldier during the fall of Fort Ticonderoga, by the historian J.D. Butler. This account, quoted in full, is not only interesting for its racially biased introduction, but also for its concise, matter-of-fact account of a black soldier's experiences. Butler's account reads as follows:

> Which of our historians might not profitably copy the following account of the evacuation of Ticonderoga, albeit it fell from the lips of a negro? "About 11 O'clock on Saturday night, orders were given by our colonel to parade. We immediately obeyed. He then ordered our tents to be struck and carried to the battery. On doing this, the orders were to take up our packs and march, which we also did; passed the general's house on fire; marched twenty miles without a halt, and then had a brush with the enemy" (OPS-Stark, pg. 44n.)

In contrast, those who fought against American troops paid particular attention to the black soldiers they saw. A letter written by a Hessian officer in Burgoyne's army, dated October 23, 1777, states that "no regiment (among the Americans) is to be seen in which there are not Negroes in abundance and among them are able-bodied, strong, and brave fellows" (OPS-Aptheker, *The Negro in the American Revolution*, pg. 34).

One true measure of the important service rendered by black soldiers was their low rate of desertion from military service. It is estimated that one-third of all soldiers during the war deserted at one time or another for varying reasons. The rate of desertion for black soldiers was much lower for several reasons. "Negroes were less inclined than white soldiers to walk off without official leave. They were not likely to have a farm that needed protection nor the kind of home that inspired homesickness. They had less to desert to" (OPS-Quarles, pg. 79). This was equally true for New Hampshire's black soldiers, whose overall rate of desertion was less than five percent. Some men, such as Cato Fisk (Epping) and Derrick Oxford (Hartford, VT) were initially reported as deserters because they failed to return home from furloughs on time. Such an occurrence was commonplace and, once their situation was fully understood, no punishment was meted out. Indeed, Cato Fisk was later awarded the Badge of

> Newmarket, April 2. 1777.
>
> RAN-AWAY from the Subscriber April 1, 1777 a NEGRO MAN named BONE, about five feet nine Inches high, between 20 and 30 Years of Age, speaks good English;— Had on when he went away, a striped Cotton and Linnen Shirt, two short Waistcoats, inside one white wollen mill'd, the other brown, with claret colour'd Sleeves, Leather Breeches, light blue Yarn Rib Stockings, & a very narrow brim'd Felt Hat: He has been in the Continental Service 19 Months and it is suspected that he will, if he can, get to the British Troops. Whoever will take up said Negro, and return him or secure him, and give information to the Subscriber, shall have Eight Dollars Reward, & all necessary Charges paid by JOSEPH KNIGHT.
> Rochester, April 3, 1777.
> N. B. All Masters or Vessels are caution'd against carrying off said Negro as they will avoid the Penalty of the LAW.
>
> LOST a Red Cornelian SEAL set in Silver, with the Letters S. M. engraved thereon—Whoever has found it, & will return it to Stephen Meed, or the Printer hereof, shall receive ONE DOLLAR for their Trouble.

Runaway slave/soldier advertisement for the slave Bone Knight. Nothing is known about Knight except what appears in this ad. Typical in most respects, the ad is unusual in that it states the slave's service in the Continental Army and his possible intention to desert to the British. *New Hampshire Gazette*, April 26, 1777. Courtesy Portsmouth Public Library.

Merit for his service as a soldier. Other men, such as Michael Sudrick (Dover), were part of mass desertions by both white and black soldiers over issues regarding food and pay. Nineteen men in his company, including Capt. James Libbey, deserted over dissatisfaction with the rations they were issued. Another form of desertion was fraudulent enlisting, whereby bounty money was taken with no intent to serve. Only one black soldier, Andrew McDaniels (Londonderry), is recorded in this category. The three most serious cases of desertion involved George Evans (Dover), Bone Knight, and William Sharper (both of Rochester). These men all deserted from their units at separate times on their own when far from home. Only Knight is thought to have had intentions to join the British, a crime punishable by death had he been caught.

Finally, in several instances, as among white families, several members of the same black family served in the war; some even fought together in the same regiment. Robert and Israel Glines, brothers of Moultonborough, both served in the war, but at different times and in different regiments. This was also the case for two other brothers, Joseph and Michael Sudrick, of Dover. Jonathan Miller (Hampton Falls) and Robert Miller (Kensington) were brothers who served together in Capt. Winthrop Rowe's company in the 2nd New Hampshire regiment in 1775. Both saw later service, but in different regiments. There is also one case of a father and son serving together. Isaac Tatten and Isaac Tatten, Jr., both of Lempster, served together in Col. Hercules Mooney's militia regiment in July of 1779 during the Rhode Island campaign.

Service as Sailors

Although the main focus of this study is on black soldiers, it is important to understand that many blacks also served as sailors during the war, helping to win the fight on the high seas. However, due to a lack of records, it is impossible to ascertain, with any reasonable degree of certainty, how many blacks saw service as sailors. It is possible that more blacks served as sailors for New Hampshire than as soldiers, but without a complete record of crew lists for the many privateers that sailed out of Portsmouth, their names will never be known. For those blacks who served from New Hampshire as sailors, there were two options. They could serve in the Continental Navy aboard one of two ships that were built at Portsmouth by congressional authorization and saw action in the war, the 32-gun frigate *Raleigh*, or the *Ranger*, a more noteworthy, but smaller ship of 18 guns first commanded by Capt. John Paul Jones. The other option, which was both more attractive and profitable, was service aboard a privateer, a privately owned vessel with congressional authorization, known as a letter of marque, to operate against enemy shipping. Sailors were subject to regular discipline in ships of the Continental Navy, and were paid a fixed wage per month, but crew members of a privateer usually operated under a more relaxed atmosphere, and shared in the profits of the sale of a captured British ship and its cargo. These proceeds were often large. The Portsmouth privateer ship *General Sullivan* captured one prize in 1780 that sold for £350,000, a sum that would ensure that even the share for the lowliest hand aboard seemed like a king's ransom. Because of the lure of privateering, the competition for sailors to man both privateers and Continental vessels was high, with the navy usually ending up on the losing end. The frigate *Raleigh* was launched in 1776, but was not ready to sail until August of 1777 because of a shortage of crew members, as well as supplies. Only two Continental Navy ships were launched and manned in Portsmouth for war service, but about 100 privateers operated from the same port. These ranged in size from the lugger *Betsey*, with two guns and a crew of 10, to the *Amphitrite*, a ship with 24 guns and 160 crew members. On average, most privateers had 8 or 10 guns, with a crew of anywhere from 30 to 50 men (OPS-Upton, pg. 108). It is likely that most of these crews contained at least one, if not more, black sailors. One other option that was open to those blacks from New Hampshire who served for another state was that of service in state naval vessels. Several states during the war, including Massachusetts and Virginia, operated their own vessels of war against the British, usually, but not always, in cooperation with Continental Navy ships. New Hampshire operated one state naval

5 Dollars Reward.

DESERTED from on board the Ship of War Raleigh, commanded by *Thomas Thompson* Esq ; Edward Thorp, an Englishman five feet six inches high, dark complexion, has a cast with one eye.— William M'Daniel, an Englishman, five feet eleven inches high, dark complexion,— And Michael Brown an American, five feet eleven inches high, dark complexion.— Benjamin Gerrish, five feet eight inches high, dark complexion,— Joseph Howard, five feet 4 inches high, brown complexion— John Allen, five feet nine and three quarter inches high, dark complexion. ———— Whoever will apprehend said deserters, and return them on board said ship Raleigh, or secure them in any of the colony gaols shall receive FIVE DOLLARS REWARD for each, and necessary Charges allowed.

PETER SHORES.
Portsmouth Sept. 18, 1776.

Military service desertion ad, *New Hampshire Gazette*, September 21, 1776. Service in the Continental Navy was not nearly as desirable as service in the more lucrative business of privateering. Some of the men listed in this ad may have been black sailors. Whatever their race, the difficulty in manning the frigate *Raleigh*, then building at Portsmouth, warranted a reward for the return of these sailors. Courtesy Portsmouth Public Library.

vessel in the war, during the failed Penobscott expedition in July and August of 1779.

Blacks were active in Portsmouth's maritime trade well before the war, helping to man colonial merchant vessels. There is no reason to believe that their role in manning New Hampshire ships during the war would be any less and, in all likelihood, was probably greater due to increased demand for sailors. Regarding their service aboard ships, whether naval vessels or privateers, most black sailors worked as ordinary seamen, performing those essential tasks that needed to be done on any sailing vessel of the time. However, some blacks who were more experienced sailors signed on as able seamen. It is equally likely that a number of blacks signed on as cabin boys or as some kind of servant. Once again, without crew lists, it is impossible to determine how many blacks from New Hampshire served as sailors during the war. One conservative estimate puts the number of men in the privateer service for the state at 3,000 (OPS-Upton, pg. 108), while those men in the Continental Navy service for New Hampshire is much lower, probably fewer than 300. Given the fact that there were about 100 privateers alone for the state, each of which may have employed one or more black sailors, a conservative estimate of the number of black sailors from the state would be anywhere from 100 to 200 men. Unfortunately, very few of these men's names are known. Caesar Lear (Portsmouth) and Peter Adams (Durham) served aboard the frigate *Raleigh*, while Scipio Gray (Portsmouth) served aboard the privateer *General Sullivan*. An unknown number of black sailors who served aboard British vessels captured by American privateers and sent into Portsmouth also served in the Continental Navy. It is unknown if men such as David Davidson and William Follet, former sailors on British merchantmen who enlisted for service on the frigate *Raleigh*, were forced to do so, or enlisted willingly to avoid detention and continue in a paid service. Finally, those from New Hampshire who saw service in Massachusetts vessels include John Barber (Portsmouth) on the *Tyrannicide*, Robinson Peters (Gilmanton) on the *Vengeance*, and Jack Driver (Portsmouth) on the *Jason*. Robert Randall (Hanover) served aboard a frigate while in service for the state of Virginia.

The Black Veteran and Pensioner

After the war ended, most black veterans found themselves in poor financial straits due to the depressed economy that then prevailed in New England. Black veterans were probably, as a whole, worse off than their white counterparts, but even white veterans suffered economic difficulties. For black veterans, their situation was often exacerbated by their newfound freedom as a result of service in the war. Not only were they now on their own to find employment to support themselves, and often a family, but they also had to find a place to live. Some blacks, such as Caesar Wingate (Rochester), and Derek Oxford (Hartford, Vt.) lived with their former masters. One man, Seco Barnard (Hopkinton), asked his former master to take him back to his old home to live, but was turned down. To support themselves, most black veterans were either farmers, such as Salem Colby (Concord), and Pomp Russell (Wilton), or laborers, like Cato Smith (Brentwood). Two men, Pomp Peters (Exeter), and Drover Minor (Londonderry), were employed as bell-ringers. Dan Martin (Durham) was a boatman, Israel Glines (Moultonborough) was a highway surveyor, and Joseph Sudrick (Dover) was a basket maker, to name just a few of the occupations practiced by black veterans. Some men were noted for their musical talents, particularly on the fiddle, and were likely in high demand at local festivals and celebrations. Two such men were Cato Fisk (Epping), and Anthony Clark (Warner). Tony Clark was so highly respected in his community that it was said about him that he "probably did more towards instructing the young people in the arts and graces of politeness and good manners than any other man of his day" (TH-Harriman, pg. 101).

One man whose postwar activities read like those in an adventure novel is Charles Bowles (Warren). After the war, he settled down as a farmer and became a Free-Will Baptist convert. Some time thereafter, he

> THE
>
> LIFE, LABORS, AND TRAVELS
>
> OF
>
> ELDER CHARLES BOWLES,
>
> OF THE FREE WILL BAPTIST DENOMINATION,
>
> BY ELD. JOHN W. LEWIS.
>
> TOGETHER WITH
>
> AN ESSAY ON THE CHARACTER AND CONDITION OF THE AFRICAN RACE
> BY THE SAME.
>
> —ALSO,—
>
> AN ESSAY ON THE FUGITIVE LAW
> OF THE U. S. CONGRESS OF 1850,
>
> BY REV. ARTHUR DEARING.
>
> WATERTOWN:
> INGALLS & STOWELL'S STEAM PRESS
> 1852.

Title page of the biography of soldier Charles Bowles. This book, written several years after he died, details Bowles's activities as a Free Will Baptist minister. It is the only known contemporary biography for a black soldier of New Hampshire.

quit farming and embarked on a ship at Boston, signing on as a cook. After three years, he left this trade and became a roving preacher in the Free-Will Baptist faith, ministering in Massachusetts, Rhode Island, New Hampshire, and Vermont, before moving to New York.

Many black veterans could support themselves, but not all were able to do so. George Knox (Enfield) and his wife signed a contract to serve as indentured servants for five years in 1785. Other indications as to the economic sufferings and privations of black veterans are found in "warning out" lists, and lists of town paupers. "Warning out" was a unique New England practice, consisting of local officials, usually the town constable or sheriff, "warning," or demanding that a certain individual, or groups of individuals, leave town by a certain date, usually within several weeks. This was often done when it appeared to town officials that a new individual in town might become "chargeable," or have to be supported by the town because he was too poor to support himself. Because of this "warning out" practice, many blacks, and whites as well, were forced to roam from town to town to eke out an existence. Many of those who were warned out of town came back, only to be warned again at a later date. Examples of such warnings for black veterans are numerous, including Aaron Small (Goffstown, 1790), London Dailey (Exeter, 1784), Boston Bell (Londonderry, 1795), and Caesar Porter (Litchfield, 1786). Those who were warned out several times include Cato Wallingford

(Exeter, 1784; Brentwood, 1799), and Jude Hall (Exeter, 1785, 1792, 1817). Perhaps the cruelest example of the "warning out" practice was that for Abigail Oliver and her son, Aaron Oliver, Jr., of Temple, in December of 1778. This occurred just eight months after the death of Abigail's husband, Aaron Oliver, a soldier for Temple who died on April 30th after his capture at the Battle of Hubbardton in July of 1777 and his subsequent release the following April by the British. Although their fate is unknown, one can only imagine the hardships endured by Oliver's widow and young son. Despite the "warning out" process, many black veterans ignored the demand and stayed in their communities, becoming town paupers who relied on public support to fill their most basic needs of food, shelter, and clothing. Such men include Peter Kent (North Hampton, 1810) and Cato Fisk (Exeter, 1787; Raymond, 1797; Poplin, 1799; Deerfield, 1801).

Warning out document for Scipio Brown. This document, dated January 3, 1769, was drawn up by the selectmen of the town of Kingston and presented to the town constable for action. It is typical of the many warnings out issued to blacks and other indigent people during the years prior to the Revolution. It is ironic that one of the selectmen who signed this document, Josiah Bartlett, was later a delegate for New Hampshire to the Continental Congress and a signer of the Declaration of Independence. New Hampshire Province Records-1769. Courtesy New Hampshire Division of Records Management and Archives.

One way the government tried to alleviate the financial sufferings of all veterans was the establishment of the pension system. Though first established as early as 1776, it was not until 1818 that the pension program was expanded to include a wider range of veterans who needed a pension to survive. However, by this time it was too late for many veterans, black and white, who had already died. At first, in 1776, by an act of the Continental Congress, disability pensions were allowed for those totally disabled as a result of their war service. Administered by the state, which was

SCHEDULE
CONTAINING the whole estate and income of *Cato Fisk* (his necessary clothing and bedding excepted,) by him subscribed; exhibited to the Court of Common Pleas for the County of Rockingham, on the 18th day of July, 1820, and annexed to his oath, viz.

This "Schedule" of property for black soldier Cato Fisk, dated July 1820, was part of his application for a government pension. In addition to a small "hut" and barn "on an other man's land," Cato had few possessions except for the basics, such as chairs, a few tables, crockery and eating utensils, and an axe. The sparseness of his belongings was typical of those of many black veterans. Pension #W14719. Courtesy New Hampshire Division of Records Management and Archives.

in turn reimbursed by the federal government, this system continued, with only slight changes, until 1818. In 1789, New Hampshire had only 83 invalid pensioners receiving compensation, a seemingly small number in relation to the number of veterans in true need of a pension (OPS-Upton, pg. 104). Many towns gave local aid and support to veterans, but it was neither required nor systematic. Not until March 18, 1818, 35 years after the war was over, was the first national pension program established by an act of Congress. This program paid ex-privates eight dollars per month, provided they could prove the need for such a pension. This program was expanded gradually over the next 20 years. In 1828, pensions were granted whether there was a need or not. In 1832, those with as little as six months of service were allowed a pension. Still later, various "widows' acts" were passed allowing compensation for families of veterans and their heirs. As late as 1899 there were still four widows left on the pension rolls whose husbands had served in the Revolutionary War.

The pension application records are some of the most useful and enlightening documents to be found for determining the economic status of black veterans. Archelaus White (Plaistow) was described in his pension application by his former master as "now very infirm and extremely poor" (Pension #S43299). Caesar Wallace (Rye) was one of the few soldiers who received a discharge from military service signed personally by George Washington. In his pension application, his "property consists of one cow purchased with money received of government" (Pension #S43250). Those who could not prove their service, or did not serve long enough to qualify, were denied pensions. Patience, the widow of William Small (Amherst), was denied a pension in 1848, at the age of 82, because his service as a waiter to an officer "affords no ground for a pension" (Pension #S45220). Robert Glines (Moultonborough) and his heirs were rejected because he had not served long enough. Perhaps the most poignant pension application, and one that is probably indicative of the financial hardships endured by many black veterans, is that for George Knox (Enfield). It states, in part, that Knox was "a very hard labouring man but lately he can not labour in consequence of his having lost the use of his right arm ... his house is a mere hovel ... and I really think he is as poor as a man can be" (Pension #S45780).

All in all, life for Revolutionary War veterans, whether black or white, was often filled with hardship. However, for the black veteran it was often doubly hard, due to his low economic and social status.

Blacks as Pioneer Settlers

Several black soldiers are also prominent for the roles they played as pioneer settlers in the establishment of new towns in western New Hampshire. Isaac Tatten was one of the first settlers in Lempster, coming there in 1767 from East Haddam, Connecticut. Silas Burdoo was the first black settler in Jaffrey, coming there in 1773 from Lexington, Massachusetts. During the Revolution, Charles Bowles, having already served as a soldier for Massachusetts, came to Warren in 1777. Although many local anecdotes and lore survive regarding his arrival in the area, there is little doubt that he was one of the town's first, if not the first, black settlers. Another man who can rightly be termed a pioneer is Israel Glines of Moultonborough, in the north-central part of the state. His activities as a surveyor and traveler in the north-country qualify him in this regard. Finally, Titus Coburn was likely an early settler in the town of Camden (now known as Washington). Pioneer activities by blacks were somewhat unusual in New Hampshire, but they were not without precedent. The town of Swanzey had, as one of its original proprietors, a freed black slave named Caezer Freeman in 1753. A portion of the town is named Mount Caesar in honor of his memory to this day. Further studies may show that the role of pioneer by black soldiers and their descendants continued after the Revolution, with the settling of new towns in Vermont, western New York, and the Ohio Territory, where many soldiers were granted land for their service during the war. Indeed, had it not been for his capture by Indians, Robert Randall (Hanover) may have been one of those soldiers who helped in settling the newly opened land to the west.

Religion and the Black Veteran

No full-length study has been completed on religion and New Hampshire's black population during the era of the Revolution and the years following, but an examination of the available records for the soldiers in this work are quite revealing and interesting. It is likely that most slaves and many free blacks belonged to the Congregational Church in their community because it was the predominant religion practiced in New Hampshire and the foundation on which many of its towns were established. Many slaves or ex-slaves who had masters who were Congregationalists also likely practiced the same religion themselves. For some black soldiers, this is demonstrated in three different ways. The first, and most obvious of these is ownership of a slave by a Congregationalist minister. Peter Stearns (Epping), Prince Walker (Concord), and Peter Adams (Durham) were all owned by prominent ministers in their hometowns. Another man in this category is Cato Baker (Dover), whose manumission from his master was aided by the Reverend Jeremy Belknap. Another identifier for those blacks who were members of the Congregational Church are baptism and marriage records. Gloster Watson (Dover), Corydon Chesley (Dover), and Silas Burdoo (Lexington, Massachusetts) are among those men recorded as being baptized. Watson has the additional distinction, like Baker, of having his manumission aided by the Reverend Belknap. Those men who are recorded as being married in the church include Richard Hunking (Dover), Boston Underwood (Kittery, Maine), Richard Black (Kittery, Maine), Edward Sands (Chichester), and Cato Fisk (Brentwood).

However, although Congregationalism was predominant in the state, it was not the most friendly toward people of color, nor was it their only option. Mirroring colonial New England society as a whole, blacks, whether free or slave, were relegated to the lesser seats in the local meetinghouse, usually at the rear of the building or in the upper gallery. With seating in the meetinghouse determined by a combination of one's social standing and wealth in the community, such arrangements clearly demonstrated to blacks that the established church viewed them as lesser members. However, the era of the Revolution brought about changes in this area as well. Newly established churches, Christian in practice, but with more liberal ideas in their form of worship, became more acceptable in New Hampshire society as a whole, and particularly attractive to blacks. Such faiths as the Free Will and New Light Baptists, the Shakers, and the well-established Society of Friends (Quakers) eagerly accepted all into their fold without regard to skin color or social standing. The most popular of these was the Baptist faith. Established in New Hampshire in 1755, this faith counted among its members black veterans Cuff Chambers (Leeds, Maine) and Prince Johonnot (Goffstown). Charles Bowles (Warren) was also of this faith, joining the Free Will Baptist Church (established in New Hampshire in 1780) and becoming a minister who spread the Gospel for over 40 years throughout New England. Another man, John Shepard (Lyme), was likely a member of a New Light or Free Will Baptist Church and may have later became a Shaker, a faith established in New Hampshire in 1782. Not to be forgotten is the Society of Friends (Quakers). This group was established early on in New Hampshire and was much persecuted before gaining some measure of acceptance. Among its members was Caesar Sankey (Dover), who belonged to the Dover Meeting prior to the Revolution.

A generation later, at least three veterans had sons who grew up to become ministers in several churches. Not surprisingly, the son of Charles Bowles was a preacher in New Hampshire, as was the son of Oxford Tash (Newmarket). The denominations they practiced in are unknown. Finally, Alexander Twilight, the son of Ichabod Twilight (Warner), gained prominence as a Congregational pastor in Vermont.

Death and the Black Veteran

It is a sad fact that the death of a black soldier did not always mean the end of the discrimination he experienced while he was living. A study of the few known gravesites for black soldiers in New Hampshire reveals some interesting facts. Prior to approximately 1800, it was customary for blacks, both free and slave, to be buried toward the rear of public burial grounds, usually without markers. If there was a marker provided, it usually consisted of an unmarked piece of fieldstone. Thus, for those black veterans who died before this time, gravestones are rare. Only two such markers for black soldiers have been found in the state, only one of which is contemporary. The gravestone of Caesar Wood (Stratham) was marked with his name, his designation as a "negro," and his date of death (1785). Prince Whipple (Portsmouth), who died in 1796, also has a marker denoting his Revolutionary War service. However, this marker is of a standard type issued to honor veterans and was placed in North Cemetery circa 1920 in a spot that may not even be Whipple's true resting place. At least two towns in New Hampshire had separate slave burial grounds. Hanover once had a slave burial ground where it is likely that such black veterans as London Dow and Robert Randall were buried. Unfortunately, the location of this burial ground is now unknown. Portsmouth also had a "Negro Burying Ground" (TH-Brewster, vol. 1, pg. 45), which was located at what

The gravestone of Wentworth Cheswill. Cheswill died in 1817 and is buried in Newmarket in a private cemetery located just west of his old homestead. This stone (with his last name misspelled) marks his Revolutionary War service, and was erected circa 1920. His original gravestone is still to be found, but is badly damaged. Nearby are the final resting places of other members of his extended family. Photograph by Glenn A. Knoblock.

is now the corner of State Street and Chestnut Street. This burial ground, about which little is known, was lost due to growth and development before 1820. Following 1800, the idea that blacks should occupy the rear portion of cemeteries was gradually abandoned. Jeremiah Crocker, who died in 1836, has a final resting place near the front of Center Cemetery in Henniker. His gravestone denotes both his service as a soldier and the fact that he was a "colored man." Similarly, Anthony Clark is buried in a highly visible section of Pine Hill Cemetery in Warner. His gravestone, dated 1856, also denotes his military service, but does not mention his race. Both Crocker and Clark died at the age of 100 years, and it is likely that, by the time of their deaths, they were remembered by townsmen more for their military service, contributions to local society, and advanced age, than for the color of their skin. Indeed, the military funeral accorded Anthony Clark was an elaborate ceremony. One final anecdote that may serve to show both the esteem given to black soldiers and the discrimination they faced concerns the funeral service of Cato Fisk of Epsom. He died at the same time as another Revolutionary War soldier, a high-ranking officer and prominent citizen from that town. The minister who delivered the sermon at the time of their deaths, the Reverend Jonathan Curtis, was criticized for mentioning Cato's name first during his sermon (Pension #W14719). Whether this was done by design or chance is unknown, but it caused enough of a controversy to be remembered many years later.

Descendants of Black Veterans

Tracing the descendants of New Hampshire's black veterans poses a formidable and daunting challenge. Research in this area has been difficult, given the lack of black family records and the relatively late attention given by experts to the field of black genealogy. Some organizations, such as the National Society for Daughters of the American Revolution, have supported and encouraged research in this area, but much more remains to be done. However, at least for a few black veterans, records concerning their descendants do exist, and the information it reveals is fascinating. Many black veterans moved to Vermont after the war, attracted not only by its better farmland, but also by freedom. Although New Hampshire did not officially abolish slavery until 1857, Vermont's 1777 State constitution prohibited slavery. When state officials learned that instances of slavery still existed, a 1786 law was passed closing any loopholes, abolishing slavery forever. One New Hampshire soldier who moved to Vermont was Ichabod Twilight. A soldier in the war for Sandown, he later married and was a resident of Vermont by 1790. His third son, Alexander, was born in 1795 in Corinth. A remarkable man, Alexander Twilight graduated from Middlebury College in 1823, the first black graduate of an American college. Afterward, he became a minister and educator. In 1836 he was elected to the Vermont State Legislature, again, the first black in America to accomplish this feat.

Another black veteran who moved to Vermont was Silas Burdoo. His family became well established in Windsor County, in the towns of Reading and Woodstock, and was held in high regard. A second cousin of Silas Burdoo, also named Silas, served in the famed 54th Massachusetts Regiment during the Civil War, perhaps inspired by the experiences and stories of his namesake. Incredibly, the participation by Silas Burdoo in the Civil War continued a family tradition of military service dating back over 100 years to the French and Indian War in 1759.

Some black veterans undoubtedly moved even farther west, but Charles Bowles is the only black soldier from the state known to have moved to New York. Settling in Malone, in northern Franklin County, Bowles was an active preacher in the Free Will Baptist faith. Several descendants of Charles Bowles also served in the Civil War, enlisting in New York regiments.

However, not all black veterans felt the urge, or had the need to go westward. Many black veterans stayed in New Hampshire, with their descendants following suit. The son of Oxford Tash (Newmarket) was Charles Tash. A resident of nearby Exeter, Tash was a man of considerable property, as evidenced by an 1847 advertisement in which he lists eight

> **For Sale!**
>
> CHARLES O. TASH offers for sale his House and Land, pleasantly situated on Water street, joining Josiah Batchelder's Carpenter's Shop. Also, one other piece of land with building thereon, joining land of Ira B. Hoitt, on said street. Also, one other House with land on the aforesaid street, formerly owned by Mrs Martha Runnels, deceased, and now occupied by Miss Elizabeth Runnels. Also, one other piece, formerly called the "Burying Ground," with 2 convenient Houses and a good Barn connected thereto, running back to Green street. Also, one other piece of land, situated on Middle street, joining land of Mr Nathaniel Conner, containing about 2 acres, more or less. Also, one other lot of land with buildings thereon, situated on Bow street. Also, one other piece of land, situated on Court street, joining the land of the late Col. Nathaniel Gilman, running back to Great River. Also, one piece of Salt Marsh, lying upon the Northerly side of Exeter River, joining land of Nathaniel Taylor and Capt. William Conner, containing 1 1-2 acres, more or less. Also, one other piece of land, situated about 4 miles from Exeter village, on the Epping and Brentwood road leading to Marshall's Corner, in Brentwood, containing 50 acres, more or less, with two-thirds of a Dwelling House and Barn thereon. The above described premises will be sold in lots to suit purchasers and at a bargain.
>
> ☞ For further information please enquire of the subscriber.
> CHARLES O. TASH.
> Exeter, April 3, 1847.

The later prosperity of the Tash family is well demonstrated by this ad that appeared in the *Exeter News-Letter* on April 5, 1847. Charles Tash, who here lists nine lots of property for sale, was the son of soldier Oxford Tash. Courtesy Exeter Public Library.

properties for sale. Sadly, Charles Tash is also known for an affair he had with a woman that ended tragically.

One black veteran whose family history is well known is Jude Hall (Kensington). His descendants stayed in the area for nearly 150 years. Jude, himself a hard fought veteran who saw action at Bunker Hill, Saratoga, and Monmouth, had two grandsons, Aaron and Moses, who fought in the Civil War. Aaron served from 1863 to 1865 in the famed 54th Massachusetts regiment, one of the first black regiments organized and allowed to fight in the war. Moses served in the U.S. 3rd Colored Infantry regiment from 1864 to 1865. After the war, he became a stone mason, and long-time resident of Epping, where he is buried.

New Hampshire's most famous black soldier is undoubtedly Prince Whipple. His family was well known in Portsmouth, and has been well researched and documented. Prince died in 1797 at the young age of 32, but his widow, Dinah, lived to the advanced age of 82, dying in 1846. With Rebecca, the wife of Prince's brother, Cuffee Whipple, she was well known for establishing and running the Ladies Charitable African School for young girls. The daughter of Prince Whipple, Esther, also lived a long life. Born in 1784, she was married and widowed twice, had six children, and supported herself as a laundress. A devout woman, she left everything in her will to Portsmouth's North Church after her death in 1868.

Finally, one remarkable fact that stands out is the tradition of military service established by the families of black veterans. Their devotion to their country during other times of war, especially the Civil War, was no doubt strengthened by the stories of grandfather's or great-grandfather's service during the American Revolution that were passed down from generation to generation. In addition to the previously mentioned descendants of the Bowles, Burdoo, and Hall families, the names of Caesar Wallace and Barzillai Lew should be added. Wallace had two probable grandsons who fought in the Civil War, while Lew had a grandson and a great-grandson who fought in the same war.

The Black Soldier as a Patriotic Symbol

The black soldier of the American Revolution has long been a symbol of New England patriotism and sacrifice. Whether fighting for his own individual freedom, or that of America, the loyalty and devotion of the "honest Continental Negro" (*New-Hampshire Gazette*, Dec. 27, 1781, pg. 3) to the cause was recognized in his own time. This is not to say that prevailing racial prejudices were set aside and forgotten. When one local paper reported that American sailors held prisoner "are confined in the common Goal [*sic*] of Halifax and are treated in a most inhuman and barbarous Manner possible,... thrown in among Negroes, Robbers &c-are told they know no distinction between them" (*New-Hampshire Gazette*, Sept. 7, 1776), it is unclear whether the "Negroes" referred to were fellow crewmen or local criminals.

One of the most persistent, and inaccurate, patriotic myths regarding black soldiers in New Hampshire was the freedom granted to them so that they could go off to fight the war. Most often, these accounts, penned by white writers, tended to first demonstrate the sagacity and patriotism of the slave owner, followed by a recognition of the former slaves' performance.

BON MOT *of an honest Continental Negro.*
The day on which the American troops at North River fired a *feu de joye* for the capture of Lord Cornwallis's army, a scouting party being on their return to camp, heard the firing ; and soon after met another party sent out as a relief :—A Negro belonging to the first, calling to one of the latter, said, *Cuffee, whas all dat firing we hear to day ?—* The other replied,—O, *my dear soul, noffing tall, only General Burgone hab a broder born to-day.*

This newspaper article records an exchange between two black soldiers on duty in New York in reaction to the capture of Lord Cornwallis at Yorktown. The humor and joy evident in this conversation seems appropriate and well earned, since black soldiers fought in most of the key battles during the American Revolution. *New Hampshire Gazette*, December 22, 1781. Courtesy Portsmouth Public Library.

The most famous of these stories involves Prince Whipple (Portsmouth), who was "sulky and in ill humor" (TH-Brewster, vol. 1, pg. 155) when going off to war with his master, Gen. William Whipple. General Whipple responded by telling Prince to "behave like a man and do your duty and from this hour you shall be free" (*ibid.*). Prince was indeed freed, but not until three years after the war ended. A variant of this same story has also been applied to Noble, the slave of Gen. John Sullivan of Durham. Little is known about Noble Sullivan, but it is unlikely that he was instantly given his freedom upon asking for it, given John Sullivan's reputation for acquiring wealth.

Finally, one of the more interesting records of the role black soldiers played in the war is their depiction in several famous paintings. The earliest of these paintings was executed by American artist John Trumbull and finished in 1786. Entitled *The Death of General Warren at the Battle of Bunker Hill, 17 June 1775*, it depicts Peter Salem, the slave of 2nd Lt. Thomas Grosvenor of the 3rd Connecticut Regiment. Salem was just one of many black soldiers, New Hampshiremen included, who fought at Bunker Hill.

Of greater interest to New Hampshire historians are several paintings depicting Gen. George Washington's famous crossing of the Delaware River on December 26, 1776. The first of these was Thomas Sully's *The Passage of the Delaware*, executed in 1813, well within living memory of the historic event. The second of these paintings, entitled *George Washington Crossing the Delaware*, was executed in 1851 by Emanuel Leutze. The first painting depicts a black soldier on horseback, while the second depicts a black soldier manning the oars in Washington's boat during the crossing. Both paintings are said to depict soldier Prince Whipple of New Hampshire. This attribution was apparently first stated in 1855 by historian William Nell and has been accepted by later historians without question.

DIALOGUE between Cuffe and Toney, about State Affairs.

Toney. HOW you du Cuffe? me no fee you dis great while.

Cuffe, I tank you Toney, I pretty well, hope you well too.

Toney. Yes Cuffe, I been berry well all along tank God. I bin in de army.

Cuffe. You bin in de army: What you go dare for? I forry you go mong dem; da better leave off he fighting, make peace; da nebber be able to pay off all he debts he got now.

Toney. You talk juft like a tory Cuffe. Merica pay all he debts eafy nuf; fave all he land; he ftock tob.

Cuffe. How he du dat? I fure he hardly pay he taxes now.

Toney. I tell you Cuffe, Merica leave of drinking trong drink, leave of tobacco, dat coft him more than half he tax. You fee now Cuffe, here be tree million folks here; one quarter part drink one glafs rum a day, tree dollars a glafs, dat make above eight hundred and twenty million dollars a year; den allow one tenth part de people ten pound tobacco a year, dat make, at four dollars a pound, twelve million dollars more; you fee now Cuffe, Merica can pay all he debts, no take he land, no take he cattle, he fheep, he horfe, he hog, no not one bit.

Cuffe. I no tink he fpend fo much for dram and bakcar, I fefs. But Toney you tink Britton he no come gin and beat him next fummer; you fee Britton he got Carlina, got Georgia away radda.

Toney. Meica no mind dat; Merica he no mad yet; he get mad he drive um all of into the fea; he got Carlina you fay; fo he be, fome part, not all do, whar good dat du him? fo he got Bofton, Phila-delphia, Rhode Ifland, he no keep um, fo he no keep Carlina long, he juft like a locuft, he fpoil all fore him den run away.

Cuffe. Ay Toney, you ftand for Merica; Merica he make poor Negro flave: Britton no make Negro flave.

Toney. Why Cuffe, you tory, Britton he no make Negro flave ha: Who make all he rum, all he fugar, he molafles? Sure Cuffe, you no fee, Britton want make all Merica flave, Negro flave tu: What he come here for? Merica he no hurt him, no fteal he tings, no meddle his fairs. O Cuffe, you go Weft Indies, you fee Britton flaves dare, fome ftarve, fome whip, fome hang up by he rib; Britton he kill twenty toufand ebbery year at Jamaica; Merica he no du fo, we bread nuf here, mea nuf, no work all Sabbar day to git bread, no kill Negroes here.

Cuffe. You tink Brittons he du fo; who tell you dis?

Toney. Me bin Weft Indies, me fee, me read, me know all about it Cuffe. I cant bear hear you fay fo more about Britton, he all Devil Cuffe, farewell:

This article, written in what is supposed to be a slave dialect, represents a conversation between two slaves, one a former soldier, the other a Tory. Printed at a bleak time when it seemed the war might never end, its purpose may have been two-fold: to encourage enlistments at a time when recruiting efforts for the Continental Army were sorely lagging, as well as to demonstrate that even an uneducated slave knew that, no matter how bad things were, Great Britain was "all Devil." Seven months later, the wisdom of "Toney" was proved when Lord Cornwallis surrendered at Yorktown, effectively ending the war. *New Hampshire Gazette*, March 26, 1781. Courtesy Portsmouth Public Library.

Unfortunately, Nell was wrong, since Prince Whipple never served under Washington, nor did his master, Gen. William Whipple. Interestingly, Portsmouth historian Charles Brewster, never hesitant to cite anecdotal history as fact, does not record Prince Whipple's presence at this historic event. Among New Hampshire's black soldiers, Prince Whipple stands out

as a legend, both in character and actions. The fact that he was not with Washington during the crossing of the Delaware, although disappointing, in no way reduces his historical stature.

The identity of the black soldiers in these paintings is now speculative at best. The soldier on horseback in Sully's painting may very well have been Washington's own slave, or, if a New Hampshire black soldier is preferred, Noble Sullivan, the slave of Gen. John Sullivan, who was with Washington at the time. Leutze's 1851 painting was done so long after the event that the depiction of a black soldier was meant solely for reasons of historical accuracy. After all, many black soldiers crossed the Delaware River that night with Washington. To ascribe any specific identity to the black oarsman in Leutze's painting is impossible. However, we do know that Prince Whipple was not present. Again, if a black soldier from New Hampshire it must be, why not Aesop Hale? He served in Col. John Glover's regiment of Marblehead mariners who performed the task of ferrying Washington's army across the Delaware that frigid night.

Opposite top: The Passage of the Delaware. This painting was done by artist Thomas Sully in 1813. It commemorates the famous crossing of the Delaware River, a prelude to the epic Battle of Trenton on December 26, 1776. The black soldier on horseback at the right has been identified, inaccurately, by many historians as Prince Whipple of Portsmouth, New Hampshire. However, Whipple was not a soldier at this time and did not participate in this campaign. It is more likely that this soldier was one of Gen. George Washington's slaves, or Noble Sullivan, the slave of Gen. John Sullivan. Photograph courtesy Museum of Fine Arts, Boston.

Opposite bottom: George Washington Crossing the Delaware. This painting was executed by Emanuel Leutze in 1851 to celebrate this famous event of 1776. As with the case of mistaken identity noted in Thomas Sully's treatment, in the caption above, the black soldier manning the oars in Washington's boat has been incorrectly identified by historians over the years as Prince Whipple. It is likely that the unknown man depicted here was a soldier in the regiment of Marblehead, Massachusetts, fishermen commanded by Col. John Glover. His men did signal duty in transporting Washington's army to safety many times during the 1776 campaign. Photograph courtesy of the Metropolitan Museum of Art, New York, AN 97.34. All rights reserved.

II. Campaigns and Engagements

Introduction

New Hampshire men were among the most experienced and hard-fighting soldiers in the American Revolution. With the exception of several regiments from New York and Delaware, no units served in more battles and campaigns than those from New Hampshire. They served in every major engagement in the northern sector of the war, including the battles at Trenton and Princeton, the Battle of Saratoga, and the Battle of Monmouth. New Hampshire soldiers were among the first to serve in the war, starting in April 1775, after the battles at Lexington and Concord, and were the last soldiers to be discharged from Continental service after the war ended. The 1st New Hampshire Regiment was the last regiment disbanded of all the American forces, being released from service at New Windsor, New York, on January 1, 1784, after nearly nine years of service.

Listed are the major campaigns, battles, and phases in which New Hampshire men participated, both in Continental and militia service. Of necessity, the information presented here in chronological order is brief, and only meant to serve as a guide in understanding the type and extent of action experienced by black soldiers during the war.

The Battle of Lexington and Concord, April 19, 1775

To bring the rebellious province of Massachusetts back into line, the British government decided upon a "decisive action" (OPS-Boatner, pg. 620). An expedition to confiscate supplies and munitions at Concord instead resulted in "the shot heard round the world," when British regulars and colonial militia clashed on Lexington's town green at sunrise, leaving 18 Americans dead or wounded. Meeting further resistance in Concord, the British were forced to retreat to Boston. Constantly harassed by colonials firing at them from behind stone fences and trees with good effect, the British force reached Boston with 269 dead or wounded. A number of blacks served in the militia regiments that fought that day, including Prince Estabrook of Lexington, who was wounded. No New Hampshire militia took part in the day's battle, but one black soldier from Massachusetts, Silas Burdoo, was a participant; he later lived in New Hampshire.

The Battle of Bunker Hill, June 17, 1775

Following the engagements at Lexington and Concord, militia units from all over New England poured into the Boston area, effectively laying siege to the British Army. During this time the Continental Army had its beginnings and each colony began to form its own regiments to defend the colonies. New Hampshire formed three regiments, commanded by John Stark, Enoch Poor, and James Reed. While the 1st and 3rd New Hampshire regiments, commanded by Stark and Reed, were stationed on the outskirts of Boston, Poor's 2nd New Hampshire regiment was kept in the state to defend Portsmouth and its important harbor. With the exception of the Battle of Bunker Hill, little action of any consequence took place. The Americans decided to fortify Bunker Hill on June 15, 1775, when they learned of British plans to fortify Dorchester Heights. However, despite orders to the contrary, the American officers instead chose to fortify nearby Breed's Hill. It is on this hill that the misnamed Battle of Bunker Hill actually took place. The battle began in earnest on June 17 at 1 PM when the British landed a number of artillery pieces and 1,500 men. On the top of Breed's Hill a hastily constructed redoubt was manned by Col. William Prescott's Massachusetts regiment, as well as portions of Massachusetts regiments commanded by Nixon, Brewer, Doolittle, and others. At the base of the hill, the British advance was blocked by a light defensive fortification known as "the rail fence" (OPS-Boatner, pg. 124). This position was already manned, but it soon became evident that the Americans would need help. This help came in the form of the New Hampshire regiments commanded by Stark and Reed. Led by Stark, the New Hampshire men advanced into position, bypassing other units who were afraid to advance due to heavy fire from British warships. In a moment of legendary calm, Stark commented that "one fresh man in action is worth ten fatigued men" (OPS-Ward, pg. 86) when Capt. Henry Dearborn suggested that they quicken their pace. Once in position, Stark built a small fortification at a vulnerable point at the end of the rail fence and manned it with his best troops. Led by John Stark, the Americans succeeded in repelling the numerically superior British attack twice, inflicting heavy casualties. However, with the Americans low on ammunition and without needed reinforcements, the third British attack succeeded. They advanced on the redoubt at the top of Breed's Hill with a bayonet charge and met stiff resistance from its defenders, who used rocks and their muskets as clubs against the British. Thirty Americans died in the redoubt before the rest retreated in orderly fashion. Black soldiers from New Hampshire fought with valor during the Battle of Bunker Hill, serving in regiments that manned the rail fence, as well as in the redoubt. Those who served in New Hampshire regiments at the rail fence include Peter Brown (Temple), Elisha Hubbard, Nathan Weston, Aaron Oliver, Ephraim Stevens, and Ezra Fuller (all of New Ipswich), Jude Hall (Kensington), Peter Kent (North Hampton), and Jonathan Small (Dunstable). Men who served in Massachusetts regiments during the battle include Jacob Danforth (Hollis), Peter Poor (Hollis), Pero Hall (Portsmouth), Prince Johonnot (Goffstown), Robin (Sandown), and Archelaus White and Scippio (both of Plaistow). The service of Danforth and Poor is notable: They were members of Capt. Reuben Dow's company from Hollis, New Hampshire, who served in the redoubt under Prescott, with Poor being one of the eight men Dow lost who died in battle.

The Invasion of Canada, September 1775 to June 1776

This campaign aimed to make Canada the 14th American colony. Despite the guidance of some of America's best military leaders, such as Gen. Richard Montgomery and Benedict Arnold, the two-pronged assault on Canada ended in disaster and defeat. The primary objective was to capture Quebec, the citadel of Canada. Montgomery's force, coming from the west, captured the city of Montreal before meeting Arnold's force on the outskirts of Quebec. Benedict Arnold had a much more difficult time in reaching Quebec. His march through 350 miles of Maine wilderness is one of the most remarkable feats in American military history. At least one black soldier from New Hampshire, Ephraim Stevens (New Ipswich), was a part of this expedition. After the failed attempt on Quebec, the remaining American force continued to occupy the area, but received no reinforcements until April of 1776. The American army, now weary and poorly supplied, was then hit by a smallpox epidemic. With the threat of British attack growing stronger, the Americans retreated. This retreat soon turned into a series of disasters and defeat. A company of 400 New Hampshire rangers, led by Col. Timothy Bedel, was ordered to defend a small fort called the Cedars, 30 miles west of Montreal. By mid–May, a British and Indian force of 600 men threatened this outpost. Though details are conflicting, the entire garrison of the Cedars was surrendered without a fight by Maj. Isaac Butterfield, who had been placed in command by Bedel, who had left the previous day, either to get reinforcements or because he was suffering from smallpox. A relief column led by Maj. Henry Sherburn was sent out from Montreal to aid the rangers, but was ambushed several miles from the fort. After a gallant fight, the entire force was overwhelmed and captured. Some of the prisoners captured at the Cedars were later tortured and killed by the Indians, including one black soldier from New Hampshire, Primas Chandler (Amherst). The rest, including Titus Freeman (town unknown) were soon released with the help of Benedict Arnold. The Canadian campaign ended in June of 1776 after yet another defeat near Trois Riviers, on June 8. The remaining American troops made a precipitous retreat, escaping the advancing British by a matter of hours. They marched to Isle Au Noix, where they set up camp. Here, thousands of men suffered from smallpox, dysentery, and malaria, and many died. In the Canadian invasion, the Americans suffered nearly 5,000 casualties, few of them in combat. Many New Hampshiremen served in this campaign, including a number of black soldiers, many of whom served in Bedel's Ranger regiment. They were London Dow (Hanover), Primas Black, John and Benajah Blackman, Fortune Negro (Concord), Stephen Lovewell (Litchfield), Prime Wheeler (New Ipswich), and Primas Chandler (Amherst).

New York City Campaign, September 15 to October 28, 1776

Forced out of Boston in early 1776, the British finally decided to move on New York. They landed troops in New York in August and, after a brief delay, fought the Americans in a series of battles. On August 27, the Continental Army was battered and defeated at Long Island, being saved only by a daring nighttime retreat across the East River. On September 15, 1776, the British forced the Americans into wild retreat at the Battle of Kips Bay, but were stymied the next day during the Battle of Harlem Heights, when the Americans held their ground. The British, ever cautious, remained inactive for nearly a month. Then, on October 12, Gen. Howe moved his British troops to envelop the city, forcing the Americans to abandon Harlem Heights and retreat to the north. On October 28, the two armies again clashed, this time at the Battle of White Plains. Washington's soldiers fought better at White Plains, but were no match for the experienced British, and retreated another five miles to a place called North Castle. Howe seemed content to rest easy, and failed to press his attacks and aggressively pursue the retreating Continental Army. He missed a fine opportunity to end the war quickly; his failure to destroy Washington's army when he had the chance would come back to haunt him, for Washington's men, though battered, had survived to fight again. Many black soldiers from New Hampshire fought in this campaign, serving chiefly in Massachusetts regiments. They include Archelaus White and Anthony Gilman (both of Plaistow), George Snell (Portsmouth), Titus McGaw (Merrimac), Charles Bowles (Warren), Oxford Tash (Newmarket), and Aesop Hale (Exeter). Hale was one of those hearty men who served in Col. John Glover's regiment of mariners that ferried the Continental Army to safety after the defeat at Long Island.

The Frigate Raleigh, *May 1776 to September 1778*

No account of New Hampshire's activities during the war would be complete without mention of the several ships that were built at Portsmouth for the Continental Navy. Their crews consisted largely of local men from the New Hampshire area, and included, as far as can be determined from surviving records, at least several black men. On May 21, 1776, the frigate *Raleigh* was launched at Portsmouth after fewer than 60 days of work. She was the first of the 13 frigates authorized by the Continental Congress to hit the water. Like many of the other frigates of the fledgling Continental Navy, her career, though active, was rather unsuccessful. She ended her service by being captured by the British navy off the coast of Maine in September 1778. Several black sailors served on the *Raleigh*, including Caesar Lear (Portsmouth), Peter Adams (Durham), William Follett (Portsmouth), Primus McIntyer (Portsmouth), and David Davidson (Portsmouth).

The Battle of Trenton, December 26, 1776

Following the New York campaign, elements of Washington's army were forced to retreat across New Jersey, being closely pursued by Gen. Lord Cornwallis. Once again, Glover's regiment of Massachusetts' mariners played a key part in saving the Americans by helping to ferry them to safety across the Delaware River into Pennsylvania. The rest of Washington's men were also due to arrive, including a force of 500 detached from the Northern army, including, among others, the three New Hampshire Continental regiments and some New Hampshire militia. Washington now had only 6,000 men fit for duty. They were defeated, demoralized, and short of supplies. Many soldiers' terms of enlistment were due to end soon, on January 1, 1777. With no guarantee that his men would stay beyond that time, Washington had to do something. He decided on a bold attack on the British outpost at Trenton, manned by 1,200 Hessian troops. The attack was to take place on December 26, the main body of the assault consisting of 2,400 troops under Gen. John Sullivan and Gen. Nathaniel Greene, led by Washington. They left camp at 2 PM on December 25 to cross the Delaware River, yet again under the guidance of Glover's men. Due to a bitter storm, floating ice in the river, and a swift current, the last man was not landed until the early morning of December 26. After a long and cold march, with many of the soldiers on their feet for over 12 hours, Washington's army reached Trenton in the early morning. The battle began at 8 AM when men under Col. John Stark, commander of the 1st New Hampshire regiment, attacked the Hessian outpost guarding the approach to Trenton. For the Americans, the surprise was complete and the Hessian force of 1,200 men was caught entirely off guard. The battle, over by 9:30 AM, was a smashing victory. The American Army had only four killed and eight wounded; the Hessians had over 100 killed or wounded and over 900 taken prisoner. All the American forces performed admirably, but Stark and his New Hampshire men were particularly effective. After driving in the Hessian outpost, they were later engaged in the lower part of town. Calling on his men to follow him, Stark led a charge that drove back a battalion of Hessians and mortally wounded their commander. The Hessians, finding their avenue of retreat blocked, were forced to surrender. With an exhausted army, a lack of supplies, and many prisoners, Washington withdrew from Trenton and returned to his camp across the Delaware River. The Battle of Trenton did much to inspire the American troops and gave them much needed confidence. Their success against the Hessians was especially important, since it helped to diminish the fearsome reputation these foreign mercenaries had gained during the New York campaign. Many of New Hampshire's black soldiers participated in this rigorous campaign. In addition to the black soldiers who served in Massachusetts regiments in the campaign, and subsequently in New Jersey, the following men also saw service; Reuben Roberts (Newmarket), Paul Long (Rye), Caesar Sankey (Dover), Peter Blanchard (Canterbury), Asa Perham (New Ipswich), Timothy Nokes (Kensington), George Knox (Enfield),

Cato Moulton (Hampton), Robert Miller (Kensington), and Prince Liberty (Somersworth).

Fort Ticonderoga and the Battle of Hubbardton, July 1777

After the disastrous campaign in Canada ended in the summer of 1776, the Americans hastened their efforts to fortify Fort Ticonderoga. This fort, originally captured by Ethan Allen and Benedict Arnold in May of 1775, was only haphazardly manned and was in poor condition. Many of New Hampshire's black soldiers served here during this time, including George Hayes, Nimshi Locke (Rye), John Reed (Canterbury), John Sampson (Portsmouth), Boston Underwood (Kittery), Caesar Small (Hampton), and Scippio Martin (Durham), to name a few. Scippio Martin is interesting in that he was an older soldier who had served in the area during the French and Indian War at Crown Point in 1760.

Washington sent reinforcements to Fort Ticonderoga in February of 1777, consisting of a number of Continental regiments, including all three of New Hampshire's regiments. However, it was not until mid-June of 1777 before the British army in Canada, now under Gen. John Burgoyne, began an offensive against the Americans by moving south with an army of over 9,000 men, their first objective being Fort Ticonderoga. On the approach of the British force the American commanders abandoned Fort Ticonderoga. Colonel Pierce Long and his New Hampshire militia, about 500 men strong, left first, transporting all available supplies, artillery, and some invalid troops. The rest of the fort's garrison, including New Hampshire's three Continental regiments, were to join Long there, going overland via Castleton, but the British pursued them quickly. The American rearguard included Col. Nathan Hale's 2nd New Hampshire regiment and Col. Ebenezer Francis's 11th Massachusetts regiment. This force, numbering about 1,000 men, included many sick and disabled soldiers, most under Col. Hale's charge. Despite the orders to proceed to Castleton, the rearguard stopped at nearby Hubbardton for the night, probably due to the many sick men, and their exhaustion from their swift retreat from Ticonderoga. The swift moving British caught up with the rearguard and attacked the Americans at dawn on July 7, 1777. They drove in an outpost company of Hale's 2nd New Hampshire under the command of Capt. James Carr during breakfast and routed them. Advancing on, the British then hit Francis's Massachusetts men, who held their lines and dealt the British heavy losses. The British were saved, however, with the arrival of fresh German troops. They struck back at the Americans and, after the death of Col. Francis, the American line broke under a bayonet charge. With this, the Battle of Hubbardton, a hard-fought victory for the British, was over. This battle was particularly disastrous for the 2nd New Hampshire regiment. Although Hale's men, under the command of Maj. Benjamin Titcomb, later rallied and came to the aid of Francis, they suffered heavy losses. Hale and 70 men under his direct command were surrounded and captured. A number of New Hampshire's black soldiers participated in this battle, including some who became casualties. They included Aaron Oliver (Temple), Asa Perham (New Ipswich), Nicholas Ventrum (Windham), Ithamar Wheelock (New Ipswich), Titus Wilson (Peterborough), and William Griffith (New Castle). Of these men, Wilson died in battle, Perham was wounded and later died, and Oliver was captured and died after his release.

The Battle of Bennington, August 16, 1777

After the American Army rearguard was mauled at Hubbardton, the entire army continued its retreat to the northwest. Meanwhile, Col. Pierce Long's force fought a pitched battle at Fort Ann before fleeing farther north to join the rest of St. Clair's force at Fort Edward. Among Long's troops who fought at Fort Ann was at least one black soldier, Peter Abbot (Kingston).

The morale of the American Army by this time was at a low point, its strength reduced to only 4,500 men, of whom 1,600 were militia. Desertions occurred almost daily. In a two-week period nearly 500 men had deserted. Of the remaining troops, "fully a third were Negroes, boys, or old men" (OPS-Ward, pg. 421). However, American fortunes were about to be reversed. The British supply line had stretched too thin, and support from local Tories had not materialized. Supplies, especially horses, were badly needed, and were known to be there for the taking to the east. Gen. Burgoyne ordered a foraging raid, led by Lt. Col. Friedrich Baum, commander of the Brunswick Dragoons. The town of Bennington, Vermont, was not Baum's original objective, but he decided to go there based on intelligence he had received that the Americans had a supply depot at Bennington, lightly guarded by only 400 militia. Opposing Baum was the veteran New Hampshire soldier, Brig. Gen. John Stark. Appointed just the month before, Stark had quickly raised about 1,800 militia, and easily outnumbered the invaders. A small skirmish was fought on August 14, 1777, after which the German commander requested reinforcements from Burgoyne.

Meanwhile, Stark withdrew his force to within several miles of Bennington, and received reinforcements from Col. Seth Warner's Vermont Continentals. They arrived at midnight on August 15, 350 men strong. Delayed by rain, Stark attacked the Germans on August 16 at 3 PM. His force of New Hampshire and Bennington militia completely enveloped the redoubts of both the Germans and the Tories, while another militia group hit the enemy rearguard. By 5 PM, with Baum mortally wounded, the first part of this battle was over. With the arrival of 600 men led by Col. Heinrich Breymann, the British renewed the fight. While Stark's forces were scattered after the first battle, and were dealing with prisoners, as well as plundering, Warner's men came on and fought the Germans to a standstill. The battle finally ended at sunset, with a third of the Germans captured, and the rest escaping under the cover of night. As John Stark stated, "had day lasted an hour longer we should have taken the whole body of them" (OPS-Ward, pg. 430). The Battle of Bennington was a smashing victory for the Americans. Their casualties were light, with only 14 killed and 42 wounded, but the Germans suffered dearly, with over 200 killed and 700 taken prisoner.

Black soldiers from New Hampshire who saw action at Bennington as militiamen include Jesse Brown (Portsmouth), Peter Blanchard (Canterbury), and Charles Bowles (Charlestown).

Victory at Saratoga, September 19 to October 17, 1777

After the victory at Bennington, American prospects for defeating Burgoyne's invasion force soared. Local militia from New York and New England answered the call to arms by the thousands. Among the New Hampshire militia groups that responded was the one raised by John Langdon, a wealthy merchant of Portsmouth, and future governor of New Hampshire. His "Company of Volunteers" included many prominent gentlemen who served as privates, including one black man, Wentworth Cheswill (Newmarket). On September 13, 1777, Burgoyne crossed the Hudson River with 6,000 men at Saratoga, and pushed southward. The American Army, reinforced by nearly 3,000 militia, now numbered 7,000 men. Having observed the British crossing, they dug in at Bemis Heights, content to wait for the British, who finally advanced to attack the American positions on September 19. The battle began when American light infantry under New Hampshire's Maj. Henry Dearborn and riflemen under Col. Daniel Morgan fired on Burgoyne's advance guard, picking off every officer.

The British then advanced with their main force. Dearborn and Morgan were quickly reinforced by the 1st and 3rd New Hampshire regiments, under the respective commands of Col. Joseph Cilley and Col. Alexander Scammell. With the 1st NH in the lead, Cilley led his men off to the left in a flanking maneuver, while Scammell led his 3rd NH straight ahead toward a clearing on Freeman's farm. The bloody battle at the farm lasted nearly an hour, before both sides retired. The fighting resumed several hours later. This time, the 3rd NH ran straight into a British force consisting of some topflight troops, and 10 pieces of artillery. In a two-hour pitched battle, the American and British troops surged back and forth, taking and retaking the artillery pieces. Scammell's 3rd NH was in trouble almost from the start, and was nearly surrounded, but received timely reinforcements from other regiments, including the 2nd NH, under Lt. Col. Winborn Adams. Finally, a spirited attack on the enemy redoubt, led by Benedict Arnold, drove the British forces off the field, ending the battle at nightfall. It had been a harrowing confrontation, one in which "both sides had battled to the limit of endurance" (OPS-Ketchum, pg. 369). In comparing American troops to their British counterparts, Col. John Glover stated that "our men were equally bold and courageous & fought like men fighting for their all" (*ibid.*). New Hampshire's Continental regiments, in the thick of the battle, suffered many casualties. The unlucky 2nd NH, battered at Hubbardton, again lost its commanding officer when Lt. Col. Winborn Adams was killed in action. The 3rd NH was also hit hard, losing Lt. Col. Andrew Colburn and 29 other men killed, wounded, or missing. Colonel Alexander Scammell called the battle "the hottest fire of canon and musquetry that ever I heard in my life" (OPS-Ketchum, pg. 363). Many of New Hampshire's black soldiers took part in this battle. Too numerous to list in full, they include such men as John Cook (Pembroke), Jude Hall (Kensington), Cato Baker (Dover), Oliver French (Epping), Samuel Wier (Peterborough), and Caesar Thompson (Concord).

Despite its heavy losses in the Battle at Freeman's Farm, Burgoyne's army was not yet defeated. Now in desperate straits, the British planned another attack the next day, but Burgoyne was persuaded against doing so because his troops needed to rest. The British army was solidly entrenched at the position it had taken after the first battle at Saratoga. Its strength, however, was now down to 5,000 men, and was continually depleted by desertions. Moreover, the supply shortage worsened daily and the Americans harassed them day and night. Certainly the tables had been turned, for the Americans were upbeat and confident. They now had over 11,000 troops with the arrival of militiamen who had taken part in the Battle of Bennington, as well as other militia groups from New York and New

England. Burgoyne started the final battle of Saratoga on October 7, 1777, when he made a reconnaissance in force, 2,100 men strong, to probe the American position on Bemis Heights. Discovering the British movement, the Americans once again responded by sending out Dearborn's Light Infantry and Morgan's riflemen in an attempt to flank the British. This time, however, they received help from the start from New Hampshire's three "battle-hardened" (OPS-Ketchum, pg. 395) Continental regiments under the leadership of Cilley (1st NH), Scammell (3rd NH), and newly-promoted Col. George Reid (2nd NH).

With the 3rd NH in the lead, the New Hampshire men swept to the left of the British position to oppose their elite Grenadiers, who held a small hill on which their artillery was based. The British attempted a bayonet charge to drive off the Americans, but were repulsed and overwhelmed by a "ferocious charge" (OPS-Ketchum, pg. 397) led by the New Hampshire Continentals. Colonel Cilley and his 1st NH men captured a cannon and eventually turned it on the retreating British. Cilley was so excited that he jumped astride the captured cannon as if it were a horse, waving his arms and yelling. Meanwhile, Col. Daniel Morgan's men poured in from the right and Henry Dearborn's men drove in from the rear. Finally, a frontal charge on the British entrenchments by the intrepid Benedict Arnold, leading New York militia and Massachusetts regiments, carried the day and the battle was over. For Gen. John Burgoyne and his army, it was the end. His force, battered and thrice beaten, was trapped against the Hudson River. With the recent arrival of 1,300 Massachusetts and 2,000 New Hampshire militiamen, he was hemmed in and unable to retreat. After some negotiating, Burgoyne finally surrendered the remainder of his army on October 17, 1777. Once again, New Hampshire troops had played a vital role in defeating the British, and fought with valor and distinction in this historic campaign. Among the many black soldiers from New Hampshire who fought in the Battle of Bemis Heights were Cato Fisk (Epping), Thomas Dunkin (Enfield), Gloster Watson (Dover), Fortain Moore (Stratham), Caesar Barnes (Merrimack), Peter Brewer (Amherst), and Sidon Martin (Lee). Brewer, a private in Cilley's 1st NH, was killed in action, and Martin died just over a month after the battle during the army's subsequent march south from Saratoga, possibly due to wounds received in battle.

Winter at Valley Forge, December 1777 to June 1778

After the victory at Saratoga, portions of Gen. Gates's Northern Army, including New Hampshire's three Continental regiments, marched south to join Washington's main army in Pennsylvania. By November 21, they reached their destination at White Marsh, 13 miles from Philadelphia. American forces subsequently marched to Valley Forge on December 16, 1777, setting up camp for the winter.

Although the winter at Valley Forge has taken its place in American legend, its circumstances are quite contradictory. Valley Forge was in a good strategic location 22 miles from Philadelphia, lying between that city and the new home of the Continental Congress at York. The area around Valley Forge had an abundant supply of water, and wood for fuel and building. Furthermore, the winter of 1777-8 was considered fairly mild. Despite this, Washington's army suffered terribly at Valley Forge, mainly due to a lack of supplies, especially food and clothing. It took several months to build enough huts to shelter 10,000 men, and without sufficient clothing many soldiers were affected by the winter weather. At one time, nearly 4,000 men lacked adequate clothing to leave their huts. Foodstuffs were also in short supply, but only because farmers in Pennsylvania and New Jersey sold their produce to the British in Philadelphia and New York City. Patriotism aside, farmers found that the British were willing to pay in hard cash, as opposed to the nearly worthless Continental paper money that Washington's officers could offer. In response to these shortages, Washington sent out foraging expeditions into Pennsylvania and Delaware to seize whatever supplies they could find. All in all, it was a tough time for the American troops. In six months, 2,500 men of the 10,000 present died. However, much good also came out of Valley Forge. Despite their suffering, the troops remained loyal to Washington, and no mutinies or mass desertions took place.

Incredibly, the Continental Army came out of Valley Forge in good fighting trim, due largely to the work of one man, Gen. Baron von Steuben. He arrived in camp in February of 1778, and began to personally train and drill the American troops in March. He began by training one model company of 100 men, and branched out from there. His results were both quick and effective, as demonstrated by the performance of Washington's army during the upcoming 1778 campaigns. Among the regiments that suffered at Valley Forge were those from New Hampshire, as well as several from Massachusetts.

Among the many black soldiers at Valley Forge were Pomp Jackson (Exeter), Drover Minor (Henniker), Brister Bennett (Chester), Fortune Fogg (Exeter), Cato Marcy (Walpole), Peter Pomp (Epsom), Richard Black (Portsmouth), Ezra Fuller (New Ipswich), and Phillip Boston (Brookline). Of the men listed above, four died at Valley Forge: Richard Black, Cato Marcy, Peter Pomp, and Ezra Fuller.

The Sloop of War Ranger, *May 1777 to May 1780*

The Continental Navy sloop of war *Ranger* was the second, and final, naval vessel built in New Hampshire that saw service during the war. The frigate *Raleigh* was the first such vessel built, but the *Ranger* had a much more successful, and colorful, career. Commanded by Capt. John Paul Jones early in her career, the *Ranger* was notable for her success at a time when this was not the norm for the Continental Navy. In April 1778 the *Ranger* terrorized the English coast, landing her contingent of marines at several places for small raids, as well as capturing the British man of war *Drake* in a hard-fought battle. Even after Jones left the *Ranger*, her success continued. In July 1779, under Capt. Thomas Simpson, she captured 11 merchant ships in a British convoy. This was the most successful cruise of any Continental Navy ship during the entire war. The following year, however, the *Ranger*'s luck ran out when the British captured her at Charleston. Many of the officers on the *Ranger* were local men, as were much of the crew. Of the 145 men recruited for her crew, many were landsmen, since most of the Seacoast's most experienced sailors were employed in privateers, or on the frigate *Raleigh*. The *Ranger* crew included at least two black men, Cato Carlisle and Scippio Africanus. Historians disagree on the origin of these men, but the statement by one noted historian that they were "two local free Negroes" is probably correct (OPS-Morison, pg. 114).

The Battle of Monmouth, June 1778

In the spring of 1778 military operations began anew when the British decided to evacuate Philadelphia and move their troops to New York. Having failed to dispatch the American Army during the previous campaign, and in an isolated position, difficult to supply, the British were forced to give up the American capitol. They began to leave Philadelphia for the Northeast on June 16. Within two days, their entire garrison, 10,000 men strong, with 3,000 Tories, had crossed the Delaware River into New Jersey. They reached the village of Monmouth Courthouse on June 26. They covered the last 20 miles in 100-degree heat on roads filled with sand. Meanwhile, Washington was quite aware of the British movements and reacted quickly. On June 25, he sent out a 1,500-man force, which included Cilley's 1st NH regiment, to harass the British. However, it was soon clear that this force would need significant reinforcement. A reluctant Gen. Charles Lee was sent out with an additional 3,500 men to take command of the lead American force. The ensuing Battle of Monmouth was an extremely confusing event. Even today, historians do not agree on all the details of this monumental battle. It started at 4 AM on June 28, when the British prepared to continue their march to New York. A rearguard force, consisting of nearly 2,000 men under Lord Cornwallis, began their march later, at 8 AM. The Americans under Lee attacked Cornwallis's men at 10 AM, but were unsuccessful. Lee then ordered Lafayette to lead three regiments against the British flank. As the Frenchman began his attack, he decided to change his position to a more advantageous one. However, this move was interpreted as a withdrawal by other units. In the confusion that followed, there was a general retreat. Some units remained calm, but others were totally disorganized. Washington, having heard the sounds of battle, arrived on the scene and soon witnessed his own army retreating. After confronting Lee about this unexpected retreat, Washington rode forward to take personal command and rally his men. He quickly organized four regiments, supported by a battery of artillery, into a line to delay the British. He then established his main line of defense at West Ravine. However, this front line was eventually pushed back by units of British dragoons and grenadiers. Despite this assault, the Americans, under the personal leadership of Washington, remained intact. New Hampshire troops, as they did at Saratoga, played a large part in the battle, and helped save the day. In a counterattack ordered by Washington, the 1st and 3rd New Hampshire regiments and the 1st Virginia regiment led a charge through heavy woods against the British right, driving them back and ending the threat. In describing the role the 1st New Hampshire regiment played in leading this charge, one historian states:

> Col. Cilley deployed his regiment into line; but there were two rail fences between the two lines of combatants. The New Hampshire men marched up and coolly took down those fences—the last one within sixty yards of the British, who poured in a heavy fire which our men did not deign to return—then deliberately shouldered arms and advanced to charge them with the bayonet. The enemy fled, filed off by their left into a swamp, and renewed the fight. Cilley's men wheeled to the right and again advanced upon them, and when within four rods halted, dressed lines, and gave them a volley from the whole battalion front. The enemy again fled and joined their main body [TH-Griffin, pg. 323].

When Washington sent an aide to inquire what regiment it was, Lt. Col. Henry Dearborn, the second in command of the 3rd NH, responded, "Cilley's of New Hampshire—full blooded Yankees, by God, Sir" (TH-Griffin, pg. 324). Following this action, the British made concerted attacks on both the American right wing and center, but were unsuccessful. British heavy artillery continued to hammer away at the Americans, but by 5 PM the battle was over, ended by heat exhaustion on both sides. In what turned out to be the longest and last important battle in the North during the American Revolution, the Americans suffered 362 casualties, including 69 killed and 37 dead of sunstroke. Once again, New Hampshire troops distinguished themselves in battle. Cilley's 1st NH regiment was called "the most distinguished corps in the battle of Monmouth, and the salvation of the army was owing to their heroic courage" (TH-Griffin, pg. 322). Some of the black soldiers from the state who participated in this battle were Caesar Wallace (Rye), Caesar Black (Sandown), Corydon Chesley (Dover), Thomas Kimball (Hillsborough), John Diamond (Epping), George Knox (Enfield), Richard Hunking and Zach Kelsey (both of Barrington), Dan Martin (Durham), John Baldwin (Hanover), and Jude Hall (Kensington).

Continental Service, July 1778 to May 1779

Following the Battle of Monmouth, New Hampshire's three Continental regiments, like most of Washington's main army, saw no fighting for the rest of the year. Several days after the battle they marched to Brunswick, New Jersey, where they celebrated July 4 in grand military fashion. Beginning on July 5, Washington marched his army north, reaching White Plains on July 24. New Hampshire's Continental regiments stayed at White Plains until September 11 when, as part of Gen. Enoch Poor's brigade, they began to march east with two other brigades. They reached Danbury, Connecticut, on September 18, where they set up camp for the winter. Only one notable event took place during this time when, on November 20, Poor's men marched to Simsbury, Connecticut, to take charge of a group of German prisoners. These men, originally part of Burgoyne's invasion force, were being marched south to Virginia. New Hampshire's troops helped guard and transport them during their travel through Connecticut, escorting them for 60 miles, to New Milford, in a week's time. The New Hampshire Continentals remained at Danbury through the winter months until their departure in April of 1779. All black soldiers who served in New Hampshire Continental regiments during this time took part in the above marches. Some of these men include Jonathan Miller (Hampton Falls), Cato Baker (Dover), Caesar Barnes (Merrimack), Primas Coffin (Epping), Robert Miller (Kensington), and Cato Wallingford (Somersworth). Most interesting are the letters that Cato Baker wrote to the Reverend Jeremiah Belknap, and his former master, Col. Otis Baker. Baker described his experiences during the year, including a bout of small pox at Valley Forge, his survival during the Battle of Monmouth, and his lack of money and clothing. These letters by Baker are important in that, as far as is known, they are the only contemporary letters written by a black soldier from New Hampshire describing his military experiences.

The Battle of Rhode Island, August 29, 1778

Although New Hampshire's Continentals were done fighting for the year 1778, New Hampshire militia units took part in the Rhode Island campaign, which began in July. Command of the attack against the British at Newport was given to New Hampshire's own, Gen. John Sullivan, who commanded a force of 1,000 Continental troops at Providence. Washington helped Sullivan by giving him some of his best brigades in the main army, under the overall command of Gen. Marquis de Lafayette. The brigades, 3,000 men strong, consisted of Gen. John Glover's men, and Gen. James Varnum's Rhode Islanders, including the newly organized 1st Rhode Island regiment that consisted of newly freed black soldiers from that state. Sullivan was later reinforced with 6,000 militia from all over New England, including six regiments from New Hampshire. One of these regiments commanded by Lt. Col. Stephen Peabody, was independent, while the other five, led by Cols. Moses Nichols, Enoch Hale, Moses Kelly, Jacob Gale, and Joshua Wingate, were part of Gen. William Whipple's brigade. On August 29, 1778, the Battle of Rhode Island began when the British, under Gen. Robert Pigot, sent three columns of troops forward in preparation to attack the Americans. Learning of this, the Americans turned and made a stand at Butt's Hill, about 12 miles from Newport. The black 1st Rhode Island regiment, commanded by Col. Christopher Greene, took a major part in this battle, showing "desperate valor" in checking the three "furious assaults" (OPS-Ward, pg. 592) by Hessian troops against the Americans. Most of New Hampshire's militia regiments took no active part in this battle. Several black soldiers from New Hampshire took part in this campaign, though they saw no fighting. They were Jeremiah Hoit (Exeter), Peter Brown (Temple), William Pharaoh (Portsmouth), George Hayes (Rochester), Peter Adams (Surrey), and Jube Savage (Temple). Several black soldiers who later moved to New Hampshire also fought in the battle, mostly as members of the distinguished 1st Rhode Island regiment. Peleg Runnals (Alton) was present, as was Barzillar Streeter (Swanzey). (Streeter may not have seen active duty, since he lists his service as that of a clerk and waiter during this time.)

Sullivan's Campaign Against the Six Nations, June to October 1779

The next operation New Hampshire Continental troops joined was Maj. Gen. John Sullivan's campaign against the Six Nations, a confederation of Indian tribes allied with the British and Tories. This campaign, carefully planned and designed by Washington, responded to petitions to Congress from inhabitants on the western frontier of New York and Pennsylvania seeking relief from the almost constant raids and attacks on their isolated settlements. Sullivan's goal was "the total destruction and devastation of their settlements and the capture of as many prisoners of every age and sex as possible" (OPS-Boardman, pg. 40). Sullivan's force was divided into three brigades, consisting of 2,300 men. New Hampshire's three Continental regiments, under Cols. Cilley, Reid, and Dearborn, were under Brig. Gen. Enoch Poor's command, along with one Massachusetts regiment.

On June 18, 1779, Sullivan's force departed Easton, Pennsylvania. It traveled slowly, due to the need for cutting 23 miles of roads for the passage of his artillery and pack-horses, and averaged less than 10 miles a day. The army reached Tioga on August 11 after fording the Susquehanna and Chemung rivers. Here they built a stockade fort, 12 miles from the Indian town of Chemung. After scouting the Indian town, Sullivan decided to attack it in force, but when his men arrived at the town on the morning of August 13, they found it abandoned. In keeping with Washington's orders, they proceeded to burn the town, 40 houses in all, and destroyed 60 acres of corn. Sullivan's army stayed at Tioga until August 26, then marched north, up the Chemung River, toward the Indian village of Newtown, near the modern day city of Elmira, New York. At Newtown, Sullivan found a force of Indians and British, led by Tories under Maj. John Butler and the Indian leader Joseph Brant, and decided to attack. In the assault, New Hampshire's three Continental regiments occupied the right wing, with New Jersey troops on the left, the Pennsylvanians and the artillery in the center, and Clinton's New York brigade in the rearguard. On the morning of August 29, Sullivan's troops advanced on the enemy, discovering his camouflaged breastworks. Mounting his attack, Sullivan's artillery pounded the British fortifications, while Poor's brigade of New Hampshire men circled to the left to attack the enemy flank and rear, and cut off possible retreat. Poor's men were slowed down by a steep hill overgrown with brush, and hit by scattered musket fire. They resorted to a bayonet charge to force their way up the hill, and to the enemy position. Matters began to worsen when American artillery fire forced the British and Indians to abandon their breastworks. In doing so, they nearly surrounded Col. George Reid's 2nd NH regiment. During the heaviest part of the fighting, Reid's men withstood the British attack and, with timely help from Dearborn's 3rd NH and a regiment of New Yorkers, forced them to retire. Threatened on all sides, the British and their Indian allies gave up the fight and retreated.

Following this battle, the only one in the whole campaign, Sullivan's men camped in the area of Newtown, sending the wounded and the heavy artillery back to Tioga. For the next two weeks, Sullivan's army marched north to Geneva, New York, and then west to Little Beard's Town (now Cuylerville). Sullivan's men, in keeping with Washington's directive, destroyed 12 towns of the Six Nations along the way, burning nearly 400 houses, some described as "neatly built," but now "reduced to ashes" (Boardman, pg. 72), an estimated 160,000 bushels of corn, and countless vegetables and fruit trees. Such devastation was shocking, even to Sullivan's battle-hardened veterans. Several officers, including Lt. Col. Henry Dearborn of the 3rd NH regiment, protested this wanton destruction, apparently without success. Sullivan's army had originally planned to march farther, but had to turn back due to a lack of supplies. On their way back to Easton, starting on September 15, the soldiers retraced their original route, stopping to destroy what they had previously missed. Several towns around Cayuga Lake in New York, containing over 100 houses, 200 acres of corn, and 1,500 fruit trees, were destroyed. By October 15, 1779, Sullivan's army returned to Easton, Pennsylvania, having marched over 500 miles in four months. After a brief, two-week stay in Easton, New Hampshire's three Continental regiments were again on the move, marching east toward Connecticut. They reached Danbury by December 1, where they set up winter camp for the second year in a row. Any black soldiers who were in Continental service for New Hampshire during this time participated in this rigorous campaign. They included, among a large number, George Knox (Enfield), Peter Abbott (Kingston), Caesar Black (Sandown), Corydon Chesley (Dover), Dan Martin (Durham), Thomas Kimball (Hillsborough), and Peter Smith (Brentwood).

Militia Service, 1779

While New Hampshire's Continental troops were busy in Sullivan's campaign in 1779, New Hampshire militiamen saw little action, and took part in no battles. With no British activity in New England of consequence, there was little need for extensive militia service. One militia artillery company was stationed in Portsmouth harbor throughout the year, while a company of scouts served at Coos, in northern New Hampshire, near Canada, for several months in the fall. The largest force of New Hampshire militia raised this year were the six companies, about 300 men, under the command of Col. Hercules Mooney. This regiment was authorized by the state in June of 1779 for the defense of Rhode Island. Most of the men were recruited in July and August, and served there until January of 1780. It was uncertain what course the British at Newport would take, but all doubts were dispelled when they evacuated Rhode Island, withdrawing all their troops and naval forces by October of 1779. A few black soldiers from New Hampshire were part of Mooney's regiment in Rhode Island. They were Peter Stearns (Epping), and Isaac Tatten, and Isaac Tatten, Jr. (both of Lempster). The Tattens, as far as is known, were the only black father and son to serve together in the American Revolution from New Hampshire. The anecdotes surrounding Stearns's enlistment are also interesting. The former slave of Epping's Reverend Josiah Stearns, Peter enlisted, along with his master's son, John Stearns. One anecdote states that Peter gladly shouldered his musket and went off to war, but another, perhaps closer to the truth, states that Peter had to be strongly persuaded by the Reverend Stearns to enlist.

Continental and Militia Service, 1780

With the focus of the war shifting to the South in the Carolinas, New Hampshire's soldiers saw no major battle action in 1780. Instead, they mostly served to garrison forts in New York, as well as guard New Hampshire's borders closer to home. The state's three Continental regiments remained at winter camp in Danbury, Connecticut, until April 1780, when they marched to West Point, New York. The regiments stationed there remained on alert because the British still controlled New York City, and Washington had to be on guard for any move they might make. While garrisoned at several points along the Hudson River during the summer and fall months, the soldiers were often called to duty at the front lines closest to the British at Tappan. Their duty usually consisted of operations against outlaws, known as "cowboys," who operated in the neutral ground between the two armies. The "cowboys," considered to be Tories, were a lawless group who mainly stole livestock from local farmers to sell to the British in New York. One major event occurred in 1780 when, on September 25, Benedict Arnold's treasonous plot to hand over the fort at West Point to the British was discovered. While Arnold was able to escape, his

British accomplice, Maj. John Andre, was not so lucky. Captured in plain clothes, and thus treated as a spy, Andre was examined by a board of American officers, including New Hampshire's Gen. John Stark, and was sentenced to be hanged. Andre's execution was carried out at Tappan in full view of the American Army, and made a lasting impression on many soldiers. One black soldier, Prince Light (Exeter), witnessed the event and, commenting on it 38 years later, remembered the shine on Andre's shoes that day. In addition to the men who served in New Hampshire's Continental regiments, several regiments of militia were also recruited from the state to help garrison West Point in 1780. These men were often called six-month men, since most served for that amount of time. Too numerous to name in full, these men include Robert Glines (Moultonborough), Tobias Cole (Somersworth), Michael Sudrick (Dover), John Jack (Greenland), Boston Pickering (Newington), and Peter Bartlett (Kingston). In addition to serving at West Point, New Hampshire militiamen also garrisoned forts around Portsmouth harbor, and saw service in several ranger companies at Coos, near the Canadian border, and at Haverhill on the state's western border. One black soldier who saw such service was Prince Taylor (Westmoreland), a private in Maj. Benjamin Whitcomb's company of Rangers "for the defence of the Western Frontier" (PSR-NHRWR, vol. 3, pg. 168).

New York City and the Siege of Yorktown, 1781

On January 1, 1781, New Hampshire's three Continental regiments were reduced by one due to a lowering of the state's troop quota. Thus, the 3rd NH regiment, commanded by Col. Alexander Scammell, was disbanded and its men consolidated with those of the 1st and 2nd NH regiments. New Hampshire's troops, along with the rest of Washington's army, lay idle at West Point and other locations along the Hudson River for the first half of the year. With the solidifying of the alliance with France, Washington now waited for the arrival of French troops to begin operations anew. With their arrival in late June, Washington at once began his campaign. He started on the evening of July 1, when a force consisting of two regiments of light infantry and an artillery unit, 800 men in all, under the command of Gen. Benjamin Lincoln, planned to attack the British forts at the northern end of Manhattan Island. The plan was to take these five outposts by surprise. Despite elaborate plans, the initial American effort failed when Lincoln's men encountered a sizeable British force returning from a foraging expedition in New Jersey. American losses in this brief skirmish numbered six killed and about 50 wounded.

The exact number of New Hampshire soldiers who were a part of Lincoln's handpicked light infantry is unknown, but at least three black soldiers from New Hampshire were participants. Pomp Peters (Meredith) and Edward Sands (Loudon) saw action, having been recruited from several Massachusetts Continental regiments. Anthony Gilman (Plaistow) was also a part of Lincoln's light infantry, having been picked from the 1st NH regiment. His experiences, especially after the battle, are most interesting, and indicate how black soldiers may have been treated by the enemy, especially Tories. Gilman was captured at Morrisania with about 40 other soldiers, but, "being a man of colour" (Pension #S32729), was sold into slavery.

It was soon clear to Washington that an attack on New York was impossible, and he considered an alternate plan to march his troops south to help Lafayette against a weaker British force under Cornwallis in Virginia. Washington's hand was forced when the French informed him that they would return with their troops to the West Indies in mid–October. With his course of action now clear, Washington directed Lafayette and his Light Infantry Corp to prevent Cornwallis' army from retreating to North Carolina. Meanwhile, Washington decided to keep half his army, mostly New England troops, in their posts in the Hudson Highlands, and marched south with the remainder of his men on August 21, 1781. This march was to be kept as secret as possible to the British in New York City. Washington did not want them to pull troops from New York to reinforce Cornwallis, so he left his New Englanders, including New Hampshire's two Continental regiments, in position to prevent such a move. Washington's army on this march numbered about 2,000 men and entailed eight Continental regiments, including Col. Alexander Scammell's regiment of light infantry. Scammell's regiment was a handpicked unit of men from New England regiments, numbering approximately 400 soldiers. The exact number of New Hampshiremen who served in this regiment is unknown. Washington's army joined that of Lafayette and, on September 28, set out from Williamsburg to meet the British army at Yorktown. As the Allied force approached Yorktown, Cornwallis, badly outnumbered, abandoned his outerworks, except several close to the York River, and withdrew his men into town. However, New Hampshire, and the entire army, suffered a loss when Col. Alexander Scammell, the former commander of the 3rd NH regiment, was wounded while reconnoitering the empty British outposts. He was captured on September 30, while acting as officer of the day, by a detachment of Tarleton's Legion of Horse, and was subsequently shot in the back and seriously wounded. He was soon after released by the British, but died on October 6.

Preparations for the siege against the British army at Yorktown were in place by the evening of October 6. Heavy artillery was hauled into place, numerous trenches were dug, and four redoubts were constructed. By October 9, an artillery barrage was started against Cornwallis's position and, by the 11th, was intensified when a total of 52 guns were put into action. The Allies continued to move toward the British lines, completing 750 yards of trenches in one night, but were delayed by the two remaining British outposts along the York River. The task of taking these two redoubts, held by British and Hessian troops, was given to a force of 800 men, 400 French chasseurs and grenadiers under Col. de Deux-Ponts, and 400 American light infantry under Lt. Col. Alexander Hamilton. Among these troops were an undetermined number of New Hampshiremen from the battalion commanded by Lt. Colonel John Laurens. The French force attacked the larger of the two outposts, called Redoubt No. 9, on the night of October 14, capturing it in less than a half an hour. At the same time, Hamilton's men attacked Redoubt No. 10, brushing aside enemy bayonets and overwhelming its garrison in 10 minutes. The exact number of black soldiers from New Hampshire who participated in this battle is unknown, but at least two, Pomp Peters (Meredith) and John Cook (Pembroke), have been identified. Peters was a private recruited from a Massachusetts Continental regiment, and recalled years later that he was at the "taking of Corn Wallace" (Pension #S45062, pgs. 36–8). Cook served in Lafayette's Light Infantry and likely took part in many military operations in Virginia. Another man, Prince Clements (Dover), may also have been present.

Cornwallis tried one last desperate attack against the Allies, but was unsuccessful. An attempt to evacuate a part of his army by boat across the York River also failed when a storm arose to disrupt the operation. Finally, out-gunned, low on supplies, and his back to the wall, Cornwallis called a truce on October 17. The next day, the two sides met and, despite his objections, Cornwallis had no choice but to accept the terms of total surrender dictated by Washington. That same day, the British and Hessian troops lay down their arms, marching out to meet the Americans and French to an old British march called "The World Turned Upside Down." Except for some minor skirmishes in the South, and on the frontiers, the war was at an end.

Additional Continental and Militia Service, 1781

While Washington's army at Yorktown was achieving its signal victory, the New Hampshire regiments, stationed at the Hudson Highlands, saw some action of their own. On October 13, 1781, the 1st and 2nd New Hampshire regiments were sent to the army's Northern Department in the Mohawk Valley to relieve the militia serving under Col. Marinus Willett. The frontier warfare in this area had continued into 1781 with no relief from the raids by Tories and Indians. The New Hampshire Continentals were sent there, with a unit of artillery, due to the threat to Tryon County by a force of 700 men, consisting of British regulars, Hessians, Tories, and Indians under Maj. John Ross. Raiding along the Mohawk River, Ross's force came within 12 miles of Schenectady, New York, before being forced to turn back. His force was pursued during its return march to Oswego, New York, by Willet's smaller force of 400 men. A sharp battle was fought at Johnstown, New York, on October 25, when Willet's army, hampered by deserting militia and nearly surrounded, was saved only by the falling darkness. Stopping for several days to regroup, Willet continued to pursue Ross, catching up with him on October 30 after marching 20 miles. In a brief battle at Jerseyfield, across West Canada Creek, Willet's men battled with Ross's Tory rearguard under the notorious Tory leader Captain Walter Butler. These battles marked the end of Tory raids in the Mohawk Valley. At the end of 1781, the New Hampshire regiments remained in the area, setting up winter camp in detachments at nearby Saratoga and Schenectady, likely to guard against possible further Tory activity in the Mohawk Valley. The winter of 1781-82, like the previous one, found New Hampshire troops experiencing a shortage of clothing. Gen. John Stark, commander of the Northern Department, wrote to Gen. William Heath on December 12, 1781, "I am obliged to detain the six months' men to do the necessary camp duty on account of the nakedness of the Continental troops" (OPS-Kidder, pg. 75). He further states that the two New Hampshire regiments only had 36 men fit for duty, the rest being "so naked that they cannot procure fuel for their own use" (*ibid.*). Stark also reports that the troops mutinied on December 10, "but by seasonable interposition of the officers it was quelled very easily. But this may be but a prelude to an insurrection of a more serious nature" (*ibid.*). Fortunately, Stark's fears were not realized. As in 1780, New England Continental troops, including those from New Hampshire and Massachusetts, were reinforced by the six months' men recruited from the state militias. Black soldiers from New Hampshire, who served for New Hampshire in 1781 include Caesar Wingate (Rochester), Caesar Wood (Stratham), and Ichabod Twilight (Sandown). Black soldiers from New Hampshire who served for Massachusetts in 1781 include Boston Bell (Loudon), Cato Boston (Dublin), Phillip Boston (Brookline), Silas Burdoo (Hampton), Pero Hall (Portsmouth), and Edward Sands (Chichester). New Hampshire's other militia service for

1781 included a company of artillery stationed at Portsmouth harbor throughout the year, a company of rangers at Coos for five months, and "sundry persons as scouts at Conway and towns adjacent" (PSR-NHRWR, vol. 3, pg. 283) from August to September.

Final Continental Service, 1782 to 1784

Although the shooting part of the war was over, for the most part, by the end of 1781, a peace treaty had not yet been signed, and the British still held New York. Thus, it was necessary for Washington to keep his army, garrisoned at various points along the Hudson River, intact and ready to march against the British, should the need arise. New Hampshire's Continental troops remained on duty in the Northern Department until November 12, 1782, when they moved back south to join Washington's main army, camped at New Windsor, New York, near Newburgh. The following year, on June 22, 1783, the 2nd New Hampshire regiment was reduced, and consolidated with the 1st New Hampshire regiment to form the New Hampshire Battalion of troops. They remained camped at New Windsor, close to Washington's headquarters, throughout 1783. Black soldiers from New Hampshire who served for New Hampshire as new recruits in these final years include Prince Lane (East Kingston), Primus Stewart (town unknown), and Cato Smith (Brentwood). One man, Peter Abbott (Kingston), served as a fifer in a ranger company in 1782 for the defense of New Hampshire's western frontier. Black soldiers from New Hampshire who served in Massachusetts regiments during these final years as new recruits include Joel Gill (Exeter), London MacGregor (Goffstown), Prince Walker (Concord), and Levi White (Londonderry). Finally, on September 3, 1783, the peace treaty between America and Great Britain was signed, and the war was officially over. By the end of November 1783, the British had evacuated New York City and what remained of Washington's army entered the city as victors. As one historian of the Revolution states, "The slender column, all that remained of the Continental Army, was spruced up to look its rather faded and worn best. It marched down Broadway amid cheers and waving flags" (OPS-Smith, pg. 1788). After being under enemy control for seven years, New York City was finally free.

With the final evacuation of the British army from the colonies, the Continental Army was no longer needed, and was quickly disbanded. By the end of November 1783, most regiments were disbanded at New Windsor and sent home. The New Hampshire men were the last state Continental regiment disbanded, serving an extra month, until January of 1784, when they were sent home. One other Continental regiment that remained in service, until June 20, 1784, was Henry Jackson's, which was organized at the end of 1783, and consisted of nine companies of veterans from the Massachusetts Line. One black soldier who was a private in this regiment was Thomas Thompson (Durham). George Washington may have had initial doubts about the use of black soldiers in the fight for independence against Great Britain, but by the war's end these doubts were dispelled. On June 7, 1783, "His Excellency George Washington" signed the discharge papers for three New Hampshire black soldiers whose time of service had expired. London Dailey (Exeter) was given his discharge for having "faithfully served" (Pension #WF5260) four years and was honored with the Badge of Merit. Cato Fiske (Epping) was also discharged that same day and awarded the Badge of Merit for having "served without any intermission" (Pension #W14719) for six years. Caesar Wallace (Rye) was also discharged by Washington personally, "having faithfully served the United States five years" (Pension #S43250).

Discharge Paper with Badge of Merit. Soldiers London Dailey, Cato Fisk, and Caesar Wallace were all discharged from New Hampshire service on June 7, 1783, and received a discharge paper, signed by Washington personally, identical to that depicted here for a New York soldier. Wallace still possessed his discharge paper in 1818 when he applied for a government pension, but it has since been lost. From James Roberts's *New York in the Revolution*, page 136.

III. The Men

Introduction

The following are the individual biographies of all known black soldiers associated with New Hampshire who fought in the American Revolution. They are broken down into three different categories: those who served solely for New Hampshire; those who saw mixed service, serving for New Hampshire, as well as another colony; and those who served for a colony other than New Hampshire. Their records show that all of these men were associated with New Hampshire in one way or another. Some were long-time residents of the state, while others may have had only a fleeting connection. This is especially true of those blacks who lived near the border between New Hampshire and Massachusetts, and often lived or worked in both at one time or another. This same movement between the two states also holds true for slave owners. Thus, several black soldiers were freemen who were held as slaves at one time in both states. The depressed economy after the war also led to many black ex-soldiers traveling between New Hampshire and Massachusetts in an effort to find employment. Due to the "warning out" practice in New Hampshire, as discussed earlier, some of these men may have only lived briefly in New Hampshire.

The Race Question

Before going into the sources and the biographies of each man, the reader should know what standards make a soldier eligible for inclusion in this work. Those soldiers that are identified in various contemporary records, described below, as being "black," "negro," or "colored" were, of course, included. In addition, soldiers who may not have been specifically identified as being black, but for whom evidence — especially their names — suggests that they were, have also been included. Some historians argue that men with such names as Cato, Caesar, Pomp, and so on cannot be included in a list of black soldiers because they are not specifically identified as such, but this seems unduly strict, especially in the case of New Hampshire's soldiers. It is likely that contemporary chroniclers assumed that such men would be known as blacks or slaves on the basis of their names, and it was not necessary to designate their race.

More difficult to determine with a full degree of certainty are those men listed in various records as "non-white." This term included not only blacks, but also Indians and others of mixed descent. Soldiers who evidence suggests were Indian are not included. This is because their service, though equally important, is outside the scope of this work. However, several soldiers are included whose race, though designated as "non-white," could not be determined with any certainty. Such soldiers have been listed, since this work seeks to be inclusive, rather than exclusive in nature. However, further research may establish that some of these men were, indeed, not black. Soldiers whose ethnic identity is in question have been identified as such.

Finally, men who have been identified as being of mixed descent can also be difficult to categorize. Referred to in the language of the day as "molatto," no designation is usually made in contemporary sources as to whether such men were of black and white, white and Indian, or black and Indian heritage. Though Wentworth Cheswill (Newmarket) was an octoroon, a person who is only one-eighth Negro, he is included in this work on the basis of his black heritage.

Sources

The primary source for this study is the published state papers for the state of New Hampshire, specifically the volumes that contain the rolls of the Revolutionary War soldiers from the state, published 1885–89. In these four large volumes are all the records pertaining to New Hampshire soldiers in the Revolution, both Continental and militia, that were then known to exist. Particularly useful are the various lists of men raised to serve in various units. Many of these rolls, or muster lists, give the barest of information, but some of them are more descriptive, giving a soldier's age, hair, eyes, and skin color, as well as his occupation. Such information is often helpful, though not foolproof, in identifying black soldiers. However, some of these lists did go so far as to identify a soldier as a slave, or as a Negro. The primary source for soldiers who served in the war from Massachusetts are the 17 volumes of *Massachusetts Soldiers and Sailors of the Revolutionary War; a Compilation from the Archives*, published in 1896. These volumes are an alphabetical listing of all known soldiers who served for the state and, similar to its New Hampshire counterpart, often give descriptions of the men listed. Even these descriptive lists must be used with caution, especially when dealing with such terms as "dark" regarding skin color. Many soldiers known to have been white were described as having "dark" skin, probably because they worked outdoors as farmers or in similar occupations for a good part of the year and had acquired a deep tan.

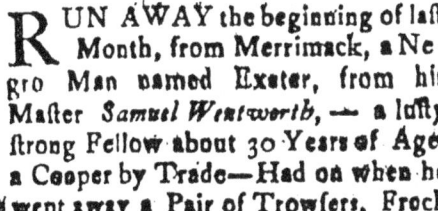

Runaway slave ad for Exeter Wentworth. With the name of Exeter, this slave was likely bought by his master at the New Hampshire Seacoast town of the same name that later served as the state's Revolutionary War capital. *New Hampshire Gazette*, August 12, 1768. Courtesy Portsmouth Public Library.

Another common method by which black soldiers can be identified is by their unusual names. Many blacks had such common given names as Jonathan, Robert, Charles, or George, to name a few, but an equal number had given names that were unusual, and traditional slave names. These names are often derived from the classic literature of Greco-Roman times. Names in this category include Caesar, Primas, Scipio, Prince, Plato, Pomp (short for "Pompey"), Fortune, Cicero, and Cato. Despite the example of Caesar Rodney, a white signer of the Declaration of Independence from Delaware, these names are usually associated with black men. There are also some other unusual, geographic-related names associated with several black soldiers who were ex-slaves. They likely indicate a location where a man was bought, or lived while still a slave. Soldiers with these names, uncommon for a white man, include Phillip Boston, Salem Colby, London Dailey, and Gloster Watson. Interestingly enough, all these men derive their names from well-known seaports in which the slave trade was practiced. Other names that are often an indication that a soldier was black specifically express the free nature of an individual. These include

The signatures of soldiers Tobias Cutler, Jude Hall, Salem Colby, and London Dailey. Found on various military and pension documents, they amply demonstrate that many black soldiers, whether free or former slave, could read and write. Courtesy New Hampshire Division of Records Management and Archives.

the surnames "Freeman," and "Liberty," both of which are found among the names of black soldiers from New Hampshire. Finally, there are several other surnames of black soldiers to consider. The vast majority usually took the same last name as that of a former master, but several soldiers are known by the descriptive last name of "Black," or "Blackman." Thus, on the rolls of New Hampshire soldiers we find the names Caesar Black, Cicero Black, John Blackman, and Benajah Blackman. In some cases, the last name "Black" or "Blackman" may have been used by an enlistment agent or officer who did not know the new black soldier's last name, or did not trouble himself to learn it. One black soldier, George Evans (Dover), is also listed in the records as George Black.

Although identifying black soldiers based on descriptive lists and name characteristics is often accurate, it was necessary to search other records to crosscheck data and verify accuracy. These records, discussed in further detail below, include government pension applications, Federal Census records, local court records, town pauper (or poor) lists, town "warning out" lists, contemporary newspaper accounts, local church records, and individual published town histories. Each of these sources, in spite of certain limitations, provided clues or, in some cases, provided the only evidence that an individual soldier was black. However, despite the abundance of records listed above, some black soldiers are identified as such in this book by name only, with nothing found to corroborate that conclusion. Where this is the case, the lack of positive evidence is so noted.

Pension applications were submitted to the federal government by the veteran himself, or his widow, in hopes of being granted a monthly sum, determined by law, to help support him, or his family. These applications are interesting because they are often the only record to be found in which a soldier's service is described in his own words. These records, too, are helpful in identifying family members, such as wives and children, and in determining where an ex-soldier may have lived. Pension applications indicate the economic status of a veteran or his family, and are generally considered a reliable record of his type and length of service.

Federal Census records are useful in determining whether a soldier was black or not. These records, started by the United States in 1790 and taken every 10 years thereafter, were intended to identify every known household in a given community, the head of the household and his or her race, as well as the number of slaves and "Free Non-whites" in a given household, if any. Like any other record, census records have their limitations which must be recognized. In many cases citizens of a given town may not have been counted due to poor or non-existent roads. In the case of counting the black population, the lack of an accurate count was even more likely. There was a sizeable population of free blacks in Newport on Coit Mountain, but the 1790 Federal Census for that town lists only one free black household. This is most certainly an example of a failure to count all people in a given locale.

Local court records, too, can be useful in determining whether a soldier was black or not, though their use is limited, since they usually concern small criminal actions, or civil suits brought against an individual over matters of trade and commerce. Mention of race in these records is often sporadic, though there are some examples of a former slave taking his ex-master to court to sue for some sort of economic redress.

Town poor lists and "warning out" lists may be considered together as records of a negative nature, and have been previously discussed at

The signatures of soldiers Wentworth Cheswill, Caesar Wallace, Michael Sudrick, and Ichabod Twilight. Found on various pension and military records, these signatures show that many, but not all black soldiers, could read and write. Compare Cheswill's signature at top, with that of Caesar Wallace below. Cheswill's signature is bold and prominent, its lively flourish indicative of his formal education. In contrast, Wallace could not write and signed his name with an X next to his name as it was written by an army official. Courtesy New Hampshire Division of Records Management and Archives.

> Rockingham, fs. } *The State of New - Hampshire* :
> To the Sheriff of our County of Rockingham
> his Under-Sheriff or Deputy, GREETING.
>
> WE Command you to Attach the Goods or Estate of Robert Wilson of Londonderry in our County of Rockingham Gentleman to the value of two hundred Pounds, and for want thereof to take the Body of the said Robert (if he may be found in your Precinct and him safely keep, so that you have him before Our Justices of Our Inferior Court of Common Pleas, next to be holden at Portsmouth within and for Our said County of Rockingham, on the first Tuesday of February Next Then and there in Our said Court to answer unto
>
> Boston Bell a Negro man of Methuen in the County of Essex & Commonwealth of Massachusetts Labourer in an Action of Trespass for that the said Robert at Bedford to wit in Portsmouth aforesaid on the 10th day of April AD 1784 with force and Arms Assaulted the said Boston and him took & imprisoned and restrained him of his Liberty and Sold him into the Continental Army for a Large Sum of Money & Compelled him the Plat there in Servitude to continue and remain for the Space of three years from the said tenth day of April against the Law of the Land and against the will of him the said Boston and other injuries he the said Robert to the Plat there & there Committed against our peace and

Court document for Boston Bell. This 1786 document records the attachment of the estate of Robert Wilson, pending a lawsuit by his former slave, and soldier, Boston Bell. Although slavery was still a legal institution in New Hampshire after the war, free blacks had the right to access the court system to resolve disputes and seek financial redress. RCR #9549. Courtesy New Hampshire Division of Records Management and Archives.

length. In issuing such lists, town officials nearly always noted when a particular individual or family on them was "black" or "Negro."

Contemporary newspaper accounts are very interesting and helpful in identifying black soldiers. Particularly noteworthy are the runaway slave advertisements, which not only describe the black man physically, but also discuss something of his character. Newspapers are also helpful for obituaries, which sometimes indicate a man's race.

Local church records are sketchy, and vary from town to town, but are useful in some cases when an individual listed in baptismal, wedding, and death records is identified by race. Some local ministers were diligent about keeping such records, but many were not, leaving a gap in the records. In addition, many of these records were privately maintained by the minister himself, and may have been lost when he moved to another town to preach, or when he died.

Finally, there are the individual published town histories. These books, many published over a century ago, are often rich sources of anecdotal information concerning slaves, ex-slaves, and free blacks who lived in a certain town. Some of these accounts have an undercurrent of prejudice characteristic of their time, and some of the most derogatory stories must be viewed with a degree of skepticism. However, there are some accounts, such as that of Anthony Clark (Warner), where a genuine measure of praise and respect is given to black individuals without hesitation or reservation.

Numbers

The number of soldiers involved in various battles has been mentioned in the text, but it may interest the reader to know the total number of soldiers from New Hampshire for the entire war, as far as can be ascertained. Although the exact number of men who served for New Hampshire, in both the militia and the Continental Army, is unknown, an estimated 16,500 men enlisted for the entire war. However, because some men re-enlisted more than once, this figure may be misleading and the number of New Hampshire men who served as soldiers may be somewhat smaller. At the start of the Revolution, New Hampshire had approximately 18,000 men of suitable age to bear arms, but the peak number of men who served in any given year was 4,483 in 1777, when New Hampshiremen turned out in large numbers to meet the threat of Burgoyne's army. The most important element of New Hampshire's military contribution was the men who formed her three Continental regiments. Through 1780, their total number was approximately 1,000 to 2,500 men at any given time. During the last three years of the war, however, with enthusiasm waning and the fact that the war had moved to the south, New Hampshire never had more than 744 men serving in its two Continental regiments, despite a quota of 1,152 men mandated by Congress.

New Hampshire Soldiers

The following 139 men served solely for New Hampshire during the war, either in militia, naval or Continental service. All town names referred to are in New Hampshire, unless otherwise indicated or, as in the case of Boston or New York, obvious. Full bibliographic details regarding these sources are listed separately at the end of the book.

ABBOTT, PETER

Abbott first enlisted in September 1776 in Capt. John Calfe's company in Col. Pierce Long's regiment, and was mustered in on September 10. Four months later, on January 25, 1777, he was enrolled in Capt. Zachariah Beal's company in Scammell's 3rd NH regiment for Continental service. He enlisted for a third time on July 31, 1781, as a six month man, serving at West Point. He saw final service from July to November 1782 as a fifer in Capt. Ebenezer Webster's ranger company in 1782 "for the defence of" New Hampshire's "Western Frontier" (NHRWR, vol. 3, pg. 295). His residence during the war is listed at different times as Kingston or Amherst, though he served for the town of Amherst during his Continental service. He may be the same Peter Abbott, a Negro servant to Samuel Abbott, who was baptized on the Isles of Shoals on July 11, 1742. Doubts about this exist because Abbott is listed in war records as being aged 18 in 1780. Were he the same man baptized in 1742, his approximate age would be 38 in 1780, not 18. This, however, may be a clerical error. His total war service lasted approximately four years.

Sources: PSR-NHRWR, vols. 1–3.

ADAMS, PETER

Peter Adams served two terms of service during the war. He first enlisted on June 11, 1778, in Capt. Peter Drowne's company in Col. Stephen Peabody's regiment of militia for service in Rhode Island. Upon enlistment he was described as Negro, 5 feet, 10 inches tall, and signed his name with an "X." His hometown is listed as Surrey. He served for only 22 days, being discharged from Rhode Island on August 8, 1778. He appears again in the records in July of 1780, listed as one of the six-month men who received a ration of rum and sugar at West Point. He may be the same Peter Adams, though it is unlikely, who served on the Continental Navy frigate *Raleigh* (see below). Peter Adams, the soldier, served for approximately seven months during the entire war.

Sources: PSR-NHRWR, vol. 3.

ADAMS, PETER

This Peter Adams served as a sailor during the war. He enlisted from the town of Durham for duty aboard the Continental frigate *Raleigh* as an ordinary seaman on February 10, 1777. He served under Capt. Thomas Thompson, but Adams's term of service is unknown. He is described in the records as a Negro. Adams enlisted in February, but he spent a long time in port at Portsmouth while the *Raleigh* was being finished. Capt. Thompson was unable to sail from the Piscataqua River until August 12, 1777, due to problems in getting the supplies he needed, as well as completing a crew for his ship. Peter Adams may have been the slave of the Reverend John Adams, a well-known patriot and minister for Durham. However, nothing further regarding Peter Adams is known.

Sources: TH-Durham; OPS-Remick.

AFRICANUS, SCIPIO

Scipio Africanus was a Negro aboard the Continental Navy sloop of war *Ranger*, commanded by Jones, when she departed from the Piscataqua River on her maiden voyage on November 1, 1777, along with 145 enlisted crewmen. Naval historian Samuel Eliot Morison calls him a "local free Negro" (Morison, pg. 114), but a local historian states that Scipio and Cato Jones (see Cato Carlisle) were former slaves of John Paul Jones from Virginia. This, however, is likely incorrect, since Morison's ample research on John Paul Jones finds no evidence that he ever owned a slave, and this story was probably fabricated by the author Augustus Buell while writing his fraudulent biography of John Paul Jones. Although little is known about Africanus, on this maiden cruise of the *Ranger* Jones first gained fame with a daring raid on Whitehaven, off the English coast, and by capturing the British sloop of war *Drake* after a hard-fought battle. Whether Scipio Africanus accompanied Jones in his other command, the *Bonhomme Richard*, is unknown.

Sources: OPS-Morison, pgs. 114, 426–27; OPS-Remick.

BAKER, CATO

Cato Baker was a Negro boy who was bought from Henry Ward, of Newport, Rhode Island, by Col. Otis Baker of Dover for 1,400 pounds, old tenor, on December 6, 1773. He was manumitted by his master, the event being witnessed by the Reverend Jeremiah Belknap of Dover, on June 4, 1777. At about this time Baker enlisted in Capt. John Drew's company in Hale's 2nd NH regiment for Continental service for an unspecified

"Strong and Brave Fellows"

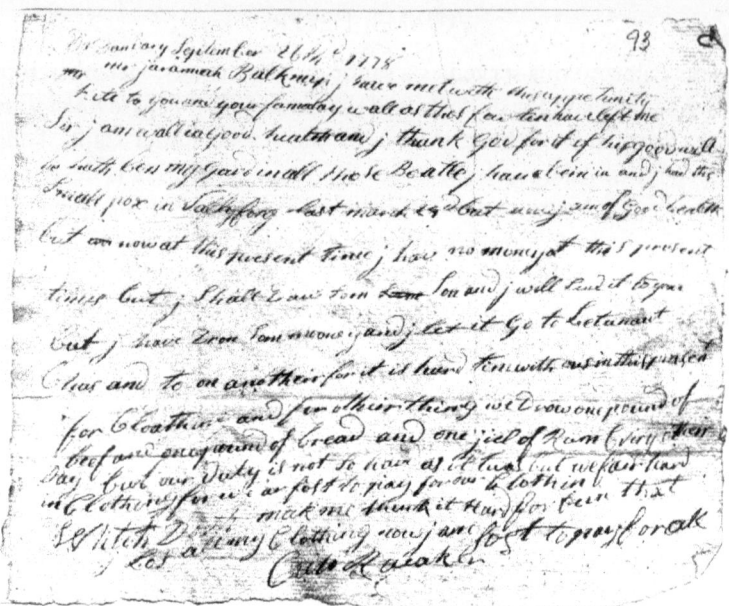

Letter from soldier Cato Baker to the Reverend Jeremy Belknap, 1778. Baker's letters are the only known surviving contemporary accounts of a black soldier for New Hampshire written during the war. Writing to his friend and the man who witnessed his manumission, Baker describes his bout of smallpox while at Valley Forge and talks about his pay and food rations. Jeremy Belknap Papers, 161.D.93. Courtesy of the Massachusetts Historical Society.

Below is a transcription of this letter. All spelling and punctuation appear in modern form. A blank indicates an undecipherable word. Words in brackets have been added to facilitate reading.

> Danbury, September 26, 1778
>
> Mr. Jeremiah Belknap, I have met with this opportunity [to] write to you and your family ____. As these few lines have left me Sir, I am well (and) in good health and I thank God, for it [is] of his good will to hath been my guard in all these battles I have been in and I had the small pox in Valley Forge last March ___, but now I am of good health. But now at this present time I have no money at this present time but I shall earn some and I will lend it to you, but I have drawn some money and I let it go to Lieutenant Chase and to one other for it is hard time with us in the present for clothing and for other thing[s]. We draw one pound of beef and one pound of bread and one gill of rum every other day, but our duty is not so hard as it was, but we fare hard in clothing, for we are forced to pay for our clothing. Which doth make me think it hard, for being that I lost all my clothing now I am forced to pay for all.
>
> Cato Baker

III. The Men

Cato Baker letter, 1779. Cato wrote this letter to his former master, Otis Baker, prior to his participation with the 2nd New Hampshire Regiment in Sullivan's Expedition on June 19, 1779. It is one of only two extant letters, both written by Cato, composed by a black soldier from New Hampshire during the war. His succinct comments about his service and the low pay he received was a sentiment held by most soldiers during the war, both black and white. Jeremy Belknap Papers, 161.D.97. Courtesy Massachusetts Historical Society.

Below is a transcription of this letter. All spelling and punctuation appear in modern form. A blank indicates an undecipherable word. Words in brackets have been added to facilitate reading.

Fishkill, June 19, 1779

To Colonel Baker, esq[uire],

Sir, upon my ____ to you, I would that you know that I am in good health at present and I hope these few lines will find you and your family in as good a state of health as they leave me. Blessed be to God for all his ___ to me. Pray Sir, don't forget to remember my love to the Reverend Mr. Belknap & all his family & all that shall give ___ ___ ___ the trouble to ask after me. Sir, I should inform you that we are a going to Susqehanna. Sir, I would not forget to let you know the ____ concerning my dissatisfaction concerning my wages for forty shillings a month. We must risk our lives & everything that is dear, so I am in hopes that the people and authority of New Hampshire will take it into their wise consideration & make the soldiers some small satisfaction, but it is my foolish opinion that they will satisfy themselves. So, I shall conclude in a word, so no more at present, but I remain your most humble servant until death.

Cato Baker

term of service, probably for three years. He was one of five black men in Capt. Drew's company. Baker maintained a friendship with both the Reverend Belknap and his former master and wrote to them during his time in the army. On September 26, 1778, he wrote Belknap from Danbury, Connecticut, telling that he had smallpox at Valley Forge but was now healthy; he also mentioned the shortage of money and clothing. The following year, on June 19, 1779, Baker wrote to Col. Otis Baker, his former master, from Fishkill, New York, telling of his good health, lack of pay, and his imminent departure for Pennsylvania to take place in Sullivan's expedition. The writings of Cato Baker (see illustrations) are rare in that they are the only known letters written by a black soldier from New Hampshire while serving in the war. After serving for approximately three years, Baker vanishes from the records after the war and his subsequent life details are unknown.

Sources: OPS-Belknap; PSR-NHRWR, vols. 2–3; US-Belknap Papers, Mass. Historical Society.

BARNARD, SECO/SEEKO

Barnard came to Hopkinton, New Hampshire, from Amesbury, Massachusetts about 1766 as the man-servant of Joseph Barnard. He was freed on the eve of the Revolution, and was described as "a man of considerable capability at all kinds of work" (C.C. Lord, pg. 271–72). He enlisted in Capt. John Calfe's company in Col. Pierce Long's regiment and was mustered into service on September 10, 1776. He was stationed at New Castle at least through February 7, 1777, when he appears on a list of men fit for the march to Fort Ticonderoga. Whether he continued his service is not known. At an unknown time during the war, Barnard returned to the Amesbury area where he lived and was married. At one point, likely after the war's end when financial hardship was experienced by many, Barnard met his old master near Amesbury and "was ardently desirous of returning to his old home with Mr. Barnard, and earnestly besought to be taken back to Hopkinton, but his appeal was resisted" (C.C. Lord, pg. 272). What further became of Barnard, who served for approximately six months, is unknown.

Sources: TH-C.C. Lord; PSR-NHRWR, vol. 1.

BARNES, CAESAR

Caesar Barnes was the slave of Thomas Barnes of Merrimack. He enlisted in Capt. Amos Morril's company of the 1st NH regiment for Continental service in January of 1777. He served until the New Hampshire regiment was disbanded in January of 1784, but it is unknown if he saw continual service, or whether he served a three-year term, as was standard, from 1777 to 1780, and then reenlisted again. It is also unknown when Barnes gained his freedom, though it was likely after his military service. His master, Thomas Barnes, petitioned the town of Merrimack in 1785 to see if it would "pay anything for services done by his Negro man" (TH-*History of Merrimack*, pg. 98). Caesar Barnes was married to Fanny, the widow of another black soldier, Pomp Peters, and had two children, John and Pamelia (also spelled "Permelia"). Barnes's son, John, was born sometime between 1784 and 1790 since he is the only Barnes' child listed in the 1790 census for New Hampshire. He stated in a pension deposition in 1835 that he was "the son and heir of Caesar, and that his father served in the New Hampshire Line" (Pension #BLWT-2102). Barnes and his family lived in Bedford in 1790, but later moved, as Caesar died in Washington, New Hampshire, on July 4, 1804. As of 1834, his children were residents of Goffstown.

Sources: PSR-NHRWR, vol. 1–3; TH-*History of Merrimack*; OPS-Kidder; CEN-1790-NH; PEN BLWT-2102.

BARTLETT, PETER

Peter Bartlett, also known as Peter Freeman, was the slave of the distinguished Josiah Bartlett, of Kingston. Josiah was a delegate to the Continental Congress, and a signer of the Declaration of Independence for New Hampshire. During the early part of the war, on December 4, 1775, Josiah wrote home to his wife from Philadelphia and talked of giving Peter "particular charge to take good care of the cattle ... not to waste hay ... to behave well until my return" (Bartlett, pg. 32). Peter Bartlett apparently did not heed his master's advice, since he was advertised as a runaway slave on February 13, 1776. How long he remained a runaway is unknown, but in 1780 he enlisted for Continental service from Kingston for three years. In May of 1782, the town of Kingston requested that they be given credit "for a black fellow named Peter who went to the Army last fall.... Said fellow is servant to Josiah Bartlett Esqr. of this town" (NHRWR, vol. 3, pg. 709). While little is known about Peter Bartlett after this time, the 1800 Census of New Hampshire enumerates one slave in the household of Josiah Bartlett. It is likely that nearly 20 years after his war service ended, Peter Bartlett was still a slave.

Sources: PSR-NHRWR, vols. 34; OPS-Bartlett.

BATCHELDER, PRINCE

Prince Batchelder was the slave of Joseph Batchelder of East Kingston. On October 28, 1760, he was given by Joseph to his wife, being described

as "My Negro Man (Prince by name)" (NHSP-vol. 37, pg. 38). In March of 1761 he was listed, though not named, on East Kingston's inventory of taxable property as a male Negro owned by Josiah Bachellor. Along with his master Josiah, Prince Batchelder enlisted in Capt. Simon Marston's company in Col. John Waldron's 18th militia regiment in January of 1776. Marston's men marched 90 miles to serve at Winter Hill, during the Siege of Boston, where they remained in service until April 1.
Sources: TR-Kingston; PSR-NHSP-vols. 26–27, 37.

BATTIS, SAMPSON

See the biography for Sampson Moore.

BLACK, CAESAR

Caesar Black, also known as Caesar Stevens, was born on August 17, 1754, in Kingston, the slave of Ebenezer Stevens. He was sold to Andrew McMillan in 1767 for 47£ 10 shillings. Black enlisted in the 1st NH regiment for Continental service in February 1777 for nine months. Later that same year, from September 8 to December 16, he was a private in Capt. Ezra Currier's company in Col. Abraham Drake's militia regiment raised to reinforce the Continental Army in New York. At this time he was going by the last name of "Stevens." Black again saw service in April of 1778, when he enlisted for one year in Capt. Caleb Robinson's company in the 2nd NH regiment. This time, he is listed as Caesar Black, "a Continental soldier from the parish of Sandown" (NHRWR, vol. 3, pg. 830). Black finished out his term, having served nearly two years in the war. After the war, times must have been hard for him. In 1799 he was warned to depart from East Kingston. A week later, on September 14, "Cesar, a Negroman" was warned out of Kingston (RCR #18299). Despite his hardships, Caesar Black lived a long life, dying at the age of 92 in Concord.
Sources: PSR-NHRWR, vols. 2–3; TH-Holmes; RCR18299.

BLACK, CICERO

Cicero Black was likely the slave of Capt. Edward Emerson of Kittery, Maine. In an inventory list dated April 22, 1769, for the estate of Emerson, he is listed as "Cicero— a Negro Boy," and was appraised at the value of 40 pounds "lawful money" (NH Provincial Probate records, vol. 25, pg. 391). On November 5, 1775, he is listed on a return of men who served at Kittery Point in Capt. Robert Follett's artillery company in Col. Joshua

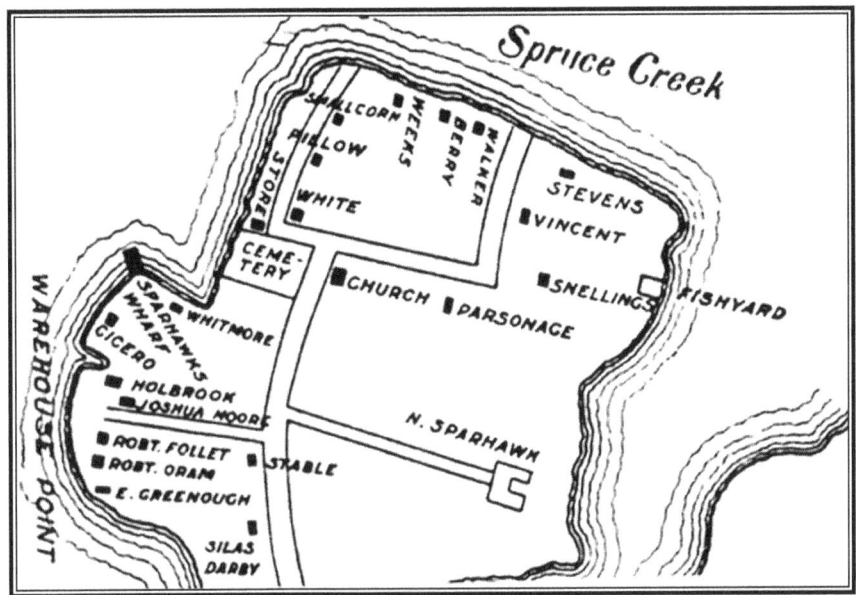

Detail map of Kittery Point, Maine, in 1775. This map shows the residence of Cicero Black, a soldier in the Revolution for New Hampshire. Living next to Sparhawk's Wharf, Cicero resided close to his future commanding officer, Captain Robert Follet. From Edward Stackpole's *Old Kittery and Her Families,* page 59.

Wingate's regiment of New Hampshire militia. His term of service was for four months. At this time, in 1775, Black, "a colored man" (Stackpole, pg. 58), lived next to Col. Nathaniel Sparhawk's wharf, close to Robert Follett, at Warehouse Point in Kittery. He continued to live in Kittery, being listed as a head of household of two free "negroes" in the 1790 Census for Maine, his name listed as Sessoro. He is also listed in the 1800 Census for Maine.

Sources: PSR-NHRWR, vols. 1–2; US-NH Provincial Probate records, vol. 25; TH-Stackpole; CEN-1790-Maine.

BLACK, GEORGE

See the biography of George Evans.

BLACK, PRIMUS

Primus Black enlisted November 26, 1775, in Capt. Charles Nelson's company, in Maj. John Brown's detachment "in service of the United Colonies"

(NHSP, vol. 30, pg. 441–42). He appears on the muster roll of Nelson's company "dated at camp near Quebec" on February 17, 1776 (*ibid.*). Brown's detachment was involved in the operations against Canada and was present at the siege of Quebec. Many of the men in his detachment were New Hampshiremen recruited from the ranger regiment of Col. Timothy Bedel. Capt. Nelson was from Lyme, New Hampshire. Nothing else is known of Primus Black, though he may be the same man as Primas Chandler, or Prime Wheeler, both black soldiers who served in Bedel's regiment.

Sources: PSR-NHSP, vol. 30.

Blackman, Benajah

Blackman enlisted in Bedel's Rangers on February 25, 1776, belonging to Capt. Samuel Young's company. On March 19, 1776, he appears on a list of men, along with "Fortune Negro" (NHRWR, vol. 1, pg. 281) who received various arms and equipment. Blackman is listed as receiving a firearm, one bayonet, and one bayonet belt. No further record of Benajah Blackman has been found. Herbert Aptheker, a noted black historian, identifies him as a Negro, primarily on the basis of his name.

Sources: PSR-NHRWR, vol. 1; OPS: Aptheker—*Negro in the American Revolution.*

Blackman, John

John Blackman is listed on the company rolls of Capt. James Osgood, in Bedel's Rangers, on June 24, 1776. He is also listed as being "left sick on the Road" during the march from Montreal which began on April 20 on a "Return of Absentees" list dated July 22, 1776 (NHRWR, vol. 1, pg. 291). It seems likely that Blackman died during this retreat from Canada, though the possibility exists that he may never have rejoined his unit and enlisted again into the Continental Army. Capt. Osgood stated that this was the case with several men who were listed on the "Return of Absentees." In either case, no further record of John Blackman has been found. Once again, Herbert Aptheker identifies him as a Negro on the basis of his name.

Sources: PSR-NHRWR, vol. 1; OPS: Aptheker—*Negro in the American Revolution.*

Blanchard, George

Blanchard was a resident of Wilton, having lived there many years. He was one of the few blacks in New Hampshire to sign the Association

Test, doing so on June 3, 1776. Blanchard saw two months' service in the war, under Capt. Benjamin Taylor in the town of Amherst's militia company. He was stationed at Winter Hill, outside Boston, in December 1775 and January 1776. George Blanchard was also one of several New Hampshire blacks who hired a substitute during the war. In 1776 he paid Israel How to serve for him "in the Canada voyage one month" (NHRWR, vol. 3, pg. 884). Blanchard, described as a "colored man," was a veterinary surgeon in Wilton (Livermore, pg. 322). His first wife, Hannah, died on December 20, 1779. They had one child, also named Hannah, who was born on June 26, 1778. Soon thereafter, as was the custom of the time, Blanchard remarried a woman named Elisabeth. They had 10 children together, as follows; James (b. 10/20/1781, d. 11/25/1781); Molly (b. 10/11/1782); Betty (b. 3/26/1784); George Washington (b. 8/25/1785, d. 4/10/1812); John (b. 12/25/1786); Anna (b. 1/21/1788); Hepsibah (b. 3/1/1790); Timothy (b. 10/1/1791); Ruth (b. 4/9/1793); and Sally (b. 4/25/1795). Blanchard's youngest son, Timothy, succeeded him as a veterinary surgeon. In 1804, the Blanchards moved to Milford, residing in the western part of town on a farm formerly owned by Peter Shedd. Blanchard died on March 10, 1824, at the age of 84. His wife Elisabeth died on August 28, 1832, at the age of 82.

Sources: PSR-NHRWR, vols. 1, 3; PSR-NHSP, vol. 30; TH-Ramsdell; TH-Livermore, et al.

BLANCHARD, PETER

Peter Blanchard saw extensive militia service during the war. On December 5, 1776, he enlisted in Col. David Gilman's regiment, in the company of Capt. Benjamin Sias for service at Fort Ticonderoga. This service lasted until March 15, 1777. Later in 1777, on July 5, Blanchard enlisted again, this time in Col. Thomas Stickney's militia regiment raised in Concord and the surrounding area. This service lasted only eight days, since the regiment was raised to reinforce the garrison at Fort Ticonderoga, but was forced to turn back when the Americans abandoned the fort, allowing it to fall into British hands. Blanchard next saw service, less than two weeks later, when he served again in Stickney's regiment. He served from July 20 to September 20, 1777, in Capt. Peter Kimball's company, seeing action at the Battle of Bennington and at Saratoga. Blanchard's final service was in Capt. Nathaniel Head's company, in Lt. Col. Daniel Reynolds's regiment of militia from August 20 to September 20, 1781. This regiment was one of several raised to protect New Hampshire's western frontier late in the war. In all his service, Blanchard is listed as being from Canterbury.

He was likely freed during the early part of the war, or just before. As late as December of 1771 he was listed in court records as a "man-servant" (RCR #1773) to William Frost of New Castle. Frost had hired Blanchard out to Daniel and Samuel Sherburne as a servant on their brig *Minerva*, for a voyage to the West Indies and back that lasted five months and 16 days. The *Minerva* was commanded by Jotham Blanchard, who may have been Blanchard's original master. Frost was suing the Sherburnes for compensation for services rendered by Blanchard during the voyage. After the war, Blanchard is listed in the New Hampshire Census records of 1790 and 1800 as being a free "non-white" resident of Litchfield. He had a wife, Dinena Coburn, from Dracut, Massachusetts, and two children whose names are unknown.

Sources: PSR-NHRWR, vols. 14; TR-Hudson, Hollis, Milford; RCR 1773, pg. 40; CEN-1790-1800-NH.

Brewer, Peter

Peter Brewer enlisted from the town of Amherst for Continental service on March 18, 1777, when he joined the 1st NH regiment in Capt. Amos Morrill's company. He served during the tumultuous summer and fall, when his regiment saw heavy action at Fort Ticonderoga and Saratoga. He was killed in action during the second battle at Saratoga on October 7, 1777, at Bemis Heights. Because Brewer was killed, he was unable to collect the bounty money due to him for enlisting. This money was refunded to the town of Amherst. On September 7, 1784, nearly seven years after Brewer's death, the town voted on a warrant presented by Capt. Bezekiel How which would allow him to collect Brewer's bounty. This warrant was dismissed by the town without payment. What relation How had with Brewer is unknown, but he may have been a former master.

Sources: PSR-NHRWR, vols. 1–2; TH-Secomb; TH-Lyford-Concord; OPS-Kidder.

Brown, Jesse

Brown was the servant of one of Portsmouth's most renowned citizens, the Reverend Arthur Brown. The Reverend Brown was the first Rector of Queen's Chapel church in Portsmouth, serving from 1736 to his death in 1773. In his will dated March 6, 1773, he gave "my servant Jesse" to his wife Mary (NHSP, vol. 22, pg. 214). Jesse Brown also appears on an inventory of Brown's estate, dated June 16, 1773, where his value is appraised at £12. Though uncertain, it seems likely that Jesse Brown was freed sometime between 1773 and 1777. He first enlisted for war service on July 21, 1777, when he joined the company of Capt. Kimball Carleton in Col. Moses Nichols's militia regiment. He is listed as being from Chesterfield, and served two months, until September 23, 1777. During this time he saw action at the Battle of Bennington and at Saratoga. Brown saw further service in 1779, when he enlisted for Continental service on July 5. He joined the 3rd NH regiment, serving under Capt. Hawkins. His term of service during this time is unknown, but he is listed on company returns dated February 9, 1780, as "now in the Regmt" at Camp Danbury, in Connecticut (NHRWR, vol. 3, pg. 41). No further record of Jesse Brown has been found.

Sources: PSR-NHRWR, vols. 2–3; PSR-NHSP, vol. 22, pg. 214.

BROWN, PETER

The identification of Peter Brown as a black soldier is tentative. He is included, however, since Massachusetts records list his complexion as "brown" (MSS, vol. 2, pg. 673), possibly indicating that he was of mixed descent. He was a freeman, as he is listed in the 1775 militia census for Temple, which also enumerated "Negros and slaves" (Blood, pg. 99), but counted none. His name appears at the end of this list, but Peter Brown was also a signer of the Association Test, further confusing matters. On the tax rolls for Temple in 1775 he is described as having "gone into ye army" (Blood, p. 99), but owned no guns or powder, and had three females in his household. Brown, along with other members of Temple's militia, was among the first New Hampshiremen to serve in the war. His enlistment began on April 19, 1775, the day of the Battle at Lexington and Concord, when men from Temple responded to the alarm and hurried to Cambridge to join the growing number of militia companies that gathered there from all over New England to lay siege to Boston. He subsequently served eight months, joining the newly formed 3rd New Hampshire regiment, under Col. James Reed, in May of 1775. Brown was among those who saw Charlestown burned by the British, and fought at the Battle of Bunker Hill. He next saw service in August of 1778, when he enlisted in Col. Enoch Hale's regiment under Capt. James Lewis. He served for 10 days, from August 18 to August 28 in Rhode Island during Sullivan's campaign. He enlisted for a final term of service on June 30, 1780, when he was one of New Hampshire's six-month men. Due to the fluctuating value of Continental currency, his bounty for enlisting consisted of a cow and 38 bushels of Indian corn. Brown, aged 26 at this time, served in Capt. Ebenezer Frye's company in Scammell's 3rd NH regiment and was stationed at West Point. In July he appears on a list of men who received a ration of rum and sugar at West Point. Brown's service ended on December 13, 1780, giving him a total wartime service of about one year and three months. What happened to Peter Brown after the war is uncertain. During the war, he lived in Packersfield for a time, but moved back to Temple. Afterwards, he may have moved to Massachusetts, and he may be the same Peter Brown who later moved to Wilna, New York, in Jefferson County. The name of his wife is unknown, though he was likely married before the war. He had two children, a daughter named Sybil (B. 2/1779), and a son named Peter. He later lived with his son, and a son-in-law, Edmund Rawson, in Wilna, and likely died in that area sometime after March of 1837 around the age of 83. It is unknown if he is the same Peter Brown who was a seaman captured by the British, returned to New Hampshire on August 11, 1782, and subsequently sent to Boston.

Sources: PSR-NHRWR, vols. 1–3; PSR-NHSP, vol. 30; TH-Blood; TR-Temple, Nelson, Stoddard, Andover, Chicester, Candia; OPS-Gilmore; PSR-MSS, vol. 2, pg. 673.

Brown, Scipio

Brown was born about 1738 and was the servant to Nathaniel Brown. He became a freeman after his master's death, before June of 1762. New Hampshire records show that Brown was quite active in land transactions prior to the Revolution, from 1762 to 1766. On June 3 and June 28, 1762 he purchased proprietor's shares in the township of Gilmanton, in partnership with James Tappin of Kingston. In September of 1764 he bought land in Raymond from Edward Scribner, and that same year, in partnership with Ephraim Currier, bought from Scribner part of a saw mill in Raymond, including the ironwork and a new saw. Brown continued his transactions in 1766 when he sold 40 acres of land in Raymond, on December 2, for £12 10s. Whether Brown's fortunes declined is unknown, but on February 21, 1769, he was warned to depart from the old parish of Kingston, having come from the east parish (East Kingston). Brown first saw service in 1775, when he enlisted on November 5 in Capt. Abraham French's company of militia under Col. Joshua Wingate. During this service, which lasted four months, Brown was stationed at New Castle. He next enlisted on September 16, 1776, from the town of Kingston in Capt. John Calfe's company of militia under Col. Pierce Long. During this time, he was again stationed at Great Island, New Castle, for about four months. From his militia service, Brown went into Continental service, enlisting into the 1st NH regiment on March 10, 1777, in the company of Captain Amos Emerson. He was paid the state bounty of £20. One source lists

III. The Men

Brown as having deserted on November 10, 1777. Soldiers were often reported as having deserted when their whereabouts and fate were unknown to company officers. However, like many soldiers during the war, Brown had fallen ill. On a regimental list of absentees dating from January of 1778, he is listed as being aged 40, having "black" complexion, hair, and eyes and six feet tall, and is listed as being "sick" at Albany, New York (NHRWR, vol. 2, pg. 437). What further happened to Scipio Brown is unknown. It is possible that he could have died from illness while at Albany.

Sources: PSR-NHRWR, vols. 1–2; NHSP, vols. 79, 97; OPS-Kidder.

Land sale transaction for Scipio Brown. This document details the sale of a quarter share of a saw mill in the town of Raymond to Scipio Brown, "a free Negro Man" in September 1764. Such transactions involving free blacks became more common in the decade before the Revolution. New Hampshire Province Deeds, vol. 75, page 444. Courtesy New Hampshire Division of Records Management and Archives.

BURNS, CAESAR

This is the same man as Caesar Barnes, listed above.

BUTLER, NEGRO

On March 3, 1778, an unnamed "Negro" slave of Lt. Henry Butler of Northwood enlisted into a regiment of state militia "now raising for the defense of Rhode Island" without his master's permission (NHSP, vol. 8, pg. 777). The New Hampshire General Assembly subsequently voted that the slave had to return the enlistment money and that "the Muster Master strike him out of the rolls" (*ibid.*). This unnamed slave tried to enlist in Col. Stephen Peabody's regiment, likely in the company of either Capts. Daniel Reynolds (Londonderry), Ezekiel Giles (Plaistow), or Samuel Dearborn

(Epping). Though Henry Butler served in the Revolution himself, rising in rank to command a militia company of his own, he apparently did not feel a moral obligation to free his slave. Henry Butler later became a selectman in the town of Nottingham, and in the 1790 Census relatives of his, both Benjamin and Zepariah Butler, are listed as having one slave each in Nottingham. One of them may have been the slave who was denied the chance to serve in the army in 1778.

Sources: PSR-NHSP, vol. 8, pg. 777; CEN-1790-NH.

CARLISLE, CATO

Carlisle, like Scipio Africanus, was a sailor aboard the *Ranger*, commanded by Capt. John Paul Jones and built in Portsmouth. Naval historian Samuel Eliot Morison refers to Carlisle as a "local free Negro" (Morison, pg. 114), but local historian Oliver Remick incorrectly states that Cato (Jones) was from Virginia and the former slave of Jones (see the biography of Scipio Africanus for details). Carlisle may have been the slave of Capt. Daniel Carlisle of Westmoreland, or, more likely, that of the Carlisle family who lived in the Seacoast area. John and William Carlisle were soldiers who saw service in forts in Portsmouth Harbor, while Alexander Carlisle of Portsmouth served as a seaman for Massachusetts. Either of these men may have been Carlisle's master. In any event, Carlisle, too, took part in the maiden cruise of the *Ranger*, a sloop of 20 guns from Portsmouth, and was aboard her when she sailed to France and was the first American vessel to have the Stars and Stripes flag saluted by a foreign power. It is unknown if Carlisle stayed aboard the *Ranger*, or followed Jones to his command in the *Bonhomme Richard* in 1779. In addition, it is also unknown if Carlisle was one of three blacks by that name, no last names listed, who enlisted for service aboard the Massachusetts privateer *Aurora* on June 16, 1781, under Capt. David Porter at Boston. These three black sailors, all with the same name, were between 24 and 27 years old, and ranged from five feet, six inches to six feet, one inch tall.

Sources: OPS-Morison, pg. 114, 426–27; OPS-Remick; PSR-NHRWR, vol. 1, pg. 291, vol. 2, pg. 430; PSR-NHSP, vol. 30, pg. 177; MSS, vol. 2, pg. 212.

CARTER, JOHN

Carter first saw war service in July of 1777, when he enlisted in Cap. Simon Marston's company in Col. Joseph Senter's regiment of militia. He served six months in Rhode Island during Sullivan's campaign and its aftermath, starting on July 1st, and was discharged on January 7, 1778. He served again in 1780, when he was enlisted by Lt. Col. Henry Dearborn to fill up the Continental Army. Carter's term of service is unspecified, but it seems likely that he was a six-month man. Four John Carters appear in the 1790 Census for New Hampshire, all listed as white. There is, however, one John Cator listed as a free non-white living in Barrington. In addition, a John Cader and Phillis Clark, both described as "black" (RCR #A14018), were warned to "depart from Deerfield forthwith" on December 16, 1793. It seems certain that the John Carter who saw military service is the same man as John Cator and John Cader. This conclusion is supported by the fact that his commander in the militia, Capt. Marston, was a resident of Deerfield, while the town "Cator" lived in during the 1790 Census, Barrington, is only a short distance from Deerfield. It is unknown if Phillis Clark was Carter's wife.

Sources: PSR-NHRWR, vols. 2–3; CEN-NH-1790; RCR #A14018.

CHANDLER, PRIMAS

Chandler was the slave of Zachariah Chandler of Amherst. He was sold for £110 by William Merchant of Boston on November 11, 1740, and delivered by John Jones. Primas Chandler is described in the records as a "Negro boy" (TH-Bedford, pg. 886). He enlisted for service by February of 1776, the exact date unknown. He served in Capt. Daniel Wilkin's company in Col. Timothy Bedel's Rangers. He was captured in May of 1776 during the battle at the Cedars, during the Canadian campaign, and was one of those men tortured and murdered by the Indians under British control. As far as is known, he is the first documented black soldier from New Hampshire to be killed in action during the war. It is not known if he was freed before the war, but he was married, and had at least one son, also named Primas. Primas, Jr., lived in Bedford and married Flora Bell. Together they had two children, named Hannah and Eri. Primus and Flora are buried together in the old town cemetery.

Sources: NHRWR, vol. 1; TH-Bedford; TH-Secomb; TR-Bedford.

CHESLEY, CORYDON

Chesley was originally from Newington and was born about 1740. He was baptized there on June 17, 1750, a "Negro boy servant" (Rowe, pg. 97) to Joseph Adams, Jr., who was the son of one of New Hampshire's most respected ministers, the Reverend Joseph Adams. "Corradon" (*ibid.*) was sold at the age of 16, on July 19, 1756, by William Shackford to James

Chesley of Dover for £600 old tenor. When his master died in late 1777, Corydon appears on an inventory list of Chesley's estate dated October 15. Along with his new suit of homespun cloth and other personal clothes and bedding, he was valued at £60. He subsequently purchased his freedom for £75 in early 1778 from Lydia Chesley, his master's widow. His certificate of manumission was drawn up by the Reverend Jeremy Belknap of Dover. It seems likely that Corydon Chesley used his bounty money for enlisting in the army to help pay for his freedom, since he enlisted two weeks before his formal manumission. Chesley enlisted on March 31, 1778, in Capt. John Drew's company for Continental service in the 2nd NH regiment. He was one of five black soldiers in Drew's company. His term of service was for three years, during which he saw action at Monmouth and marched in Sullivan's campaign against the Six Nations in Western Pennsylvania and New York. Chesley's final term of service was performed in 1781, from September 17 to the 27, in the company of Capt. Joshua Woodman in Col. Daniel Reynold's regiment of "Militiey" defending New Hampshire's western border. After the war, he married Judith Cole, a white woman, in 1790, and lived in Dover. They had at least two children. The first, whose name and date of birth is unknown, died in infancy on February 9, 1796, and is listed in the mortality records for Dover's Society of Friends (Quakers) by Deacon Benjamin Peirce simply as "Corodon's Child" (Society of Friends, pg. 18). Another child, a daughter named Lydia, is later recorded as marrying "Gamby," a Negro man (Canney, pg. 187). Corydon Chesley lived long enough to receive a pension for his war service. This pension began on April 19, 1819, but was discontinued after May of 1820, when proof of poverty or hardship was required. Because Chesley owned sufficient property, his name was dropped from the pension rolls. Corydon Chesley died on March 1, 1831, at the age of 91.

Sources: PSR-NHRWR, vols. 1–4; PSR-NHSP, vol. 30; CEN-NH-1790; TH-Rowe; OPS-Canney; PEN-SF45635; GSP-Society of Friends, pg. 18.

CHESWILL, WENTWORTH

Wentworth Cheswill ranks as one of Newmarket's most distinguished citizens of his time. Though he served briefly as a soldier in the Revolution, he is more notable for his family background, as well as his own achievements in civil affairs. Cheswill's grandfather, Black Richard, was the slave of David Lawrence of Exeter. In a deed dated September 8, 1707, Lawrence gave to Black Richard his future freedom, promising "that if my said Negro Man do honestly and faithfully serve me two years from the last day of September in the year one Thousand, Seven Hundred and Seven

A handwritten deed, dated October 18, 1717, recording the sale of 20 acres of land from Joseph Hilton to Richard Cheswill, the grandfather of soldier Wentworth Cheswill. This is the earliest known record of land ownership by a black man in New Hampshire. US-New Hampshire Province Deeds, vol. 9, page 6. Courtesy New Hampshire Division of Records Management and Archives.

the said Negro Man shall be free..." (NHSP, vol. 7, pg. 328). After he gained his freedom, Black Richard took the name Richard Cheswill, though it is often reported as Caswell. How he decided upon this surname is unknown, but perhaps it was to honor an individual who helped him after he gained his freedom. Though the rest of Richard Cheswill's life is somewhat shrouded in mystery, he did take part in several land transactions in Newmarket. On October 18, 1717, he purchased 20 acres, "a certain portion or piece of land," from Joseph Hilton of Exeter (NHSP, vol. 9, pg. 6). Less than two weeks later, on October 29, 1717, Richard Cheswill of Exeter, "Negro," sold the same parcel of land to James Rundlett (*ibid.*, pg. 9).

Richard Cheswill had one son, Hopestill, by a woman whose identity is uncertain. She may have been a white woman whose name was Jane Cate. Cate had an illegitimate child named Clement Cate that she claimed was fathered by Clement March of Greenland. Dr. Clement March, later Col. March, was the son of Dr. Israel March, and was one of Greenland's leading citizens in adulthood. However, he never admitted to his supposed liaison with Jane Cate, and never accepted Clement Cate as his son. Clement Cate later adopted his supposed father's surname of March, giving rise to much confusion among latter day historians and genealogists. Known as a somewhat shady character, Clement Cate/March later became the keeper of the local almshouse, and was probably Hopestill Cheswill's half brother. There is no record of any marriage for Richard Cheswill. Jane Cate later settled down and married Henry Beck in Greenland in 1733. It has been asserted by local historians that Hopestill Cheswill's half brother was Paul March, but this is incorrect. There is no doubt that Paul March, baptized in Greenland in 1716, was the son of Dr. Israel March. Hopestill Cheswill's date of birth is unknown, but likely occurred sometime between 1725 and 1728. He learned the trade of a housewright, which, perhaps not coincidentally, was the trade of Jane Cate's father, John Cate, who lived in Portsmouth. Hopestill lived in Newmarket, but often worked in Portsmouth, and is known today for the gambrel-roofed dwellings he built. He framed the house of Paul March in Portsmouth in 1743, which later became the popular Bell Tavern, a gathering place for local patriots prior to the Revolution. This is Hopestill Cheswill's only direct connection to Paul March.

Hopestill Cheswill was involved in a number of land transactions in Newmarket, beginning in 1733, when he bought a piece of land on the south side of the Piscassic River from Samuel and Elizabeth Rawlins. In 1741 he bought 20 acres of land from John Taylor from Edward Hilton's mill grant, and in 1743 bought 20 acres from Ephraim Folsom. This land Cheswill bought ran from his own gate along the Piscassic River to the bridge that crossed it, the path being known as Hope's Path. It was in the house on this tract of land that Wentworth Cheswill was born. In 1749, Hopestill bought one-eighth of Wadley's mill from John Smart, as well as another 20 acres of land near Hope's Path from Samuel and Susannah Dudley.

At an unknown date before 1746, Hopestill Cheswill married Catherine Keniston, about whom little is known. She was probably a descendant of the local Keniston families of Greenland or Stratham. Hopestill was likely of mixed race; his wife was white. By the time their only child, Wentworth Cheswill, was born on April 11, 1746, it is highly likely, given their mixed ancestry, that the family was considered by most as being white. After the birth of Wentworth, who was named after New Hampshire's royal governor, his parents survived for an unknown number of years. In 1756, they sold to Wentworth, aged only 10 years, the land and buildings they had acquired from John Smith at Clark's bridge near Hilton's mill. Wentworth Cheswill would improve on his land holdings over the years, and built a mansion, with large elm trees on the north side of Wadley Road. At his death he owned a considerable amount of land on both sides of Wadley Road, as well as a large farm in Durham.

Wentworth was educated at prestigious Dummer Academy in Byfield, Massachusetts, no small achievement for the grandson of a former slave. On September 13, 1767, at the age of 21, he married Mary Davis (b. 2/19/1750) of Durham. During their long life together, they had 13 children. Cheswill, who was at times, at least early in life, referred to as a "yellow man" or "mulatto" (Kaplan, pg. 200), was appointed justice of the peace for Rockingham County in 1768. A resident of the town of Newmarket, he was chosen to carry dispatches to patriots in Exeter in October of 1775. In April of 1776, he was a signer of the Association Test for Newmarket. His sole stint of military service began on September 29, 1777, when he enlisted in Col. John Langdon's militia regiment of volunteers to help reinforce the Continental Army at Saratoga. He served for one month and three days, his service ending after the defeat of Burgoyne, on October 31, 1777. Langdon's company was "composed of men of rank and position" (NHRWR, vol. 2, pg. 418) in the Seacoast area who volunteered to serve as privates. Langdon himself was later a delegate to the Constitutional Convention in Philadelphia, and governor of New Hampshire. Cheswill was paid the same as all the other privates in this company, no matter what prominence in society they had. Following his service, Cheswill served the town of Newmarket in a variety of positions. In 1778 he was elected as a delegate to New Hampshire's constitutional convention, but apparently did not serve. In March of 1780 he was voted town selectman, and from

1783 to 1787 served several times as selectman and assessor. He also served in several other capacities, including town clerk, auditor, moderator, and coroner. During this time, he was also a well-known builder, like his father, and a shareholder in the Newmarket Social Library. One local resident, commenting on Wentworth as an historian, stated that "He was in the habit of collecting facts relating to the town of Newmarket and its settlement ... and was systematic and accurate in making and arranging his collections" (Newmarket Club of Boston file, undated). In 1806 he ran for a state senate seat, but lost. He was also active in financial affairs, and made large numbers of small loans over the years to area men, some of whom he was forced to take to court in order to be repaid. In short, Wentworth Cheswill was a prominent citizen of Newmarket at all levels, political, financial, and social.

Esquire Wentworth Cheswill died on March 8, 1817, of typhus fever, and was buried two days later. At his death he left behind an extensive library and collection of manuscripts, as well as his mansion. His widow, Mary Cheswill, survived him by 12 years, dying on June 22, 1829. Both were buried in a small cemetery in town, just west of Cheswill's own homestead. Located near the downtown area, their gravestones, though damaged, can still be seen today. The Cheswill children are as follows: Paul, b. 8/4/1768, d. 1832, married, seven children; Thomas, b. 8/20/1770, d. 2/28/1841, had 14 children by two wives. Thomas lived in the old house where his father was born, and was deacon in the church of Newmarket, where he often preached; Samuel, b. 2/28/1772, death date unknown, married, four children; Sarah, b. 4/28/1774, d. 11/9/1829, married, no children; Mary, b. 12/30/1775, married, d. 3/23/1853; Elizabeth, b. 1/9/1778, d. unmarried 7/7/1800; Nancy, b. 3/7/1780, married; Mehitable, b. 3/1/1782, married 1807, d. 1/2/1856; William, b. 2/20/1785, d. at Dover, unmarried, 10/21/1806; daughter, died at birth on 3/4/1787; Martha, b. 4/27/1788, died unmarried 7/20/1867; daughter, died at birth on 10/2/1790; and Abigail, b. 2/8/1792, died unmarried 3/31/1855.

Sources: GSP-Noyes, et al.-pgs. 132–33, 140, 457; PSR-NHSP-Province Deeds, vol. 7, pg. 328 and vol. 9, pgs. 6, 9; OPS-Brighton, pg. 88; TH-George; TH-Brewster; NEW-undated collections of Historical Committee of the Newmarket Club of Boston; PEN-W24831, pg. 212 for John Rollins; PSR-NHRWR, vol. 2; OPS-Kaplan.

Church, Job

Church is listed as a black soldier primarily on the basis of a description of him found in military records. He was a private in Capt. Richard

Shortridge's company in the 2nd NH regiment, serving in the year 1776. His date of enlistment is unknown, as is his length of service. On a sick list for the 2nd NH regiment covering January 1, 1776, to July 8, 1776, made at Chimney Point near Fort Ticonderoga, he is listed as being from Newbury, Massachusetts, and 24 years old. Church is described as five feet, eight inches tall with "black" hair and eyes (NHRWR, vol. 1, pg. 310). The fate of Church is unknown, but it seems likely he may have been one of hundreds of men who died during the disastrous retreat from Canada in 1776 due to illness.

Sources: PSR-NHRWR, vol. 1.

CLEMENTS, PRINCE

Clements, described as a "black" man (NHRWR, vol. 3, pg. 244), enlisted in the 2nd NH regiment for Continental service on April 11, 1781, in the company of Capt. James Carr. He is listed as being 22 years old, and five feet, five inches tall. His hometown is listed as Dover. His term of service was for three years, the same as several other black soldiers who enlisted about the same time, including Cato Hale, Caesar Wood, Caesar Wingate, Michael Sudrick, Tumbril Pickering, and Tobias Cole. Unfortunately, Clements died during his service on November 20, 1781. His manner and place of death are unknown. Though it is strictly conjecture, he could have died from wounds received at the Battle of Yorktown if he was one of the New Hampshiremen selected to join Washington's army. He may have died from illness when the 2nd NH regiment was stationed in the Northern Department in late 1781, setting up winter camp in several detachments at Schenectady and Saratoga, New York.

Sources: PSR-NHRWR, vol. 3.

CLOUGH, CAESAR

Clough saw two terms of service during the Revolutionary War. He first enlisted in February of 1778, in the company of Capt. Ezekiel Worthen, in Col. Stephen Peabody's regiment of militia, and saw service in Rhode Island. His term of service was unspecified, but it probably lasted one month. He again enlisted on March 9, 1778, this time for Continental service in the company of Capt. Caleb Robinson, in the 2nd NH regiment. His term of service was for three years, and he is listed as hailing from Hampton. On July 22, 1778, he was at Camp North Castle, near White Plains, New York, with the rest of his regiment, but later, in August, he is reported as sick at Brunswick, New Jersey. After this report, Caesar disappears from the records, perhaps an indication that he, like so many others, died from his illness. Caesar did have a wife, Priscilla Glasgo, whom he married in Exeter on December 9, 1777, just before joining the army. Both were identified as "Negros" (Bell, pg. 58). The fact that Priscilla (also known as Cill) Clough married another black soldier (see below) a year and a half later seems a sure indicator that Caesar Clough died while in the army.

Sources: PSR-NHRWR, vols. 1–2; PSR-NHSP, vol. 30; TH-Bell.

COFFIN, PRIMAS

Primas Coffin, also known as Prince, was the slave of two different Coffin families. In the *Boston Newsletter*, dated August 4, 1768, he is described as a "Negro man Partly Molatto ... 30 years — A well set fellow born in this country" owned by Zaccheus Clough of Durham. The ad further stated that "Said Negro was lately owned by the Rev. Mr. Coffin Kingston. He can play well on the violin." The Coffins, originally from Exeter, had a long history as slaveholders. The Reverend Peter Coffin's father, Captain Eliphalet Coffin, owned three Negro slaves at his death. One of them, Jack, was left to the Reverend Coffin in a will dated January 15, 1735, with the condition that he could possess him only "after his mother has done with him" (NHSP, vol. 32, pg. 523–4). Jack may have been the father of Primas Coffin. Five years later, in May 1740, the Reverend Coffin moved to East Kingston to serve as the minister there. Among the occupants of the parsonage was Primas Coffin, "whose birthdays were carefully recorded with those of the white children of the family" (Shipton, vol. IX, pg. 289). Later in life, his third master was Enoch Coffin of Epping, who still owned one slave in 1790.

Primas Coffin, a resident of Epping, first saw service on February 13, 1777, when he enlisted for Continental service in the company of Capt. James Norris in the 2nd NH regiment. His term of service is unspecified, but it was likely for three years. During this time, he participated in all the grueling campaigns that the 2nd NH was involved in, including the retreat from Fort Ticonderoga, Saratoga, Monmouth, and Sullivan's campaign against the Six Nations. While on furlough in the spring of 1779, he married Cill Clough in Exeter on May 19th. Both were listed as "Negroes" (Bell, pg. 58). Primas returned to the army to serve out his term, but re-enlisted soon after, on June 28, 1780, serving at the garrison at West Point, in New York, until late July of 1781. However, this time he went by the name Primus, or Prince Lane. During his time in the service from 1779 to 1781, Primus was friends with another black soldier, London Dailey, who, nearly 40 years later, stated that "the said Prime Lane and myself were frequently together, we both being black men" (Pension #S44489).

Following this term of service, Primus Lane had a brief, but active,

III. The Men

taste of civilian life. The Rockingham County Court passed two judgments regarding Lane during this time. The first, in April, 1782, awarded "Primus Lane a Negro Man of Kingston ... Labourer" £20 against Jonathan Greeley of Kingston for 90 days of work from August, 1781 to April, 1782, the spinning of 34 "Seains of Yarn," one pair of woman's stockings, and for "watching cattle one night" (RCR #5054). However, the second judgment, also in April, went against "Primus Lane alias Coffin a Negro Man of Kingston" (RCR #5070) to the sum of £18. Dr. Joseph Tilton of Exeter provided "Sundry Medicines and Attendance from February 7, 1780, to July 5, 1781, for him and wife inclusively" (*ibid.*).

Eight Dollars Reward

RAN-away the 24th of *July* Instant from *Zaccheus Clough* of *Durham*, in *New Hampshire*, a Negro Man partly Molatto named *Primus*, about Thirty Years of age, a well set Fellow, born in this Country, speaks good English; (said Negro was lately own'd by the Rev. Mr *Coffin* of *Kingston*,) had on when he went away a Blue Serge Coat, a grey lappcil'd Jacket lin'd with red Baise, a pair of Deerskin Breeches of a light colour, a Beaver Hat, a pair of blue yarn Stockings: He can play well on a Violin. Whoever apprehends said Negro and brings him to his said Master, shall have EIGHT DOLLARS Reward and all neceffary Charges paid by ZACCHEUS CLOUGH.

N. B. All Masters of Vessels and others, are cautioned against secreting or carrying off said Negro, as they would avoid the penalty of the Law.

Durham, July 30th. 1768.

Runaway slave ad for Primas Coffin. This ad for runaway Primus Coffin, also known as Primus Lane, describes his "Deerskin Breeches," and his prowess at playing the violin. *Boston News-Letter*, August 4, 1768. Courtesy Dimond Library, University of New Hampshire.

Primus Lane enlisted for the third time in May of 1782, this time for the town of East Kingston. This term of service was for three years. During this time, until the New Hampshire Brigade disbanded in January of

This document details the medical service rendered by Dr. Joseph Tilton to black soldier Primus Coffin and his family during 1780 and 1781. RCR #5070. Courtesy New Hampshire Division of Records Management and Archives.

1784, there were many payments to Prince's wife by the town of East Kingston for her support. After the war, Primus Lane/Coffin remained in the area and made his living as a farmer. When he applied for a government pension in September of 1819 he lived in Deerfield, in Rockingham County, and stated he was 80 years old. A former officer in the 2nd NH, Daniel Gookin, testified that he knew Primus Lane and that "Part of the time he was my waiter or servant" (Pension #S44489). Lane began receiving a pension for his war service on November 6, 1819. When it came up for renewal in 1820, he was a resident of Meredith, in Strafford County, and testified that he was 80 years old, with no family. Following this, nothing further regarding Lane is known.

Sources: PSR-NHRWR, vols. 1–3; PSR-NHSP, vol. 30, pg. 298; NHSP, vol. 32, pgs. 523–4; TR-East Kingston; TH-Bell; PEN-S44489; RCR #1782, #5054, #5070.

Colby, Salem

Salem Colby was born a slave about 1760, his master being Hannah Bowers of Billerica, Massachusetts. Bowers sold the young boy to Lot Colby, of Rumford, New Hampshire, for 45 shillings sterling on May 2, 1761. He first saw service on March 1, 1780, when he voluntarily enlisted, likely with his master's consent, in the company of Capt. Nathaniel Hutchins in the 1st NH regiment for Continental service. He first served as Capt. Hutchins's waiter, but later served as a regular soldier. He states in his pension application that he was in no battles, but in several "skirmishes." He also stated that he received a "blow" while in the service and that "in consequence ... he has always been a cripple" (Pension #SF38619). He later served under Capts. Daniel Livermore and Daniel Clapp, and was discharged from service at Newburgh, New York, on July 1, 1783. After the war, he was given his freedom. He lived for a time, with a white wife, in Newport in "quite a colony of negroes" (Wheeler, pg. 252) on Coit Mountain and its vicinity. He later moved to Vermont with his wife, practicing the trade of a farmer in West Fairlee. In April of 1818, when he applied for a government pension for his service, his age is listed as 58. When he applied for the continuation of his pension in July of 1820, his age was listed as 61, while his wife, whose name is not given, is listed as being 57 years old. Salem Colby died on April 18, 1834, but the amount due on his pension was not paid until February 11, 1835, the "reason it had not been called for before being that the only surviving heir has been absent to the state of Massachusetts until within a few weeks" (Pension #SF38619). Whether this surviving heir was his wife or a child of his is unknown.

Sources: PSR-NHRWR, vol. 3; PSR-NHSP, vol. 30; TH-Lyford-Concord; TH-Wheeler; TR-Croydon and Newport; PEN-SF38619, pgs. 101–02.

COLEMAN, PLATO

Coleman, listed as a "black" man, enlisted "voluntarily" in the New Hampshire militia as a six-month man, serving from June to December 5, 1780 (NHRWR, vol. 3, pg. 61). His age was listed as 24, his height as five feet, five inches. Coleman, who was from Newington, could not write and signed his name with an X. He was mustered in at Kingston on July 4 and marched from there to West Point, New York. He appears on a list of men who received rations of rum and sugar while at West Point, and on November 2, 1780, is listed as being sick at Morristown, New Jersey. He was discharged on December 5, 1780, and was paid a blanket allowance and travel money, but none of the wages that were due him. In court records dated February 24, 1783, his master, James Coleman, relinquished "all my rights and demands I have to said servant's state wages" (RCR-Probate #5296). However, the parish of Newington, not Plato, received Coleman's wages and clothing bounty. What happened to Plato Coleman is a mystery. He may have died shortly after the end of his service, or he may simply have moved away as a freeman, leaving his old master and the town of Newington to argue over who received the bounty money that may have helped to buy his freedom.

Sources: PSR-NHRWR, vol. 3; RCR-Probate #5296.

COOK, JOHN

Cook was a "West Indie lad" who was brought to Pembroke by his master, Nathan Waite, from the state of Massachusetts (NHRWR, vol. 3, pg. 791). He lived with Waite in Pembroke for "about two years before going into the Army for Ticonderoga" (*ibid.*). It is unclear when Cook gained his freedom, but it seems likely that it was after his war service. His master stated in September of 1781, that he "furnished him with everything Necessary for each campain," and that he "never Disposed of him to no person living" (*ibid.*). Waite's attempts to gain reimbursement from the town of Pembroke in 1781, 1783, and 1787 for Cook's war service all failed.

Cook first saw service when he was mustered into the company of Capt. William Barron, out of Col. Daniel Moore's militia regiment for service in Canada on July 22, 1776. While at Fort Ticonderoga, Cook reenlisted in May of 1777 in the 2nd NH regiment for Continental service, serving in Capt. Frederic Bell's 3rd company of Dover men. Cook subsequently took part in the 2nd NH regiment's actions at Fort Ticonderoga, Saratoga, and Valley Forge. His company commander, Capt. Bell, was wounded at the Battle of Freeman's Farm, and died soon after. It is unknown if Cook fought with his regiment at the Battle of Monmouth, since he is listed in June of 1778 as "tending to the sick" at Valley Forge (NHSP, vol. 30, pg. 468). His medical service, though he was likely untrained, is unique among New Hampshire's black soldiers. Muster rolls at this time list his age as 17, and his residence as Dover. After the expiration of his initial enlistment, Cook enlisted again with the 2nd NH on June 17, 1779, this time serving for one year, for Nottingham West. Cook's final term of service came in 1781, when he enlisted yet again with the 2nd NH, this time for three years, in the 6th company of Capt. Jeremiah Fogg. Cook was subsequently one of the New Hampshire men who was picked to serve in Lafayette's Light Infantry Corp in 1781. He was among a group of New Hampshire men paid a $15 bill of credit as a "Gratuity for our faithful services" (NHRWR, vol. 3, pg. 241) at camp on the James River in Virginia on May 10, 1781. Later that year, as part of Lafayette's Corps, Cook would see much action, culminating in the Yorktown campaign in October to capture Cornwallis.

After the war, John Cook was a resident of Exeter, from which he was warned to depart in March of 1784. In 1790, he was still a resident of Exeter. Cook applied for, and received, a government pension for his war service on April 13, 1818, stating that his discharge certificate was taken by "the person who bought his land" (Pension #SF45694). When his pension was up for renewal, Cook stated on August 15, 1820, that he was 58 years old, had no family living with him, and his occupation was that of a laborer.

Sources: PSR-NHRWR, vols. 1, 3; PSR-NHSP, vol. 30; CEN-NH-1790; PEN-SF45694.

COTTON, JOSEPH, JR.

Little is known of Joseph Cotton, Jr. He was the son of Joseph and Nancy Cotton, and had two brothers, Eleazor and James. All, except Joseph Jr., were the property of William Cotton, of Portsmouth. Joseph Cotton, Jr.'s master was Eliza Cotton, likely the widow of William. Cotton may have later been sold to George Osborne, since he served in Capt. Osborne's company of minutemen for the defense of Piscataqua Harbor in 1775. Later, in July of 1776, Cotton enlisted as a marine corporal aboard the Continental Navy frigate *Raleigh*, which was being built and fitted out at

Portsmouth. The muster roll lists his height as five feet, three inches, and his complexion as "black" (NHGR, vol. 2, pg. 184). George Osborne also served on the *Raleigh* as captain of marines. What further became of Joseph Cotton, Jr., is unknown. The 1790 Census for Portsmouth lists only one man named Joseph Cotton. He is listed as being white, and is not the same individual.

Sources: PSR-MSS, vol. 4; Portsmouth South Church records, pg. 243; GSP-NHGR, vol. 2, pg. 184.

Cutler, Tobias

Tobias Cutler was the slave of Col. Enoch Hale of Rindge. He was born about 1758, and was said to have been promised his freedom at the age of 21. Cutler did not gain his freedom in 1779, but was given it upon enlisting in the Continental Army for Rindge on March 24, 1781, with the consent of his master. Upon his enlistment, the town "voted the said Tobe be Received & Deemed a Legal Inhabitant" (Stearns, pg. 169). Cutler enlisted in the 2nd NH regiment, serving in the 4th company under Capts. McGregor and Livermore. The muster rolls list Cutler as being sick at Albany, New York, in January and February of 1782. He likely served until late 1783, or January 1784, when the NH battalion was disbanded. Tobias Cutler was an influential man in Exeter's small black community. He was a leader in local military turnouts and celebrations. He married Dorothy, the daughter of two ex-slaves named Caesar Paul and Lovely Rollins of Stratham. Tobias and Dorothy had two children, Mary and Rufus (b. 3/2/1797, d. 11/4/1864). Mary married Samuel Baker and moved to Boston, while Rufus married Diana Cilley (b. 10/2/1796) of Deerfield on March 12, 1825. Like his father, Rufus Cutler grew to prominence in Exeter's black community and, with the aid of former black soldier London Dailey, helped form a society for its benefit. There were many descendants of the family of Rufus, who lived in Exeter well into the 20th century.

The activities of Tobias Cutler are also recorded in the local courts. In 1805–6, he was sued by James Burley for a note he refused to pay. He lost, and was forced to pay $9.41, plus $5.26 in court costs. In 1813, Tobias sued Josiah Bartlett of Stratham, but lost again, and had to pay $21.16, plus court costs of $7.55. Cutler died on September 13, 1834, at the age of 76, and was buried in Exeter's Winter Street Cemetery, where his gravestone, and that of his wife Dorothy, can still be seen.

Sources: PSR-NHRWR, vol. 3; TH-Bell; TH-Stearns; New-*Exeter News-Letter*.

DAILEY, LONDON

Dailey enlisted for Continental service in July of 1779 from the state militia of New Hampshire. He joined the 2nd NH regiment and served in Capt. Caleb Robinson's company. London came from, and served for, the town of Gilmanton. On the muster rolls for June 1, 1782, he is listed as being on command at Schenectady, New York, but by December of 1782 was stationed at West Point. Dailey was discharged after four years of service on June 7, 1783. His discharge certificate was personally signed by Gen. George Washington, and attested to his faithful service. In addition, he is one of the few men from New Hampshire known to have been honored with the Badge of Merit. This award was probably similar to the modern day Good Conduct medal. Prior to the end of his service, London Dailey married a woman named Margaret in Exeter on March 11, 1781. He continued to live in Exeter after the war, and was one of the most distinguished men in its black community. However, he was also involved in a number of court actions brought against him. In February of 1811 Prince Light, another black veteran from Exeter, "had taken from him by Daily [sic]" (RCR-Civil-#1015) four loads of manure, a hand sled, and 30 pounds of feathers, all to the value of $13.33. He filed suit against Dailey for payment five years later, and won a judgment of $20 against him on November 25, 1816. London Dailey, however, was either unable, or refused to pay Light. The debt remained unpaid in February of 1817. On October 6, 1820, London Dailey, listed as being a resident of Deerfield, was arrested and committed to jail in Exeter for a judgment of $50.75, plus $5.62 in damages, against him by Samuel Chamberlain of Exeter.

Despite his financial woes, London Dailey was still active in the community. In the *Exeter Watchman* (page 3) for July 22, 1817, there is a notice for "the people of colour throughout the state" to meet at his residence to form a society "beneficial to said people" (see illustration). Often referred to as "Lunnon," Dailey was known as a skilled gardener, and Margaret was well known by Phillips Academy students for the fine cake and ale she served. The Dailey home was described as "quite a comfortable cottage," and "everything about the interior of the house was a pattern of neatness" (*Exeter News-Letter*, December 12, 1879). London and Margaret had a sizeable family, including four boys, Robert, Abraham, Jerry, and Jack. When Margaret Dailey died is unclear, but on March 22, 1820, Dailey was married again, this time to Nancy Barhew. In 1818, Dailey applied for and received a government pension for his war service. On June 28, 1820, in an application for the renewal of his pension, Dailey listed his age as 72, and that he had a wife and two children, ages nine and one year old, living with him. Dailey and his family later moved to Epsom, where he died on June 8, 1832. His second wife, Nancy, applied for, and received, a widow's pension in 1853. Living in Boston, Nancy Dailey deposed on July 7, 1853, that she was aged 80 and remained a widow. In September of 1853, her two sons, Robert Dailey (aged 53) of Salem, Massachusetts, and Abraham Daily (aged 47), of Boston, testified that they were the sons of London Dailey. On March 28, 1855, Nancy Dailey, aged 81, applied for and received 60 acres of bounty land "due her as a widow of London Dailey, Revolutionary Soldier" (Pension #WF5260), having already been granted 100 acres.

Sources: PSR-NHRWR, vols. 2–3; PSR-NHSP, vol. 30; RCR-Civil #1015; RCR #41724; TR-Gilmanton; NEW-*Exeter-Watchman*, *Exeter News-Letter*; PEN-WF-5260-BLWT.

NOTICE.

THE people of *colour* throughout the State are respectfully invited to appear at the residence of LONON DAILEY in Exeter, on Wednesday the 13th day of August next at 10 o'clock in the forenoon, for the purpose of forming a society beneficial to said people. The particular objects of the society will be made known at the time and place aforesaid.

Per order of LONON DAILEY.
RUFUS E. CUTLER, *Sec'y.*

N. B. An Oration will be pronounced on said day at 3 o'clock in the afternoon.

Exeter, July 22, 1817.

This unusual ad details a meeting scheduled to be held in Exeter at the home of black veteran London Dailey. Whether or not the proposed "society" for "people of colour" was ever formally established is unknown. Secretary Rufus Cutler was the son of soldier Tobias Cutler. *Exeter Watchman*, August 12, 1817. Courtesy Exeter Public Library.

DAVIDSON, DAVID

Davidson was a sailor during the Revolution who enlisted at Portsmouth in June of 1776 for service aboard the Continental frigate *Raleigh* for one year. Enlisting as an able seaman, his wages were listed as being eight dollars per month. At the time of his enlistment, Davidson was then living aboard a vessel called the *Nelly*. This was a 300-ton British vessel, commanded by Lyonel Bradstreet, captured by an American privateer and brought into New Hampshire. Davidson, likely a member of its crew, is described as being five feet, six and a half inches tall, of "black" complexion, and "Creole" (NHGR, vol. 3, pg. 25). His designation as a Creole, a person of mixed Spanish or French and Negro descent, makes it likely that David Davidson originally came from one of the Southern colonies or the West Indies. Since the *Raleigh* did not sail from the Piscataqua River until August of 1777, it is unknown if Davidson was still a crew member, as his original enlistment would have expired in June of 1777. Nothing further regarding Davidson is known.

Sources: OPS-Remick, pg. 218; NEW-*Freeman's Journal; New Hampshire Gazette*, August 31, 1776; GPS-NHGR, vol. 3, pg. 25.

DEARING, CATO

Cato Dearing was the slave of Capt. Ebenezer Dearing of Portsmouth. Little is known about him, other than the fact that he accompanied his master to war. Ebenezer Dearing was 1st lieutenant in the field artillery companies of Doctor Hall Jackson and Capt. George Turner in 1775, and commanded his own artillery company in 1776-77 in Col. Pierce Long's militia regiment. In July of 1777 he advertised his slave Cato, a "Negro Man" (*Freeman's Journal-New Hampshire Gazette*, July 26, 1777, pg. 4) as having run away from Fort Washington in Portsmouth Harbor. Cato was described as being "about Forty Years old, about five Feet six Inches tall, thick set, had on a gray Jacket, and Leather Breeches, blue Yarn Stockings" (*ibid.*). A 30-shilling reward was offered for his return. Because Capt. Dearing was at Fort Ticonderoga with Long's regiment during the time this advertisement appeared, it is likely that Cato ran away in February or March of 1777, just before Long's regiment marched to Fort Ticonderoga. It is possible that Cato ran away at this time because he had no desire to go off to war such a long distance from home. It is unknown if Cato Dearing succeeded in his bid for freedom, but the 1790 Census for Portsmouth lists Ebenezer Dearing as the owner of two slaves. One of these may have been Cato.

Sources: NEW-as above; PSR-NHRWR, vol. 1; CEN-1790-NH.

DIAMOND, JOHN-JACK

John Diamond enlisted for the town of Epping into Continental service in February of 1778 for three years, or the duration of the war. Joining Capt. Caleb Robinson's company in the 2nd NH regiment, "He promised to obey his officers and the army's rules and regulations and to carry with him into the service a cartouche box, knapsack, and blanket" (NHRWR, vol. 2, pg. 450–51). On March 9, 1778, he was mustered in service and was paid the Continental bounty due him. On July 22, 1778, he was mustered in at Camp North Castle, near White Plains, New York. At some point, Diamond served as the personal waiter or servant to Col. George Reid, the commander of the 2nd NH regiment. In an order dated

June 7, 1780, it was requested that the Board of War "deliver to the bearer, Jack Diamond, one pair Leather breeches, one pair overalls, one shirt, he waits on Col. Reed [sic]" (NHRWR, vol. 4, pg. 364). How long Diamond served Reid is unknown, but on July 15, 1780, he was transferred to the infantry. The last known record of John Diamond is dated March 24, 1781, when the town of Exeter billed the state of New Hampshire for supplying Diamond's family while he was in the army. The New Hampshire Census for 1790 lists Susanna Diamond of Exeter as a black head of household for a family of four. Susanna was likely John's widow. He may have died during his service, or afterwards, between 1781 and 1790.

Sources: PSR-NHRWR, vol. 1–4; PSR-NHSP, vol. 30.

DICKINSON, CASTOR

Very little is known about Castor, also known as Caesar, but the men he was associated with were very prominent in New Hampshire. Dickinson also holds the distinction of being one of only a few black soldiers who served in both the French and Indian War, as well as the Revolution. He was originally the slave of Capt. Robert Rogers, the Ranger hero of the French and Indian War. In 1761, Rogers married Elizabeth, the daughter of the distinguished Reverend Arthur Browne, of Portsmouth. On December 20, 1762, Dickinson and Sylvia, a Negro woman, Pomp, a Negro boy aged 12, and an Indian boy named Billy, were sold by Rogers, "Captain of one of His Majesties Independent Companies of Foot in South Carolina," to the Reverend Browne. Soon thereafter, on December 22, Dickinson, aged "about 28" (NH Province Deeds, vol. 69, pg. 58–60), was sold by Browne to his brother Marmaduke of Newport, Rhode Island, to be held in trust for Elizabeth, his daughter. Prior to the American Revolution, Dickinson became a free black, and was married to Fan, the slave of John Clogstone of Dunstable, whose freedom, and that of their children, he had purchased after 1781. Before this, in 1774, Clogstone had promised Fan that her children would be free when she reached the age of 21, if she paid him £20, or if she served him until she was 30 years old for only £10. Clogstone also promised that if Fan had other children, they would be free if she brought them up herself. Fan was still a slave in 1782, when Clogstone agreed to free her and her children for £13 lawful silver money, $680 in Old Tenor and Continental currency, and 10 bushels of Indian corn.

Although Castor is listed as one of Old Dunstable's soldiers of the Revolutionary War, his length and type of service is unknown. Since his name does not appear in New Hampshire's Revolutionary War rolls, it seems likely that he may have served briefly in one of the local militia companies. His Revolutionary War service is unknown, but Dickinson was a soldier for a short time during the French and Indian war. While still a slave to Robert Rogers, he served under Capt. Thomas Bell as a private at Fort William and Mary at New Castle for five months and three days. His name spelled as Sesor Deckson, he served from December 18, 1757, to May 10, 1758, and was paid a total of £22 13s. 7d. for his term of service, the same as other soldiers who were white. He served at Fort William and Mary yet again, from December 15, 1758, to May 10, 1759, with his name spelled on the rolls as Ceazer Dickson. Nothing further is known about Dickinson after the war.

Sources: PSR-NHRWR, vol. 1, pg. 20; PSR-NHSP, vol. 69, pg. 58–60; TH-Fox; CH-Hurd-*Hillsborough*; OPS-Potter, pgs. 198 and 222; Hillsborough City Deeds, vol. 3, pg. 630, vol. 9, pg. 306.

Dow, London

London Dow, a former slave, was a native of Africa and was born about 1719. When he was brought to the colonies is unknown, but prior to coming to Hanover, New Hampshire, he was a slave in the Peters family of Hebron, Connecticut. The date of his arrival in New Hampshire is unknown, but he may have been one of the four male slaves listed in the 1773 Census for Hanover. It is also unknown whether Dow had any association with the Wheelock family, who brought the first slaves to the town when they established what would later become Dartmouth College. Nothing further is known of Dow prior to his military service. On November 26, 1775, a "London" (no last name listed) enlisted in Capt. Robert Cochrane's company as a private, in Maj. John Brown's detachment of the Green Mountain Boys. The Green Mountain Boys were recruited as a Continental regiment from the territory between New York and New Hampshire known as the New Hampshire Grants, which later became the state of Vermont. Dow was also present with his company, at camp near Quebec, on February 16, 1776, and was likely a participant in the siege of the British stronghold. He must have been a man of some size and strength, since he was probably over the age of 50 when serving in the army. Dow had a wife named Peggy, and apparently no children, but little else about him is known. He is listed in the New Hampshire Census for 1800 as a resident of Hanover, the head of a family of two non-whites, and is reported to have died in 1819 at the age of 100 years. Peggy Dow, his wife, died in 1820, at the age of 80.

Sources: TH-J.K. Lord, pgs. 301–02; OPS-Roberts, pgs. 60–61.

Downing, Simon

Simon was probably the "Negro" slave of Richard Downing of Newington (NHRWR, vol. 3, pg. 514). He enlisted on July 9, 1782, in the New Hampshire Battalion of Continental troops for a term of three years, and was paid the state bounty. He likely served until the New Hampshire Battalion was disbanded in early 1784. Although no further records have been found that mention Simon by name, the 1790 Census for New Hampshire lists Richard Downing of Newington as having in his household two slaves. It seems likely that one of these was Simon.
Sources: PSR-NHRWR, vol. 3.

Duce, Cato

Cato Duce served two terms in the Revolutionary War. He first enlisted on May 25, 1775, in Col. Enoch Poor's newly formed 2nd NH regiment, in the company of Capt. Winthrop Rowe. Duce's regiment was stationed in the Seacoast area for the defense of the Piscataqua River. Duce's length of service in 1775 is unknown, but it was probably for six months. On October 4, 1775, he appears on a list of men who were paid four dollars coat money at Medford, Massachusetts. This money was paid to many of the New Hampshire men who enlisted in 1775 to allow them to buy a regimental coat, or as reimbursement for having already purchased one. He also served in the New Hampshire Battalion late in the war, enlisting on May 1, 1782, as a private in the 5th company of the 2nd NH regiment. A year later, on May 21, 1783, he appears on the muster roll of Maj. William Scott's 4th company of the NH Battalion. Again, Duce's length of service is unknown, but he likely served until late 1783, or to January of 1784. Duce's family was apparently well known in Exeter, but there is little information on him, and nothing further is known of him, at least under the name of Cato. Several possibilities exist. He may have died prior to 1790, since he is not listed in the census for that year in Exeter. Another possibility, which seems likely, is that he dropped his slave name, Cato, and took the name Robert. Name changes among newly freed slaves were not uncommon. Robert "Bob" Duce was well remembered. He and his wife lived in Exeter, though Bob was a "seafaring man, and, of course, was often away from home" (*Exeter News-Letter*, December 12, 1879). Robert Duce's wife, like London Dailey's wife, Margaret, was also known for the cake and ale she served, and for the neatness and cleanliness of her home. Bob Duce was well remembered for his heroics in 1807 or 1808, when the store of Clark Dean caught fire. He "perched himself on the ridge pole of the store next to it and fought the fire like a salamander" (*ibid.*). His bravery is further demonstrated by the fact that the two stores were no more than eight feet from each other. Bob Duce was listed in the 1790 census for Exeter as "Bob Bombaway Duce" (NH Census-1790, pg. 67). The origin of this nickname is unknown, but perhaps it is in relation to his Revolutionary War service. One final, less plausible, theory is that Robert Duce was a son, or brother of Cato Duce. What became of Robert "Bob" Duce after 1807 is unknown. Neither Cato or Robert Duce appear in New Hampshire pension records.

Sources: PSR-NHRWR, vols. 1, 3; TH-Bell; PEN-NA-M881-roll 506; NEW-*Exeter News-Letter;* CEN-NH-1790.

Dunkin, Thomas

Thomas Dunkin was the slave of John Dunkin of New Grantham. He enlisted in the 1st NH regiment on March 17, 1777, joining the 4th company of Capt. John House as a private. He apparently enlisted to serve for the nearby town of Enfield, since he appears on a list of men who joined the army for that town, dated February 17, 1779. Thomas Dunkin's term of service was for three years and, on a list dated April 23, 1778, his hometown is listed as Hartford, Vermont, his age "about 30," his height 5 feet, 8 inches, and his "complection D.black, nativity unknown" (NHSP, vol. 11, pg. 611). Nearing the end of his service, Dunkin appears on the rolls of the 1st NH regiment, 4th company, dated January 1, 1780. Three other black soldiers also served in this company at the same time. They were George Knox, Derrick Oxford, and Robert Miller. Dunkin is one of the few black soldiers who did not receive his freedom after the war. The 1790 Census for New Hampshire still lists one slave for John Dunkin of New Grantham. This was Thomas Dunkin. He continued to live in slavery until at least 1798, when town records still indicate that he was a slave of John Dunkin. Whether, or if, Thomas Dunkin ever received his freedom is unknown. One source erroneously lists Dunkin as having died in the course of his service.

Sources: PSR-NHRWR, vols. 1–2; PSR-NHSP, vol. 11, pg. 611.

Evans, George

George Evans was the "Negro servant" (Wentworth, pg. 174) of Benjamin Evans of Dover. On January 4, 1776, he was married by the Reverend Jeremiah Belknap, of Dover, to Phillis, the "Negro servant" (*ibid.*) of Solomon Emerson. Soon thereafter, before enlisting, George Evans made out a will, leaving all his property to Phillis. On June 5, 1777, "George — a negro man" enlisted as a private from Madbury in Capt. John Drew's company in the 2nd NH regiment (NHRWR, vol. 1, pg. 618). His term of service was for three years, and his age was listed as 36. His place of abode was listed as Barrington. George saw action right away, fighting with the 2nd NH on the retreat from Fort Ticonderoga, and was in the Battle of Hubbardton, where the 2nd NH was hit hard. From July 7 to October 8, 1777, George Evans is listed as missing. What happened to him during those two months is unknown. He may have been captured and released by the British, or he could have become separated from his unit and spent the time trying to find and rejoin his unit. However, on a list of absentees for the 2nd NH regiment, dated January of 1778, he is listed as having deserted at Poughkeepsie, New York. On this list he is described as George "Black," aged 36, height 6 feet, and "black" complexion (NHRWR, vol. 2, pg. 442). What further became of George Evans, and whether he ever returned to New Hampshire, is unknown.

Sources: NHRWR, vols. 1–3; TH-Stackpole; OPS-Wentworth.

Fisk, Cato

Cato Fisk was the slave of Dr. Ebenezer Fisk of Epping. After his master's death, Cato appears on an inventory list of Dr. Fisk's estate, dated January 2, 1777, and was appraised at the value of £25. He likely gained his freedom soon after, since he enlisted for Continental service on May 1, 1777, for three years, from the town of Epping. A document dated February 26, 1778, states that he was "to furnish or carry with him into the service a cartouche box, knapsack, and blanket," and that he would "promise obedience to the officers set over us, and to be subject to the rules and regulations that are or may be appointed for the Army" (NHRWR, vol. 2, pgs. 450–51). Fisk served in Capt. William Rowell's company in the 2nd NH regiment, and served with that regiment in all the major northern campaigns. Though not recorded, Fisk must have re-enlisted in 1781, since he continued in his service until 1783. Muster rolls for his company dated February 16, 1783, list him as having deserted, because he did not return from his home furlough on time. However, such an occurrence this late in the war, when the fighting had ceased, was not uncommon, and it is unlikely that Cato Fisk was the subject of any disciplinary action. Fisk ended his service on June 7, 1783, when he was discharged with the Badge of Merit, having "served without any intermission" (Pension #W14719). His pension records state that he was "a drummer in the Army — A fiddler at home" (*ibid.*). Soon after the war, Fisk married a black woman named

Elsa Husow (also spelled "Alice Wooso") in Brentwood, the ceremony being performed by the Reverend Nathaniel Trask. They had three children, James (b. 1792, declared insane in 1820), Ebenezer (b. 1796), and Nancy (b. 1790, still alive in 1838). It is likely that other members of the Husow family also lived with Cato Fisk and his wife. A descendant of one of these may have been Sarah Huso, who died in Exeter in 1879 at the age of 83. Life for Cato Fisk and his family after the war was a tough one, and probably typical of that of many black veterans. On February 7, 1787, he was warned to depart Exeter, along with 18 other blacks. That same year he is also listed as a pauper for the town of Exeter. Fisk continued to live in Exeter, where he and his wife and children are recorded in the 1790 Census. During the late 1790s, Cato Fisk and his family moved about the area frequently. He is listed as a pauper for the town of Raymond in 1797, for Poplin (now Fremont) in 1799, and for Deerfield in 1801. In April of 1818, he received some relief when he was granted a pension for his war service. According to pension records, in July of 1820 he was a resident of Deerfield, and earned his living as a laborer at the age of 61. Soon after, he moved to Epsom, since he died there on March 24, 1824. One interesting local anecdote states that the minister for Epsom preached a sermon on the death of Cato Fisk and another Revolutionary War veteran, the well known Gen. Michael McClary, but offended some members of his parish by mentioning Cato's name before that of the general.

Sources: PSR-NHRWR, vols.1–3, PSR-NHSP, vol. 30, pg. 284; Pen-#W14719; RCR-Probate records, vol. 23, pg. 451; TR-Fremont.

Fogg, Jockey

Jockey Fogg was a slave of the McClary family of Epsom, New Hampshire. Likely owned by Capt. Michael McClary, who served in the 3rd NH regiment from November 1776 to September 1778, Fogg was his "servant in the Army," and "used to speak of his horse as a large, powerful iron-gray, four year old stallion, so exceedingly vicious that none could mount or govern him but the Captain. He could spring upon his back and, by the power of his arm, govern him with the greatest of ease" (French, vol. 4, pg. 41). Accompanying his master, Capt. McClary, Fogg was in the thick of battle, being present at the Battle of Trenton in 1776, Fort Ticonderoga and Saratoga during Burgoyne's campaign in 1777, and at the Battle of Monmouth in 1778. Nothing further of Fogg is known, but he likely gained his freedom at war's end. Michael McClary continued his residence in Epsom, but is not listed as a slave owner in the 1790 Census for that town.

Sources: TH-French; CEN-NH-1790.

Follett, William

Follett enlisted for service as a sailor aboard the Continental Navy frigate *Raleigh* at Portsmouth on August 22, 1776. The *Raleigh* was then being built and outfitted by her captain, Thomas Thompson, in the Piscataqua River, but was not destined to sail until a year later. Follett enlisted for one year at the rate of eight dollars per month and, like fellow enlistee David Davidson, was described as having a "black" complexion, and as "Creole" (NHGR, vol. 2, pg. 181). His height was listed as 5 feet, 11 inches. Since the *Raleigh* did not sail until just 10 days prior to the end of Follett's term of service, it is unknown for certain if he was still aboard the ship when she departed Portsmouth on her maiden voyage. Nothing further regarding Follett is known.

Sources: OPS-Remick, pg. 218; GSP-NHGR, vol. 2.

Fortune

Known only by the name "Fortune Negro" (NHRWR, vol. 1, pg. 281), this man was a member of Capt. Samuel Young's company in Col. Timothy Bedel's Rangers. He first appears on payroll lists for his company on February 26, 1776. On March 19, 1776, while at Orford, he was issued a firearm, a bayonet, and a belt. On April 25, 1776, he was mustered in with his company "at garrison Montreal" (NHRWR, vol. 1, pg. 285). Having taken part in the failed invasion of Canada, Fortune was still a member of Bedel's Rangers on June 24, 1776, when he is listed with his company at Isle aux Noix. Nothing further is found for Fortune after this date. He may have been one of the many soldiers who died at Isle aux Noix due to disease, or he may have lived to enlist and fight again, perhaps under a more complete name.

Sources: NHRWR, vol. 1; PEN-NA-M881-roll 536.

Fox, Benjamin

Fox first served in the war when he enlisted on November 5, 1775, in Capt. Smith Emerson's company in Col. Joshua Wingate's regiment of militia. Stationed on Seavey's Island, Fox served for four months, mostly engaged in the defense of Piscataqua harbor. He was also listed as a six-weeks man in Capt. Stephen Clark's company that was stationed for the winter of 1775-76 at Winter Hill, near Boston. Later in 1776, on July 11, Fox enlisted in the 1st NH regiment, though he apparently did not join, since he is listed as a "deserter," and described as 19 years old, "black" complexion, and five feet, two inches tall, belonging to the "Government" of New Hampshire (NH State Archives-Rev. War Records, folder 3, item 38). Possibly preferring to be stationed closer to home, Fox enlisted several months later, on September 30, 1776, in Capt. Mark Wiggins' company in Col. Pierce Long's regiment stationed at New Castle. His term of service is unknown, but continued well into the fall of 1777. He is listed on a group of men who were "Fit to march to Ticonderoga" (NHRWR, vol. 1, pg. 515), and indeed, did go there. As a private in Long's militia regiment, he saw heavy action at the fall of Fort Ticonderoga in July 1777 and continued action during the Saratoga campaign. He was probably released from service in September or October of that year. Like many men, he was reimbursed by the state for the loss of his personal belongings at Fort Ticonderoga, being paid just over two pounds (NHRWR, vol. 3, pg. 529).

Fox does not show up again until after the war when, in March 1786, the town of Raymond voted to abate Fox's poll tax for the year 1785. At this same time, Fox is listed as a landowner. Benjamin Fox received a pension for his militia service starting on April 1, 1833, at the age of 73.

Sources: PSR-NHRWR, vols. 1, 3, and 4; PSR-NHSP, vol. 30, pg. 366; PEN-NA-M881-rolls 523, 559; TR-Raymond; NH State Archives-Rev. War Records.

Freeman, John

Freeman enlisted in Timothy Bedel's company of Rangers on June 15, 1775, and was discharged on December 31, 1775. He served a total of 6 months and 17 days. Enlistment records state his age as 24, and his residence as Hanover. No further records are found regarding John Freeman, and he is only identified as a black soldier based on his last name.

Sources: PSR-NHRWR, vol. 1; OPS-Aptheker, *Negro in the American Revolution*.

Freeman, Moody

Like John Freeman, Moody Freeman also enlisted in Bedel's Rangers on June 15, 1775. His rank, however, was that of corporal, and his age was listed as 22, and his residence as Hanover. He served 6 months and 17 days. Freeman again saw service from October 28 to November 18, 1776, when he was a private in Col. Jonathan Chase's militia regiment. This unit marched from Cheshire County to reinforce the army at Fort Ticonderoga after its disastrous defeat in Canada. Freeman served once more, again as a corporal, in Chase's militia regiment, from July 4 to July 11, 1777. This time, the men marched from Cornish and towns adjacent to reinforce the Fort Ticonderoga garrison during Burgoyne's offensive. After his military service, no further record of Moody Freeman is found. He is identified as a black soldier solely on the basis of his last name, thus leaving a good deal of doubt. The possibility exists that he was the slave of Lt. Jonathan Freeman, who served in Chase's regiment at the same time, and was also a resident of Hanover.

Sources: PSR-NHRWR, vols. 1, 2, 4; OPS-Aptheker, *Negro in the American Revolution.*

FREEMAN, PETER

See the biography of Peter Bartlett.

FRENCH, OLIVER

Oliver was the slave of Gould French of Epping, who advertised him as a runaway slave in the October 25, 1775, edition of *The New Hampshire Gazette* (see illustration). Oliver is described as a "Negro Man," aged 23, and "a well built strait Limb'd Fellow, about six Feet high, speaks slow." Whether Oliver was ever caught and returned to his master is unknown. In March or April of 1777, he enlisted in the 2nd NH regiment for three years, in Capt. James Norris's first company. He was listed simply as "Oliver," with no last name, and came from the town of Epping. Whether

> RANAWAY from his Mafter Gould French of Epping, a Negro Man named Oliver.— He had on when he went away, a dark colour'd homefpun Coat with red Lining, a red Jacket, and carried with him another—He was about 23 Years of Age, a well built ftrait Limb'd Fellow, about fix Feet high, fpeaks flow, had on a Moofe Skin Breeches—Whoever takes up faid Negro, and confines, or returns him, fo that his faid Mafter may have him again, fhall have Five Dollars Reward, and neceffary Charges paid by me,
> Epping, Octob. 25. 1775.   GOULD FRENCH

Runaway slave ad for Oliver French. One interesting aspect of these is the descriptions of clothing worn at the time by slaves. French was one of three runaway slaves advertised at the same time. All later became soldiers in the Revolution. *New Hampshire Gazette,* November 2, 1775. Courtesy Portsmouth Public Library.

Oliver served out his full term is unknown, since there are no further records regarding him.

Sources: PSR-NHRWR, vol. 1; NEW-*New Hampshire Gazette*; TH-Sanborn.

GLINES, ISRAEL

Israel Glines's identification as a black soldier is tentative, based on one census record that categorizes him as a free, non-white individual. It is likely that he was of mixed descent, but it is unknown if he was either part black or part Indian. Glines came to the area of Moultonborough some time before 1770 with his brother Abraham. They were said to come from Durham, but no record of them has been found there. There is record of a William Glines, who signed several petitions to the New Hampshire General Court in 1715/16 as a member of Oyster River Parish. It is unknown if William Glines was the father of Israel Glines. Israel Glines was known as an explorer and hunter in this region and traveled well into the White Mountains, leaving his mark on the map of New Hampshire. In *Lucy Crawford's History of the White Mountains*, the author notes that an Indian stream formerly called Sinoogawnock was now called Israel River. She further states that it was named after an "old man named Israel Glines, who hunted and fished about and in its waters previous to any settlement along its borders" (pg. 185). Mount Israel, in the Sandwich Range, just north of Moultonborough, was also named after Israel Glines. Both of these natural features are still found on New Hampshire maps today. Glines eventually settled down in Moultonborough, where he built a log cabin next to a spring at the base of Red Hill before 1770. He is also credited as being the first to plant apple trees in the area.

His war service began when he enlisted in Capt. Ebenezer Green's company, in Bedel's Rangers, on February 1, 1776, for one year. He then marched to his unit's headquarters at Orford, 53 miles distant from his hometown of Moultonborough. On April 25, 1776, he was with his unit at garrison at Montreal, where he received his bounty, advance pay, and wages. Two months later, on June 24th, Glines was at Isle aux Noix. From there, his unit went to Mount Independence, near Fort Ticonderoga, and then proceeded to Albany, New York. On November 5, 1776, he signed for the firearm and bayonet belt he had received upon his enlistment at Orford. Glines's service ended on January 15, 1777, when he was discharged at Saratoga, New York. Although Israel Glines had marched a long distance, he took part in no battles during his time in service. He returned to his home in Moultonborough where, on March 28, 1780, he was voted one of the town's seven highway surveyors. He is recorded as living in the town in the 1790 Federal Census. Listed as "Ezruel Glimes," he was enumerated as a free white male, head of a household that included three white females. The identity of the other members of his household is not known. On October 17, 1799, Israel Glines married Margaret Paine in Center Harbor at the house of her father, Amos Paine. Over the years they had six children, Affa (b. 3/26/1800), Burnham (b. 1805), Dustin (b. 1807), Amos (b. 1815), Lydia (b. 1810), and Hannah (b. 1813). The 1800 Census also lists Israel Glines and his family as white, but the 1810 Census lists them as being non-white. Thus, it may be that the Glines were of mixed descent. On April 24, 1818, at the age of 60, Israel Glines received a government pension for his war service. Glines's pension was renewed in 1820, and continued until his death on July 23, 1835, in Moultonborough. In 1848, Israel Glines's widow, Margaret, now aged 70, applied for a widow's pension based on his service. Despite some confusion about when Margaret and Israel were married, her request for a pension was approved on September 20, 1849. Margaret Glines died soon after, on April 28, 1850. The Glines's oldest daughter, Affa, worked for the family of Hosea and Joanna Sturtevant as a maid when she was 15 years old, and later married Luther Willoughby on April 20, 1820, and lived in the town of Holderness. Affa and Luther Willoughby had six children, the grandchildren of Israel and Margaret Glines. They were: John (b. 8/14/1820), Daniel (b. 2/24/1822), Lu Setta (b. 9/12/1823), Benjamin Burnham (b. 2/29/1828), Luther Perry (b. 3/23/1831), and Charles Henry (b. 7/31/1834).

Sources: TH-Topalian; TH-Stackpole; PSR-NHRWR, vol. 1; TR-Moultonborough, vol. 1; CEN-NH-1790, 1800, 1810; PEN-W1851; OPS-Crawford, pg. 185.

GLINES, ROBERT

Like Israel Glines, the identification of Robert Glines as a black soldier is tentative. He was a six-month man for New Hampshire, enlisting in Capt. Daniel Livermore's company in the 3rd NH regiment on June 27, 1780. After being mustered in at Kingston by Josiah Bartlett, he proceeded to West Point. From West Point, he moved with his unit to its several bivouacs at Orange and Hackensack Ridge, in New Jersey. The 3rd NH returned to West Point on the news of Benedict Arnold's treason, and went into winter camp there. Glines was discharged on December 6, 1780, having served 5 months and 25 days. Glines was originally from Canterbury, being born there in 1762. He moved with his family to Moultonborough in 1766. On January 4, 1787, he was married to Anna Smith and, about

1796, moved to Campton. His application for a pension was rejected in 1832 due to his short service. His heirs reapplied for a pension in 1862, but were again denied, for the same reason. Robert was possibly Israel Glines's brother, since both came to Moultonborough at about the same time, and are listed as co-defendants in several court cases. Like Israel, he is referred to in the 1790 Federal Census as a free white resident of Moultonborough, but is listed in the 1810 Census as being non-white.

Sources: PSR-NHRWR, vol. 3; PEN-NA-M881-roll 527; CEN-NH-1790, 1800, 1810.

Gray, Scipio

Scipio Gray, originally from Boston, served as a sailor aboard the Portsmouth privateer ship *General Sullivan* in 1778-79. The story of how Gray arrived in Portsmouth is an interesting one. The brigantine *Elizabeth*, owned by Richard Hart, sailed from Montserrat, West Indies, in October of 1775, bound for Portsmouth with a cargo of rum and sugar. On October 27 she was seized by a British naval vessel and taken into Boston as a prize. When the British evacuated Boston in March of 1776, the ship was loaded with Tories and their belongings, destined for Halifax, Nova Scotia under Capt. Peter Ramsey. Among those on board were four slaves: Adam, owned by John Rowe; Belinder, owned by Benjamin Austin; Brada, a woman owned by widow Kitcath; and Scipio Gray, owned by Harrison Gray. The *Elizabeth* was retaken by an American privateer while en route to Halifax and was subsequently brought to Portsmouth, her original destination the year before, for sale. As historian Richard Winslow points out, on the reverse side of the legal notice published regarding the sale of the *Elizabeth* in the *Freeman's Journal-New Hampshire Gazette*, dated July 20, 1776, there is reproduced the full text of the Declaration of Independence, "with no mention of freedom for blacks such as those aboard the prize *Elizabeth*" (Winslow, pg. 30).

Whether or not Scipio Gray was granted his freedom is unknown. He may have been the unnamed subject in an advertisement that appeared in the *Freeman's Journal-New Hampshire Gazette* on October 22, 1776, describing "A genteel sprightly NEGRO FELLOW" available "To be SOLD for a Certain Time, or Let by the Month ... is extremely desirous of belonging to a Captain of a privateer or going in one." If this man was indeed Scipio Gray, then his wishes eventually came true, since in late 1778 he was engaged for service aboard the Portsmouth privateer *General Sullivan*, a ship of 18 guns and manned by 100 men. Her commander, Capt. Thomas Manning, was granted a letter of marque on November 16, 1778. Sailing

III. The Men

> To be SOLD for a CERTAIN TIME, or Let by the month, A genteel fprightly NEGRO FELLOW, in fine health, about eighteen years of age; he can be recommended for many good qualities, has ferved at fea and land; waits on company well, and is extremely defirous of belonging to a Captain of a privateer, or going in one, as may be agreed. For further particulars enquire of the printer.

Slave for sale or lease advertisement. This ad likely advertises the availability of slave Scipio Gray, who was on board a British ship bound from Boston to Halifax that was captured by an American privateer and sent to Portsmouth. True to the ad, Gray did indeed ship out on a privateer. *New Hampshire Gazette*, October 22, 1776. Courtesy Portsmouth Public Library.

soon after from the Piscataqua River, the *General Sullivan* captured a number of prizes, including the brig *Union* and the *Mary*, a ship of eight guns with a cargo of flour, wheat, and oats, bound from Quebec to New York. Scipio Gray served as one of the prize crew for an unnamed vessel captured by the *General Sullivan* in late 1778 or early 1779. However, as was so often the case, the prize ship was retaken by the British and her prize crew, Scipio Gray included, were captured on January 9, 1779. It is unknown if Gray and the other men from the *General Sullivan* were first imprisoned in Canada, probably at Halifax, but on July 3, 1779, they were committed to the notorious Old Mill Prison in Plymouth, England. A large number of American seamen were incarcerated during the war at this infamous prison, some of whom died; some were paroled or exchanged. The fate of Scipio Gray, however, is unknown.

Sources: GSP-New England Historical and Genealogical Record, January 1865, pg. 138; OPS-Winslow, pgs. 17, 18, 25, 28–30, 41, and 53; NEW-*The Freeman's Journal*.

GREELE, ENOCH

Greele enlisted in Col. Enoch Poor's 2nd NH regiment on June 12, 1775, for an undetermined amount of time. Serving in Capt. Philip Tilton's company, he is listed as being aged 21, a resident of Kingston, and his occupation as that of husbandman (farmer). He later moved to Rumney, where the 1800 Census lists him as a non-white head of household for a family of four, one of whom was a white female over the age of 45. Greele, whose name is also spelled "Greely," is also listed in the 1810 Census for New Hampshire.

Sources: PSR-NHRWR, vol. 1; CEN-NH-1800-1810.

GRIFFITH, WILLIAM

William Griffith served several tours of duty during the American Revolution. His first started on November 5, 1775, when he enlisted as a private in Capt. Robert Follett's company, in Col. Joshua Wingate's militia regiment, to defend Piscataqua Harbor. In muster rolls he is listed as William "Negro" (NHRWR, vol. 1, pg. 237). Griffith next served in 1776, when he enlisted in Capt. John Calfe's company in Col. Pierce Long's regiment on September 10, and was stationed at New Castle. Shortly thereafter, on September 20, he was married to Elizabeth Anderson of New Castle. Griffith served in Long's regiment until at least January 13, 1777, when he was one of a group of soldiers certified as being fit to march to Ticonderoga. Griffith was part of the militia sent to relieve the dwindling garrison at Fort Ticonderoga during the winter of 1776-77. While at Ticonderoga, in April of 1777, Griffith re-enlisted in the 2nd NH regiment of Col. Nathan Hale, in Capt. Frederick Bell's company. He served with the 2nd NH during its retreat from Ticonderoga, and took part in the defeat at Hubbardton. Griffith, described as aged 50, five feet, eight inches tall, dark complexion, black hair and eyes, and hailing from New Castle, appears on a list of absentees for the 2nd NH regiment, dated January 10, 1778. He is listed as being left at "H Town," and "missing" (NHRWR, vol. 2, pg. 441). Due to the casualties the 2nd NH suffered at Hubbardton, and the large number of prisoners taken by the British, it seems likely that Griffith was either killed or captured there. There are no further records on William Griffith of New Castle to shed any light on his possible fate. However, the name of William Griffith does appear on a list of British prisoners, dated March 1781 to March 1783, that were received by the commissary of prisoners for New Hampshire, Moses Woodward. He is listed as a seaman who was received on September 15, 1781, and was subsequently sent to the Penobscot region of Maine. It is impossible to ascertain whether this is the same Griffith as described above and, if so, whether he deserted the American cause, or whether he was captured at Hubbardton and later pressed into British naval service.

Sources: PSR-NHRWR, vols. 1-3; TR-New Castle, vol. 3, pg. 225; TR-Portsmouth, vol. 11, pg. 318.

Hale, Cato

Cato Hale enlisted for Continental service on May 22, 1781. He served as a private in the 1st NH regiment in Capt. Ebenezer Frye's company. A resident of Atkinson, he is described as "Negro," aged 18, and five feet, eight inches tall (NHRWR, vol. 3, pg. 245). His term of service was for three years. Cato was the slave of widow Hale of Atkinson, and likely was freed after his term of service expired in 1784. In 1785, the town paid "widow" Hale for "a servant she had in the Army" (Barnum, pg. 216), and in that same year the neighboring town of Hampstead set Cato Hale's tax at nine shillings. Nothing further is known of Cato Hale after the war.

Sources: PSR-NHRWR, vol. 3; OPS-Kidder; TH-Barnum; TR-Hampstead, vol. 1, pg. 687.

Hall, Jude

Jude Hall is likely New Hampshire's best-known black soldier of the American Revolution. More information is known about this heroic and colorful individual, both factual and anecdotal, than about most other soldiers. In addition, his descendants lived in the area well into the 20th century, and have been well documented.

Hall was born sometime between 1744 and 1755, depending on which records are consulted. His military records indicate he was born in 1755, although subsequent pension records indicate an earlier date of 1744. Because birth dates for slaves were seldom recorded, it is unlikely that even Hall himself knew, for certain, when he was born. Prior to the American Revolution, Hall was the slave of Philemon Blake, and worked on his farm in Kensington. He was later sold to Nathaniel Healey, but was said to have resented being sold, and ran away from his new master. There is no evidence that states when he was freed, but anecdotal information indicates that he was given his freedom and 100 dollars for serving throughout the war, from 1775 to 1783.

Hall is distinguished for his long record of service during the war. No black soldier, and few white soldiers, served as long as he did. He first saw service when he enlisted on May 10, 1775, in Capt. Jacob Hind's company in Col. James Reed's "Regiment of Foot" (the 3rd NH). He was with his regiment at the Battle of Bunker Hill, on June 17, 1775, and was said to have been "thrown headlong by a cannonball striking near him" (Sawyer, pg. 201). This must have been quite a blast, as Hall, nearly six feet tall, is described by contemporaries as a powerful man who could "lift a barrel of cider and drink from the bunghole" (Sawyer, pg. 202). Hall further appears on muster rolls for Reed's regiment on August 1, 1775, and on a list dated October 4, 1775, he appears as one of those soldiers who received a payment of four dollars coat money at Medford. Hall served in Reed's regiment until November 13, 1776. However, he did not remain out of service for long. In December of 1776 he enlisted in Capt. Elijah Clayes's company in Hale's 2nd NH regiment for three years. In his previous term of service, Hall had enlisted for the town of Kensington. This time, he apparently enlisted for the distant town of Amherst. This would later be a source of contention. Jude Hall served in all the campaigns of the 2nd NH regiment throughout the war, and was a battle-hardened veteran. He is listed on the 2nd NH regiment's roll of absentees, dated January 10, 1778, at Valley Forge. He is described as "a Negro," 23 years old, five feet, ten inches tall, with "black" complexion, hair, and eyes (NHRWR, vol. 2, pg. 444). He is listed as having been left at Albany, New York. However, Hall soon after rejoined his regiment, since he was conspicuous in the grueling Battle of Monmouth in June of 1778. In this, the longest and largest battle of the war, fought in 100-degree heat, Hall gained the nickname "Old Rock" (Nell, pg. 119), no doubt for the strength, endurance, and courage he displayed.

In December of 1779, with his three-year term near its end, Jude Hall decided to continue his service, re-enlisting in the 2nd NH regiment. With the death of Clayes, Hall's original company commander in Sullivan's Campaign, the previous month, Hall now served under Capt. William Rowell. In this, his third consecutive term of service, he served for the duration of the war, and is listed as serving, once again, from Kensington, though Amherst still claimed him. Hall continued with his regiment through the next several years, mainly being on station at, or near West Point and the Hudson Highlands. From January to February 15, 1783, he was absent on leave, and likely returned home to Kensington for a much-deserved furlough. When Hall ended his service is unknown for certain. It may have been in November of 1783, when some New Hampshire soldiers were released from service, or, more likely, it was in January of 1784, when the New Hampshire Battalion was disbanded.

After the war, the experiences of Jude Hall were much like those of other black soldiers. On November 30, 1785, Hall, described as "a Black Negro fellow" (RCR #8983) was warned to depart Exeter, and was told "not to persume to dwell hear any longer." On January 21, 1786, Jude Hall and Rhoda Paul (born 1765) published their intention to marry. Later that same year, on October 30, the town of Kensington, nine years after the fact, finally voted to pay Hall for his military service in 1777.

Between 1786 and 1802, Jude and Rhoda had 10 children, four of whom were born before 1794. They were, as follows; George, Dolly, Nathaniel, William, Clarissa (b. 1792), Aaron, James, Rhoda (b. 1802), Betsey, and one whose name is unknown. It is stated that Hall and his family, at some point, lived with Enoch Rowe of Exeter for 14 years. Hall and his family of five are listed in the 1790 Census as being residents of Exeter and as free, non-whites. The 1800 Census is identical, except that the Hall family now numbered six people. From the records, it is evident that Jude Hall and his family moved about the area. In June of 1792, Jude, a "Negroe man," along with his wife, Rhoda, and four children, was warned to depart Stratham "forthwith" (RCR #13190). On February 28, 1795, Jude and Rhoda and their five children were warned from Exeter. Jude and his family, at least for a time, lived in "a cabin in the Exeter woods" (*Exeter News-Letter*, April 2, 1926), close by "Jude's Pond," near present day Drinkwater Road. Hall was said to be "a famous fisherman" (*ibid.*, December 5, 1879). With the turn of the century, Jude Hall and his family continued in the area. The year started out on a high note when, on January 21, 1800, Jude won a judgment from the Rockingham County Common Pleas Court for damages sought against the town of Amherst for its refusal to pay him the enlistment bounty promised him 24 years earlier, back in 1776. Despite this apparent windfall, times continued to be hard for Hall and his family. On February 7, 1817, they yet again were warned out of Exeter, along with 18 other blacks. Later that year, in July, Hall sought to bill the town of Exeter for support for him and his daughter Clarissa. Less than a year later, on April 6, 1818, at the age of 75, Jude Hall's government pension for his wartime service commenced.

Life was not only hard for Jude Hall and his wife, but for his grown children as well. Three of his grown sons were kidnapped and sold into slavery at different times. James Hall, at the age of 18, was kidnapped by David Wedgewood of Exeter and forcibly carried to Newburyport, Massachusetts. He was put on board a ship owned at that port, commanded by Capt. Isaac Stone, and shipped to New Orleans. There, he was jailed and sold as a slave to a Frenchman from Kentucky who treated him poorly. Wedgewood kidnapped James from the home of Jude Hall while Jude was absent, over a four-dollar debt. The fate of James Hall after this is unknown. Aaron Hall, a seaman, was kidnapped from Providence, Rhode Island in 1807. Unable to read or write, he was likely kidnapped and sold in return for a debt of $20 that he mistakenly signed for in the amount of $200. On his way home to Exeter, he was overtaken at Roxbury, Massachusetts and sent to sea, never to be heard from again. William shipped out on the bark *Hannibal* from Newburyport, Massachusetts, but was sold into slavery in the West Indies. After 10 years, however, he was able to escape and later served as the captain of a collier (coal carrying vessel) operating between Newcastle-Upon-Tyne and London, England. Jude's oldest son, George Hall, was well known in Exeter for many years. About 1820, when "the colored people celebrated the abolition of slavery in New Hampshire" (*ibid.*, December 5, 1879), he was mentioned as being one of many individuals who marched through the streets of town, accompanied by a drum and fife band. To celebrate this event, a bit of "verse" was printed soon after, reading, in part, "Yesterday was training day ... George Hall was corporal, and Ben Jake commander" (*ibid.*). The aforementioned Ben Jake was Benjamin Jacob Paul, a black man who was married to Betsey Hall, Jude's daughter. Unlike most of the members of Exeter's black community, Ben Jake was regarded as a troublemaker. Local legend states that a plan was devised about 1834 to rid the town of Ben Jake. He was arrested and jailed under false pretenses, during which time a mob of men surrounded Ben's house, moved his family and their goods out, then demolished the house. Once released, Ben Jake was homeless and, having no recourse with local authorities, left town and later died in Strafford County. Ben Jake, while married to Betsey Hall, had two children, Mary Ann and Parker, by another woman who lived with them, named Betsey Greene. Parker must have taken after his father, since it is recorded that he "died in the New Hampshire state prison" (*ibid.*).

Despite his age, Jude Hall was not destined to fade into obscurity. In 1822 he became the center of attention with his involvement in the case of John Blaisdell, on trial for the murder of John Wadleigh. Hall was said to be a witness to the event, which happened near his home by Jude's Pond. Although defense lawyers painted Jude Hall as a character of the shadiest sort, it soon was evident that he was guilty of nothing more than, perhaps, stretching the truth, rather than perjury. After this notorious event, Hall continued on for several more years until his death on August 21, 1827, at the age of 84. He was accorded the honor of being buried in the "old yard" at Exeter, off Winter Street, in the northeast corner (Sawyer, pg. 202). The exact location is unknown today, though a monument was erected in Hall's honor in 2000, in the back corner of the old burial ground, not far from the grave of another black soldier, Tobias Cutler. Following the death of Jude Hall, his widow Rhoda went to live with their daughter Rhoda Cook in Belfast, Maine. She collected a widow's pension until her death there in 1844.

After Jude Hall's death in 1827, his descendants remained in the area for nearly the next hundred years. The most notable among them are the grandsons of Jude Hall, Moses and Aaron Hall. They were the sons of George Hall, Jude's son, and together they carried on their grandfather's tradition of serving their state and country, by serving as soldiers in the Civil War. Moses U. Hall was born about 1835 in Exeter. As a young man, one of his occupations was that of a sleigh driver on cold winter mornings for Judge Henry French, and his sons William and Daniel Chester French, the future sculptor of note. One area resident said that "after the faithful driver had deposited his small charges, he drove his team home and then walked back and became a fellow pupil of his young masters" (*Exeter News-Letter*, April 2, 1926). This "stalwart young colored man" (*ibid.*) enlisted into the Third U.S. Colored Infantry regiment of the Union Army as a private on August 5, 1864, at the age of 29. He served 14 months before being mustered out of service on October 31, 1865. During this time, his unit served as a heavy artillery regi-

Monument stone for soldier Jude Hall. Hall is buried in the Winter Street Cemetery in Exeter, New Hampshire. He lies in an unknown spot to the rear in an area designated for black burials. His original gravestone disappeared sometime around 1900. This monument, detailing his extraordinary service, was erected in 2000. Photograph by Glenn Knoblock.

ment at Jacksonville, Florida, and later saw duty around Lake City and Tallahassee. After the war, Moses later moved to Epping and practiced the trade of a stone mason, working around the Epping-Exeter area. He was said to be "skillful ... industrious and well liked" (*Exeter News-Letter*, April 19, 1926). One local historian states that several of the buildings he worked on may still be in existence today. Moses lived out the last years of his life with his daughter Stacy, and died in her home in Haverhill, Massachusetts, on April 3, 1926, at the age of 92. His body was brought

The gravestone of Moses Hall and his wife Eliza. Moses died in Haverhill, Massachusetts and was brought back to his long time home of Epping, New Hampshire, for interment. Like his grandfather, Jude Hall, Moses was a soldier, serving in the 3rd United States Colored Infantry Regiment during the Civil War. Photograph by Glenn Knoblock.

back to Epping for burial, and laid to rest alongside his wife Eliza, who died in 1919.

Moses's older brother, Aaron C. Hall, also saw service in the Civil War. Born in 1830, he enlisted for service on September 29, 1863, in the 54th Massachusetts regiment. This unit gained renown as the first black regiment enlisted in the North. Married at the time of his enlistment, practicing the trade of a laborer, and hailing from Exeter, Hall served as a private in Company B until August 20, 1865. During this time, the 54th Massachusetts, already famed for its heroic attack on Fort Wagner, South Carolina, on July 18, 1863, took part in actions around Savannah, Georgia and Olustee, Florida, as well as aiding in the siege and bombardment of Charleston. At war's end, the 54th Massachusetts was among those Union regiments that held control over Charleston, and served garrison duty at the Citadel, the former bastion of Southern military aristocracy, before being released from service.

Though both Moses and Aaron Hall were born after the death of Jude Hall, there is one thing we can be certain of: Both boys grew up listening to the stories of Jude Hall and his actions and adventures during his long service as a soldier in the American Revolution. One may speculate that, perhaps, they served as an inspiration to both men later in life to serve their country when the call for arms came out to fight for a different kind of freedom.

Sources: PSR-NHRWR, vols. 1–3; PSR-NHSP, vol. 30, pg. 286; CEN-NH-1790-1800; TH-Bell; TH-Sawyer; TR-Kensington, vol. 1, Exeter, vol. 1, Amherst, vol. 2, Stratham, vol. 3; RCR #11517, #3190, #8983, #9740, #184231,

#459992; OPS-Oesterlin; OPS-Nell, pg. 119; OPS-Quintal, pgs. 118–119; NEW-*Exeter News-Letter*, December 5, 1879, and April 2, April 9, 1926.

HAYES, GEORGE

George Hayes was the slave of Reuben Hayes of Rochester. On May 10, 1762, "George, my Negro Man" (NHSP, vol. 22, pg. 447) was willed by Hayes to his wife, Abigail. She was given the direction to use George "to her own disposal" (*ibid.*). In a list of Reuben Hayes's estate, dated September 20, 1762, George was valued at £1000. When George Hayes gained his freedom is unknown, but it was likely before the Revolution. He served three terms of militia service during the war, starting on August 29, 1776, when he enlisted in Capt. John Drew's company in Col. Isaac Wyman's regiment for service in Canada. This first term of service lasted only a month. He next saw service in 1777, when he served from September 8 to November 30 in Capt. Daniel McDuffee's company in Col. Stephen Evans' regiment, which joined the Continental Army at Saratoga as reinforcement during the campaign against Burgoyne. George Hayes's final term of service was from August 1 to August 25, 1778, when he served in Capt. John Hill's company of Wakefield men in Col. Joshua Wingate's regiment, which served in Rhode Island. After his war service, George Hayes continued to live in the area. Although not listed in the 1790 Census for New Hampshire, he does appear in the 1800 Census, still a resident of Strafford County. At the advanced age of 73 years, on March 4, 1831, his government pension commenced. He is not to be confused with another black soldier, George Evans, also known as George Black.

Sources: PSR-NHRWR, vols. 1, 2, 4; PSR-NHSP, vol. 22, pg. 447; vol. 30, pg. 366; vol. 37, pg. 298.

HILL, DAVID

Hill is yet another black soldier for whom little information has been found. He enlisted for service on June 26, 1775, in Capt. Richard Shortridge's company in Poor's newly-formed 2nd NH regiment. On August 1, 1775, he is on a list of men paid for travel money, a coat and blanket allowance, and for having served one month and eight days. On October 4, 1775, Hill is on a list of men paid four dollars for a regimental coat at Medford. The following year, on July 8, 1776, Hill was reported as being absent due to illness from Capt. Shortridge's company, then at Chimney Point, near Fort Ticonderoga. He is described as being 21 years old, five feet, seven inches tall, with "black" eyes and "black" hair (NHRWR, vol.

1, pg. 310). On this roll, Hill is listed as being from "Eastown" in Strafford County (*ibid.*). After this, no definite further record of Hill is found. Whether he was one of the many men who died at Ticonderoga in late 1776 due to rampant disease and illness is unknown.

Sources: PSR-NHRWR, vol. 1.

HOIT, JEREMIAH

Jeremiah Hoit served one brief term of militia service in the American Revolution. He served as a private in Capt. Ebenezer Webster's company of Salisbury men in Gen. William Whipple's Brigade of New Hampshire Volunteers, who served in the Rhode Island campaign. His term of service lasted from August 5 to August 27, 1778. Jeremiah Hoit appears again in the records in 1791, when "Gerry Hoit, a Negro" (Oesterlin, pg. 61), is listed as a pauper for the town of Exeter. No other records have been found regarding Jeremiah Hoit.

Sources: PSR-NHRWR, vol. 2; OPS-Oesterlin.

HUBBARD, ELISHA

Though Hubbard is one of the few black soldiers who served as a non-commissioned officer, very little is known about him. A resident of New Ipswich, he is found on a list of rate-payers, dated September 15, 1774, for a portion of Reverend Stephen Farrar's salary as town minister. This record serves to indicate that Hubbard was a free black while living in New Hampshire, not a slave. He enlisted for service in the war early, on April 23, 1775, in Capt. Ezra Towne's company of New Ipswich men in Col. James Reed's newly formed 3rd New Hampshire regiment. His rank was that of sergeant, making him, as far as is known, New Hampshire's highest ranking black soldier. At the time of his enlistment, his age was 25, he was five feet, nine inches tall, his complexion was brown or black, his eyes black, and his occupation was that of a farmer. His birthplace was listed as Connecticut, the exact town being unspecified. As part of Reed's 3rd NH regiment, he took part in the Battle of Bunker Hill, and was still with his unit in October of 1775, when he received payment for a regimental coat at Medford. How long Hubbard continued in service is unknown, since no further records of his service have come to light, though we know that he, at least, served six months. Whether he died during his service, after October 1775, is unknown, but no further record of Hubbard is found after the war ended. He is not to be confused with a white soldier named Ephraim Hubbard, of Chesterfield.

Sources: PSR-NHRWR, vol. 1; TR-New Ipswich, vol. 2, pgs. 801, 817; PSR-MSS, vol. 8, pg. 428.

HUNKING, RICHARD

Richard Hunking, also known as "Dickie," was one of three slaves brought to Barrington by Capt. Mark Hunking, a West Indies trader (Wiggin, pg. 42). On December 26, 1774, Richard, a "Negro servant," was married to Julie, a "Negro servant" of Stephen Evans of Dover by the Reverend Jeremy Belknap (*ibid.*). This wedding, which took place with the consent of their masters, is said to have been the last wedding of Negro slaves ever performed in New Hampshire. Richard was promised his freedom in his master's will, dated April 19, 1776, when Mark Hunking gave "My Negro Man Dickey his freedom and discharge him from any obedience unto my heirs after my decease, releasing unto him all claim that any person under me may pretend to have unto him" (SCR-Probate, vol. 1, pg. 506). Soon thereafter, Richard Hunking was freed, and on May 16, 1777, he enlisted as a free Negro for Continental service. He joined the 2nd NH regiment in the company of Capt. John Drew of Barrington. Enlisting in the same company as Richard Hunking were five other free blacks: Zach Kelsey, Cato, Gloster Watson, George Evans, and Corydon Chesley. Hunking's term of service was for three years and, as far as is known, he served out his term. Richard Hunking appears in the records one last time, on December 2, 1782, when only his "Negro Bed and Bedding" (*ibid.*, pg. 515) are listed in an inventory and appraisal of Mark Hunking's estate. This could indicate that Richard may have died during his service, his few possessions being left behind at Hunking's residence, or he may have, despite his absence from the records, finished out his service and continued to live with Hunking after the war. If so, while "Dickie" was a free man, he was likely still employed by Mark Hunking, and relied on him for such necessities as his bed and bedding.

Sources: PSR-NHRWR, vols. 1–3; TH-Wiggin; US-Strafford County Probate records, pgs. 506, 515.

JENNESS, PAUL

See the biography of Paul Long.

JENNESS, PRINCE

There is very little information on Prince Jenness. In the town history of Rye, it is simply stated that he was "given his master's liberty to enlist in the Revolutionary War," and that he was one of 38 Rye men "lost" during the war (Parsons, pgs. 213, 255). Prince may have enlisted with his former master, Job Jenness, in Capt. Zachariah Beal's company in Scammell's 3rd NH regiment in January of 1777. Job Jenness died at Valley Forge on December 31, 1777. Another possibility is that Prince took the last name of "Liberty," enlisting in the 2nd NH regiment in November of 1776. See the service record for Prince Liberty for further details.

Sources: TH-Parsons, pgs. 213, 255.

KELSEY, ZACH

Zach Kelsey was born in approximately 1725 and began his war service on May 7, 1777, at the advanced age of 52 years. He enlisted in Capt. John Drew's company in the 2nd NH regiment for Continental service. His activities prior to the war are largely unknown, though he was a free man by 1772, when he was warned to depart the town of Exeter on November 13. Kelsey's first term of service was for three years. Soon after his term of service was up in 1780, he re-enlisted as a six-month man. He re-enlisted for yet another term of service, date unknown, and received his final discharge at Newburgh, New York, in January of 1783. After the war, Zach Kelsey continued to live in Exeter. Referred to in military and town records as a "Negro" (NHRWR, vol. 2, pg. 619), "Zack" is listed in the 1800 Census for New Hampshire as a resident of Exeter and a free, non-white head of household for a family of six people. Anecdotal information states that he lived in squalid poverty and had a large family, including a wife nicknamed "Yellow Beck," and one young son, Josh, who went to sea and was later sold into slavery while his ship visited a Southern port. Zach Kelsey began receiving a government pension for his service on March 17, 1819, at the advanced age of 94. When he was placed on the pension roll in 1818, there were only nine other men on the roll as old, or older than Zach. The two oldest men were aged 102 and 104 years old! If pension records are accurate, Zach Kelsey lived to be 104 years old, dying in Gilford on May 21, 1829. His pension records, describing him as "a man of colour" (Pension #544478), also list a wife named Rachel. Although listed in records as Zach Kelsey, he also used the last name of "Robinson," at least while living in Exeter.

Sources: PSR-NHRWR, vol. 2, 3; PSR-NHSP, vol. 30, pgs. 298–99; CEN-1800-NH; NEW-*Exeter News-Letter*-12/11 and 12/18, 1941; PEN-#544478.

KENT, PETER

Kent served an undetermined term in the Revolutionary War, first enlisting on June 10, 1775, in Capt. Hezekiah Hutchins's company in Col. James Reed's newly formed 3rd NH regiment. Kent enlisted from the town of North Hampton and fought with the 3rd NH at the Battle of Bunker Hill. On August 1, 1775, he appears on a list of men paid for their time in service. At this point, Kent had served one month and 24 days. Kent next appears on a list of men, dated October 16, 1775, paid four dollars coat money at Medford, Massachusetts. After this, Kent disappears from the military records. Peter Kent appears one last time in October of 1810, when he is listed as a pauper in North Hampton. He was paid by the town selectman at the rate of 29 cents a week, adding up to a total of $3.19 by December 31, 1810, after which he moved to the town of Deerfield. No further records of Peter Kent, and his subsequent fate, have been found.

Sources: PSR-NHRWR, vol. 1; OPS-Oesterlin.

KIMBALL, THOMAS

Thomas Kimball was a free black who enlisted for Continental service on March 23, 1778. Recruited by Col. Noah Lovewell, the local mustermaster in the Amherst area, Kimball joined Capt. William Rowell's company of the 2nd NH regiment, along with another black recruit, Caesar Wallace. Kimball, whose term of service was for three years, was paid the £100 bounty for enlisting on June 7 of that same year, and served for the town of Amherst. Though uncertain, it is likely that Kimball lived in Amherst. After his first three-year term was ended, Kimball enlisted for another term of service, prior to December of 1781. This time, Kimball joined the 1st NH regiment, in Capt. Amos Morrill's company. This term was apparently for the remainder of the war. During this second term, Kimball served for the town of Hillsborough, and is identified in their records as a "Negro" (NHRWR, vol. 3, pg. 508). Nothing is known of Thomas Kimball's life before or after the war.

Sources: PSR-NHRWR, vols. 1–3.

KNIGHT, BONE

Bone Knight was the slave of Joseph Knight of Rochester. All that is known about him appears in an advertisement in the ironically named *Freeman's Journal–New Hampshire Gazette*, dated April 26, 1777. Bone, listed as a "NEGRO MAN," is described as being between 20 and 30 years old, five feet, nine inches tall, and "speaks good English." After having "been in the Continental Service 19 Months," he ran away on April 1, 1777, it being "suspected that he will, if he can, get to the British Troops." No record of his enlistment or service has been found in New Hampshire or Massachusetts to indicate what regiment he may have served in. He apparently enlisted about September 1775. Though instances of slaves deserting their masters to gain freedom with the British was common in the South, Knight is the only black soldier from New Hampshire known to have such intentions. Whether or not he was successful in his endeavor is unknown.

KNOTT, JESSE

Knott's listing as a black soldier is very tentative, based on name association only. There is, however, no existing description of him in military or census records to confirm his identification as a black soldier. Living on the slope of Coit Mountain in Newport was a black man named Robert Nott. It is speculated that Jesse Knott (his name was also spelled as "Nott" in military records) may have been a relative of his, possibly his son. The name is rather unusual in New Hampshire, and is not commonly found. Jesse Knott first saw service in 1775, when he enlisted on May 8 in Col. James Reed's 3rd NH regiment in the company of Capt. John Marcy. As a private in Marcy's company, Knott took part in the Battle of Bunker Hill. He is listed on a company muster roll for the 3rd NH dated August 1, 1775, by which time he had served three months and one day. If subsequent records are correct, Jesse Knott was only 15 years old at the time of his service in Marcy's company. The following year, Jesse Knott served another term of service when he enlisted in the company of Capt. Samuel Weatherbee in Col. Isaac Wyman's militia regiment raised to reinforce the Northern Army. Knott is listed in company records dated August 20, 1776, as serving for the town of Westmoreland. On November 5, 1776, the regiment was stationed at Mount Independence, near Fort Ticonderoga, doing garrison duty. How long Knott served at Mount Independence is unknown. However, in early 1777 he enlisted with the 1st NH Regiment under Capt. Jason Wait. He is listed on a roll of Wait's company dated May of 1778. Knott is listed as living in Walpole and being aged 18. As part of Wait's company he saw action during the heavy fighting that took place in 1777 during Burgoyne's campaign. During the fighting at Saratoga on September 19, 1777, Knotts's commander, Capt. Wait, was captured during the battle at Freeman's Farm. Subsequent records state that Knott served until his death on July 18, 1778. It is unknown if he died due to wounds received at the Battle of Monmouth, which took place on June 28, 1778, or whether he died due to illness from his recent time at Valley Forge. Knott's place of death is also unknown. At the time of his death, the 1st NH regiment was in New York, heading for camp at White Plains. There is no documentary evidence showing that Jesse Knott ever lived on Coit Mountain in Newport, but the towns he served for during the war are near that locale.

Sources: TH-Wheeler, pg. 253, PSR-NHRWR, vols. 1–2; OPS-Kidder, pg. 146.

KNOX, GEORGE

George Knox is one of those few black soldiers, like Jude Hall, who is fairly well known, through official records, as well as through local lore, legend, and tradition. His birth date is unknown, but was between 1733 and 1745, depending on which records are consulted. Records state his birthplace as Westfield, Connecticut. Given the fact that he knew Eleazor Wheelock, the founder of Dartmouth College, and worked for his family, it seems likely that he came to the Hanover area around 1770, the year Dartmouth was established. From this time, until his death in 1825, Knox lived in the area. His name is remembered by a pond, a brook, and a hill in Enfield which are named after him. Although Knox worked for Wheelock and the new college, most historians agree that he was not a slave. It seems most probable that he was, instead, an indentured servant.

Knox first saw service in the Revolution in late 1776, when he enlisted in Capt. Joshua Hayward's company in Col. David Gilman's regiment of New Hampshire militia. Serving as a private for three months and eleven days, from December 5 until March 15, 1777, Knox and his regiment served garrison duty at Fort Ticonderoga for a short time, then were likely sent to New Jersey to take part in the pivotal battles at Trenton and Princeton. Days after his first term of service expired, George Knox enlisted to serve again, on March 17, 1777, in the 1st NH regiment, in the company of Capt. John House. His term of service is unspecified, but it was likely for one year. It is not surprising that Knox enlisted under Capt. House, since he was a Hanover resident, and may have had a prior acquaintance with George Knox. One year later, in April of 1778, Knox re-enlisted in the 1st NH regiment, continuing in Capt. House's company. This time his term of service was specified as both during war and, at a later date, three years. Knox was promised a bounty of $20 for this enlistment, but had not received payment by May 8, 1778, when Capt. House certified that Knox had, indeed, enlisted into his company and regiment, and was due the bounty money. At the time of his re-enlistment, Knox is described as "malato Dark" (NHSP, vol. 11, pg. 611), five feet, ten inches tall, aged 32 years, and hailing from Enfield. Knox continued in service with the 1st NH regiment until his discharge on May 1, 1781. Having served continuously from March of 1777 to 1781, Knox took part in all the important northern campaigns his regiment was involved in. Knox was discharged from camp in New York on May 1, 1781, "having faithfully served," and was allowed to draw 15 days of provisions from the "Public Magazines" prior to his journey home (McRoberts, pg. 455). His discharge paper was issued and signed by Col. Alexander Scammell, the commander of the 1st NH.

Although much has been written about Knox's service, some of it is in error. It has been asserted that he served in the militia regiment of Col. Jonathan Chase, under Capt. John Wheelock, son of the founder of Dartmouth College, and worked as a servant to Pvt. James Wheelock, Capt. Wheelock's brother, from September 22 to October 24, 1777. However, Knox's name does not appear on the list of soldiers for Chase's regiment, and it seems likely that he has been confused with another soldier named George Noice. This error may also have resulted from the fact that Knox appears on a list of soldiers, dated February 17, 1779, who enlisted into Continental service from Col. Jonathan Chase's militia district. As stated before, Knox was a member of the 1st NH regiment during the time in question.

After the war, Knox, like many black veterans, led a hard life, plagued by financial hardship. He married his first wife, Peg, before 1785, and their first child, whose name is unknown, was born about April of 1784. Though George Knox was a free man, he and his wife signed an agreement on September 12, 1785, to become the indentured servants of James Wheelock of Hanover for five years. In return for working for Wheelock, and agreeing not to damage or waste his goods, and promising "never to be absent day or night unlawfully," George and Peg were promised payment of £100 at the end of their indenture, less "decent and comfortable cloathing" and "the comfortable maintenance of their child" (Quinlan, pg. 59). This money was to be paid in the form of "either wild Land well situate & calculated for a good farm-or in grain or cattle at the current market price" (*ibid.*). Knox served out the term of his indenture, but it is unknown what kind of payment he received. Local tradition has stated that Knox "was discovered in a systematic course of thieving," and that "he transported his plunder" to his house in Enfield (Chase, vol. 1, pg. 398). One source also states that in January of 1778 his illegal activities were discovered, and that he was judged guilty during a meeting on February 20, 1778, and was given a fine and sentenced to be given "fifteen stripes on the naked body, which Knox duly received" (*ibid.*). No records have been found to verify such legends, but there is probably some truth to them. However, one must call into question whether these activities occurred in 1778, rather than at some point after the war ended. As far as can be determined, Knox was a soldier in the 1st NH regiment during January and February in 1778. Unless Knox was home on furlough, it is impossible for him to have been involved in such actions at that time.

George Knox first lived in Enfield, in a cabin on the north side of George Pond, a short way behind modern day Route 4A. To the east is George Hill, and Knox Brook flows from George Pond into Lake Mascoma. However, by 1790 Knox had left Enfield and moved to nearby Thetford, Vermont, where he is listed in the 1790 Census as the head of household for a family of four. Local land records indicate that Knox bought 30 acres of land in 1792 for £17. It is unknown if this land was purchased as a result of his indenture with James Wheelock.

Like many other details of his life, the family of George Knox has also been difficult to determine with any amount of certainty. He had three wives, Peg Woodward, Jemima, and Catherine Minor. Peg, Knox's first wife, probably died before 1788, since in June of that year he had a child named Henry born by a new wife, named Jemima. George and Jemima had two other children, James (b. September 1790), and Harvey (b. April 1792). When Jemima died is uncertain, but Knox married Catherine Minor, his third wife, in May of 1812. They had three children, including Ermanda (b. 1815), Harriet (b. 1818), and, incredibly enough, George, Jr., born on July 4, 1824, just a year before the death of George Knox. One of Knox's wives, probably Jemima, was said to be white, as well as the most difficult of all his wives. Knox and his family are listed in Vermont Census records for 1790, 1800, and 1810. The 1800 Census lists his household as having six non-whites, and one white woman. What became of Knox's children is unknown. Knox and his last wife, Catherine, are buried together in a small plot on land he once farmed. According to his gravestone, he was 92 years old at the time of his death.

Knox applied for a government pension for his service and was granted a pension in December of 1818. In July of 1820 the continuance of this pension was debated and questioned, with Knox declaring under oath "that I have not since that time by gift, sale or in any other manner disposed of any property or any part thereof with intent thereby so to diminish it as to bring myself within the provisions of an act of Congress to provide for certain persons" (McRoberts, p. 459). His property at the time, which was valued at $310.66, included his farm, valued at $150, and one "Old mare, 8 Sheep, 4 Lambs, 1 small hog, 1 Old Cart, 1 old gig, 1 plough, one Desk, 1 old Table, 2 Old Chairs, 1 old ax, 1 old hook, shovel" (*ibid.*).

The gravestones of soldier George Knox and his family in Thetford, Vermont. Knox died in 1825 at the age of 92. His gravestone, worn and weathered, is barely legible today, located in a forlorn spot off a dirt country road. Photograph by Glenn Knoblock.

He also states that his wife Catherine is 45 years old and "sick and unable to do any labour," and that his daughter Hariot, aged two, "is a cripple," and that he is "from old age unable to labour for a great measure" (*ibid.*, pgs. 459–60). Unfortunately for Knox, the matter was not settled for over a year. A local court official, Joseph Reed, at the request of George Knox's neighbors, sent a letter to John C. Calhoun, the secretary of war, dated March 14, 1821. In this letter he describes the delay in forwarding Knox's paperwork and details his general misery:

> Knox is about 80 years of age has been a very hard working man but lately he can not labour in consequence of having lost the use of his right Arm ... and his health otherwise very poor — his wife has been sick a number of years — with a cancer one of her breasts has already been amputated and she has a white swelling on one of her knees and probably will not live long allso one child that is a cripple and always will be he has no friends to assist him — his schedule of property amounts to about $310 — but I am certain it was appraised much above its real value but since that time however a considerable part of it has been expended to pay Debts and nursing Bills — his home is a mere hovel and has not any furniture at all and I really think he is as poor as a man can be and live. The small piece of land mentioned in his schedule is very poor and Stoney and will provide nothing with out great labour and is worth but little. I live in the same town with Knox and have been acquainted with him 18 years — he

has always Sustained the caracter of an Honest hard labouring man and served faithfully 3 or 4 years in the Revolutionary war.... I feel it is my duty to Advise the Department of War with his present situation [*ibid.*, pgs. 461–62].

After further delay, Knox was finally granted a continuance of his pension on August 2, 1821. The above letter regarding the situation of George Knox describes financial circumstances that were probably applicable to many black veterans of the time. A few years later, on July 28, 1825, George Knox died on his farm in Thetford. Buried by the side of his last wife, Catherine, his gravestone can still be seen today in a small plot enclosed by a stone wall, a hundred yards or so off a small country back road.

Sources: PSR-NHRWR, vols. 1–4; US-McRoberts—"Revolutionary War Soldiers of Enfield"; TH-Chase; OPS-Quinlan; PEN-#S40904; CEN-Vermont 1790–1800–1810; PSR-NHSP, vol. 11.

LAIGHTON, JOHN

Laighton served as a private in Capt. David Place's company in Col. Joshua Wingate's militia regiment for the defense of Piscataqua Harbor. He appears on a company muster roll dated November 5, 1775, but the date and length of his enlistment is unknown. He also appears on a list of men raised in the company of Capt. Joseph Badger, Jr., to serve in Col. Isaac Wyman's regiment sent to reinforce the Continental Army in Canada. These men were mustered into service at Gilmanton on July 19, 1776. How long Laighton served during this term is also unknown. After the war, John Laighton, his name spelled "Laden," appears in the records as a "Negro" (Oesterlin, pg. 71) pauper for the town of Deerfield in 1793, and on December 19, 1793, "John Laden and Phillis Clark—two Blacks" (RCR #14018) were warned to depart town. Nothing of Laighton after 1793 is known.

Sources: PSR-NHRWR, vol. 1; RCR #14018; OPS-Oesterlin.

LANE, PRIMAS

See the biography of Primas Coffin.

LEAR, CAESAR

Caesar Lear was the slave of Capt. Tobias Lear, a shipmaster who lived on Hunking Street and owned a farm on Sagamore Creek in Portsmouth. On June 16, 1777, Caesar enlisted for his master's son, Tobias Lear, Jr., for service for one year as an able seaman aboard the Continental Navy frigate *Raleigh*. The *Raleigh*, a ship of 32 guns, was then being outfitted and manned at Portsmouth by her captain, Thomas Thompson. Caesar Lear sailed with the *Raleigh* on her maiden voyage on August 12, 1777, and, as a member of her crew, took part in the capture of a small schooner on August 15, and another small vessel on September 2. He received his baptism under fire a few days later, on September 4, 1777, when the *Raleigh*, working against a 60-ship British convoy bound from the West Indies to England, attacked the British sloop of war *Druid*, which carried 14 guns. After a fight of 45 minutes, the *Raleigh* had severely disabled the *Druid*, killing her captain, master, and six of her crew, and wounding 21. The *Raleigh* lost one man killed and two wounded. Following this action, the *Raleigh* set course for France, where she received the full complement of guns she had been unable to get in Portsmouth. She set sail for America in December of 1777, in company with the ship *Alfred*, carrying 20 guns. On the way back, on March 9, 1778, the two ships encountered two British men of war, the *Ariadne*, with 20 guns, and the *Ceres*, with 16 guns. Due to poor judgment and a lack of co-operation between the American captains, the *Alfred* was lost to the British and the *Raleigh* sailed alone to Boston. Her captain, Thomas Thompson, was subsequently censured and stripped of his command. It is likely that once the *Raleigh* reached Boston, Caesar Lear's service was over. Nothing further regarding him is known. Caesar's service allowed his master's son, Tobias Lear, Jr., to accomplish greater deeds. Just a youth of 17 in 1777, Tobias Lear, Jr., later served as President George Washington's private secretary.

Sources: GSP-NHGR, vol. 3, pgs. 24, 72; OPS-Remick, pg. 218; OPS-Miller, pgs. 234–35, 314–15; TH-Brewster, vol. 1, pgs. 267–68.

Liberty, Prince

Prince Liberty enlisted for Continental service on November 8, 1776, in Capt. James Carr's company in the 2nd NH regiment. Though it is uncertain, he may have enlisted from Somersworth. As a private in Carr's company, he likely saw battle at Trenton and Princeton. However, his service was short lived: He is reported as being dead on June 18, 1777. At this time, the 2nd NH regiment was stationed at Fort Ticonderoga. What Prince Liberty died from is unknown. As stated earlier, he may be the same man as Prince Jenness of Rye, who enlisted in the army and died during his service. Details on both men are lacking to state conclusively whether or not they are one and the same.

Sources: PEN-NA-M881, Roll #512.

Light, Prince

Prince Light likely began his life as a slave. He was probably first the slave of John Light, a militia captain and innholder of Exeter. He may be the slave who was listed as Peter, "a Mullato Boy" (NHSP, vol. 20, pg. 525), valued at £300 in an inventory of Capt. Light's estate dated June 28, 1757. Probably sold after the death of his master, he may have been given the name Prince when he became the slave of Ephraim Robinson of Exeter. In 1768 Prince "my Negro man" (NHSP, vol. 30, pg. 190) was bequeathed by Robinson to his wife Mary, but it was stipulated that if she should remarry, or die, Prince was to go to his son Samuel. At some point between 1768 and 1780, Prince changed his last name to Light. Whether this was because he was sold to a new master, or this was a name he took upon gaining his freedom is unknown. He may have been a servant to Capt. Robert Light after his service with the Robinsons. In addition, it is unknown when Prince Light gained his freedom. He first saw war service on July 16, 1776, when he enlisted, as Prince Robinson, in Capt. William Harper's company in Col. Isaac Wyman's regiment for three months. This regiment was raised by the state to help reinforce the Continental Army in Canada. Prince Robinson next saw service on September 8, 1777, when he enlisted in Capt. Zebulon Gilman's company in Col. Nicholas Gilman's regiment to reinforce the Northern Continental Army at Saratoga during Burgoyne's offensive. Robinson served for just over three months before being discharged on December 15, 1777. Both his regimental and company commanders were residents of Exeter. He enlisted for a final term of service on June 28, 1780. Now going by the last name "Light," he is listed as being 37 years old and was paid for his travel to Worcester, Massachusetts, before proceeding to West Point, New York. Light also appears on a list for July of 1780 at West Point, being one of New Hampshire's six-month men who were issued a half a pint of rum and one pound of sugar. Prince Light ended his final term of service on December 5, 1780, having served five months and twenty days. While stationed at West Point, Light was a witness to the execution of Maj. John Andre, the British spy who worked with Benedict Arnold in his failed plot to deliver the fort at West Point to the British. In his pension application in 1818, nearly 40 years after the event, Light still remembered the shine, "like a glass bottle" (Pension #S44511), on Andre's shoes as he was being led to the gallows.

After the war, Light continued to live in the Exeter area. On March 5, 1798, he was warned to depart the neighboring town of Kingston, having come from Exeter. He is also listed as a town pauper for Kingston in 1798. On March 16, 1800, he was married to Phillis Currier in Exeter. It is unknown if they had any children together, though Prince is known to have had a son named Mark Robinson, perhaps by a previous wife. Prince and his wife were often employed by area farmers in pulling flax to make a living. Financial hardships must have befallen Prince and Phillis, since they were jailed in Exeter from August 17, 1813, to August 15, 1815. What their crime was is unclear, but it seems likely that they were jailed as debtors. In addition to helping area farmers, Light was a farmer himself. He was forced to sue fellow black veteran London Dailey of Exeter in 1816 for items that he provided to him in 1811, but the amount he was owed was still unpaid in early 1817. Prince, described as "short, thickset, and good natured" (*Exeter News-Letter* December 11, 1941), applied for a government pension for his war service in 1818, and began receiving it in March of that same year. When he applied for a renewal of his pension, on July 5, 1820, a man named John Kimball of Exeter served as his guardian. Kimball deposed that Light was aged 75, and had living with him his wife, who was aged 65. A listing of Light's personal estate at this time proved his dire need for a pension. Except for his clothing and bedding, Light's estate was valued at a meager $2.20, and included one table, two chairs, a pail, two tea cups and saucers, six plates and platters, a brown mug, two brown bowls, a shovel, two iron spoons, and two knives and two forks. Based on this estate appraisal, Light's pension renewal was approved, but didn't last long. Prince Light died soon thereafter on January 30, 1821, at the supposed age of 78. He is probably buried in the rear section of the old cemetery on Winter Street in Exeter, but no stone marks his grave.

Sources: PSR-NHRWR, vols. 1–3; PSR-NHSP, vol. 20, pg. 525, vol. 30, pgs. 286–7; NEW-*Exeter News-Letter*, 12/11 and 12/18, 1941; PEN-S44511.

LOCK, NIMSHI

Nimshi Lock served as a soldier in the Revolution for the town of Rye. He was the slave of Capt. Joseph Lock, who sold him, along with all his land, dwellings, livestock, "tools for husbandry work," and "half of the Iron Work of one Grist Mill" (NH Province Deeds, vol. 67, pgs. 336–7), to his son, Jeremiah Lock, for bills of credit amounting to £10,000 on February 15, 1763. This deed also provided that "Nimshi a Molater Boy" would be his son's slave "until he is thirty years of age" (*ibid.*). It is unknown how old Nimshi Lock was when this deed was executed, but it is possible that Lock was freed before gaining the age of 30 so he could serve in the war. His master since 1763, Jeremiah Lock, was a resident of Rye, and a signer of the Association Test. Though it is only speculation, perhaps he freed Nimshi in the spirit of patriotism that then prevailed, or, equally likely, he may have promised Nimshi his freedom if he enlisted in the army. In either case, Nimshi Lock first saw service in 1775 in the company of Capt. Joseph Parsons in Col. Joshua Wingate's regiment of militia. It is uncertain when he enlisted, and for how long. Listed by his first name only, Lock appears on a list of men entitled "Return of what Remains" (NHRWR, vol. 1, pgs. 247–48), dated November 5, 1775, and was stationed at Newcastle. Several weeks later, on November 22, he is listed as one of Parson's "minute men" (NHRWR, vol. 4, pg. 26) who may have gone to Winter Hill, near Boston, in December of 1775. Lock appears in the records one last time in September of 1776, when he was listed in Capt. Jonathan Robinson's company in the militia regiment of Col. Thomas Tash. This regiment helped to reinforce the battered American Army in New York after the failed Canadian invasion. For his enlistment, Lock received a six-pound bounty payment. After this, Nimshi Lock disappears from the records, and is said to have been one of the Rye men lost during the war. It seems likely that Lock was one of those soldiers who succumbed to illness while stationed at Fort Ticonderoga, or the vicinity, during the winter of 1776-77.

Sources: US-NH Province Deeds, vol. 67, pgs. 336–7; PSR-NHRWR, vols. 1, 4; TH-Parsons, pg. 153.

LONG, CAESAR

Caesar Long was a Revolutionary War soldier from Hampton about whom little is known. He first appears in New Hampshire records as a plaintiff in court action in the town of Hollis in 1757. Whether he was a free black or a slave is unknown. In 1758, Long was a plaintiff in another court action, this time in Hampton. He is also mentioned in a petition to the New Hampshire Assembly, dated January 28, 1760, by one Nathan Blake of Hampton. Blake states in his petition that he returned home after serving in Col. John Goffe's New Hampshire regiment under Capt. Jeremiah Marston, and that he was taken sick and broke out with smallpox. He further states that his family all left home, and that "nobody was with him for some days but one Caezar Long" (NHSP, vol. 12, pgs. 122–3). Whether Long was his slave or servant is unknown. In 1761 Caesar Long was involved in court action yet again when he was the complainant against Walter Neal of Hampton for £40 due him, with interest of 15 percent. Neal appealed the court's decision against him, but it was upheld on January 29, 1762, in Long's favor. Long may have originally come from the town of Raymond or Chester, and was possibly the slave, at one time, of either Benjamin or Joseph Long of Chester. Caesar Long, his last name spelled "Loney" (NHRWR, vol. 1, pg. 351), served one unspecified term of service in the war, starting on July 10, 1776, when he enlisted in Capt. Samuel Nay's company in Col. Joshua Wingate's regiment of militia raised to help reinforce the Continental Army after the failed invasion of Canada. Nay's company, composed of mostly Hampton men, was among those units ordered to "repair to Charles Town on Connecticut River" (*ibid.*) before proceeding to join the Continental Army. Nothing further of Caesar Long is known.

Sources: PSR-NHRWR, vol. 1; PSR-NHSP, vol. 12, pgs. 122–23; TR-Hollis, vol. 6, pg. 94.

LONG, PAUL/PETER

Paul Long, also known as Paul Jenness, was a soldier in the Revolution from the Rye–North Hampton area. He is probably the same man as Peter Long, who was advertised on November 2, 1775, as a runaway slave from Rye. Peter Long was described by his master, Marifield Berry, as "a Negro MAN ... about six feet high, talks good English — He had on when he went away a light colour'd homespun Coat, knit Jacket and dark brown Breeches, is about 25 Years of Age — Whoever will take up said Negro and confine him in any of his Majesty's Gaols, so that he may be had, or return him to his Master, shall have Ten Dollars Reward" (*New Hampshire Gazette*, November 2, 1775).

Town legend states that Paul, along with Prince, were the slaves of Job Jenness of Rye, and that Paul was "given his liberty to enlist" (Parsons, pg. 213) when war began. Paul Long first enlisted for service in July of 1776, when he served for six months in Capt. Samuel Nay's company in Col. Joshua Wingate's regiment of militia raised to reinforce the Northern Continental Army. Long continued his service while stationed at Fort Ticonderoga on December 5, 1776, when he enlisted for four months in Capt. Joseph Parson's company in Col. David Gilman's regiment. Long served in Capt. Parson's company until March 11, 1777, and likely took part in the battles at Trenton and Princeton. Long served one last term of service, for eight months in Scammell's 3rd NH regiment, from May of 1777 to January 1, 1778. During this short term of service, Long took part in the major battles at Saratoga, serving first in Capt. Richard Weare's company, than that of Capt. Isaac Frye. Little is known of Paul Long after the war. He was a resident of North Hampton, and received a government pension for his service beginning in April 1818, at the age of about 68. In a pension document dated July 4, 1820, he is said to be totally blind, and without any family. Paul Long died at the approximate age of 76 on May 28, 1826.

> RUNAWAY from the subscriber a Negro MAN named Peter Long, about six Feet high, talks good English——Had on when he went away, a light colour'd homespun Coat, knit Jacket and dark brown Breeches, is about 25 Years of Age.— Whoever will take up said Negro, and confine him in any of his Majesty's Goals, so that he may be had, or return him to his Master, shall have Ten Dollars Reward and necessary Charges paid by MARIFIELD BERRY.
> Rye, October 16. 1775.

Runaway slave ad for Peter Long. Long was one of three runaway slaves advertised on this day. Whether he was captured or returned voluntarily is unknown, but return he did, since he enlisted for service in July 1776. *New Hampshire Gazette*, November 2, 1775. Courtesy Portsmouth Public Library.

Sources: PSR-NHRWR, vols. 1–3; NEW-*New Hampshire Gazette*: TH-Parsons; Pension #S44516.

Lovewell, Stephen

Lovewell, also spelled "Lowell" and "Lowal" (NHRWR, vol. 1, pgs. 171, 174) was a "colored" man from the Dunstable-Litchfield area (Hurd, *Hillsborough*, pg. 166). He may have been the slave of Noah Lovewell, but there is no evidence to substantiate this. Nothing is known of Stephen Lovewell's status as either a free black or as a slave. Born about 1756, he served as a private in Col. Timothy Bedel's Regiment of Rangers from July 8 to December 16, 1775, in Capt. John Parker's company. Company rolls dated August 2, 1775, describe him as a 19-year-old husbandman (farmer) from Litchfield. On December 16, 1775, Stephen "Loval" "got home from Canedey" (NHRWR, vol. 1, pg. 177) with other men of Parker's company "allowing 15 day travel for there march from said Canedey" (*ibid.*). Nothing further is known of Stephen Lovewell after this time.

Sources: NHRWR, vol. 1; CH-Hurd-*Hillsborough*; TH-Fox.

Marcy, Cato

Cato Marcy was a resident of the town of Walpole who practiced the blacksmith's trade. He is said to have had a shop on a farm "near where the old meeting house once stood" (Aldrich, pg. 47) in Walpole. While Cato was a free black at the time of his enlistment, he probably served as a slave at some point prior, possibly to Capt. John Marcy of Walpole, who commanded a company in Reed's 3rd NH regiment. Cato Marcy enlisted sometime in 1777 in the 1st NH regiment for Continental service in the company of Capt. Jason Wait. His length of service is unspecified. He appears on a list of men in Wait's company dated May 27, 1778, and is listed as being 31 years old. The Walpole town history states that Marcy died of "disease or wound" (*ibid.*) sometime thereafter. No further record of Cato Marcy is found, and one can only speculate as to his fate. He may have been a casualty at the Battle of Monmouth, where the 1st NH saw heavy fighting in June of 1778. One old town resident, Thomas Bellows, in talking about the 12 men from Walpole who fought at Saratoga, stated that he "never was able to recall the name of the twelfth one," and after some hesitation would say "no matter, twas a black man anyway" (*ibid.*). A sad remembrance, indeed, for a man who sacrificed his life for his town and country.

Sources: PSR-NHRWR, vols. 1–2; TH-Aldrich, pg. 47.

Martin, Dan

Dan Martin was one of four black soldiers from Durham who served in the Revolution. In addition to the name Martin, he also went by the last names of Woodman and Freeman. Although he is known under the name Martin in census records, pension records use the name Woodman. In any event, he was the slave of John Woodman of Durham. In Woodman's will, dated August 14, 1775, he provided that his son, Jonathan, would have "his Negro man named Dan" and all his "work and service during his natural life" (Strafford County Records-Probate, vol. 1, pg. 261). It was further stipulated that, should Dan outlive Jonathan, he could "choose for himself whether to remain in the family where he is or surve either of my daughters" (*ibid.*). Dan, listed only as "a Negro," enlisted on June 28, 1777, for a term of three years in Hale's 2nd NH regiment, in the company of Capt. Benjamin Titcomb of Dover (NHRWR, vol. 2, pg. 653). He was paid a bounty of £20. Just prior to this, and probably with the aid of the bounty money due him, Dan Martin purchased his freedom from John Woodman for £60 lawful money. With this transaction, John Woodman signed a document stating that he had sold Dan "his time for life, liberating & making him a free man to all intents as tho' he had been born free" (Stackpole and Thompson, pg. 252). Even in those times, when the ideals of freedom were debated and discussed, masters who freed their slaves often only did so with the promise of financial compensation. It is unknown if Dan Martin joined his regiment in time to take part in the flight from Fort Ticonderoga, and the disastrous defeat at Hubbardton on July 7, 1777. However, he did serve in the company of Capt. William Rowell, after Titcomb was severely wounded at Hubbardton, and took part in all the subsequent engagements in which the 2nd NH saw action, including Saratoga, Monmouth, and Sullivan's campaign against the Six Nations. After the war, Martin returned to Durham, where he practiced the trade of a boatman, working on the boats that carried freight to Portsmouth via Oyster River and Great Bay. He lived on the landing, near the wharves and the Gleason house. Court records for June 1788 indicate that Martin was living in Durham when he sold "a certain piece of land in the town of Pittsfield" (RCR #A11116) to James Jenkins, a resident of Lee. The land in question was sold for £16 16s. with the proviso that the bill of sale would be null and void if, within one year, Dan Martin paid Jenkins the purchase price "in coined Gold or Silver with lawful interest" (*ibid.*). This indicates that Martin, while living in Pittsfield, likely became indebted to Jenkins and was forced to deed to him his land in order to pay off what he owed. However, over a year later, in July 1789, Dan Martin was still living in Pittsfield on the very land he had sold, forcing Jenkins to go to court to seek "an Action of Ejectment" (*ibid.*). Whether or not Jenkins was successful is unknown. In 1790, Dan Martin was still a resident of Pittsfield, but by 1800 had moved to Epsom with his family. Martin was married, according to Greenland town records, to Sally Barnes in 1800, and likely left town shortly thereafter. He is known to have had at least one son, named Archelaus, after the brother of his former master. Martin, listed as Dan "Woodman," received a pension for his service in April of 1819 at the age of 71. Martin later returned to Durham, and then removed to nearby Greenland, where he lived out the remainder of his years. Sources, however, differ as to his date of death. The Durham town history states that Martin died in June of 1839 at the age of 91 and was buried in the Chesley-Young burial lot in that town. Greenland town records, which are probably more accurate, show that Martin was attended to in his final days, at town expense, by Benjamin Berry, and that he died on December 22, 1838. The fact that the town also records expenditures to Samuel Hughes, for tolling the bell at Martin's funeral, and John Hatch, for making Martin's coffin, likely indicates that Martin was buried in Greenland.

Sources: PSR-NHRWR, vols. 2, 3; TH-Stackpole and Thompson; RCR #A11116; US-Strafford County Records-Probate, vol. 1, pg. 261; PEN-Draper, vol. 62, pgs. 114–119, TR-Greenland.

Martin, Jubil

Little is known of Jubil Martin. Listed as a "Negro man," he appears on a list of men in Capt. Stephen Clark's company of militia dated November 22, 1775 (NHRWR, vol. 4, pg. 24). Captain Clark, a resident of Epping, went with a portion of these men to Winter Hill in December 1775, during the Siege of Boston. Three other black soldiers, Sidon Martin, Ceaser Macling, and Timothy Nokes, also appear on this list, though only Jubil and Sidon Martin are designated as being "Negro" men. After the war, Martin probably lived in Portsmouth, at least for a time. He may be the man listed by the sole name of "Juba" who appears in the 1790 Census for Portsmouth as a free, non-white individual in a household of four free, non-whites. Jubil Martin later moved to Exeter, which had a sizeable free black population. Living on the road to Epping, "he owned and cultivated a small farm, seemed to live quite comfortably" (*Exeter News-Letter,* December 5, 1879).

On January 29, 1813, he sued Thomas Pendexter, a joiner of Durham, in the Rockingham County Common Pleas Court for $300. On March 24, 1809, Martin, listed as a husbandman in court records, had loaned money to Pendexter, which was to be paid back, with interest, in three years. On August 31, 1813, Jubil Martin recovered judgment against Pendexter and was awarded $265.65, plus an additional 17 cents for the cost of the court writ directing the county sheriff to collect the debt from Pendexter.

Martin was involved in the courts again when, on December 21, 1815, he was ordered to appear before the Common Pleas Court in Portsmouth in January of 1816 to answer the demands of Elizabeth Connor, a "Widdow" of Brentwood (RCR #A39865). Elizabeth Connor was the wife of Benjamin Connor, "late of Canaan in the County of Somersett & State of Massachusetts" (Ibid). After her husband's death, she lived with Jubil Martin as his common-law wife for an unknown period of time. However, in her court action, she "complains that the said Jubil Martin hath diforced [sic] her," and "whereof she hath nothing," demanded that Martin "instantly and without delay" return to her "her reasonable dower," which consisted of "a certain tract of land with the buildings standing, their cow situate partly in Exeter ... & partly in Brentwood ... bounded northerly on the road leading from Exeter to Epping Meeting house" (*ibid.*). Elizabeth Connor also sought the return of another tract of land in Epping.

Jubil Martin had one known child, a daughter named Mary. The name of her mother is unknown.

Sources: PSR-NHRWR, vol. 4, pg. 24; CEN-1790-NH; NEW-*Exeter News-Letter*; RCR #A36362, #A39865.

Martin, Scipio

Scipio Martin, his name often given as Sip or Sippo, was the slave of Timothy Emerson of Durham. At the death of his master in 1755, Martin, then aged 26, became the property of Emerson's widow Mary. In April of 1758, with the consent of Mary Emerson's new husband, Dr. Joseph Atkinson, Martin enlisted under the name "Sippo Negro" (NHRWR, vol. 1, pg. 21) as a private in the company of Capt. Thomas Tash in Col. John Hart's regiment. This regiment was raised for the expedition against Crown Point. Martin saw another term of service in the French and Indian War when he enlisted again in 1760, first in Capt. Phillip Johnson's company in Col. John Goffe's regiment, and then in Capt. Ephraim Berry's company, for a total of nine months' service. During this time, Johnson's company was employed in cutting a 26-mile-long road from Keene west to the Green Mountains. Berry's company was used in the expedition for the invasion of Canada. After 1760, Martin became a free man, and was married in Portsmouth on January 15, 1775, for the first time using the last name Martin. Already a veteran, he served one short term of service in the Revolution.

Referred to here by his first name only, Scipio Martin enlisted for service in 1776. The fact that he was listed separately in this return of men, with his captain not yet chosen, indicates that black soldiers were not always readily accepted for service in the first years of the war. PSR-NHRWR, vol. 2, Folder 5, item 80. Courtesy New Hampshire Division of Records Management and Archives.

He enlisted in Capt. Joseph Badger, Jr.'s company in Col. Joshua Wingate's regiment of militia in July of 1776. This regiment was raised by the state to help cover the Continental Army's retreat from Canada. Scipio Martin, listed as "a black" (*ibid.*, pg. 338), was enlisted by Deacon James Knowles with the designation "Captain not Chosen" (*ibid.*). Martin last appears on a list of men, described as "Able bodied Effective" and "well Accoutred" (*ibid.*, pg. 363), dated August 29, 1776, who were paid their bounty and wages for one month of service, as well as a travel allowance for going to Fort No. 4 at Charlestown. Nothing further of Scipio Martin is known.

Sources: PSR-NHRWR, vol. 1.

MARTIN, SIDON

Sidon Martin was the slave of Samuel Thompson of Durham, and is listed in the inventory of his estate in 1755, valued at £400 old tenor. By the time of the Revolution, Martin was a free black, enlisting for his first term of service in September of 1775 in Capt. Smith Emerson's company in Col. Joshua Wingate's regiment of militia. Serving for four months, until December 1775, Martin was stationed on Seavey's Island in Portsmouth harbor for the defense of the Piscataqua River. Martin again enlisted for militia service in Capt. Stephen Clark's company, appearing on a muster roll dated November 22, 1775. He may have been one of Clark's company that went to Winter Hill in Boston in December of 1775. Martin, his name given as "Sider Martain — Negro" (NHRWR, vol. 2, pg. 620), next served in 1777, when he enlisted for Continental service on April 20 in Capt. Michael McClary's company in Scammell's 3rd NH regiment. His term of enlistment was for three years and he was paid the state bounty of £20 for enlisting. His residence was listed as Lee, and town returns designate him as a "Negro" (NHSP, vol. 19, pg. 298). Sidon Martin later served under Maj. James Norris, but is listed as having died while in service on November 12, 1777. Though this is only speculation, it is possible he died from wounds he may have received at Saratoga, where the 3rd NH saw heavy fighting.

Sources: PSR-NHRWR, vols. 14; PSR-NHSP, vol. 19, pg. 298.

McDANIELS, ANDREW

McDaniels is identified as a black soldier based on a description of him. Little is known about him other than that he enlisted for Continental service in Capt. Ebenezer Frye's company in the 1st NH regiment in February of 1777 and was paid a state bounty of £20 for doing so. However, McDaniels was a deserter and never saw service in the 1st NH. On a list of absentees for the regiment dated January 10, 1778, he is listed as a "Tranchen Person" (transient), aged 25, with a "dark" complexion and "black" hair and eyes, and five feet six inches tall (NHRWR, vol. 2, pg. 438). He deserted at Derry even before joining the 1st NH. While it was not uncommon for men to accept a bounty payment and then desert, few blacks are recorded as doing so. Nothing further of McDaniels is known.

Sources: PSR-NHRWR, vols. 1, 2.

McIntyer, Primus

Primus McIntyer enlisted for one year of service aboard the Continental Navy frigate *Raleigh* as ordinary seaman on August 5, 1776, at Portsmouth. He was described as being American, five feet, seven inches tall, with black hair. However, when he reported for duty, he was discharged. The reason for his discharge is unknown. He may have been physically unfit for service, or, more likely, may have been a slave who enlisted without his master's permission. He was possibly the slave of Neal McIntyer, a Portsmouth merchant, but could also have been a slave of Mecum McIntyre of nearby York, Maine. Mecum McIntyre advertised for a runaway slave named Cato McIntyre just two years before in 1774.

Sources: GSP-NHGR, vol. 3, pg. 65.

McLain, Caesar

Caesar McLain, his last name also spelled "Macling" (NHRWR, vol. 4, pg. 25), served one short term during the Revolution from the town of Hampton. He appears on a list of men in Capt. Stephen Clark's company, along with Jubil and Sidon Martin, both listed as Negro men, dated November 22, 1777, at Portsmouth. Some of these men went to Winter Hill in Boston in December of 1775. Although the race of Jubil and Sidon Martin was identified, Caesar's was not. After the war, Caesar McLain appears in the census records for 1790 as a free, non-white resident of Hampstead, with one other person, likely his wife, in his household. After this, nothing further of Caesar is known.

Sources: PSR-NHRWR, vol. 4; CEN-NH-1790; TR-Hampton.

Miller, Jonathan

Jonathan Miller was a free black or "mulatto" (Brown, pg. 242) from Hampton Falls who was born about 1756. The Miller family, including Jonathan and his brother, and fellow soldier Robert, lived on "Murray's

Row" in Hampton Falls and were described as "mulattoes" (Brown, pg. 298). Their father was Robert Miller, Sr., who was a veteran of the Colonial Wars and was a resident of Hampton Falls as early as 1738. Robert Miller, Sr.'s life will be discussed in greater detail in the biography of his other son, and namesake, Robert Miller, Jr. Jonathan Miller first saw service in 1775, when he enlisted, along with Robert, in Capt. Winthrop Rowe's company in Col. Enoch Poor's 2nd NH regiment. Serving a six-month term, Jonathan enlisted on May 29, and was described as being aged 20 and practicing the trade of a fisherman. He appears on the payroll of Rowe's company on August 1, 1775, being paid his wages and blanket and coat money. He appears on another list, dated October 4, 1775, as being one of the soldiers paid $4 for a regimental coat. After this first term of service, Jonathan Miller enlisted again on April 20, 1776, in Capt. Nathan Brown's company in Col. David Gilman's militia regiment raised for the defense of Piscataqua Harbor. This term of service was short, since Miller enlisted again, on July 12, 1776, this time in Capt. William Harper's company in Col. Isaac Wyman's militia regiment destined for Canada. Miller served under Harper until December 1, 1776, and was paid the town bounty for enlisting. Whether race was an issue, the town selectmen of Hampton Falls voted on July 12, 1776, to pay Miller an "equal" bounty with other soldiers "that is gone in the Canada Service" (Brown, pg. 242). Miller next enlisted, for a fourth tour of duty, in Capt. Richard Weare's company in Col. Alexander Scammell's 3rd NH regiment for Continental service on February 18, 1777. His term of service was for one year, and he was paid the state bounty for enlisting. During this term, Miller saw heavy fighting with his regiment at Fort Anne, in New York, where Capt. Weare was killed, as well as at Saratoga. Miller re-enlisted with the 3rd NH on May 19, 1778, continuing in the same company as before, now commanded by Weare's successor, Capt. Isaac Frye. This time, his service was to be for three years. From June 1778, probably after the Battle of Monmouth, to January of 1779, Jonathan Miller is reported as sick in the army hospital in Pennsylvania. On February 5, 1780, he is reported as having deserted camp, but was likely on furlough. On April 19, 1781, while on furlough at home, and his term of service expiring, Miller re-enlisted again in the 3rd NH regiment and was paid the state bounty for doing so. Returns list him as being 25 years old, of "dark" complexion, and six feet tall (NHRWR, vol. 3, pg. 244). Interestingly enough, the following day, April 20, 1781, a resident of Seabrook, James Man, charged Miller and another man, Eliphalet Rawlins, with making a "Violent Assault" on him and "chased him with clubbs from said Hampton Falls to Seabrook and then and there Threatened him in fear of his life or bodily hurt" (RCR #6226). Miller, despite a plea of not guilty, was indeed found "Guilty of threatning the Said James Man in a high handed manner whereby he appears to be in great fear and Terror" (*ibid.*). The nature of this dispute is unknown, but Miller was forced to pay a fine and court costs, amounting to nearly £109. He also had his land and personal property "Levied" to the value of £1,000 for his "Good behaviour & keeping the peace ... Untill the Next Court of General Sessions" (*ibid.*) was held. Since Jonathan Miller subsequently served in the army and was out of the area, no further mention of the matter is made.

Throughout 1781 and 1782, the town of Hampton Falls paid Miller £18 for sundry supplies to his family. With six months left in his term, on June 8, 1783, Miller hired Joseph Green as a substitute to serve in his place as a soldier and serve his time out. Miller gave a power of attorney to his commander, Capt. Isaac Frye, to draw all his remaining pay, and a note to this effect was signed at Newburgh, New York, where the remaining New Hampshire Battalion was stationed. Miller was later forced to sue Frye for the pay due him, and won a court action against him on April 22, 1785, in the amount of £12. Following his extensive career as a soldier, nothing is known of Jonathan Miller, other than the fact that he continued to reside in Hampton Falls for an undetermined amount of time. However, he is not listed in the town census for 1790.

Sources: PSR-NHRWR, vols. 13; PSR-NHSP, vol. 30, pgs. 489, 491, 493; TH-Brown; TR-Hampton, vol. 1, pg. 228, vol. 2, pg. 33; TR-Hampton Falls, vol. 2, pgs. 107–108; RCR #6226, #8308.

MILLER, ROBERT

Miller was a soldier in the Revolutionary War from Kensington. He was the brother of Jonathan Miller of Hampton Falls, and lived in that town before moving to nearby Kensington at an unknown date. The Miller family's roots date to the early 1700s, starting with Neb Miller, the slave of Col. Christopher Toppan of Hampton (Dow, pgs. 287–88). His son was likely Robert Miller, Sr., who was living in Hampton Falls as early as 1738 as a free man. On November 10, 1738, Robert Miller, Sr., and his wife, whose name is unknown, were warned out of Hampton Falls, ordered to "Depart forthwith out of this Parish of hampton Fals ... Miler and his wife came into the Parish ... the last of August past" (Hampton Falls Town Records-loose item). Robert Miller, Sr., started his family's tradition of military service in 1745 when he was one of over 600 New Hampshire men recruited to fight in the war with France. Serving in the Hampton Falls company of Capt. Edward Williams, Miller saw action at the Siege of Louisburg, on

Cape Breton Island, Canada. The expedition against the French fortress, organized by Massachusetts and led by William Pepperell, was composed of over 3,000 men from Massachusetts and the District of Maine, while the rest came from New Hampshire. They landed near Louisburg on April 30, 1745, and by June 17 the fort capitulated. Little fighting of consequence took place, but many men were lost due to sickness, including at least five men from Hampton Falls. Of all the Hampton Falls men who served, only one casualty is stated as being directly due to enemy fire. Robert Miller, though he survived, is listed as having his "arm shot off" (Brown, pg. 240). Robert Miller later petitioned the New Hampshire Royal Government for assistance on July 14, 1747, stating "That your Petitioner at the Unfortunate Attack of the Island Battery in the Siege of Louisbourgh Met with a Shot by which he lost one arm which Renders him Incapable of Labouring for the Support of himself & a Large family..." (NHSP, vol. 18, pgs. 317–18). Because Miller went in the pay of Massachusetts for his service at Louisburg, he first asked that government for assistance, "But was Denied Any because He Belonged to New Hampse" (*ibid.*).

Robert Miller, Sr., next appears in the records on January 3, 1753, when he was charged by Meshach Weare, the Justice of the Peace for Hampton Falls, "that he had the Carnal Knowledge ... at Several times" of the body of Katharine Bryan, "Singlewoman," and "that she is now with Child and that the said Robert Did beget the same on her body" (Governor Weare Papers, vol. 13, pg. 91). This child was likely his son, and namesake, Robert Miller, Jr., who was born about 1753. Nothing further regarding Robert Miller, Sr., is known.

Robert Miller, Jr., grew to manhood in circumstances unknown and followed in his father's footsteps as a soldier. He first saw service on May 29, 1775, when he enlisted as a private in Capt. Winthrop Rowe's company in Poor's 2nd NH regiment. On a list dated June 3, 1775, he is described as being a "husbandman" (farmer) and aged 21. Listed separately from white soldiers, he is described as a "Molatto," and his enlistment was apparently conditional, stating, in part, "if the committee accept him" (NHRWR, vol. 1, pg. 111). At the bottom of this list is the final count of men enlisted for Rowe's company, which states "Total officers & Rank and file 66 including the Molatto" (*ibid.*). Robert Miller, however, was accepted for service, and by August 1, 1775, he had served for two months and eight days. On October 4, 1775, he appears on a list of men who received a payment of four dollars for a regimental coat at Medford. It is unknown when Miller's first term of service ended, but he enlisted again in January of 1776, probably for one year, in Capt. Joshua Abbott's company in Col. John Stark's 1st NH regiment for Continental service. Appearing on company rolls

> Province of
> New Hampsh. ss.
> At a Justices Court held at Hampton falls
> the third day of January 1753 before
> Meshech Weare Esq. one of his Majestys Justices
> of the Peace for the Province aforesaid —
>
> Robert Miller of Hampton falls aforesaid Husbandman
> being Charged by Katharine Bryan of Hampton falls
> aforesaid Singlewoman that she is now with Child
> and that he the said Robert Did beget the same on her
> body.
> Upon the Examination of the said Robert Miller
> It is Considered by the Court
> That the said Robert Miller do Recognize unto his majesty
> in the Sum of fifty Pounds new tenor Bills of Credit on
> the Province aforesaid with two Sureties in the
> Sum of twenty five Pounds like Bills Each
> for the appearance of the said Robert Miller before
> his majestys Justices of the Peace for the Province
> aforesaid at their General Quarter Sessions of
> the Peace for the Province aforesaid on the first
> tuesday of March next then and there to abide &
> Receive what shall be injoyned by the said Court
> Concerning the Premises And in the mean time to be
> of the good behaviour
> Meshech Weare

The closest thing to a birth certificate for any black soldier is this court summons to the father of Robert Miller in 1753 to answer the charge of "Carnal Knowledge" with Katharine Bryan, "Singlewoman." US-Meshach Weare Papers, vol. 13, pgs. 90-92. Courtesy New Hampshire Division of Records Management and Archives.

dated in April and November of 1776, Miller fought with the 1st NH at New York City, and subsequently saw garrison duty at Mount Independence, near Fort Ticonderoga late in the year. Robert Miller saw his next tour of duty when he re-enlisted in the 1st NH, this time under Capt. John House, on February 17, 1777. Serving a term of three years, Miller fought with the 1st NH in all the major northern campaigns, including Saratoga and Monmouth. He was discharged from service on January 22, 1780, having served his country for nearly five consecutive years. Little is known about Robert Miller after the war. He does not appear in any census records, though North Church records from Portsmouth list as a parishioner a man named Robert Miller, aged 76, on February 26, 1807. Whether this is the same man as the soldier Robert Miller is unknown.

Sources: TH-Sawyer, pgs. 238–40; TH-Dow, pgs. 287–88; TH-Brown, pg. 240; PSR-NHSP, vol. 18, pgs. 317–18; US-Weare Papers vol. 13, pgs. 90–92; PSR-NHRWR, vols. 1–3; OPS-Kidder; North Church records, vol. 1, pg. 114.

MOORE, FORTUNE

Fortune Moore, who also went by the name "Fortunatus" (NHRWR, vol. 3, pg. 845), was a free black soldier who enlisted for Continental service for the town of Stratham. Little is known about him, but he is probably the same man as Fortune Negro, who was warned to depart Portsmouth on December 31, 1764. He enlisted in Capt. Michael McClary's company in Scammell's 3rd NH regiment in April of 1777, his term of service specified as during the war. His name was spelled in the records at this time as "Fortain" (NHRWR, vol. 2, pg. 597). In a list of soldiers for the town of Stratham dated February of 1779, Moore is referred to as "a melatto belonging to Stratham during War" (NHRWR, vol. 3, pg. 845). As a private in the 3rd NH, Moore took part in some of the heaviest fighting during the war at Saratoga and Monmouth. Though undocumented, Fortune may have been a slave at one time to Thomas Moor, a resident of Stratham.

Sources: PSR-NHRWR, vols. 2, 3; TR-Portsmouth.

MOORE, SAMPSON

Sampson Moore was the slave of Col. Archelaus Moore of Canterbury. He was born there in 1752, and lived most of his life in Canterbury, Dunbarton, or Loudon. Moore served several short terms in the Revolution. He first enlisted on April 19, 1775, at the age of 23, after hearing about the fight at Lexington and Concord. In a local militia regiment under Capt. Benjamin Sias, he served for one month during the Siege of Boston. Sampson next saw service in September of 1777, when he enlisted again under Capt. Sias in Gen. John Stark's militia regiment raised to reinforce the Continental Army at Saratoga. Moore marched with his regiment to Fort #4 Charlestown, then to Manchester, Vermont. From Manchester, the regiment marched to Saratoga, where it stayed one night before going to nearby Fort Edward, where Moore spent the rest of his time in service. During his stay at Fort Edward, Moore served mostly in scouting parties under Capts. Sias, Joshua Abbott, and John Ford. Sampson Moore, now using the last name "Battis" (NHRWR, vol. 2, pg. 387) enlisted for a final term of service in July of 1781 for three months. He served under Capt. Nathaniel Head and spent part of this time marching to West Point, but only got as far as Danbury, Connecticut, before being ordered back to Springfield, Massachusetts, and, later, Fort #4 Charlestown. During this time, Sampson and his unit heard of the defeat of Cornwallis at Yorktown and "the troops had a day of rejoicing" (Pension #S13961). Moore was discharged from service in November 1781, but was listed as having deserted on November 22, just three days before the rest of his company was discharged. The record stating he was a deserter was likely due to a clerical error or miscommunication, since Moore later states that he was "verbally discharged" from service (*ibid.*). Prior to the Revolution, Moore was promised his freedom by his master for "good fighting" (Potter, pg. 335n) in the war, and this promise was apparently kept. In addition, Sampson was also given a one hundred-acre lot in the southwest part of Canterbury, known locally as "New Guinea" (*ibid.*). After the war, Moore married Lucy, a slave of William Coffin of Concord, and purchased her freedom by working for Coffin for one year. Local tradition calls Moore a "fine specimen of a Negro," and a man who was "well recollected by the people of Concord" (*ibid.*). Moore was also said to have been given command of a "Battalion" of state militia in 1800, and was given the "honorary title" of "Major" by Governor Gilman (*ibid.*). Sampson was also remembered for attending election and muster day events dressed in his regimental uniform, and was called "a famous fiddler" who "for many years afforded fine fun for frolicsome fellows in Concord with his fiddle on election day" (Bouton, pg. 252). At the age of 82, on August 28, 1832, Moore applied for a government pension for his war service, and was placed on the pension rolls as of February 16, 1833. Sampson must have died soon after since he disappears from the records.

Moore also went by the name of Sampson "Battis" on other occasions, such as the 1790 Census for New Hampshire, for reasons that are unclear. Though it is speculation, it may be that his father was John Battis, a slave of Robert Thompson of Durham. John Battis and two female slaves, Nan and Page, are listed in probate records for Thompson's estate after his death in 1753.

Sources: PSR-NHRWR, vols. 2–4; OPS-Potter, pgs. 252–3; TH-Bouton, Lyford, *History of Canterbury*; CH-Hurd, *Merrimac*; PEN-S13961; PSR-NHSP, vol. 30, pgs. 348, 397; US-NH Provincial Probate record, vol. 20, pg. 409.

Moulton, Cato

Cato Moulton was the slave of Col. Jonathan Moulton of Hampton. Cato was sold several times as a slave before being owned by Moulton, and is said to have preferred the name Elisha Bartlet, "as he has said that

TEN DOLLARS REWARD.

RUN away from the Subscriber, on the 19 h of October laſt, a Negro Boy named CATO, about eighteen Years old, five Feet and a Half high, or full a thing more ; had on when he went away a blue dull l round Jacket with Cuffs and without Lining ; an under Jacket without Sleves of blue Serge, both almoſt new : a new Pair of leather Breeches, made of Moose Skin, carried with him three Check'd Shirts, two of which were Cotton and Woolen, the other Linnen, with large Checks, feveral Pair of Stockings of different Colours, and a wooden Quart Bottle of Rum. His Pack was feen by a Boy not long before he went away, and his Things were then done up in one of his Check'd Shirts. A more likely, well built, active and cunning Boy is feldom to be feen ; he plays well on a Fife, and carried one with him : It's probable he is making his Way for New York, and it's likely he will ſteer his Courſe by Way of Cohefs, as he once lived at Orford, and ale y hinted it to one of his Maſters that he ſhould go that Way. Whoever will take up faid Runaway and con vey him to his Maſter, ſhall receive TEN DOLLARS Reward, and all neceſſary Charges paid by me

JONATHAN MOULTON.

Hampton October 21, 1775.

N.B. 'Tis likely he will change his Name, perhaps call himſelf Eliſha Bartiſt, as he has faid that was his Name with one of his Maſters and his right Name. It don't appear at any Time when he hinted of running away that he gave any Reafon for it, but it is fuppoſed he was deluded away by fome Perſon or Perſons. Notwithſtanding as he has heretofore been a faithful Boy, if he will return and behave well his Maſter promiſes to forgive him his Crime, and truſt him as tho' it had not happened.

Runaway slave ad for Cato Moulton. This unusually detailed ad for Moulton was one of three such ads that appeared on the same day. Cato was later returned, since he saw service in 1776 as a fifer in a regiment of militia. *New Hampshire Gazette*, November 2, 1775. Courtesy Portsmouth Public Library.

was his name with one of his Masters and his right Name" (*New Hampshire Gazette*, November 2, 1775, pg. 1). Little is known about Cato Moulton, but much can be gathered from a runaway slave advertisement placed in the *New Hampshire Gazette* dated November 2, 1775, by Jonathan Moulton. Cato, who ran away on October 19, is listed as being about 18 years old, five and a half feet tall, and is described as follows: "A more likely, well built, active and cunning Boy is seldom to be seen; he plays well on a Fife, and carried one with him: It's probable he is making his Way for New York, and it's likely he will steer his Course by way of Cohose, as he once lived at Orford." The name "Cohose" probably refers to the town of Cohoes, on the outskirts of Albany, New York; Orford is in New Hampshire, near the Vermont border. It may be that Moulton was held as a slave at both these locations. In addition, he was also described as wearing a blue jacket with cuffs and without a lining, an "under Jacket without Sleves of blue Serge" and "a new Pair of leather Breeches made of Moose Skin." Cato also carried with him three "Check'd Shirts, two of which were Cotton and Woolen, the other Linnen, with large Checks, several Pair of Stockings of different Colours, and a wooden Quart Bottle of Rum," all of which were "done up in one of his Check'd Shirts."

Despite his action of running away, Cato was well liked by his master, since he states in his advertisement that "Notwithstanding as he has been a faithful Boy, if he will return and behave well his Master promises to forgive him his Crime, and trust him as tho' it had not happened." Whether Moulton returned on his own, or was captured and returned is unknown, but he was reunited with his master. On September 21, 1776, he enlisted from his master's militia regiment as a fifer in Capt. William Prescott's company in Col. Thomas Tash's regiment of militia. This regiment was raised to reinforce the Continental Army in New York after the failed Canadian campaign. How long he served under Prescott is unknown, but it was for only several months at the most. On December 5, 1776, he enlisted again as a fifer in Capt. Benjamin Sias' company in Col. David Gilman's regiment of militia. During this time, Moulton served at, or around Fort Ticonderoga, and may have been part of the New Hampshire militia sent to New Jersey to take part in the campaigns at Trenton and Princeton. He served for three months and one day during this term, his enlistment ending on March 15, 1777. However, soon after, in April of 1777, he re-enlisted for yet another term of service, this time for three years. He joined the company of Capt. Richard Weare in Scammell's 3rd NH regiment for Continental service. After the record of this enlistment, no further record of Cato Moulton is found. If, as seems likely, he served out his term with the 3rd NH, he took part in some of the heaviest fighting in the war at Fort Anne, where his captain was killed, as well as at Saratoga and Monmouth.

Sources: PSR-NHRWR, vols. 1–2; NEW-*New Hampshire Gazette*, Nov. 2, 1775.

OLIVER, AARON

Aaron Oliver was a freeborn black from the town of Temple. Born in Malden, Massachusetts, in 1750, he enlisted, at the age of 25, in Capt. Ezra Towne's company in Reed's 3rd NH regiment on April 23, 1775, following the alarm at Lexington. Oliver was described as being five feet, ten inches tall, with "black" complexion and eyes (MSS, vol. 11, pg. 635). His occupation was that of a farmer. Later records list Oliver as a "mulato" (*ibid.*). Oliver's first term of service was for an undetermined time, but lasted at least six months, since he was on company rolls dated August 1, 1775, and in the census for households in Temple, dated October 28, 1775. The Oliver household is listed as having one female, two boys under the age of 16 and one man in the army, though none are listed as being "Negro" (Blood, pg. 78). Oliver served for a second time in 1776, when he enlisted on July 18, 1776, in Capt. Joseph Parke's company of New Ipswich men in Col. Isaac Wyman's regiment, which joined the Northern Army at Ticonderoga. This term of service lasted about one month. Aaron Oliver enlisted for a final term of service on March 24, 1777, when he joined the company of Capt. Isaac Frye in Scammell's 3rd NH regiment for Continental service. This term of service was for three years. However, Oliver was one of many New Hampshire soldiers who were captured at the Battle of Hubbardton on July 7, 1777, following the flight from Fort Ticonderoga. Oliver remained in captivity with the British for nearly nine months before being released on April 3, 1778. Less than four weeks later, on April 30, 1778, Aaron Oliver died. His death was likely due to his weakened state during his imprisonment, with its unsanitary living conditions and malnourishment, or any number of common diseases, such as smallpox, typhus, diphtheria, dysentery, or malaria. After the death of her husband, Abigail Oliver, along with her son, Aaron, Jr., suffered further when they were warned out of Temple in December of 1778. This would seem to be one of the cruelest examples of the warning out process in New Hampshire. There are no records that have been found that show the town of Temple paid any relief to Aaron Oliver's widow, or gave aid to his family. Following this, nothing further is known of Abigail Oliver and her family.

Sources: PSR-NHRWR, vols. 1–3; TH-Kidder, pg. 78; Blood, pg. 829; TR-New Ipswich-vol. 22, pg. 87; PSR-MSS-vol. 11, pg. 635.

Parsons, Samuel

Little is known about Samuel Parsons. He is identified as a black soldier based on his description in military records. He served as a private in Capt. Frederick Bell's company in Poor's 2nd NH regiment sometime between January 1st and July 8, 1776. He appears on a list of soldiers for the 2nd NH which were either sick or absent, and is described as being 30 years old, five feet, three inches tall, with "black" hair and eyes (NHRWR, vol. 1, pg. 310). His residence is listed as Marblehead, in Essex County, Massachusetts. The list mentioned above is dated July 8, 1776, at Chimney Point, near Fort Ticonderoga. A Samuel Parsons is also listed as serving in Capt. William Barron's company in Col. Moses Nichol's regiment of New Hampshire militia, raised to help garrison West Point, New York. Parsons served for three months and sixteen days, from July 6 to October 22, 1780. It is unknown if this is the same individual as the man from Marblehead.

Sources: PSR-NHRWR, vols. 1, 3; PSR-MSS, vol. 11, pg. 976–78.

Perham, Asa

Asa Perham was the son of Samuel Perham of New Ipswich, a veteran of the French and Indian War. Samuel Perham saw military service in 1755 when he enlisted in the company of Capt. Peter Powers of Hollis on May 1, serving until October 21, 1755. Captain Powers's company was part of a regiment of 600 men commanded by Col. Joseph Blanchard and raised for the expedition against Crown Point. The men rendezvoused at Stevenstown, New Hampshire, at a place called Salisbury Fort. Here, they built batteaus for the transport of troops and supplies down the Connecticut River. Blanchard's regiment then went to Fort Number 4 at Charlestown, and from there to Albany, New York. It subsequently fought a battle on Lake George with French forces before its return home. Whether Samuel Perham was already an old man, or worn out by his military service is unknown, but he did not long survive after the French and Indian War ended.

Asa Perham is identified as a black soldier based on his physical description in military records. Both his mother and father died in March of 1760, leaving Asa and his six brothers and sisters without parents. The children were to be cared for by a relative, Lemuel Perham, but this did not happen to the satisfaction of some of the townsmen of New Ipswich. On January 2, 1761, 13 men petitioned the Probate Court

> that Lemuel Perham may no Longer administer on ye Estate of ye Deceasd for he has Taken no Care to pay anything for keeping Sd Children and hath Taken ye Chief of ye Stock into his own hands which he might have Sold for the Support of ye Children which he Refused and Tels those which have the Children that they must keep them or provide places for them which they cannot by reason of there being no money for their Support and there is no body to Let them out for any Term of Time the oldest of sd five is Eleven years old and ye administrator has paid Towards Cloathing Sd Children Eighteen Shillings and Sixpence in Sterling money, the most of sd Children Remain at the places that in pity they ware taken to when their parents ware Sick — We therefore Desire that your Honour would be pleased to Consider us in our Difficulties as an Infant Plantation and be pleased to Give a Letter of administration to Capt Reuben Kidder and of Gaurdeenship for he appears a man of Truth and fidelity and we make no Doubt he will Take faithfull Care of ye poor fatherless and motherless Children that we as Inhabitants may not be at ye Cost to Bring them up when we Believe there is Estate Enough to pay all ye Debts and bring up sd Children if Prudently managed... [NHSP, vol. 36, pgs. 544–45].

The court approved the petition and on January 20, 1761, awarded guardianship of five of the Perham children, Asa, Elizabeth, Mary, Lydia, and

Sarah, all aged younger than 14, to Reuben Kidder. The two oldest children, Samuel and Amos, both "minors," were awarded to Benjamin Adams, a yeoman of New Ipswich and signer of the petition (*ibid.*).

Nothing further is known about Asa Perham's life as a youth prior to his military service.

On December 5, 1776, at the age of 19, Asa enlisted in Capt. Francis Towne's company in Col. David Gilman's regiment of New Hampshire militia raised to reinforce the Continental Army at New York. He may have seen action in New Jersey at the decisive battles of Trenton and Princeton. He served under Capt. Towne for three months and eight days, until March 12, 1777. Soon after, in April of 1777, Perham enlisted again, this time in Capt. James Carr's company in Col. Nathan Hale's 2nd NH regiment for Continental service. Stationed with his regiment at Fort Ticonderoga, Perham saw heavy action during the retreat from that location, and took part in the heavy fighting during the Battle of Hubbardton, on July 7, 1777. Records are unclear what happened to Asa Perham at Hubbardton. On a return of absentees for the 2nd NH regiment, dated January 10, 1778, Perham is listed as having been left at Hubbardton, but the cause of this absence is not specified. Perham is described in this list as having "black" hair, eyes, and complexion, aged 20, and five feet, eight inches tall (NHRWR, vol. 2, pg. 443). Since Capt. Carr's company bore the brunt of the initial British attack at Hubbardton, and suffered many casualties and captured men, it seems likely that Asa Perham was either wounded or captured, or possibly both. The New Ipswich town history states, rather vaguely, that he died of sickness in the army, or soon after he was brought home. It seems likely that Perham was wounded at Hubbardton, and died shortly thereafter, or that he was captured by the British, and died soon after his release.

Sources: OPS-Potter, pgs. 129–32, 143; PSR-NHSP, vol. 36, pgs. 544–45; PSR-NHRWR, vols. 1–2; TH-Kidder, pgs. 86, 98–99.

PICKERING, TUMBRIL

Tumbril Pickering enlisted as a soldier late in the war from Greenland. He enlisted on April 28, 1781, in the 2nd NH regiment, in the 7th company commanded by Capt. Samuel Cherry. Pickering is described as a "negro," 18 years old, and five feet, six inches tall (NHRWR, vol. 3, pg. 507). His term of service was described as being "during the war" (*ibid.*). Pickering was paid the state bounty for enlisting. In a list dated June 30, 1781, Tumbril Pickering is described as a "black" (*ibid.*, pg. 245) soldier for the town of Greenland. Nothing further is definitely known about

Tumbril Pickering, but he was probably the slave of Nicholas Pickering of neighboring Newington, who placed an ad in *The New Hampshire Gazette*, dated March 12, 1781, warning and forbidding anyone from trading with or crediting a "Negro Lad" of his. Since this occurred just after Tumbril Pickering's enlistment, it was likely an attempt by his master to keep him from spending the bounty money he had just received.

THIS is to forbid any Person or Persons trading with, or Crediting a Negro Lad belonging to Nicholas Pickering, of Newington.

This brief notice likely concerns soldier Tumbril Pickering of Greenland and was placed a month before his enlistment for military service. It may indicate that this "Negro Lad" was trading illegally in the name of his master, or that Pickering was trying to prevent his slave from spending the bounty money he would soon receive for his enlistment. *New Hampshire Gazette*, March 12, 1781. Courtesy Portsmouth Public Library.

Sources: PSR-NHRWR, vol. 3; NEW-*New Hampshire Gazette*.

POMP, PETER

Peter Pomp was a slave who served in the war from the town of Epsom. Born about 1747, he was the slave of Maj. Andrew McClary. In a 1775 state census, only one slave was listed for all of Epsom, this being Peter Pomp. When Maj. McClary was killed at the Battle of Bunker Hill by a stray cannonball, on June 17, 1775, Pomp was part of his estate to be settled. In an inventory of McClary's estate in 1776, he is described as "one male negro named Peter about 19 years old" (RCR-Probate, vol. 23, pg. 386). Though uncertain, it seems likely that Pomp remained a slave of the McClary family for an undetermined time, but may have been freed to serve in the war. He enlisted for Epsom on January 24, 1777, in Capt. Michael McClary's company in Col. Alexander Scammell's 3rd NH regiment for Continental service. His length of service was listed as "during war" (NHRWR, vol. 1, pg. 570). On February 6, 1777, Pomp was paid the state bounty for enlisting and mustered into service. Throughout 1777, he served with the 3rd NH at Fort Ticonderoga, and took part in the bloody battles at Fort Anne and Saratoga. After the defeat of Burgoyne, Peter Pomp marched south with his regiment to winter at Valley Forge, Pennsylvania. However, like many men, he became ill during the long winter. He is listed on regimental rolls as being "sick in camp at Valley Forge" from February 21 to March 15, 1778. On March 15, 1778, it is recorded that "Peter Pomp, an African" (Hurd, *Strafford*, pg. 457) died at Valley Forge.

The gravestone of Peter Pomp. This monument details the service of Peter Pomp, a soldier who was the slave of Maj. Andrew McClary. McClary was killed at the Battle of Bunker Hill, but Pomp went on to serve in the war until his death at Valley Forge in 1778. Though Pomp was buried at his place of death, this stone was erected circa 1920 to honor his memory. Photograph courtesy of T.J. Rand.

Sources: PSR-NHRWR, vols. 1–3; CH-Hurd, *Merrimack*; CH-Hurd, *Strafford*; OS-RCR-Probate, vol. 23, pg. 386.

POOR, PETER

Little is known about Peter Poor and his inclusion in this list is somewhat speculative. Poor, whose last name is also given in some records as Power, enlisted on May 15, 1775, for service in the company of Hollis, New Hampshire, men commanded by Capt. Reuben Dow. This unit was mustered into Col. William Prescott's regiment of Massachusetts troops shortly after the outbreak of war at Lexington and Concord. Poor is listed as serving one month and six days before he was killed at the Battle of Bunker Hill on June 17, 1775. He was one of eight Hollis men killed that day in the heavy action that took place in the redoubt on top of Breed's Hill. The possibility that Poor was a black soldier comes from a voucher that was issued by the selectmen of Hollis nearly a year later, on March 14, 1776. It states that "Capt. Reuben Dow is the only proper person to receive the clothing that is due to Peter Poor, a transient person who enlisted in his Company, and last resided in this Town and went away in debt. Said Poor was killed in Bunker Hill fight" (Worcester, pg. 161). The use of the word "transient" is one that was most often applied to free blacks who had no real home and drifted from town to town. Rarely applied to white enlistees, the term "transient" has also been found in records for two known black soldiers, John Webb and Andrew McDaniels. If, indeed, Poor was a black soldier, he was not the only one in Dow's company. Jacob Danforth also served in Dow's company and fought at Bunker Hill. Like Poor, he is not listed in military records by race.

Sources: TH-Worcester, pg. 161; PSR-MSS, vol. 12, pgs. 560, 646.

Reed, John

John Reed first saw service in December of 1776, when he enlisted in Capt. Francis Towne's company in Col. David Gilman's regiment of New Hampshire militia. This regiment was raised to reinforce the Continental Army in New York, and may have fought in the battles of Trenton and Princeton in New Jersey. The length of Reed's service in Gilman's regiment is unknown, but was probably for two or three months. Reed next saw service in 1777, when he was part of Col. Samuel Ashley's militia regiment, in the company of Lt. James Robertson. This regiment marched from Chesterfield to help relieve the garrison at Fort Ticonderoga. Reed saw service for only 13 days, from June 29 to July 11, 1777. However, Reed was back in action less than two weeks later, enlisting as a private under Capt. Kimball Carlton in Col. Moses Nichols' militia regiment. This regiment marched from Chesterfield and towns adjacent on July 22 and was part of Gen. John Stark's Brigade raised to meet the threat of the advancing British under Gen. Burgoyne. As part of Nichols' regiment, Reed took part in the Battle of Bennington, where the victorious Americans dealt a serious blow to Burgoyne's army. Reed served during this term until September 23, 1777, having served a total of two months and two days. Once again, Reed enlisted for yet another term of service. Though the time is not recorded, it was probably immediately at the end of his militia service, while in the Saratoga vicinity, that Reed enlisted in the 1st NH regiment for Continental service in the company of Capt. Ebenezer Frye. His term of enlistment is not certain, but was likely for three years. As part of Col. Joseph Cilley's 1st NH regiment, Reed took part in the second battle of Saratoga at Bemis Heights, where the New Hampshire Continentals stopped a British charge and defeated their renowned grenadiers in a bloody battle. On a list of absentees for the 1st NH regiment, dated January 10, 1778, at Valley Forge, Reed is listed as a "negrow" of Canterbury, aged 30, five feet, eight inches tall, with "black" hair and eyes (NHRWR, vol. 2, pg. 438). He is listed as being sick, and was left at Fishkill, New York. After the Saratoga campaign, the New Hampshire Continentals marched south toward winter quarters at Valley Forge, Pennsylvania. They stopped at Fishkill, New York, on the Hudson River, on November 2, 1777, and stayed there for several days. During this time, there was a mutiny in the brigade over pay issues, and one captain and one soldier were killed. It is unknown when Reed rejoined his regiment, but there is nothing to indicate he was out for any extended time. There is no record of when John Reed was discharged from service with the 1st NH, so it is uncertain whether or not he participated in that regiment's subsequent actions at Monmouth and Sullivan's Expedition. Reed, however, was not yet done serving. He served as a six-month man in 1780 and was stationed at West Point. His name appears on a list of men, dated July of 1780, who received a ration of a half-pint of rum and one pound of sugar. John Reed saw one final term of service in 1782, when he enlisted for three years on July 30 and was paid the state bounty for doing so. Reed likely served with the New Hampshire Battalion at West Point until it was disbanded in January of 1784. After the war, little is known of Reed, except that he was a free non-white inhabitant of Croydon in 1790.

Sources: PSR-NHRWR, vols. 2–3; CEN-1790-NH; TH-Lyford, *History of Canterbury*, pg. 145.

ROBINSON, JACK

Jack Robinson enlisted for service in Col. Enoch Poor's 2nd NH regiment for Continental service in the company of Capt. Philip Tilton. His exact enlistment date is unknown, but it was prior to July 1776. Robinson's name appears on a list of men sick and absent from his regiment, dated July 8, 1776, at Chimney Point, near Fort Ticonderoga. Robinson is described as being 30 years old, six feet tall, with black hair and eyes. His residence is listed as Andover, Massachusetts. Nothing further is known about Robinson and it is unknown if he, like so many others at this time, died from his illness.

Sources: PSR-NHRWR, vol. 1, pg. 309.

RUSSELL, POMP

Little about Russell is known, but he was likely one of the youngest black soldiers to serve in the war. He came from the town of Wilton and was probably a former slave. He was born circa 1765 in Charlestown, Massachusetts, and came to New Hampshire under unknown circumstances. He enlisted for military service on July 20, 1777, at the supposed age of 12 years, serving in the company of Capt. John Goss in Col. Moses Nichols' militia regiment. Under the command of Gen. John Stark, this unit took a key part in the ensuing Battle of Bennington. Russell served under Goss for two months and eight days, being discharged on September 27 in the vicinity of Saratoga, New York. Details about Russell after the war are scarce. He lived in Packersfield (Nelson) until 1805, being taxed annually in that town from 1789 to 1804. His holdings during this period consisted of one or two cows, 30 acres of land, and a house. Pomp Russell is listed in the 1790 Census for New Hampshire as living in Packersfield, the head of a household of three free blacks, likely including a wife and son. Russell, who may have had another son, later moved to Maine, dying at Wells in 1838.

Sources: PSR-NHRWR, vol. 2; OPS-Gilmore; PEN-NA-M881-#549.

Rymes, Thomas

Tom Rymes was the former slave of Samuel Rymes of Portsmouth. He appears early in the records, on January 28, 1748, when he is listed as a friend and associate of Tobey Buss, a Negro servant of John Buss, who confessed to the crime of breaking and entering. On November 26, 1755, Thomas Rymes is listed in an inventory of his late master's estate, valued at £300 old tenor. Whether Rymes continued as a slave after this time is unknown. However, he next appears in the records on April 2, 1776, when he enlisted as a private in the company of Capt. Caleb Hodgdon in Col. Pierce Long's militia regiment. He was stationed in the Seacoast area, being paid 40s. upon enlistment, and an additional 52s. and $2 blanket money on August 23, 1776, while at New Castle. His term of service is listed as being one year or less, and his residence was Berwick, Maine. Rymes, his name also spelled as "Rines," served in Long's regiment under Hodgdon, and later Capt. Abraham Perkins until December 7, 1776. Soon after this term of service ended, Rymes turned his eye to the sea, signing on as a crewmember on board the privateer sloop *Charming Polly*. However, this vessel was captured by the British on May 16, 1777, and some of her crew, Rymes included, were taken to England as prisoners. At an unknown time afterwards, Thomas Rymes died at the infamous Old Mill Prison in Plymouth, England, where many captured American sailors were held and treated poorly.

Sources: PSR-NHRWR, vol. 1; GSP-NEGHR, January 1865, pg. 75.

Sampson, John

John Sampson was a soldier from Portsmouth who first saw service in 1776, when he enlisted in Capt. James Arnold's company in Col. Joshua Wingate's regiment of New Hampshire militia. This regiment went to Fort

Ticonderoga to provide relief for the army after the failed Canadian invasion. It is unknown when Sampson enlisted, or for how long. His name appears on a list of soldiers, dated July 20, 1776, who received a bounty and advance wages for their service. It is likely that Sampson enlisted for six months, beginning in July of 1776. He next saw service when he enlisted in Capt. Ebenezer Frye's company in the 1st NH regiment for Continental service on January 1, 1777. It is most likely that Sampson enlisted for this second term of service right at Fort Ticonderoga, after his term of militia service expired. His term of service was likely specified as being the duration of the war, since he served in the 1st NH up to December of 1781. As a member of Frye's company in the 1st NH, Sampson took part in all the campaigns of his battle-hardened regiment. After the war, Sampson, at least for a time, continued to live in the Seacoast area. The 1790 Census for New Hampshire lists him as a free black residing in Exeter with one other person, likely his wife. Nothing further of John Sampson is known after 1790.

Sources: PSR-NHRWR, vols. 1–3; OPS-Kidder, pg. 156.

SANKEY, CAESAR

Caesar Sankey, his name also spelled as "Ceazar" (NHRWR, vol. 1, pg. 540), was a free black from Dover. He first appears in the records in 1774, when he was married to Sarah Sharp of Dover on November 23. Caesar and his wife may have been nominal members of the Quaker faith, since there is an entry in the Friends Records, dated February of 1777, stating that Caesar and Sarah were "disowned … neither of them members till now" (NHGR, vol. 5, pg. 30). Their child, Simon (born January 31, 1776), was "disowned" in 1802 (*ibid.*). The Quakers had a strong presence in the Dover area, and it would not have been unusual for a free black to be accepted as a member. Caesar "Sankee" (Pension #S41124) first saw military service in December of 1776, when he enlisted as a private in Capt. Samuel Wallingford's company in Col. David Gilman's regiment of New Hampshire militia raised to reinforce the Continental Army at New York. Sankey, his name also listed as "Carson" (NHRWR, vol. 1, pg. 447) served under Wallingford from December 5, 1776, to March 15, 1777. During this time, it is probable that Gilman's regiment took part in the pivotal battles at Trenton and Princeton in New Jersey. Sankey's company commander, Samuel Wallingford, later served as a commander of Marines aboard the ship *Ranger*, commanded by Capt. John Paul Jones, and was killed during a battle with the British sloop *Drake* in late April of 1778. Sankey served one final term late in the war when he enlisted in March of

1781 in the 1st NH regiment. He served nine months during this term and was stationed at West Point. Sometime after the war, by 1810, Caesar Sankey moved north to Moultonborough, where he is listed in the 1810 Census as being a free black with four other family members, presumably his wife Sarah and several children. By 1819, he was living in Portsmouth, and his first wife Sarah was likely deceased sometime earlier. On November 29, 1819, "Mr. Ceasar Sankey and Lydia Gardner, people of colour, both of this town" (Pension #S41124) were married. Like many other free blacks, Sankey later moved to Vermont. In September of 1830, at the age of 74, he resided in Pomfret and applied for a government pension for his war service. He did not apply for a pension earlier because "he could not obtain evidence to prove his service" because "his discharge certificate was destroyed when his house was burned years ago" (*ibid.*). Caesar Sankey's pension application was finally approved and he began receiving a payment of eight dollars per month on December 10, 1831. After this, nothing further of Caesar is known, though it seems likely he passed his remaining years in Pomfret.

Sources: PSR-NHRWR, vol. 1; TR-Portsmouth, vol. 11, pg. 376; GSP-NHGR, vol. 5, Jan. 1908, pg. 30; PEN-S41124.

SANNO, PETER

Peter Sanno saw service in the Continental Navy when he enlisted for service aboard the frigate *Raleigh* on February 23, 1777, at Portsmouth. His term, as ordinary seaman, was for three years. His complexion is listed as being "black" and his nationality as "African" (NHGR, vol. 3, pgs. 69, 76). However, although Sanno enlisted at Portsmouth, he was not from New Hampshire. His place of residence was listed as the sloop *Granville*. Sanno was one of seven men, but the only black sailor, who listed the sloop as their residence. The other men were listed as being from "North Britain" (*ibid.*). The *Granville* was captured by local privateers and brought into Portsmouth, with her crew agreeing to serve in the *Raleigh* rather than suffer imprisonment. Nothing further of Sanno is known.

Sources: GSP-NHGR, vol. 3, pgs. 69, 76.

SHARPER, WILLIAM

Sharper is one of the few black soldiers who deserted during the war. He enlisted sometime in 1777, date unknown, in the 1st NH regiment for Continental service under Capt. Amos Emerson for three years. On a list of absentees for the 1st NH regiment, dated January 10, 1778, at Valley

Forge, Pennsylvania, Sharper is described as being aged 35, five feet, eight inches tall, with "black" complexion and hair, and "yellow" eyes (NHRWR, vol. 2, pg. 437). He is listed as having "desarted," with the notation that he did so at "Sopers" (*ibid.*). This last notation is not positively understood. There is no geographical location that corresponds to the word "Sopers," nor any further reference to it concerning other soldiers who were absentees. One possibility is that it refers to the name of an individual. There was an officer in the 1st NH early in the war, 1st Lt. Joseph Sopers, who resided in Canterbury. It may also be that Sopers helped recruit soldiers for his old regiment, including William Sharper, and that Sharper disappeared after signing enlistment papers. On the absentee list, Sharper is listed as being from Rochester, but enlisted for the town of Lee. Nothing further is known of William Sharper after his desertion.

Sources: PSR-NHRWR, vol. 2.

SHEPARD, JOHN

John Shepard enlisted for Continental service in April of 1777 for three years in the 3rd NH regiment under Capt. Benjamin Stone. He enlisted for the town of Boscawen, but was a resident of Rumney. His name appears on a list of men from Col. Thomas Stickney's militia district, dated March 12, 1779, of men who enlisted into the service of the state, according to the returns made by the respective captains of New Hampshire's Continental regiments. No further record of John Shepard is found in later rolls of the 3rd NH regiment. Such records are incomplete, and it is uncertain whether Shepard served his full term of service. However, there is nothing that would indicate his lack of service. Little else is known about John Shepard. He may be the same man who settled in Canterbury in 1767. Shepard appears in the records in 1790, when he is listed as a free non-white inhabitant of Lyme, a town close to Rumney, in the Federal Census for New Hampshire. The soldier John Shepard may also be the same man who belonged to the New Light Baptist Church near Canterbury and, upon hearing reports about the Shaker religion from a peddler who visited their settlement in New York, was sent by his church to visit the Shaker village at Harvard, Massachusetts. Following this visit, a rift in the New Light Church resulted, with some members joining the Shakers, and others adapting some of their practices only. Some years later, on October 3, 1795, John Shepard was appointed a clerk in the Free Will Baptist Church in Canterbury headed by Elder Benjamin Randall. This John Shepard should not be confused with the white soldier named John Shepard, who served in the 2nd NH regiment and came from the Seacoast area.

Sources: PSR-NHRWR, vol. 2, pg. 607; CEN-1790, NH; OPS-White and Taylor, pgs. 90–91; TH-Lyford-Canterbury, pg. 319.

SHERBURNE, POMP

Sherburne was a soldier in the war from Londonderry. He first saw service in 1778, when he enlisted for six months in Col. George Reid's 2nd NH regiment. He next saw service in 1780 from June 27 to December 5 as a six-month man. At this time, Sherburne was 43 years old, and was stationed at West Point. Here, in July of 1780, he appears on a list of men who received a ration of a half-pint of rum and one pound of sugar. While on a furlough home in 1780, he married Florissa Taggart, a "coloured girl of the neighborhood" (Draper, vol. 45, pg. 241). He was said to have purchased her freedom prior to his marriage with a portion of the bounty money he received for enlisting. It was probably during this time that he was later remembered by a fellow resident of Londonderry for the uniform coat and cocked hat he wore. On February 15, 1781, Sherburne re-enlisted for three years in the 2nd NH regiment under Capt. James Carr. However, it is said that he was a waiter to Col. George Reid, the regimental commander, "for some time" (*ibid.*, pg. 239). In April of 1783, he was reported "sick at N. Hampshire" (NA-M-881, Roll 517)), and was probably home on leave during this time. Such an occurrence was not unusual this late in the war, when the fighting was over. In November of 1783 Sherburne was discharged at West Point and was said to have died soon after. This, however, is inaccurate, as he appears in the 1790 Census for Londonderry, where he is listed as the non-white head of a family of five individuals. He and Flora had one son, Jesse Sherburne, who was born about 1781, while his father was in the army. Jesse was later given to Polly Pinkham, of Londonderry, presumably after the death of his parents. He later lived with Polly and her husband, Capt. James Dickey, in Acworth. Once Jesse Sherburne was freed, at an unknown date, he moved to Newport, where he lived in the "colony of negroes" (Wheeler, pg. 252) on Coit Mountain. Jesse, who practiced the trade of a "boot-black" (shoe shiner) is referred to by Newport's town historian as "a very clever man, given to fun and poetry" (*ibid.*). In meeting the town minister one day, he said "Sir, you shines the souls of men; I shines their uppers" (*ibid.*). Just when Pomp Sherburne died is unknown. After his death, his wife Flora married Boston Bell, another black soldier, from Londonderry.

Sources: PEN-Draper, vol. 45, pgs. 239–241; PEN-NA-M-881, Roll 517; Cen-1790-NH; TH-Wheeler, pgs. 252–3.

Small, Caesar

Information regarding Caesar Small is very scant. In 1774 "Cezar" Small was warned to depart Hampton along with his unnamed wife (RCR #3269). He likely had a wife named Dinah, who was formerly the slave of William Godfrey of North Hampton. In July of 1776 Small enlisted in the company of Capt. Samuel Nay in Col. Joshua Wingate's regiment of New Hampshire militia that went to Fort Ticonderoga. Small was mustered in on July 10, 1776, and presumably served with his company in New York. Nothing further is known of Small's service, but he is reported as having "died from exposure in the army" (Dow, pg. 287) in 1777. His widow, Dinah, later married Phillip Burdoo and lived in Hampton until her death on January 11, 1825. See the service record of Silas Burdoo for further information on Dinah.

Sources: RCR #3269; PSR-NHRWR, vol. 1; TH-Dow, vol. 1, pg. 287.

Smith, Cato

Cato Smith enlisted for service in the New Hampshire Battalion on May 3, 1782, for three years. He was paid the state bounty of £20 for enlisting for the town of Brentwood. Because the New Hampshire Battalion was disbanded in January of 1784, Smith saw less than two years service. After his service, he returned to Brentwood, where he got into trouble. On October 19, 1786, Smith, described as "a negro labourer, late of Brentwood" (RCR #9623), broke into the house of Edward Stevens and took eight sheets, one shirt, and four skeins of yarn. Cato Smith pled guilty and was ordered to pay £3, plus court costs. Less than a month later, on November 15, Smith stole a horse from Joseph Wadleigh, and later that night broke into the house of John Lyford and stole, "among other things," eight pounds of butter (RCR #9625). Once again, he pled guilty, and was fined £16, plus court costs. It is unknown whether Cato Smith was considered a common criminal, or whether he was driven to commit his crimes due to severe financial hardship. Nothing further of Smith is known after 1786.

Sources: PSR-NHRWR, vol. 3; US-RCR #9623, #9625.

Stearns, Peter

Peter Stearns was the slave of the Reverend Josiah Stearns of Epping. He was said to have been raised as if he were one of the children in the Stearns family. One anecdote states that the Reverend Stearns once promised to thrash the next boy who left the garden gate open. One day, he found the gate wide open and "compelled the reluctant Peter to name the culprit" (Sprague, pg. 577). When the Reverend Stearns was told that he himself was the guilty party, he "compelled Peter to cut sticks and thrash him" (*ibid.*). There are several anecdotal accounts of how Peter Stearns came to be a soldier in the Revolution. One account states that,

> touched by the typical quickening of social conscience which accompanied the Revolution, he (Reverend Stearns) told Peter that if he would enlist with the other Stearns boys, he could have his freedom. When the offer was declined, Stearns said "if you will not take your liberty, I shall treat you as they did the Hebrew servants in old-times— bore your ear through with an awl to the door-post, and make you serve forever." This convinced Peter [*ibid.*].

Another account states the reason for Peter becoming a soldier in a more patriotic fashion. In talking about the Reverend Stearns, it states

> some of his sons were in the field during a great part of the Revolutionary contest. He had held a Negro as property; but though he had given the boy advantage for mental and moral improvement with his own children, he felt the inconsistency of holding a fellow human being in legal bondage while thus struggling for National independence, and pronounced him henceforth free, whereupon Peter, in company with his master's sons, shouldered his musket and did good service in the common cause as a freeman [Hurd, Rockingham, pg. 229].

Whether Peter Stearns served in the war willingly or not is unknown. However, he enlisted on August 12, 1779, to serve in Col. Hercules Mooney's regiment of state militia raised for the defense of Rhode Island. Stearns, designated "a Negro" (NHRWR, vol. 2, pg. 629), was paid a £60 bounty for enlisting, the same as John Stearns, the Reverend Stearns's son. However, it is unknown if either man served in Mooney's regiment. Their names are not found on any company rolls for that regiment, and another source states that Peter and John Stearns enlisted for Continental service for one year. Peter Stearns does not appear in any further military records, so it is unknown what service he performed. He may have served in the company of Maj. Daniel Reynolds's company in Mooney's regiment, since the lieutenant for that company was Peter Stearns, another son of the Reverend Stearns. If so, the former slave, Peter, probably served for six months, because Mooney's regiment served until December of 1779. Another possibility is that Peter served in the 3rd NH regiment, in the company of Maj. James Norris. John Stearns served for one year in the 3rd NH under Norris, even though he was listed as enlisting for service in Mooney's regiment for Rhode Island. Since John and Peter Stearns enlisted together, it seems likely they may also have served together in the 3rd NH regiment. In either case, since Peter's name does not appear on any company rolls, it is probable that he was considered more as a servant to one of the Reverend Stearns's sons than a soldier. What further became of Peter Stearns after he was freed and enlisted for military service is unknown.

Sources: PSR-NHRWR, vols. 2–3; OPS-Sprague; CH-Hurd, *Rockingham*.

STEPHENSON, CATO

Cato Stephenson, signing his name with an X, enlisted for service aboard the Continental Navy frigate *Raleigh*, outfitting at Portsmouth for one year on March 19, 1777. An ordinary seaman who was five feet, four inches tall, with a complexion listed as "black: Affrican" (NHGR, vol. 3, pg. 22), his hometown was listed as Casco (Maine). For unknown reasons, however, he was released from service.

Sources: GSP-NHGR, vol. 3.

STEVENS, CAESAR

See the biography of Caesar Black.

STEVENS, EPHRAIM

Stevens is identified as a black soldier based on a description of him while in the army. He was born about 1758 in New Ipswich. It is unknown if he was freeborn, and nothing is known of his parents. On December 15, 1772, at the early age of 14, he was warned out of Plaistow, having come there from Atkinson. Several years later, on April 23, 1775, Ephraim Stevens enlisted as a private in Capt. Ezra Towne's company in Col. James Reed's 3rd NH regiment. Stevens was 17 at the time, his occupation listed as that of a farmer. He is described as five feet, seven inches tall, with "black" (TH-Kidder, pg. 78) complexion, hair, and eyes. As part of Reed's 3rd NH, Stevens fought at the Battle of Bunker Hill. On August 1, 1775, Stevens was paid for three months and sixteen days of service, as well as blanket and coat money. Shortly thereafter, he was on the roll of Capt. Samuel McCobb's company in Col. Benedict Arnold's detachment for Canada. McCobb was formerly a company captain in Col. John Nixon's

Massachusetts regiment. Arnold's force was raised from among the troops surrounding Boston to launch a surprise attack on the city of Quebec, via an overland march through the wilds of northern Maine. Ephraim Stevens was likely chosen, or volunteered, for service in Arnold's force due to his youth and strength. Stevens went with Arnold's force on its epic march through the desolate wilds of Maine, at least for part of the journey. However, Capt. McCobb's company was part of Arnold's force that was commanded by Col. Roger Enos of Connecticut. When disputes arose among Arnold and some of his officers over remaining food supplies, a portion of his men, led by their own officers, deserted at the half-way point and returned to Massachusetts. The man most responsible for this action was Col. Enos himself, who returned with the forces under his command on October 9, 1775. They included Capt. McCobb and his company, with, as far as is known, Ephraim Stevens. The soldiers themselves were not punished for this desertion, since they were following their officers' orders; Col. Enos was not so lucky. He was cashiered from the army for his supposed cowardice. Stevens, however, saw further service. From June 29 to July 12, 1777, he was a private in Capt. Joseph Brown's company in Col. Enoch Hale's regiment of militia that marched from New Ipswich to help relieve Fort Ticonderoga. Unfortunately, Fort Ticonderoga was abandoned by the American forces, so Hale's militia only reached Fort #4 on the Connecticut River before being ordered back. They reached Rindge on July 3, and on the following day received orders to march to Rutland, in Vermont, "where they met our Army on their retreat" (NHRWR, vol. 2, pg. 92). Later that month, Stevens saw his last term of service in Capt. Steven Parker's company in Col. Moses Nichol's regiment in Gen. John Stark's Brigade of New Hampshire militia. Serving under Capt. Parker from July 19 to September 26, 1777, Stevens fought at the Battle of Bennington, and then marched to Stillwater, New York, to join the Northern Continental Army under Gen. Horatio Gates. Following his extensive military service, Ephraim Stevens nearly disappears from the records, though he continued to live in New Ipswich. He is not listed in Federal Census records, but town records show a daughter born to Ephraim and Jerusha Stevens on December 4, 1794. Whether Stevens and his family continued to live in New Ipswich, or subsequently moved is unknown. However, he still lived in Hillsborough County when he was placed on the government pension rolls on June 8, 1819, at the age of 70. He is the only known black soldier from New Hampshire to have served in Benedict Arnold's expedition.

Sources: PSR-NHRWR, vols. 1–3; PSR-NHSP-vol. 30, pg. 272; OPS-Bird, pg. 112–13; TH-Kidder, pgs. 78, 88, 90.

STEWART, PRIMUS

Virtually nothing is known about this black soldier, other than the fact that he enlisted for Continental service for three years on June 19, 1782, in the New Hampshire Battalion stationed at West Point. He is probably the same man as Primus Stuart, who is recorded as enlisting for the same term and the same regiment on July 15, 1782. He likely served until the New Hampshire Battalion was disbanded in January of 1784.

Sources: PSR-NHRWR, vol. 3, pg. 285.

STOCKBRIDGE, JOHN

Stockbridge saw service in 1778, from February 1 to March 31, 1778, in Capt. Joseph Taylor's company in Col. Timothy Bedel's Rangers. This regiment was raised for an expedition into Canada that was later cancelled. Stockbridge appears in the 1790 Census for New Hampshire as a free, nonwhite inhabitant of Unity. His identity, however, as a black soldier, is questionable. He could have been an "Indian" who served for New Hampshire. There was a group of "Indians" known as the Stockbridges, who lived in Western Massachusetts and fought with the colonists against the British.

Sources: PSR-NHRWR, vol. 3; CEN-NH-1790.

SUDRICK, JOSEPH

Sudrick was a soldier in the war from Dover. He first enlisted in the army on July 30, 1779, in the 1st NH regiment, in the company of Capt. Jeremiah Gilman. His term of service was for one year, and he was paid the £60 state bounty for enlisting. Though unrecorded, Sudrick enlisted again, probably in July of 1780, in the 1st NH for an unspecified term. This time he likely served for three years or during the war. In 1781, Sudrick transferred to the 2nd NH regiment under Col. George Reid, likely in the company of Capt. George Aldrich. He served with the 2nd NH, and, subsequently, the New Hampshire Battalion, through 1783. In March of 1783, Sudrick served in the company of Capt. Isaac Frye, his last name spelled as "Sutherick" (NHSP, vol. 30, pg. 493). Joseph Sudrick had a wife and one child, whose names are unknown. Sudrick did not survive long after the war ended. He is recorded as having "drowned about the year 1794" (Pension #BLWT-2312). Joseph was the brother of another Revolutionary War soldier, Michael Sudrick. In 1843, the Probate Court of Strafford County, New Hampshire issued a certificate stating that Joseph Sudrick's only surviving heir was his niece, Catharine Glidden, wife of Asa Glidden, and daughter of Michael Sudrick. Because she was the only surviving heir to Joseph Sudrick, Catharine Glidden applied for, and was granted, 100 acres of land as compensation for her uncle's service.

Sources: PSR-NHRWR, vols. 2–3; PSR-NHSP, vol. 30, pg. 493; PEN-BLWT-2312.

SUDRICK, MICHAEL

Michael was the brother of Joseph Sudrick of Dover. During the war, he served five different terms. The first came in 1776, when he enlisted on September 3 in Capt. John Brewster's company in Col. Pierce Long's Battalion of militia stationed at New Castle. He served here for nearly four months. He was one of his regiment's men who received advance pay for the march to Fort Ticonderoga, but on January 22, 1777, he appears on a list of 47 men who refused to march, possibly due to grievances over pay. Sudrick next saw service on September 8, 1777, when he enlisted in Capt. James Libby's company in Col. Stephen Evans's regiment of militia raised to reinforce the Continental Army at Saratoga. However, problems in Evans's regiment arose over rations, and a large part of Libby's company, including its top officers and many men, including Sudrick, deserted on October 20 and returned home. Michael Sudrick's third term of service came nearly two years later when he enlisted on July 30, 1779. Michael, designated "a melato" (NHRWR, vol. 3, pg. 244), was paid the £60 bounty for enlisting for one year. The regiment he served in was not designated, but it was likely the 2nd NH regiment. Sudrick enlisted for a fourth time on August 30, 1780, in the state militia for the defense of Piscataqua Harbor, around Portsmouth. Here, Sudrick served for six months in the small company of Lt. Samuel Piper. Sudrick's fifth term of service began on May 12, 1781, when he enlisted in Capt. James Carr's company in the 2nd NH regiment for three years. At this time, Michael Sudrick was described as aged 27 and five feet, eight inches tall. He was discharged from the service on December 17, 1783, at West Point.

After the war, Sudrick lived in Dover but soon moved to Northwood. He was married to Bridget Hart (born about 1769) of Epping on April 7, 1789, by Reverend Robert Cutler. They had a daughter named Catharine, who later married Asa Glidden. Available court records show that times were tough for Michael Sudrick, forcing him to borrow money he could never pay back. As early as January 1799 Sudrick was sued by one Neptune Adams and was forced to pay $19.25 in damages and court costs. In 1821, the Epping firm of Samuel, George, and John Plumer won a judgment against Sudrick for non-payment of debt in the amount of $50.

Sudrick was jailed but was bailed by Jonathan Clark of Northwood. The Plumers won similar judgments against Sudrick in 1823 and 1826, with the result that he was jailed each time. In 1823, in another court action, Joel Virgin of Northwood was awarded $50 for non-payment of debt by Sudrick. Similar judgments against him were won by Edward Nealley of Lee in 1825 and George Sullivan in 1828.

By March of 1818, now 64 years old, Michael Sudrick was living in Nottingham and working as a basket maker. He applied for, and was granted, a government pension for his service. He died at Northwood on June 6, 1832. Hiram Morrison, a neighbor of the Sudricks, testified that "I know he died about that day because on the 7th of June 1832 I made his coffin and on June 8, I attended his funeral" (Pension #W25175). Because he died intestate, Michael Sudrick's estate, what little there was, was administered by Joel Virgin in 1833. The probate court that granted Virgin the power of administration states, in part, that Sudrick "died leaving neither widow or child" (RCR #14087). Since this was not true, one must wonder if Joel Virgin sought to administer Suderick's estate in hopes of recovering money due him from the court judgment awarded him back in 1823. Sudrick's widow, Bridget, survived him for at least 20 years, and applied for a widow's pension while living in Epping in August of 1852, at the age of 87. Her claim was allowed on February 3, 1853.

In many ways, Michael Sudrick's military service was typical of most soldiers during the Revolutionary War. He fought in no great battles and spent a lot of time on garrison duty at several different forts, both near and far. Disputes over pay and rations, or lack of rations, was a constant source of irritation and dissatisfaction for many soldiers, and Sudrick had his share. Yet, he continued to serve his new country, no doubt inspired by both a sense of patriotism and the monetary reward offered by the state for his service as a soldier.

Sources: PSR-NHRWR, vols. 1–3; PSR-NHSP, vol. 30, pgs. 290–91; SCR-Court of Common Pleas Minute Book, Jan. 1799; RCR #9776, #6862, #6325, #4642, #4089, #14087; PEN-W25175.

SULLIVAN, NOBLE

Noble Sullivan was the slave of John Sullivan of Durham. A well-known lawyer in town, John Sullivan was an active patriot who served in the New Hampshire militia before the war. He served two terms in the Continental Congress before his appointment as a brigadier general in 1775. A year later, Sullivan attained the rank of major general and faithfully, if not always with success, served as one of Washington's most trusted officers until he resigned from the army in 1779. Sullivan owned a number of slaves, among whom was Noble, who were employed in rowing Sullivan downriver to Portsmouth when he had business there to attend. Anecdotal information suggests that Noble accompanied Sullivan when he went off to war, having "shrewdly suggested that it would be a great satisfaction to know that he was indeed going to fight for *his* liberty. Struck with the reasonableness and justice of this suggestion, Gen. S at once gave him his freedom" (Nell, pgs. 119–20). Nothing further is known about Noble; whether he fought in the war is undocumented. If he did do so, it was likely as personal attendant to Gen. John Sullivan. If this is the case, Noble Sullivan likely saw significant action, since Sullivan served at the Siege of Boston, was captured at the Battle of Long Island, and was a major participant in Washington's crossing of the Delaware River as a prelude to the historic Battle of Trenton. Given all these possibilities, one may even speculate that it was Noble Sullivan who was depicted as the black soldier on horseback in Thomas Sully's 1819 painting of Washington crossing the Delaware.

Sources: TH-Stackpole; OPS-Nell; OPS-Boatner, pg. 1070.

Sweat, Pomp

Pomp Sweat was the "Negro slave" (Remick, pg. 220) of John Sweat of York, Maine. On January 30, 1777, he signed up to serve aboard the Continental Navy frigate *Raleigh*, then outfitting at nearby Portsmouth. He apparently served in place of his master, since he is recorded as going "for ye John Sweatt Esq. Of York" (NHGR, vol. 2, pg. 87). Nothing further regarding Pomp Sweat is known.

Sources: OPS-Remick, GSP-NHGR, vol. 2.

Tatten, Isaac, Jr.

Isaac Tatten, Jr., was the son of Isaac Tatten, the first settler in the town of Lempster. Father and son served together in the Revolutionary War from New Hampshire, the only known black father and son to do so. Little is known about Isaac, Jr., including where he was born, or his age. Since his father came to New Hampshire from Connecticut, it is possible that Isaac, Jr., was born in either colony. Isaac, Jr., enlisted with his father on July 19, 1779, for a six-month term in Capt. Ephraim Stone's company in Col. Hercules Mooney's regiment of state militia for service in Rhode Island. Both father and son, as well as the other enlistees, signed an oath to "Promise Obedience to our Officers as Good Soldiers" (NHRWR, vol. 2, pg. 662), and were paid the state bounty for enlisting. The Tattens were discharged on January 4, 1780, having served five months and seventeen days. Although his father served another term of service in the Vermont State militia, nothing further is known of Isaac Tatten, Jr.

Sources: PSR-NHRWR, vol. 2.

THOMPSON, CAESAR

Caesar Thompson was a slave from the town of Concord who enlisted for three years of Continental service in 1777. He served in Capt. Amos Coburn's company in Scammell's 3rd NH regiment. Nothing further is found of him in military records to indicate when his service began or ended. The 1790 Census for Concord lists widow Sarah Thompson and one slave in her household. This was very likely Caesar, though nothing else definite is known about him.

Source: PSR-NHRWR, vol. 1; CEN-1790-NH.

THOMPSON, PRINCE

Prince Thompson enlisted for Continental service from Canterbury on February 17, 1777, in the 1st NH regiment of Col. Joseph Cilley. He was likely a slave at some point prior to his military service, when he joined the company of Capt. Ebenezer Frye. His term of service was specified as being for the war's duration and he was paid the state bounty of £20 for enlisting. He was discharged from service on May 17, 1781. By this time, no doubt, he was a hardened veteran, having fought at Saratoga, and having possibly taken part in several other campaigns. However, Thompson also appears to have performed other duties during the war. His name, listed as "Prince Negro" (NHRWR, vol. 2, pg. 437), appears on a list of absentees for the 1st NH regiment, dated January 10, 1778, at Valley Forge, Pennsylvania. He is listed as being in Capt. Frye's company, but at the time was "with Gen'l Gates" (*ibid.*) at Albany, New York. General Horatio Gates was the commander of the American Army during the Saratoga campaign, but it is unknown when Thompson joined Gates's command, and for how long he was with Gates. It is also unknown in what capacity he served Gates, whether as a servant or as a bodyguard. Before the war, he may have been the slave of Robert Thompson, a former resident of Durham who moved to Canterbury. Nothing further regarding Prince Thompson is known.

Sources: PSR-NHRWR, vols. 1–3; OPS-Kidder.

Underwood, Boston

Boston Underwood was the "Negro servant" (NEHGR, vol. 63, pg. 173) of Capt. John Underwood of Kittery, Maine. On July 11, 1773, he was married to Silpha, a servant to Lady Pepperell, by Reverend Benjamin Stevens in Kittery. His name appears on a list of soldiers in Capt. James Arnold's company in Col. Joshua Wingate's regiment of New Hampshire militia destined for Fort Ticonderoga, dated July 20, 1776. He was mustered and paid wages and the state bounty at this time. Following this entry, nothing further of Boston Underwood is known.

Sources: PSR-NHRWR, vol. 1; GSP-NEHGR, vol. 63 (1909).

Varrell, William

William Varrell was a black soldier from Rye who served two six-month terms during the war. The first began on September 25, 1776, when he enlisted in Col. Pierce Long's regiment of militia under Capt. John Calfe. Varrell was stationed at New Castle for the defense of Piscataqua Harbor and served until January 7, 1777. At this time, Varrell was quite young, only 15 or 16 years old. He next saw service in 1780 when he enlisted in the New Hampshire Battalion stationed at West Point, New York, as a six-month man. Varrell, who signed his name with an X, was described as aged 19, five feet, ten inches tall, but with a "light" complexion (NHRWR, vol. 3, pg. 61). He served from June 27 to December of 1780. Varrell last appears in the records on August 3, 1800, when he was married at North Church in Portsmouth to Lydia Currier. Both man and wife were described as being black. Nothing further is known of William Varrell after 1800.

Sources: PSR-NHRWR, vols. 1 and 3; North Church Records, vol. 1, pg. 159.

Ventrom, Nicholas

Ventrom was a black soldier from Windham who served in the Continental Army. His last name is spelled a variety of ways in military records, including Vintrom, Vixtrom, Vixton, and Vickstrum. He first saw service on July 11, 1776, when he enlisted in Capt. John Nesmith's company in Col. Joshua Wingate's militia regiment for duty at Fort Ticonderoga. Ventrom served in the militia until his time expired in February of 1777, but while at Fort Ticonderoga he immediately re-enlisted with the 2nd NH regiment of Col. Nathan Hale under Capt. James Carr. At the time of his enlistment with the 2nd NH on February 17, 1777, Ventrom was 28 years old. He fought with the 2nd NH regiment during the retreat from Fort Ticonderoga and at the Battle of Hubbardton. Ventrom next appears in the records on a list of absentees for the 2nd NH regiment, dated January 10, 1778. He is listed as aged twenty-six years old, five feet, ten inches tall, and is described as having "black" hair, eyes, and complexion (NHRWR, vol. 2, pg. 443). He is described as being left at Hubbardton. Because Ventrom does not appear in any subsequent records, it seems likely that he was one of those soldiers captured or killed at the Battle of Hubbardton on July 7, 1777. This is even more likely when it is considered that Ventrom was in Carr's company, which bore the brunt of the initial British attack and suffered many men wounded and captured. Though it is sheer speculation, Ventrom may have been killed outright during the battle, or, like Col. Nathan Hale himself, may have been taken prisoner and died while in captivity in New York.

Sources: PSR-NHRWR, vols. 1–2.

WALLACE, CAESAR

Wallace was a slave who served in the Revolutionary War from 1777 to 1783. Tradition states that he was probably the slave of Lt. Samuel Wallis of Rye. However, there is no available evidence, other than the similarity of their names, to support this theory. In 1820, he stated that he enlisted at Newbury, Massachusetts and "was in the Indian Country at the battle of Herkimer — at Bunker Hill — he entered in 1777 + served until the close of War" (Pension #43250). If true, then Wallace likely came from Massachusetts and served with a master, name unknown, who saw action at Bunker Hill in 1775, and at the Battle of Oriskany (Herkimer) in 1777. Unfortunately, there are no records from the state of Massachusetts to confirm this service. Wallace's stated participation in the Battle of Herkimer is most interesting, since only one New England regiment, the 9th Massachusetts under Col. James Wesson, served in that area. Given this, it is likely that Wallace served first in the war as a slave of Massachusetts, gaining his freedom in late 1777 or early 1778, prior to enlisting for the state of New Hampshire on March 23, 1778, in the company of Capt. James Norris in the 2nd NH regiment for Continental service. Caesar, his name spelled "Seaser Wallas" (NHRWR, vol. 1, pg. 586), enlisted for the town of Newton, though his residence is listed as Rye. His term of service was specified as three years. During this time, he took part in the Battle of Monmouth and was later stationed at West Point and the surrounding area. On a list of men dated February 14, 1781, Wallace is listed as being in the company of Capt. Caleb Robinson in the 2nd NH regiment. While in the army, Wallace's duties varied. In July 1778 he was stationed as a headquarters guard, and in December he was on fatigue duty, likely helping to gather food and firewood. For much of 1779, however, he saw little duty. In May he was listed as being "confined" and from June to September was listed as "sick-absent," preventing his participation in Sullivan's campaign against the Six Nations (National Archives-M-880-#2799). Wallace continued to be sick at Danbury, Connecticut, in October 1779, but presumably returned to active duty the following month. From February to June 1780 he was listed as being "on guard," while from August to October he was "on command" at Constitution Island, on the Hudson River (*ibid.*). Wallace's later time at Constitution Island must have been both exciting and trying, since it was during this time that the treachery of Benedict Arnold at nearby West Point was discovered. After his original term of service was up in 1781, Wallace re-enlisted for another term. He received a furlough on February 15, 1783, and returned home to New Hampshire. Though listed briefly as a deserter, he did nothing more than return late from his furlough, arriving back at camp in April. Caesar Wallace served for nearly two more months until he was discharged on June 7, 1783.

Wallace's discharge certificate was personally signed by Gen. George Washington and attested that "Ceazer" had "faithfully served the United States five years" (Pension #S43250). Wallace is one of only a few black soldiers known to have received such a certificate. While on furlough from his service, Wallace married Katy Duce in Exeter on March 25, 1783. After his discharge, he and his wife lived in Exeter for a time. However, on March 18, 1784, Caesar and Catherine (Katy) Wallace were warned to "immediately" depart Exeter "to their legal residence," along with three other black veterans, Fortune, London Dailey, and Cato Wallingford (RCR #7181). Where Wallace's legal residence was at this time is unknown for certain, but it may have been Rye or Gilmanton. In 1790, the Census records for New Hampshire list Wallace as being a resident of Gilmanton, heading a family of four free blacks. About 1793, a daughter, Lucy, was born to Caesar and Katy. Whether they had other children or not is unknown. Two black men from Exeter, the town where Wallace was married, served during the Civil War for New Hampshire, and were likely his grandsons. Freeman Wallace, aged 23, served in the U.S. Navy aboard the USS *Ohio* and USS *Cyane*, enlisting in 1863, and his brother, James Wallace, aged 22, enlisted in 1864. He served for one year in the 127th US Colored Troop Regiment.

Caesar Wallace and his family continued in Gilmanton for an undetermined time before moving to Meredith. On April 23, 1818, Wallace, "a

Man of colour aged about eighty years," applied for a government pension (Pension #S43250). This pension was granted on December 10, 1818, for the standard rate of $8 per month. When he applied for a continuation of his pension in 1820, he stated that his property consisted of "one cow purchased with the money received of Government" (*ibid.*). His wife, Katy, was still alive at the time, being 72 years old, while Wallace stated that he was "aged about ninety years" (*ibid.*). He spent the last six or seven years of his life back in Gilmanton, under the guardianship of John Page, Jr. He was appointed Wallace's guardian on August 7, 1821, likely due to Wallace's advanced age. Page probably acted as his guardian until sometime in 1827 or early 1828. On March 6, 1827, he signed for a $48 payment for money due Wallace. Since this was the last pension payment to Caesar Wallace, it seems likely that he died soon thereafter, though his date of death is not recorded. He is buried, along with his family, on the Piper Farm above Meredith Center in an unmarked grave.

Caesar Wallace, the Revolutionary War soldier, should not be confused with another slave owned by Samuel Wallis of Rye. This slave, referred to by both the name Caesar Wallace and Caesar Seavey, was purchased by Wallis in July 1778 for £150 from Capt. William Parker, master of the private armed schooner *Friends Adventurer*. Caesar Seavey was later married to a slave named Phyllis and lived in Salem, Massachusetts, after the war before eventually returning to Rye. Phyllis, also owned by Wallis, along with Caesar, were said to be the last slaves held in Rye, living in the Wallis farmhouse on Brackett Road. Caesar Seavey died in Rye on November 18, 1821, at the age of 81 and, along with his wife, was buried on the Wallis homestead.

Sources: PSR-NHRWR, vols. 1–3; PSR-NHSP, vol. 30, pg. 304–05; vol. 7, pg. 31; TH-Bell; TH-Parsons; TH-Hanaford; PEN-NA-M-880-#2799; RCR #7181; PEN-S43250; OPS-Ayling; OPS-Hatcher, vol. 4, pg. 155.

WALLEY, PRINCE

Walley enlisted from the town of Acworth for Continental service on July 8, 1779. His term was for one year in the 2nd NH regiment, but his company was not identified. On July 29, 1779, Walley, his name also spelled Wally, was paid six pounds billeting money for the journey from Keene to Springfield, Massachusetts. On August 9, 1779, Walley was paid the £60 state bounty for enlisting. While Walley was on the march with other new recruits, the 2nd NH regiment was engaged in Sullivan's expedition in western New York. It is unknown where Walley spent the first months of his service, but it was likely at West Point, New York, performing garrison duty before joining his regiment at Danbury, Connecticut, where it spent the winter of 1779-1780. Prince Walley appears several times in town records after the war. In 1789 he was taxed by the town of Bedford one shilling and six pence as a "non-resident" (Bedford TR, vol. 2, pg. 26). In 1790 he was assessed a five shilling tax in Bedford for "defraying state expenses" (*ibid.*, pg. 31). What these state expenses were for is unclear. Two years later, on December 26, 1792, the New Hampshire House of Representatives voted on Walley's personal application to pay him "the money due him as a soldier in the Continental Army" (*ibid.*, pg. 36). By this time, Prince Walley went by the name Prince Cesar, since the New Hampshire House also certified that "Prince Cesar is the same person with Prince Cesar alias Prince Wally mentioned in the depreciation books" (TR-Bedford, vol. 3, pg. 714). Whether this application was for wages never paid Walley, or the Continental bounty for enlisting is unknown. Following this application to the state, nothing further of Prince Walley, alias Prince Cesar, is known.

Sources: PSR-NHRWR, vols. 23; TR-Bedford, vol. 2, pgs. 26, 31, 36 and vol. 3, pg. 714; PEN-NA-M858, roll 10, #3175.

WALLINGFORD, CATO

Cato Wallingford was the slave of Col. Thomas Wallingford of Somersworth. Following his master's death, Cato is listed in an inventory of Thomas Wallingford's estate, dated September 28, 1771, and was valued at £45. Richmond, Phillis, and Dinah, three other slaves owned by Wallingford, are also mentioned in this inventory. Cato continued as a slave to Wallingford's wife, Elizabeth, and was likely still a slave when he enlisted for military service in 1777. Cato Wallingford enlisted in March of 1777 for Continental service in the 2nd NH regiment under Capt. James Carr. Carr was a resident of Somersworth and probably knew Cato. Since Cato Wallingford's term of service was for three years, he participated in every major campaign in which the 2nd NH saw action, including the fight at Hubbardton, the Saratoga campaign, the Battle of Monmouth, and Sullivan's expedition against the Six Nations. When his term was up in 1780, he re-enlisted for an undetermined time of service, possibly six months or a year. It is likely that Cato Wallingford paid for his freedom after the war with the bounty money he received for enlisting.

There seems to have been a dispute between Somersworth town officials and "Madame" Wallingford in 1782, since the town "treated" with Elizabeth Wallingford "respecting her negro Man" (Somersworth TR, vol. 1, pgs. 463, 655). Wallingford eventually was paid the town bounty of £15, but it is likely that Mrs. Wallingford received the state or Continental bounty, perhaps in compensation for granting him his freedom. After the war, Wallingford lived in Exeter, where he was warned out on March 18, 1784. The 1790 Census for New Hampshire finds Cato Wallingford a resident of Gilmanton with one other free black, likely his wife Pegg. He later moved back south to the Exeter area, where he is found one last time in the records, when he and his wife were warned to depart Brentwood within 14 days on January 21, 1799. Nothing further is known of Cato Wallingford after 1799.

Sources: US-RCR-Probate, vol. 24, pgs. 58–9; PSR-NHRWR, vol. 3; TH-Bell; TR-Somersworth, vol. 1, pgs. 463, 655; RCR #17750.

WATSON, GLOSTER

Gloster Watson was a slave who was baptized in Portsmouth in 1749, his master being Joseph Libby. In July 1758, at the age of eight, he was sold to Dudley Watson of Dover. After serving over 25 years as a slave he was given his freedom on June 4, 1777. Gloster was freed by his master's son, Thomas Watson, likely under the influence of Reverend Jeremy Belknap. Prior to this time, on May 16, 1777, Watson was allowed to enlist for Continental service in the 2nd NH regiment under Capt. John Drew. Watson, whose term of service was for three years, was described as a "negroman" (NHRWR, vol. 1, pg. 618), aged 26, from the town of Dover, but serving for neighboring Barrington. As a soldier in the 2nd NH, he took part in all of that regiment's subsequent campaigns, including the Battle of Hubbardton and the action at Saratoga. His name appears on a list of absentees for his regiment, dated January 10, 1778, at Valley Forge, Pennsylvania. Watson is described as a "negro," five feet, six inches tall, with "wool" hair and "white" eyes and was listed as "sick," being left at Poughkeepsie, New York (NHRWR, vol. 2, pg. 444). He was probably left there between October 31 and November 2, 1777, during the New Hampshire Brigade's march south from Saratoga to join Washington's main army. Gloster Watson eventually recovered from his illness and likely took part in the Battle of Monmouth in 1778 and Sullivan's Expedition against the Six Nations in 1779. He was discharged at West Point, New York, on May 10, 1780, after his three-year term was up. After the war, Watson returned to live in Dover. Nothing specific is known about his life afterward, but this "man of colour" seems to have been held in high regard (Wentworth, page 97). His death, at the age of 57, was recorded in the local press on January 18, 1806, an honor seldom accorded to free blacks.

Sources: PSR-NHRWR, vols. 1–3; OPS-Belknap; OPS-Wentworth; TH-Parsons.

WESTON, NATHAN

Weston was a native of Reading, Massachusetts, likely free born, who moved to New Ipswich several years before the war began. He enlisted for an unknown term of service on May 4, 1775, in Capt. Ezra Towne's company in Col. James Reed's newly formed 3rd NH regiment. Weston is listed as being aged 30 and a carpenter. He is described as being five feet, five inches tall, with black complexion and eyes. He fought with the 3rd NH at Bunker Hill on June 17, 1775, and is listed on the muster rolls for his company dated July 11 and August 4, 1775. He also appears on a list of men paid four dollars coat money on October 12, 1775, at Medford, Massachusetts, but is listed as being absent. Nathan Weston served another term during the war in 1777, enlisting for a 14-day stint in June and July as a corporal in Capt. Josiah Brown's company in Col. Enoch Hale's regiment of militia. Though his term was short, Weston is one of only two black soldiers from the state known to have served as non-commissioned officers during the war. Weston marched with his regiment from New Ipswich on June 29, 1777, in an attempt to reinforce the beleaguered American garrison at Fort Ticonderoga. However, with the capture of the fort by Burgoyne's forces, Hale's militia was ordered to turn back before reaching its destination. Weston and his fellow soldiers reached Rindge, New Hampshire on July 3, and the following day marched to Rutland, Vermont, to meet elements of the retreating Continental Army. Weston served until July 12, when Hale's militia was disbanded and its men sent home. Nathan Weston had a wife named Hannah and a son, James, who was born on March 8, 1772. Nothing further regarding Weston is known.

Sources: PSR-NHRWR, vols. 1–2; TH-Kidder; TR-New Ipswich, vol. 1, pgs. 67–8; PSR-MSS-vol. 16, pg. 917.

WHEELER, PRIME

Wheeler is identified as a black soldier on the basis of his first name, which is a derivative of the popular slave name Primus. He enlisted for military service on July 15, 1775, in Capt. John Parker's company in Col. Timothy Bedel's Regiment of Rangers for service in Canada. He was probably the slave of 2nd Lt. Seth Wheeler of New Ipswich. He was mustered in with his company on September 28, 1775, at camp in St. John, Canada, and returned home on December 31, 1775, along with Seth Wheeler and other members of his company. Wheeler was paid for five months and seventeen days of service, as well as blanket and coat money. Nothing further of Prime Wheeler is known after his Canadian service. Seth Wheeler

saw later militia service in the war as a private, but there is no indication that Prime Wheeler served with him.
Sources: PSR-NHRWR, vol. 1.

WHIPPLE, PRINCE

Prince Whipple is another well-known black soldier who served in the Revolution for New Hampshire. His life is well documented, and much has been written about him. However, there have also been several aspects of his life and service that have been misstated so often that, over the years, they have been perceived as factual. He was a native of Amabou, on Africa's Gold Coast, who was born about 1756. Tradition states that he and his brother Cuffee were the sons of an African prince who were sent to this country to be educated, but were instead sold into slavery at Baltimore by an unscrupulous ship's captain. They were then brought to Portsmouth as slaves and sold, along with a number of other slaves, prior to 1766, at the age of 10. They were purchased by Capt. William Whipple, a well-known sea captain and former slave trader of Portsmouth. William Whipple retired from sea life about 1760 and was a wealthy merchant in town. He is remembered today as a signer of the Declaration of Independence for New Hampshire in 1776, as well as for his services as a general of several militia regiments during the war.

It has been stated that Prince Whipple saw service in 1776, and was present with Gen. Washington at the historic crossing of the Delaware River, prior to the surprise attack on Trenton on December 26, 1776. Two well-known paintings of Washington's crossing are even said to depict Whipple. The first, painted by Thomas Sully in 1813, depicts a black soldier on horseback near Washington, along with several other mounted officers. The second, and better-known, painting was executed by Emanuel Leutze in 1851. It depicts Washington standing in a rowboat as it moves through the ice-laden Delaware River. One of the oarsmen depicted is black. It has been asserted by several black historians that the black soldier in question in both these works is Prince Whipple. However, there is no available information to support this theory. Contrary to the statement of historian William Nell, William Whipple was not an aid to Gen. Washington, and saw no active military service at this time. Whipple was the commander of a local militia district at this time in New Hampshire, but never served under Washington. Both William Whipple, and his slave, Prince, first saw service in 1777. Gen. William Whipple commanded a militia regiment at Saratoga in September of 1777, and subsequently was in charge of escorting Burgoyne's captured army, along with Gen. John Glover, to

Cambridge, Massachusetts, in November. Prince Whipple enlisted for service on September 27, 1777, serving in Whipple's brigade as his servant for a total of one month and seventeen days. For his service, which ended on November 12, 1777, he was paid at the rate of two pounds per month.

One anecdote that is often quoted, but is inaccurate, at least in part, describes how Prince Whipple acted at the beginning of his first term of service. On being ordered to get the horses ready by Gen. Whipple to start their journey, "Prince appeared sulky and in ill humor. His master upbraided him for his misconduct. 'Master,' said Prince, 'you are going to fight for your liberty, but I have none to fight for.' 'Prince,' replied his master, 'behave like a man and do your duty, and from this hour you shall be free.' Prince wanted no other incentive" (Brewster, pg. 155). In fact, Prince was not freed on the eve of his service in the Saratoga campaign. He did not gain his freedom until nearly seven years later, in February of 1784. A similar story is to be found in New Hampshire Revolutionary War lore for the slave of Gen. John Sullivan of Durham (see the biography of Noble Sullivan), leading one to believe that such accounts of conversations between masters and their slaves are based more on patriotic myth and legend than actual fact.

Prince Whipple served a second term during the war in 1778, when he was, once again, on the payroll for Gen. William Whipple's militia regiment to Rhode Island. Listed as a "servant" (NHRWR, vol. 2, pg. 580), he served in Rhode Island with his master from August 3 to September 5, 1778. For his service of one month and three days, he earned £2½, while Gen. Whipple was paid £41½. However, this money was not paid to Prince directly, but to William Whipple.

Prince Whipple is unique among all of New Hampshire's black soldiers in that he is the only black man, as far as is known, to have been on the company rolls as a servant and earned wages as such. Many officers during the Revolution, from captains on up, often had personal servants, but most were hired by the officers themselves, and were not paid for their service by the state. The fact that Prince Whipple was an exception to this rule leads to the possible conclusion that he acted as more than just a servant to Gen. Whipple. Very much trusted by his master, it is likely that Prince, in addition to serving his master, also acted as a bodyguard and an aide-de-camp of sorts. The fact that Whipple placed a great amount of trust in Prince is demonstrated by the following anecdote: Prince was "once entrusted by the General with a large sum of money to carry from Salem (Massachusetts) to Portsmouth. He was attacked on the road, near Newburypory (Massachusetts), by two ruffians; one he struck with a loaded whip, the other he shot, and succeeded in arriving home safely" (Nell, pg. 199).

Although Prince Whipple was greatly trusted by his master, there was one thing that he still desired, and that was his freedom. Still a slave after serving two stints in the military, he tried another approach when, on November 12, 1779, he was one of 20 Portsmouth slaves who signed a petition seeking to gain their freedom. Whether this was done with the consent of his master is unknown, but unlikely. Sent to New Hampshire's House of Representatives, the slaves' request for freedom was tabled after only a brief review. Freedom for Prince Whipple and the others would have to wait.

Following the war, Prince continued as a slave to William Whipple, likely continuing as his personal servant during Whipple's service as state legislator (1780–84), and during his term as an associate justice of the New Hampshire Superior Court (1782–85). Prince Whipple was finally freed in February of 1784, a year before his master's sudden death. After Gen. Whipple's death in 1785, his widow, Catherine, gave Prince and his brother, Cuffee, the use of a lot of land at the back end of her garden on High Street in Portsmouth. They soon bought a small two-story house and moved it to this plot of land, living there the rest of their lives. Prince Whipple had a large and well-known family, some of whom continued to live in Portsmouth well into the 19th century. He married Dinah Chase, a former slave, on February 22, 1781. Dinah was born into slavery and was owned by Reverend Stephen Chase of New Castle. Because of Reverend Chase's occupation, and position in society, it is likely that Dinah was better educated than most slave girls. During the Revolutionary War, Dinah was sent to Hampton where, at the age of 17, she was admitted to the church there under Reverend Thayer. She was freed at the age of 21, in 1781, and very soon after married Prince Whipple, with whom she was probably already acquainted. Prince and Dinah had at least six children. They were: Esther (baptized 12/19/1784); Susannah (baptized 5/14/1785); Robert (baptized 4/27/1787); Jeremiah (baptized 12/6/1789); Elizabeth (baptized 11/22/1791); and Hannah (baptized 1/5/1794). On March 3, 1791, a funeral for one of Prince's children was given in Portsmouth by the Reverend Joseph Buckminster. It is unknown if this was for another child, or for one of his above-named children. Unfortunately, Prince Whipple was unable to enjoy his freedom for a long period, nor did he live to see any of his children grow into adulthood. He died of a fever on November 21, 1796, at the young age of 40.

One Portsmouth historian states that Prince Whipple

> was a large, well-proportioned and fine looking man, and of gentlemanly manners and deportment. He was the Caleb Quotem of the old-fashioned

semi-monthly assemblies and at all large weddings and dinners, balls and evening parties. Nothing could go on right without Prince, and his death was much regretted by both the white and coloured inhabitants of the town; by the latter of whom he was always regarded as a leader [Brewster, pg. 155].

Prince Whipple was buried in Portsmouth's North Cemetery. His grave, marked by a monument that notes his Revolutionary War service, is the only known marked grave for any black soldier in Portsmouth, and one of only a few found for black veterans in the entire state.

Following the death of Prince Whipple, members of his family continued to live in Portsmouth for the next 70 years or so. His brother, Cuffee, lived in Portsmouth until his death about 1820. Like Prince, he was well known in town, and is described as "prominent among the dark gentry of the day" (*ibid.*). Prince's widow, Dinah, also continued to live in Portsmouth, where, along with Cuffee's wife Rebecca, she established and ran the Ladies Charitable African School. This was probably a dame school, meant to prepare young girls for public school. However, times were not always easy for Dinah. As an impoverished widow, she received financial support from North Church in 1825, 1844, and 1846. Her burden was considerably eased in 1832, when Catherine Whipple, Gen. Whipple's widow, died, and her heirs gave Dinah a small house on Pleasant Street for life, along with a small annuity. She lived on Pleasant Street with two of her grown daughters, Elizabeth Smith and Esther Mullinaux, until her death in 1846 at the age of 86. Portsmouth's North Church, with which she had long been associated, paid her funeral expenses of $8.62.

Little is known of Prince Whipple's sons. However, one daughter, Esther, has had her life well documented. Born in 1784, she married a mariner of Portsmouth named William Mullinaux in April of 1801. They had two children, William Prince (b. 1801) and Anna (b. 1813). Frequently at sea, her husband failed to return from a voyage, and his fate was unknown to Esther. Giving her husband up for lost, Esther remarried in 1815. However, in 1817, North Church officials learned that Esther was still lawfully married to her first husband, William Mullinaux. She was admonished by the church and her confession read aloud to the assembled church congregation on December 6, 1817. In 1827, Esther's second husband died, but she married yet again, having three more children, Elizabeth (b. 1828), Richard (b. 1828), and Horace William (b. 1831). Following the death of her mother, Dinah Whipple, in 1846, Esther lived on Water Street, now Marcy Street, and earned a living as a laundress. By 1851 she had saved enough money to buy a small house on the north side of Walden Lane, where she lived until her death in 1868, at the age of 83. She left everything in her will to Portsmouth's North Church.

Sources: PSR-NHRWR, vol. 2; TR-Portsmouth-vol. 3, pg. 95; TH-Brewster-vol. 1, pgs. 154–56; OPS-Nell, pgs. 198–99; OPS-Cunningham.

WHITE, POMP

Pomp White is identified as a black soldier on the basis of his name. The name Pomp is short for the name Pompey, a classical Roman name often given to slaves in the Colonial era. White first saw service in 1776 when he enlisted in Capt. James Arnold's company in Col. Joshua Wingate's militia regiment. He served for three months and eight days, from July 20 to the end of October 1776. Wingate's regiment was raised following the Continental Army's retreat from Canada in the summer of 1776 and was to "repair to Charles Town on Connecticut River," and from there to "join the northern army wherever it might be found" (NHRWR, vol. 1, pg. 339). Pomp White served a second term of militia service in 1777. On September 17, 1777, he joined the company of Capt. Nicholas Rawling in Col. Abraham Drake's regiment, in Gen. William Whipple's militia brigade raised to reinforce the Continental Army at Saratoga. He served for three months during the Saratoga campaign, taking part in the battle at Bemis Heights on October 7, and was discharged on December 15, 1777. Nothing further regarding Pomp White is known.

Sources: PSR-NHRWR, vols. 12.

WHITE, SAMUEL

Samuel White was the Negro slave of John Langdon, a wealthy merchant and prominent patriot of Portsmouth who served in the Continental Congress, led several militia regiments during the war, and later served as a senator and governor of New Hampshire. Referred to as "Colonel Langdon's man" (National Archives, M881-#539), White enlisted for service on September 8, 1777, in Capt. Nicholas Rawling's company in Col. Abraham Drake's regiment in Gen. William Whipple's militia brigade raised to reinforce the Continental Army during the Saratoga campaign against Burgoyne. However, he deserted after only one month and twenty-one days' service on October 29, 1777, after taking part in the battle at Bemis Heights on October 7. His name, listed only as Samuel, with no last name, appears on a list of men who served in Rawling's company dated

January 15, 1778. Where, and why, White deserted is unknown, and nothing further regarding him is found in any records. Samuel White should not be confused with two other men who served in Rawling's company, Samuel White Cate, a white soldier who also deserted, on October 1, and Pomp White, another black soldier.

Sources: PSR-NHRWR, vol. 2, pg. 325; PEN-NA-M-881, roll 539.

WIER, SAMUEL

Wier was a "colored man" (Annett, vol. 1, pg. 148) from the town of Peterborough who enlisted for the town of Jaffrey on May 18, 1777, for Continental service. His term specified as three years, Wier joined the company of Capt. William Scott in Col. Joseph Cilley's 1st NH regiment. As a soldier in this battle-tested regiment, he took part in the Saratoga campaign and was wounded there during some of the fiercest fighting of the war. Wier's name appears on a list of absentees for the 1st NH, dated January 10, 1778, at Valley Forge, Pennsylvania. He is listed as being wounded and left at Albany, New York, and is described as age 30, five feet, eight inches tall, and "black" complexion (NHRWR, vol. 2, pg. 434). How long Samuel Wier was out of action due to his wounds is unknown, but he did recover and return to service until his discharge on May 18, 1780. Following his military service, Samuel Wier, his last name also spelled as "Weir," disappears from the records. He is not to be confused with a white soldier of the same name from Walpole, or with Samuel Weare of Hampton Falls.

Sources: TH-Annett, vol. 1; PSR-NHRWR, vols. 2–3; OPS-Kidder, pg. 159.

WILSON, TITUS

Wilson was a black soldier from Peterborough about whom little is known, except that he was the slave of Robert Wilson. Described as a "colored man" (J. Smith, pg. 391), it is unknown if Titus was freed before his military service, or was still a slave. He enlisted for Continental service on April 1, 1777, in Capt. William Scott's company in Cilley's 1st NH regiment. Captain Scott was also a resident of Peterborough, and may have known Titus Wilson. Wilson was paid the state bounty of £20 for his enlistment, as well as an additional £8 for travel from his hometown to Fort #4 at Charlestown, where he was mustered into service. Wilson soon traveled with other new enlistees to serve garrison duty at Fort Ticonderoga in New York. However, with the threat of Burgoyne's advancing army, the

American Army retreated from Fort Ticonderoga on July 5, 1777. While most of the American forces escaped from Ticonderoga intact, including New Hampshire's Continentals, Wilson's exact fate is unclear. His name appears on a list of absentees for the 1st NH regiment, dated January 10, 1778, at Valley Forge, Pennsylvania. Titus Wilson is described as 30 years old, five feet, eleven inches tall, with "black" complexion and "yaller" (yellow) eyes (NHRWR, vol. 2, pg. 434). He is further listed as being "with ye enemy-prisoner" (*ibid.*). However, Peterborough's town history states that he died at Mount Independence, near Fort Ticonderoga, on July 7, 1777.

There is no doubt that Wilson was lost on the retreat from Ticonderoga, but several possibilities exist as to how this occurred. He may have may been one of the many soldiers who fell sick at the fort, and was part of the group of sick and invalid soldiers who were escorted on the retreat from Ticonderoga by Hale's 2nd NH regiment. Hale's men were attacked by the British on July 7 at Hubbardton, and in the battle that ensued, many men were lost or captured. It is highly likely, given the date mentioned by Peterborough's historian, that this was where Wilson was either killed or captured. A lesser possibility is that Titus Wilson was one of those soldiers the Americans left atop Mount Independence to man the cannons in an attempt to slow down the British advance and give the American Army a chance to escape. These men failed in their duty and were captured on July 6, 1777, when British soldiers "found them dead drunk by a cask of Madeira" (Wolkomir, pg. 62). Whether Titus Wilson was killed outright, or died as a prisoner, remains a mystery, but, in either case, he stands as one of those black soldiers who paid the ultimate price while fighting for American independence.

Sources: OPS-J. Smith, pg. 391; PSR-NHRWR, vols. 1–2; TH-Smith; OPS-Kidder, pg. 159; OPS-Wolkomir, pg. 62.

WINGATE, CAESAR

Wingate was a slave from Rochester who served late in the war in the New Hampshire Battalion. He was first the slave of Capt. Jonathan Ham of Rochester and was brought here from "the South" (McDuffee, vol. 1, pg. 71). Wingate was said to be trained in cultivating tobacco, making it probable that he came from the colonies of either Virginia or Maryland. Several anecdotes have been carried down over the years regarding Wingate, one of which involves his introduction to the cold New England climate. When he awoke to find the ground covered in snow on a winter's day, he allegedly thought it was sugar until he went outside and tried to gather it.

He was also very religious, and was overheard reciting the following prayer for his master by Capt. Ham's doctor: "O Lord, do sabe Massa Ham, Massa Ham a berry good man, Mass Ham good to make Plow, Massa Ham good to make Harrow. O Lord, don't take Massa Ham. If you must take some body, take old Bickford, he ain't good for nothin'" (*ibid.*, pgs. 550–51). When the doctor told Capt. Ham about Wingate's prayer, it "so heartened him" that he "soon was on the mend" (*ibid.*).

Wingate later became the slave of Judge Daniel Wingate of Rochester, and enlisted for Continental service for three years on June 6, 1781, for "Rogerstar" (Rochester) (NHRWR, vol. 3, pg. 245). He was described as age 31, "Negro" (*ibid.*), and five feet, seven inches tall, and served in the New Hampshire Battalion stationed at West Point, New York. Wingate probably served until January of 1784, when the New Hampshire forces were disbanded, but the Rochester town history states that he was still in the army on November 21, 1785. It does not mention what unit he was serving in. Caesar Wingate was not freed from slavery until after the war, but continued to live with his master, Judge Wingate, on Chestnut Hill Road in Rochester. Nothing further about him is known.

Sources: PSR-NHRWR, vol. 3; TH-McDuffee, vol. 1, pg. 71, vol. 2, pgs. 550–51.

Wood, Caesar

Caesar Wood was a slave from the town of Stratham who was owned by Dr. Wood. Prior to being a slave for Dr. Wood, he was the slave of Capt. George March of Stratham, a Tory who refused to sign the Association Test in 1776. It is unknown when Dr. Wood purchased Caesar from Capt. March, but it was likely early in the war years. Many men who refused to sign the Association Test and were branded as Tories were ostracized by their communities and forced into financial hardship for their political views. It is possible that Capt. March was forced to sell Caesar for the cash he might bring. Caesar Wood enlisted for Continental service on May 26, 1781, in the company of Capt. James Carr in Reid's 2nd NH regiment. His term of service was for three years. He is listed in the military records as a "Negro" (NHRWR, vol. 3, pg. 245), age 20, and five feet, five inches tall. His age, however, was incorrect, since he was born about 1743, making him about 37 years old at the time of his enlistment. There is no record as to whether Caesar Wood received any bounty for his enlistment, or whether he was freed prior to his enlistment. However, in 1782, Dr. Wood is listed as being "paid in full 42 pounds for his negroman" (Nelson, pgs. 165–66). It is probable that this was when Caesar Wood was formally freed,

The gravestone for Caesar Wood, a soldier from Stratham. This worn and weathered stone, now preserved in the Stratham Historical Society, is the oldest known gravestone in New Hampshire for a black soldier. Such markers were seldom provided for blacks, whether free or slave. Caesar, who was the slave of a local Tory, was buried in a private family plot that is now difficult to locate. From *Historic Burial Grounds of the New Hampshire Seacoast*. Photograph by Glenn Knoblock, courtesy Arcadia Publishing.

Dr. Wood likely receiving the bounty money for his enlistment as compensation for granting him his freedom.

Caesar Wood served his term doing garrison duty at West Point, New York, for most of the time, but probably took part in some of the operations against the Tories and their Indian allies in western New York late in 1781 by the New Hampshire Continentals. He was likely released from service in December of 1783, or in January of 1784, when the New Hampshire Battalion was disbanded for good. Unfortunately, times were hard for Wood after the war and he had little time to enjoy his newfound freedom. He evidently had good feelings for his former master, Capt. March, since he returned to Stratham after the war to live with him and look after him due to March's impoverished state. Local tradition states that Caesar Wood and his former master ate a great deal of mutton "which they neither raised nor bought" (*ibid.*). Unfortunately, less than two years after he was done with his military service, Caesar Wood died in 1785 at the age of 42. The reason for his death is unknown to us today. He was evidently held in high esteem, since he was buried in a private family plot in Stratham, and given a homemade gravestone to mark his final resting place. His gravestone was inscribed with the name "Caesar Negro" (Knoblock, pg. 80), along with his age, and year of death. This gravestone stood for many years before it was eventually removed and later sold to a local antique dealer. However, it was tracked down by a resident of Stratham and purchased for that town's historical society, where it still resides.

Sources: PSR-NHRWR, vol. 3; TH-Nelson, pgs. 165–66, 200–201; OPS-Knoblock, pg. 80.

WOODMAN, DAN

See the biography of Dan Martin.

Soldiers with Service to New Hampshire and Other Colonies

The following 34 men served for both New Hampshire and other colonies' forces during the Revolutionary War. Almost all of these men served for Massachusetts, due to that state's proximity to New Hampshire, though several served in the state forces of Vermont for protection of her frontier late in the war. As of this writing, no black soldiers have been identified who served for both New Hampshire and the colony of Connecticut, while only two men, sailor Dodge Collins and soldier Reuben Roberts, are identified as serving for both New Hampshire and Rhode Island. Given the distance between those colonies and New Hampshire, such combined service would have been a rarity. Soldiers from the District of Maine are grouped with those from Massachusetts, since Maine was a part of that colony before, during, and after the war, until it gained statehood in 1820. In regards to which colony was served first by a particular soldier, approximately two-thirds of the men listed below served for New Hampshire first in the war, before serving elsewhere, and the remainder served for New Hampshire after first serving another colony. However, despite this disparity, three black soldiers, Reuben Roberts (Newmarket), Robin Hanson (Plaistow), and Archelaus White (Plaistow), tried to enlist for service in New Hampshire in 1775 when the war began, but were rejected by local officials. They served in Massachusetts regiments before they later served in regiments from their home state.

Although the movement of free blacks between Massachusetts and New Hampshire, both during and after the war, was a frequent occurrence, it may not have always been on a voluntary basis. Historian Herbert Aptheker states that "Many free Negroes were ordered out of Massachusetts" (*American Negro Slave Revolts*, pg. 226) in 1800 because "suspicions of the designs of the Negroes are entertained and we regret to say there is too much cause" (*ibid.*). The cause in this case was the revolt led by a slave named Gabriel in the area of Richmond, Virginia. Slave revolts in the South, particularly the Carolinas, Louisiana, and Virginia, occurred on a frequent basis, but they were usually small and unorganized. This was not the case with the revolt led by Gabriel. Described as "a twenty-four year old giant of six feet two inches," and possessed of both "courage and intellect" (*ibid.*, pg. 219), Gabriel formed a well-organized revolt involving some 1,000 slaves. However, despite being kept secret for several months, the plot was betrayed at the last minute by several of the slaves involved. This betrayal, along with a terrible rainstorm, caused the revolt to fail. Hundreds of slaves were captured and jailed, and at least 35 slaves were executed, including Gabriel. He was initially given a stay of execution, in hopes that he would talk, and was even interviewed personally by Governor (later President) James Monroe. Despite his impending fate, Gabriel kept his resolve and "met death with fortitude" (*ibid.*, pg. 223). Despite the fact that this event took place far to the south, its implications were far reaching and spread fear as far north as New England. How many blacks were ordered out of Massachusetts is unknown, but it is likely that at least a small number moved to New Hampshire as a result. Though it is impossible at this late date to determine with any degree of accuracy the identity of such individuals, several black veterans, including Thomas Griffin, Jacob Danforth, and William Davison, who moved to New Hampshire around this time, may have been among them.

BARBER, JOHN

John Barber first saw war service in July of 1776 when he served for one month in the company of Capt. John Drew in Col. Isaac Wyman's regiment of New Hampshire militia. This regiment was raised to reinforce the Continental Army during its Canadian operations, and rendezvoused at Haverhill on the Connecticut River in mid–July. Barber was paid three pounds in wages for his service, as well as a six-pound bounty for enlisting. Barber, likely a resident of Portsmouth, is probably the same individual who served the following year in the Massachusetts State Navy as a "boy" on the brigantine *Tyrannicide*, which carried 14 guns, under Capt. Jonathan Haraden (MSS, vol. 1, pg. 587). Later records regarding his age indicate that he was about 15 at the time he served under Capt. Haraden. This service lasted from October 1, 1777, to May 8, 1778. The John Barber who served in the Massachusetts State Navy may be the same individual who enlisted for a nine month term in the army later in 1778, arriving at Fishkill, New York on June 9. Described as being aged 18, five feet, four inches in height, with "dark" (*ibid.*) hair and gray eyes, Barber joined the 1st Massachusetts regiment under Col. Joseph Vose, but was subsequently sent to Gen. Jonathan Warner. It is very likely that Barber acted as a servant for Warner, who was in command of Massachusetts militia regiments in the West Point area. After the war, John Barber is listed in the 1790 Census for Portsmouth as a free non-white, with one other person in his household. Little else is known about him, but he does appear in the 1840 census of New Hampshire Revolutionary War pensioners, dated June 1. He is listed as being aged 78, and lived in Lyman with one Libbeus Hastings.

Sources: PSR-NHRWR, vol. 1; PSR-MSS, vol. 1; CEN-1790-NH; PSR-NHSP, vol. 30, pg. 414.

BLACK, RICHARD

Richard Black is notable not only for his military service and the supreme sacrifice he made, but also for his ancestry. His great great grandfather was a slave known as Black Will, later William Black. Black Will was the slave of Maj. Nicholas Shapleigh of Kittery. When Maj. Shapleigh died in 1683 the settlement of his estate provided that "A Neger called black Will: to bee Mis Shapleighs dureing her life" (York County, Me., Deeds, Book III, Fol. 126). Black Will continued to be owned by Shapleigh's widow, but lived on three acres of land, "reserved to his the said Negros use" (York County, Me., Deeds, Book IV, Fol. 52). While still a slave, Black Will fathered one child. In 1691 he had a child by a "notorious tart" (Clark, pg. 101) named Alice Hanscom (later Metherell), who was white. This child was his first son, known as both William Black Junior and William Negro Junior. Black Will gained his freedom on February 13, 1701, when he became the possession of the widow Shapleigh's nephew, John Shapleigh. The deed that gave Black Will his freedom, executed at Kittery, in the province of Maine, states in part that Shapleigh "doe release and for ever set free one Negroe man comonly called Black Will which was formerly Majr Nicholas Shapleighs and now in my possession" (York County, Me., Deeds, Book VI, Fol. 88).

One local source states that John Shapleigh "nobly gave him his Liberty. It may be that the spirit and speeches of Richard Saltonstall, who first advocated the utter abolition and annihilation of slavery in New England actually vibrated in the Maine atmosphere; and John Shapleigh breathed it in and gave Will his freedom" (Willis, vol. 1, pg. 81). Following this, Black Will continued to live in Kittery. In 1708 he helped gain the freedom of another local slave, Anthony Freeman (Tony), from his master, Charles Frost, by bounding his 100 acres of land to protect the town of Kittery from Freeman becoming a burden upon them. Will further helped Freeman by allowing him to build his dwelling on his own land. In 1712 Black Will had a son, Joshua, by a woman named Elizabeth Brooks, but it is unknown if they were married. In Black Will's will, proved January 1, 1728, he names a wife, Sarah, as well as his two sons and two grandchildren. Black Will Junior "kept house" (Noyes, et al., pg. 94) with Elizabeth Turbet, and had two children, Elizabeth and William. Black Will Junior was active in real-estate transactions, with local records showing a tract of 30 acres he bought from Alexander Ferguson in 1714, and the sale of a portion of 80 acres of land he owned in 1725. He is probably the same man, though it could also have been his son, who was the Black Will, "a mulatto man" (*ibid.*), who owned New Cape Newagen Island in Harpswell in 1739. In 1760 William Black sold his half of the 100 acres of land in Kittery formerly owned by his grandfather Black Will.

Black Will's second son, Joshua, married a woman named Mary. They had 12 children, as follows: Benjamin (b. 4/19/1719); Jonathan (b. 2/15/1721); Mary (b. 1/23/1723); Joshua and Henry (twins, b. 12/27/1724; Henry died 2/1725, Joshua died 5/3/1742); Thomas (b. 8/5/1728, d. 1729); Sarah (b. 5/13/1730); Amanda (b. 3/8/1731); Catharine (b. 5/15/1734); Thomas (b. 10/1735); Margery (b. 7/28/1738, d. 8/1738); and Margery (b. 8/19/1739). It is likely that Richard Black, born about 1741, was the son of either Benjamin or Jonathan Black, though Black Will Junior, or his son, William Black, could also have been his father. He is probably the same man as the Richard Black who married Mary Miles in Kittery on March 31, 1757. A relative of Richard Black, Thomas Black, likely his uncle, saw service in the French and Indian War. In his will dated April 30, 1756, Thomas Black, a "labourer" of Kittery, "bound on an expedition in His Majesties Service, and not knowing whether ever I shall return" bequeathed his possessions, including a gun, to his brother Henry and sister Margery (Maine Wills, pg. 807).

Richard Black, a negro from Kittery, Maine, first saw military service in 1776, when he enlisted on September 23 in the company of Capt. John Calfe in Col. Pierce Long's regiment of militia "stationed at New Castle at the entrance of Piscataqua Harbour" (NHRWR, vol. 1, pg. 380). Black served until about February of 1777. Company rolls indicate he was paid for service at least through January 7, 1777, but his name appears on a list of men, dated February 25, of soldiers who did not march to Fort Ticonderoga. However, while Richard Black did not travel with Long's regiment, he did go to Fort Ticonderoga. On February 20, 1777, he was mustered into service in the company of Capt. Daniel Wheelwright in Col. Ebenezer Francis's 11th Massachusetts regiment at nearby York, Maine. Receiving the Continental and state bounties for enlisting, Black was paid, too, for his rations until he marched on March 22, 1777, for Fort Ticonderoga. Black, described in company rolls as aged 36, "dark" (MSS, vol. 2, pg. 99) complexion, and five feet, eight inches in height, fought with the 11th Massachusetts during the retreat from Fort Ticonderoga, and was in the thick of battle at Hubbardton, where his regiment fought fiercely and lost its commanding officer. Richard Black also fought at Saratoga, and marched with his regiment to Valley Forge, Pennsylvania, after its assignment to the main army under Washington on October 27, 1777. However, Black did not long survive. He is reported as having died at Valley Forge on February 1, 1778, the cause not listed, but likely due to illness.

Sources: GSP-Noyes, et al., pg. 93–94; PSR-York County (Me.) Deeds-Book 3, fldr. 126-Book 4, fldr. 52- Book 6, fldr 88-Book 16, fldr 8; TH-Willis, vol. 1, pg. 81; OPS-Clark, pg. 101; PSR-Maine Wills, pg. 806; PSR-NHRWR, vol. 1; PSR-MSS, vol. 2.

Boston, Anthony

Anthony Boston, also known as Tone or Toney, was a "Negro" (NHRWR, vol. 2, pg. 754) from Boscawen who completed four terms of service during the war, beginning on May 27, 1775, when he enlisted in the company of Capt. Jeremiah Clough in Col. Enoch Poor's 2nd NH regiment. Boston appears on Clough's company roll dated August 1, 1775, having been in service for two months and ten days. His name also appears on a list from either September or October of men "that has not drawn blankets" (NHRWR, vol. 1, pg. 194) in Clough's company. It is unknown when Boston's term with the 2nd NH ended. He enlisted again for New Hampshire on February 14, 1778, in Capt. William Tarleton's company in Col. Timothy Bedel's Regiment of Volunteers. This term of service was short, ending on about March 31, 1778. Two months later, Anthony Boston, now a resident of Newburyport, Massachusetts, enlisted for service in the company of Capt. Amasa Soper in the 5th Massachusetts regiment. Boston, who enlisted on June 15, 1778, for nine months, was described as having "black" (MSS, vol. 2, pg. 292) eyes, hair, and complexion. He primarily served garrison duty at West Point, New York, but was reported sick, at least for a time, at Fishkill, New York, on the east bank of the Hudson River. Whether Boston continued with the 5th Massachusetts regiment for uninterrupted service after his enlistment expired in March of 1779 is unknown, but records indicate that he did re-enlist with the 5th Massachusetts, in the company of Capt. Sylvanus Smith, on May 17, 1781, for three years. He appears on subsequent company rolls through February of 1783, though in February of 1782 he is listed as being "on command at the Blockhouse" (*ibid.*) while at West Point. Anthony Boston's service ended in February of 1783 when he found a substitute to take his place.

Boston was "succeeded by Francis Cisco" (MSS, vol. 3, pg. 466), a black from Taunton, Massachusetts. Cisco's records state that he "served in place of Boston, negro" (*ibid.*). Anthony Boston is one of only a few black soldiers known to have hired substitutes to take their place, and, as far as is known, is the only black soldier known to have found another black soldier as a replacement. Other than his military record, nothing is known of Boston, though, given his name, it is likely that he was a slave at or from the city of Boston at some point in his life.

Sources: PSR-NHRWR, vols. 1–3; PSR-MSS, vol. 2, pg. 292, vol. 3, pg. 466; TH-Coffin.

BOWLES, CHARLES

Bowles is, without a doubt, one of the most interesting black soldiers to serve in the Revolution. There is a wealth of material, though obscure in nature, that documents his life and career, including some colorful anecdotal material that illuminates his somewhat dubious character. As a result, Bowles comes down to us through history, not as an idealized portrait of the black soldier fighting for his freedom, but as more of a down to earth individual, with all the foibles and faults that all men, black or white, are endowed with.

Bowles was born in Hanover, Massachusetts, on October 20, 1760, supposedly the child of an "African" (Lewis, pg. 5) father and a white mother. A biography of Bowles, published in 1852, states that his mother was the daughter of Col. Daniel Morgan, the famous commander of a rifle regiment during the Revolutionary War. However, there is nothing at all in the records that would validate this wild claim. Bowles apparently lived with his father, presumably as a free black, for a time, but when he was a young child, he was placed in the care of a Mr. Jones in Lunenburg, Massachusetts. In 1773, Jones died, and Charles was said to have been "placed" in the family of a Tory (*ibid.*). His biographer further states that Bowles served as a waiter to an officer in the "Colonial army" in 1775, "at the tender age of fourteen," serving in this capacity for two years before enlisting in the Continental Army (*ibid.*). Charles Bowles did begin his military service in 1775, but there is nothing in the records to indicate it was as anything but a regular soldier.

Records show that Bowles enlisted from Salem, Massachusetts, on April 23, 1775, in the company of Capt. Micajah Gleason in Col. John Nixon's regiment. Bowles fought with Nixon's regiment throughout 1775 and 1776. Since Nixon's regiment was newly formed in June of 1775, only a portion of his men fought at Bunker Hill. It is unknown if Gleason's company was among them. However, Nixon's regiment was in the thick of battle in New York in 1776, taking an active part in the New York City Campaign. Bowles's regiment, now designated as the 6th Massachusetts (4th Continental Infantry), was sent to New York about April 29, 1776, to join the brigade of Gen. William Alexander, Lord Stirling. The 6th Massachusetts regiment took part in the heavy fighting there throughout the late summer and early fall months, including the action at Harlem Heights where Bowles's company commander, Capt. Gleason, was killed on September 16. Bowles also took part in the Battle of White Plains and was among those men in service in September and October of 1776 at North Castle, New York. As part of Washington's main army in late 1776, Bowles's regiment retreated across New Jersey and crossed the Delaware River to set up camp at Valley Forge. They also took part in the important victory at Trenton, New Jersey, against the Hessians on December 26, 1776, and later at the Battle of Princeton. Bowles continued his service with the 6th Massachusetts to the end of January 1777 before returning home. Already, by the age of 16, Bowles was a battle-hardened veteran.

Soon after returning to New England, Charles Bowles moved to northern New Hampshire, probably in the spring of 1777. He settled in the small town of Warren, in the vicinity of Lake Tarleton on its eastern shore. The area where he lived became locally known as Charleston, derisively named according to several historical anecdotes. One account states that Bowles was known for "his love of self" (Bixby, pg. 258), and that "he acted as though he owned the whole place so folks began to call it Charleston," and that even after he moved away, "the name has stuck" (*ibid.*). A second anecdote states that the area of Charleston, around Lake Tarleton, was so named because Bowles only stopped there a short time, and said he was frightened away by the immense bull-frogs which inhabited Tarleton Lake; that every night he could hear them singing out, "Charles Bowles! Charles Bowles! We are a coming, we are a coming! Don't run, don't run," and that he would not stay there for the whole district. His friends laughed at him and called the place Charles' town — Charleston" (Little, pg. 307n). Whether there is any truth to these legends is unknown, but there can be no doubt that Charles Bowles soon made his presence known in the area. The probability that Bowles was one of the few blacks in the area, free or otherwise, likely further contributed to his notoriety. Bowles only lived along Lake Tarleton for a short time, before moving to several other locations around Warren. He later lived on the north side of Beech Hill, as well as "on Sentinel Mountain west of the flats" (Bixby, pg. 40).

Charles Bowles evidently succeeded in establishing a home for himself quite soon in Warren, or maybe he had the desire to fight again. In any case, he enlisted on July 24, 1777, in the company of Capt. Jeremiah Post, a resident of the neighboring town of Orford, in the militia regiment of Col. David Hobart, as part of Gen. John Stark's Brigade. Stark's force was authorized and raised in July due to the threat from Burgoyne's army. As part of Post's company, Bowles fought in the Battle of Bennington on August 16, 1777, where his commander, Capt. Post, was severely wounded and died. Following this action, Hobart's regiment went to Stillwater, near Saratoga, New York, to take part in the actions against Burgoyne's main army. Charles Bowles served for two months and five days before being discharged on September 25. Bowles returned home for the fall and early winter of 1777, but in February of 1778 enlisted again, this time for Continental service, for the town of Andover, in the 1st NH regiment under Capt. Amos Emerson. He was paid the £20 bounty for enlisting, as well as eight pounds for his travel to Charlestown at Fort #4. His term of service was for either two or three years, the confusion over the exact term being a later source of contention. During this second term of service in New Hampshire, Bowles fought with the seasoned 1st NH regiment at Monmouth, New Jersey, and in Sullivan's campaign against the Six Nations. However, in the early part of 1780, Bowles is listed as a deserter. Bowles claimed his term of service was for two years and at an end in February of 1780, but his officers claimed his enlistment was for three years. Disputes like this were common at this point during the war, and Bowles later returned from home to duty at West Point, New York, under a general pardon that had been issued to men in his situation. Bowles evidently made up the time he missed, since he served until about February of 1782 before being permanently discharged from duty.

After the war, Charles Bowles returned to Warren. He set to work clearing 100 acres of land in the northern part of town near "old Coventry" (*ibid.*). He felled trees, sowed a bushel and a half of grain, and built himself a house. On April 14, 1784, he married Molly Corliss (born March 3, 1768, at Salem, New Hampshire). Between 1784 and 1803, Charles and Molly Bowles had nine children born at Warren: James (b. 12/19/1784); Molly (b. 12/12/1787); Charles (b. 1/24/1789); Elenor (b. 5/18/1792); Jesse (b. 2/26/1795); Euna (b. 5/17/1797); Hannah (born 3/3/1799); Jonathan (b. 1/12/1801, d. 8/23/1803); and Sarah (b. 5/20/1803). During his time in Warren, Bowles was a respected and well-known citizen. He is referred to as "a young stalwart man of dark complexion" and as "a good man, religiously inclined, somewhat given to preaching," but also as one who was "somewhat of an egoist and quite stuck on himself" (Little, pgs. 285–6). Bowles had a gift for preaching, but he also ran a store in Warren for a time after 1789. He is also remembered for his large appetite. Invited to the house of

Squire Jonathan Merrill, legend has it that he ate an entire quarter of lamb "and nearly everything else on the table ... thereby depriving the Squire and his family of their morning meal," forcing Merrill's wife "to do another cooking that morning" (*ibid.*, pg. 413n).

What happened to Charles Bowles and his family after 1803 is based on his biography, written by Elder John Lewis and published in Watertown, New York, in 1852, partially based on a journal Bowles kept. While in Warren, Bowles became a member of the Free Will Baptist faith and is said to have struggled in his mind on what course the rest of his life should take. It is very possible he was driven to action by the death of his son Jonathan in the summer of 1803. Not long after, at an unspecified date, Bowles left his family and signed on as a ship's cook out of Boston. He evidently sailed the seas for three years before being persuaded to pursue a career as a preacher by a woman who met him while his ship was in port for repairs. She stated that she had seen him in a dream and that he was "the instrument in the hands of God" for an "extensive Revival" that was to occur (Lewis, pg. 12). He was led to a place in the country to preach, and after some initial doubt, "the gospel took hold of his heart ... his duty was now plain" (*ibid.*, pg. 13). Bowles soon after went home, but found his resolution shaken when "he met with the opposition of his wife," Molly, as well as others "whose duty it was to encourage him, all frowning in coldness upon his new undertaking" (*ibid.*). Whatever opposition Bowles met he ignored, and he simply left his wife and family. In 1808 he preached in Asburnham, Massachusetts, as well as other places as an itinerant minister in the Free Will Baptist faith. In 1813 he preached in Gloucester, Rhode Island. By 1816, Bowles had moved to Vermont, preaching first at Williamstown before settling in Huntington, living with one of his daughters and her children.

Free Will Baptist records state that he met with much opposition wherever he preached. He was very active as a preacher in the towns of Richmond, Duxbury, Waterbury, Stowe, and Middlesex, Vermont. To catalogue all of the revival meetings and Free Will Baptist yearly meetings that Bowles attended and presided over would be rather tedious, but some of the highlights include the following: In 1817 he organized churches at Hinesburg, Duxbury, Shelburne, and Huntington, Vermont; in 1819 he organized a church in Stowe, and also began receiving a government pension for his war service. In 1820 he visited Warren, where he saw his children, but no mention is made of his wife. In 1823 he organized a church in Enosburg, Vermont, and in 1824 he went to Canada for a brief time, enjoying "great liberty in preaching" (Lewis, pg. 179). In 1837, Bowles moved to Hopkinton, New York, where his son, Charles Bowles 2nd, lived and worked as a preacher. The "Elder" Bowles bought a small farm that he leased to his son. He continued to be an active Free Will Baptist minister, preaching in Dickinson and surrounding towns. In 1841 he established a church at Malone, New York, whose members resided in both Malone and the village of Constable, New York. However, in 1842, now over the age of 80, and his voice worn out by "long use" (*ibid.*, pg. 212), Charles Bowles sold his farm in Huntington and boarded with a Mr. Fuller, likely in the town of Constable. He died the following year on March 16, 1843, at the age of 82. He was buried in the Irish Street Cemetery in Constable on March 18, 1843, during a violent snowstorm. A gravestone was paid for by his Free Will Baptist flock in Constable, and can still be seen today.

During his nearly 40 years as a preacher, Bowles encountered much prejudice and opposition, both due to his race, as well as his religious affiliation. During one revival meeting, he was threatened with being thrown into a pond from a rail if he continued his preaching, but preached with such power that many were converted instead. His manner of preaching was called "simple and practical, never attempting to make any display either of ignorance or learning" (*ibid.*, pg. 26). When asked at one time by a fellow minister if he had any regret that he was a black man, Bowles replied "No—never. Hundreds have been led to Christ and converted just by my colour" (*ibid.*, pg. 148).

Although Charles Bowles's children are known, their fate, for the most part, is a mystery. His son, Charles Bowles 2nd, was the town minister for Bridgewater, New Hampshire, from 1825 to 1829 before moving to New York. He died in Pitcairn, New York, in late 1850, leaving behind at least one son. Two of Bowles's likely descendants, either grandchildren or great-grandchildren, fought in the Civil War. William Bowles, aged 23, and Samuel Bowles, aged 21, enlisted together at West Bangor, New York, near Malone, as privates in the 98th New York Infantry on October 20, 1861. William attained the rank of officer, becoming a 2nd lieutenant, and served until August 31, 1865, being mustered out of the service at Richmond, Virginia. His brother, Samuel, also received promotions, attaining the rank of sergeant, but was reduced back to a private for unknown reasons. He later reached the rank of corporal before being mustered out of the service at Albany, New York, on November 23, 1864. Like Charles Bowles, William and Samuel saw a fair amount of action during the war, the 98th New York having participated in the historic battles at Fair Oaks, Cold Harbor, and the Siege of Petersburg.

Sources: PSR-NHRWR, vols. 1–3; TH-Little, pgs. 285–6, 307, 413; TH-Bixby; PSR-MSS, vol. 2, pg. 346; OPS-Lewis; OPS-Lawrence; OPS-*Free*

III. The Men

> ELD. CHARLES BOWLES died on the 16th of March, in Malone, N. Y. in the 82d year of his age, in the full prospect of a blessed immortality. He had been nearly blind for some years; but continued to preach Christ and him crucified till within a few weeks of his death. We have no particulars of his religious experience or ministerial labors. We believe, however, that he traveled extensively and was very useful.

Above: The obituary of soldier turned evangelist Charles Bowles. Bowles served for both Massachusetts and New Hampshire during the war and afterward became a Free Will Baptist minister. He preached throughout New England before moving to northern New York. From the *Free Will Baptist Registry*, 1844, page 75.

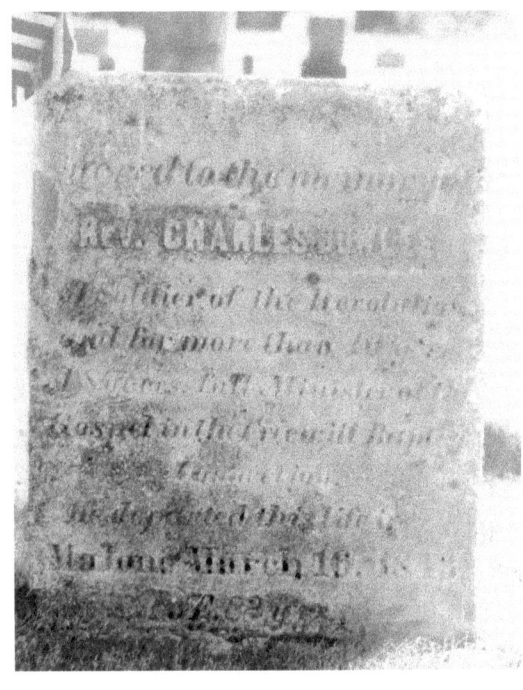

Right: The gravestone for soldier Reverend Charles Bowles. This "Soldier of the Revolution" died in Malone, New York, on March 16, 1843, and is buried in the Irish Street Cemetery in the nearby village of Constable. His gravestone details the two most important aspects of his life, his service in the war and his career as a "Successful Minister of the Gospel in the Free Will Baptist Connection." Photograph courtesy Ed Doherty and Kevin Roddy.

Baptist Cyclopedia, pg. 63; OPS Seaver, pg. 805; OPS-*Free Will Baptist Registry*, pg. 75: Internet-HDS-www.Civilwardata.com.

COLE, TOBIAS

Tobias Cole was probably the slave of Amos Cole of Somersworth sometime before the war. In 1761, on an inventory of taxable property for the town, Cole is listed as owning one slave, whose name is not stated. In all likelihood, Tobias Cole gained his freedom just prior to the American Revolution. His documented military service began on September 8, 1777, when he enlisted in Capt. James Libby's company of Dover men in Col.

Stephen Evans's regiment of New Hampshire militia, raised to reinforce the Continental Army at Saratoga. The unit Cole joined was an unhappy one. Cole served his full term, which ended on December 15 of that same year, but 19 out of the unit's 55 men, including Capt. Libby, deserted after serving only a part of their time due to a dispute over rations. Following this term, the military career of Cole is somewhat confused. He may have served in the company of Capt. Peter Drowne in Col. Evans's regiment of militia raised to serve in Rhode Island. This service lasted from June 15 to December 30, 1778. Unfortunately, no records survive from this time that describe his physical characteristics or indicate his residence. However, Massachusetts records also list the service for Tobias Cole during this time. He enlisted for service in June 1778 in Col. Rufus Putnam's 5th Massachusetts regiment for nine months. His residence was listed as Sanford (present-day Maine), his age 25 years, height five feet, ten inches, and complexion as "dark" (MSS, vol. 3, pg. 788). He served garrison duty with the troops in and around West Point, arriving at Fishkill, New York, that same month. Whether this is the same Tobias Cole who served earlier for New Hampshire is unclear, but likely. However, this time conflicts with that of the service listed for Tobias Cole in Rhode Island, leaving some doubt about which records are correct. In any event, no further records are found regarding Tobias Cole's service in the 5th Massachusetts regiment.

Tobias Cole saw further duty during the war when he enlisted in Capt. Timothy Emerson's company in Col. Thomas Bartlett's regiment of New Hampshire militia, serving garrison duty at West Point from June 3 to October 26, 1780. Cole saw one final term of service when he enlisted in the company of Capt. James Carr in the 2nd NH regiment for a term of three years. Captain Carr may have known Tobias Cole since he was also a resident of Somersworth. Cole enlisted on May 8, 1781, for three years, serving most of his time on garrison duty in New York. He was discharged at West Point in October 1783. On a descriptive list of new recruits, Cole is described as being age 19, five feet, seven inches in height, with a "dark" (NHRWR, vol. 3, pg. 245) complexion. Cole's town bounty for his service in 1781–2 for Somersworth was paid to other individuals, including Elizabeth Hanson. Since the Hanson family were known as slave owners, it is possible that Tobias Cole was her slave and gave his town bounty money in return for his freedom.

After the war, Tobias Cole is listed as a resident of Sanford, Maine, in the 1790 Census. On April 25, 1818, he applied for a pension for his war service. Cole claimed to have served in the battles of White Plains and Long Island in 1776, even though surviving records indicate his service began in 1777. One possibility is that Cole was a servant to an officer who fought

during this time. By 1818, however, Cole was a resident of Troy, Pennsylvania, in Bradford County. His age was listed as 55, his occupation that of a farmer. When he applied for a continuance of his pension in 1820, he listed a wife named Elizabeth, and two daughters, Sarah (age 15), and Margaret (age 7). Nothing further regarding Tobias Cole after 1820 is known.
Sources: PSR-NHRWR, vols. 2–3; PSR-MSS, vol. 3; Pension #SF40849; CEN-1790-Maine.

COLLINS, DODGE

Collins enlisted for naval service for one year as an ordinary seaman on June 13, 1776, on the Continental frigate *Raleigh*, then building at Portsmouth. He is described as "black complexion, African" (Remick, pg. 219), five feet, eight and a half inches in height, with a hometown of Worcester, Massachusetts. Whether Collins was aboard the *Raleigh* when she finally sailed in August of 1777, after his term of service would have expired, is unknown. He may be the same D. Collins who was listed as a seaman and one of 94 prisoners taken in "vessels armed for war in Rhode Island" (NHGR, vol. 3, pg. 23), and released on November 29, 1778, in exchange for an equal number of British prisoners of the same rank by Gen. John Sullivan. Nothing further regarding Collins is known.
Sources: OPS-Remick; GSP-NHGR, vol. 3.

DANFORTH, JACOB

Jacob Danforth saw extensive military service during the war. He first served in 1775, while living in the town of Hollis, when he was in the town's minuteman company led by Capt. Reuben Dow that marched to Cambridge, Massachusetts, on the Lexington alarm on April 19, 1775. Six days later, on April 25, 1775, Danforth enlisted for further service in Col. William Prescott's Massachusetts regiment, along with many other Hollis men, in Capt. Dow's company. There is little doubt that Danforth and the rest of Capt. Dow's company would gladly have enlisted in service for the state of New Hampshire. However, spirits were running high, and it would be a month before New Hampshire was able to raise her own regiments. Thus, Dow's Hollis company enlisted under Prescott. As part of Prescott's regiment (designated the 7th Continental Regiment on June 14, 1775), Danforth and the rest of Dow's company took part in the historic Battle of Bunker Hill, occupying a position in the hastily built redoubt on the top of Breed's Hill. Dow's company, in particular, was in the thick of things when the British stormed the American position and resorted to the bayonet to drive them off the hill. Captain Reuben Dow's Hollis company lost seven men in the fierce hand-to-hand fighting that resulted.

Following the battle, Danforth continued as part of Dow's company under Prescott until about August 1, 1775, having served for three and a half months. He then joined the regiment of Col. Ebenezer Bridges's Massachusetts State Troops under Capt. Jonathan Stickney. His term of service is unknown, but he is on company return of men at Cambridge, dated September 25, 1775, and on a list of men, dated November 16, 1775, who received payment for coat money at Cambridge. This term of Danforth's service probably ended in December of 1775. However, he was not done serving. A year later, on February 15, 1777, he enlisted again, this time in the company of Capt. James Bancroft in Col. Michael Jackson's 8th Massachusetts regiment. Danforth's term of service was for three years, with his residence listed as both Hollis and Wilmington, Massachusetts. He was credited as a soldier for Wilmington. As part of the 8th Massachusetts, Danforth took part in the Saratoga campaign, encamped at Valley Forge in the winter of 1777-78, and fought at the Battle of Monmouth in 1778. Following this, the 8th Massachusetts was assigned to the Army's Highland Department, performing garrison duty in and around West Point, New York. During his three years of service, Danforth served under Capt. Bancroft and Capt. Ebenezer Cleaveland, as well as in the regimental major's company, until his discharge at West Point on February 12, 1780.

Following his service with the 8th Massachusetts, Danforth may have gone to sea. He is likely the same Jacob Danforth who served on the armed ship *Mars*, sailing from Boston under Capt. James Nivens, for nearly two months, from April 20 to June 12, 1781. He is also likely to be the same Jacob Danforth who served in the company of Capt. William Bird in Col. Webb's regiment of Massachusetts militia raised from Middlesex and Suffolk counties to reinforce the Continental Army at West Point. Danforth served from August 17 to December 1, 1781, during this term for a total of three months and 22 days.

Following the war, Jacob Danforth, listed as "a person of colour" (Portsmouth Town records, vol. 11, pg. 251), moved to Portsmouth, where he married Sally Kimball, also "coloured" (*ibid.*), on October 24, 1802. The Danforths had at least two children, both of whom died young. One son, whose name is not known, died at Portsmouth in July of 1810 at the age of five, and was buried on July 5. Another son, Jacob Danforth, Jr., died of a fever in Portsmouth at the age of 24, and was buried on February 17, 1828. The veteran Jacob Danforth is listed in the 1827 city directory for Portsmouth as a hostler (one who takes care of horse and mules) at the Simes stable on Jaffrey Street. Nothing further regarding his family is known.

Sources: TH-Worcester, pgs. 147, 171; PSR-NHRWR, vols. 1–3; PSR-NHSP, vol. 30; PSR-MSS, vol. 4; TR-Hollis, vol. 1, pg. 352, vol. 2, pg. 70, vol. 6, pg. 246; TR-Portsmouth, vol. 11, pg. 251; US-Portsmouth's North and South Church records; OPS-Portsmouth City Directory, 1827, pg. 66.

DAVISON, WILLIAM

Davison's identification as a black soldier is somewhat tentative. A William "Daverson" (NHRWR, vol. 1, pg. 252) appears on a list of men in Capt. Henry Elkins's company of militia stationed at Fort Washington for the defense of Piscataqua harbor. Listed as a "fifer" (*ibid.*), Daverson enlisted on November 23, 1775, for an unknown term of service. He may be the same man as the William Davison who served from July 8 to October 1, 1777, as a fifer in Capt. Joseph Balch's company in Col. Thomas Croft's Massachusetts militia artillery regiment, likely raised to reinforce the Continental Army during the Saratoga campaign. Given this artillery service, the William Davison who served for six days, June 15–21, 1775, as a matross in Capt. Samuel Trevett's company in Col. Richard Gridley's Artillery regiment may also be the same man. This William Daverson enlisted from Salem, Massachusetts, and saw later service in 1775, from May 25 to October 6, under Capt. Nathan Brown in Col. John Mansfield's regiment (5th Massachusetts regiment) during the Siege of Boston. It is impossible to sort out all the William Davisons listed in the Massachusetts records, and reconcile them with William Daverson of New Hampshire with any degree of certainty, but it seems likely, given some similarities, that they may be one and the same individual. A William Davison lived in Portsmouth in 1810, and married a woman, designated as "colored" (Portsmouth Town Records, vol. 2, pg. 313), named Ann-Marie Fogg, making it probable that Davison himself was either black, or possibly of mixed descent. Three William Davisons are listed in New Hampshire's 1790 Census, but none are listed as being non-white. However, given the inaccuracies of the census-taking process, it is possible that the William Davison of Rye, a neighboring town of Portsmouth, is the same man who performed the military service listed above.

Sources: PSR-NHRWR, vol. 1, pg. 252; PSR-MSS, vol. 4; TR-Portsmouth, vol. 2, pgs. 313, 423 and vol. 8, pgs. 169, 485, 663; CEN-1790 NH.

DEGO, PETER

Nothing is known about Dego, except his military service. He first saw service in 1775 when he enlisted in the company of Capt. Charles

Dibbel in Col. John Patterson's 1st Massachusetts regiment. It is unknown when in 1775 he enlisted, or for how long. He was reported as a "negro" (MSS, vol. 4, pgs. 638). A certificate dated November 16, 1775, states that Dego was discharged on October 7, 1775, when his company under the command of Capt. William Goodrich marched to Quebec. He is also listed as having not received a regimental coat. Dego next enlisted in December of 1775 for New Hampshire service in Capt. Jonathan Wentworth's company of Somersworth men in Poor's 2nd NH regiment. However, he deserted several months later, in February of 1776. He was designated a "negro" (NHRWR, vol. 1, pg. 308), and his name appears on a list of men who were sick or deserted, dated July 8, 1776, at Chimney Point, near Crown Point, Lake Champlain. Peter Dego is described as being 30 years of age, and five feet, nine inches in height. He returned to Massachusetts service late in 1776 as a private in Capt. John Walton's company in Col. John Brooks's 8th Massachusetts regiment. This service lasted two months and one day, from September 27 to November 16, 1776. Dego's name appears on a roll of men stationed at North Castle, New York. As part of the 8th Massachusetts, Dego took part in the Battle of White Plains on October 28, 1776. The day his service ended was a dark day for the Continental Army, since Fort Washington, in New York, was surrendered to the British on that day, resulting in nearly 3,000 American troops being taken prisoner. Dego next saw service in 1777, when he enlisted again for Massachusetts on February 1, 1777, for three years.

Engaged by the town of Stockbridge, Massachusetts, Dego served in the company of Capt. John Chadwick in Col. Samuel Brewer's 12th Massachusetts regiment. During this time, Dego was stationed at, or around, Fort Ticonderoga, later taking part in the Saratoga campaign. The 12th Massachusetts regiment was with the main army at Valley Forge in the winter of 1777-78, and also fought at the Battle of Monmouth in New Jersey in 1778 before returning north late in the year to serve garrison duty at West Point and the surrounding area. Although Dego appears on the payroll of the Continental Army from February 1, 1777, to May 8, 1780, indicating that he served out his three-year term, he is listed as having deserted at one time, the date given as October 30, but without a year specified. Dego served his entire time with the 12th Massachusetts regiment, though he served an extension of his term, from January to May 8, 1780, in the company of Capt. James Means, with Hartwood, Massachusetts, indicated as the town for which he served. However, other records state that Dego re-enlisted for the town of Pittsfield, Massachusetts, on November 29, 1779, for three years. Whether the records are incorrect, or Dego deserted is unknown. He resumed his service, however, in August of 1780, when he enlisted as a six-month man on August 1 from Natick, Massachusetts.

Listed as a "negro" (MSS, vol. 4, pg. 361), aged 25 and five feet, eleven inches in height, Dego joined the 6th Massachusetts regiment and was "marched to camp" (*ibid.*) at Springfield, Massachusetts on August 2, 1780, by Lt. Benjamin Pike. Following his military service, nothing further of Peter Dego is known. It is believed, though uncertain, that all the Massachusetts service listed above was for the same individual, despite the wide geographical distances among the towns that were served. However, the possibility exists that there were two black soldiers by the same name and, if this were the case, it would be difficult to identify which soldier served for New Hampshire.

Sources: PSR-MSS, vol. 4, pgs. 361, 638; PSR-NHRWR, vol. 1, pg. 308; OPS-Heitman.

FREEMAN, TITUS

Freeman is identified by black historian Herbert Aptheker as a black soldier, primarily on the basis of his name. The surname Freeman is a name commonly used by both blacks and whites, but the first name Titus was one often given to slaves in colonial times. Titus Freeman, his first name also spelled "Tytus" (NHRWR, vol. 1, pg. 275), first enlisted for service in New Hampshire during the war. He enlisted about February of 1776 in Capt. James Osgood's company in Col. Timothy Bedel's Regiment of Rangers for Continental service, his term of service and town for which he served not specified. He appears on a list, dated March 28, 1776, of men in Osgood's company who were paid for one month of service, as well as blanket money and their bounty for enlisting. Taking part in the invasion of Canada, Freeman was among Osgood's men at garrison in Montreal on April 15, 1776. As part of Bedel's regiment, Freeman took part in the action at The Cedars, near Montreal, and was captured there by the British, along with the rest of Osgood's company, when the fort was surrendered about May 19. Titus Freeman and the men captured at The Cedars were soon released on May 28 due, in large part, to efforts by Benedict Arnold, who wanted to prevent their massacre by the Indian allies of the British. He is likely the same Titus Freeman who subsequently enlisted for Massachusetts service in July of 1780. His name appears on a list of men, dated July 2, 1780, who were raised to reinforce the Continental Army. Freeman arrived at Springfield, Massachusetts, on July 2 and was received by Maj. Peter Harwood of the 6th Massachusetts regiment. The following day, Freeman was marched to camp under the command of Lt. Daniel Frye of Baldwin's Artillery Artificer regiment. This was a unit in the Continental Army similar to a modern-day combat engineer battalion. Its function was to carry out construction projects around West Point, maintain the army's wheeled vehicles, and build and repair roads. How long Freeman served at West Point, and whether he was with the 6th Massachusetts regiment there, or with Baldwin's Artificer regiment is unknown. However, his term of service must have been four months or less, since he re-enlisted for another term of service on October 30, 1780, in Capt. Alexander Hodgdon's company in Col. Ebenezer Thayer's regiment of Massachusetts militia raised to reinforce the Continental Army at Rhode Island. During this time, Freeman served for three months and eight days, until January of 1781. However, almost immediately he re-enlisted yet again, this time for three months in Capt. Wise's company in Brig. Gen. John Fellow's regiment of Massachusetts militia. On company rolls, Freeman is described as either aged 31 or 37 years old, with a "black" (MSS, vol. 6, pg. 54) complexion, and five feet, two inches in height. He was also reported as a "Negro" (*ibid.*) who enlisted for the town of Boston. Following the end of his final term of service, about April of 1781, nothing further regarding Titus Freeman is known.

Sources: PSR-NHRWR, vol. 1; OPS-Martin, pgs. 213–14; PSR-MSS, vol. 6; OPS-Aptheker, *Negro in the American Revolution*; OPS-Wright, pg. 137.

FULLER, EZRA

Fuller first saw service on April 23, 1778, just four days after the battles at Lexington and Concord, when he enlisted in the company of Capt. Ezra Towne in Col. James Reed's 3rd NH Regiment of Foot. Fuller, a resident of Mason, is described as being a native of Lynn, Massachusetts, a farmer, five feet, seven inches in height, with "black" (MSS, vol. 6, pg. 161) complexion and eyes, and aged 21. As part of the 3rd NH, Fuller took part in the historic Battle of Bunker Hill on June 17, 1775, being among the men of Reed and Stark who repulsed the initial British assaults and gave their vaunted troops heavy casualties. Following this, on June 30, 1775, Fuller, for reasons unknown, joined the Continental Artillery regiment of Col. Richard Gridley, serving as a matross in the company of Capt. Edward Burbeck. Described as aged 18 and five feet, eight inches in height, Fuller's name appears on regimental rolls dated August 1 and October 7, 1775. How long Fuller served with Gridley's Artillery regiment is unknown for certain, but likely ended sometime between October and December of 1775. Fuller served again for Massachusetts, for a brief time, in 1776 as a private in the company of Capt. Noah Lankton in Col. Mark Hopkins's 1st Berkshire County Massachusetts militia regiment. Fuller served for 21 days, from July 15 to August 4, 1776, having marched to the Hudson Highlands, in New York, to help support the Continental Army after the failed Canadian invasion. Following his second tour of duty for Massachusetts, Ezra Fuller returned for a second tour with New Hampshire. On May 2, 1777, he enlisted in Scammell's 3rd NH regiment in the company of Capt. Isaac Frye, his residence now listed as Temple. As part of Scammell's 3rd NH, Fuller fought at Fort Ticonderoga and Saratoga, where the 3rd NH was particularly noted for its bravery under fire. Fuller was with the 3rd NH at Valley Forge in December of 1777, but from January to March of 1778 went home to Temple on furlough, along with Amos Fuller, the son of David Fuller, and a fellow soldier in Frye's company.

Amos Fuller had previously been a tax collector for Temple, but it is unknown what his relation was to Ezra Fuller. They may have been related family members, or Ezra Fuller may possibly have been a slave of David or Amos Fuller sometime before the war. Whatever their relation, the men shared the same fate. They returned to Valley Forge in April of 1778 and are listed as being sick in camp during April and May. In June they are listed as being sick in the hospital at Valley Forge. Ezra Fuller died on July 1, 1778, at the hospital in Valley Forge, and Amos Fuller died two weeks later, on July 14. Whether they were related by blood, or simply an ex-slave and his master's son, it would be interesting to know if Ezra and Amos Fuller lived their final days together suffering side by side. Or, perhaps, they were separated, each uncertain of the other's fate and dying a lonely death far from home.

Sources: PSR-NHRWR, vols. 1–3; PSR-NHSP, vol. 30; PSR-MSS, vol. 6, pg. 161; TH-Kidder, pg. 78; TH-Blood, pg. 116; TR-Mason, vol. 1, pg. 757; TR-New Ipswich, vol. 2, pg. 819.

GILMAN, ANTHONY

Anthony Gilman was a "man of colour" (Pension #S32729) who enlisted for war service, for one year, from the town of Plaistow in December of 1775. He enlisted as a fifer in the company of Capt. Jeremiah Gilman, also a Plaistow resident, in Col. John Nixon's 6th Massachusetts regiment (also known as the 4th Continental regiment). Though uncertain, it is highly likely that Anthony Gilman was acquainted with Capt. Gilman, and may have been his slave prior to his military service. As part of Nixon's 6th Massachusetts, Gilman served during the Siege of Boston, and in early May of 1776 was sent to New York for operations there against the British.

The 6th Massachusetts was part of Gen. William Alexander, Lord Stirling's Brigade at first, and then, on August 12, joined the main army under Washington. Gilman took part in several battles during the disastrous New York City campaign, including the battles of Long Island, Harlem Heights, and White Plains through the summer and fall of 1776.

In December of 1776, Anthony Gilman enlisted for three years, "without leaving the service" (*ibid.*), in the company of Capt. Nathaniel Hutchins in Col. Joseph Cilley's 1st NH regiment for Continental service. Ironically, Capt. Jeremiah Gilman also joined the 1st NH regiment, just the month before, serving first as captain, and then as major before ultimately reaching the rank of lieutenant-colonel. Anthony Gilman served this term for the town of Plaistow, though the town of Charlestown was at first listed. As part of New Hampshire's most distinguished regiment, Gilman took part in the actions at Fort Ticonderoga and Saratoga in 1777. Gilman was reported sick in camp in February of 1778 at Valley Forge, but recovered and fought in the Battle of Monmouth in June. From December 26, 1778, to February 26, 1779, Gilman was on a 60-day furlough, during which he likely returned home, but was back on duty, "on command at the lines," in late February at Danbury, Connecticut, and later New London. In 1779, Gilman took part in Sullivan's campaign with the 1st NH, and served with his regiment on garrison duty at and around West Point, New York, in 1780. Anthony Gilman re-enlisted with the 1st NH in January of 1781, continuing his string of uninterrupted service since December of 1775. As part of Capt. Daniel Livermore's company, Gilman was reported as "taken prisoner of war" (NHRWR, vol. 3, pg. 219n) on February 15, 1781. He was part of a detachment of soldiers under Gen. Hull sent out from West Point to Morrisania, New York, to drive out the "Cowboys" (Pension #S32729), a lawless group of Tory refugees who harassed the contested territory between New York City and West Point to the north. Gilman later stated that he was captured with about 40 other men and taken to New York City as a prisoner, where he was kept for several weeks. Following this, Gilman was sold as a slave to one John Falkenham, whom he served for a year before being sent to Annapolis-Royal in Nova Scotia, Canada. Gilman further states that he was a slave in Canada for six months before he escaped and returned home, after which "the war was then over" (*ibid.*). Following his war service, little is known about Gilman. In May of 1818, he was a resident of Manchester, in Essex County, Massachusetts, when he applied for a pension for his war service at the age of 77. His pension was granted, but no data was given regarding his family.

Another former Gilman slave was also carried off as a captive to Canada during the French and Indian War, nearly 25 years before. Maj. John

Gilman of Exeter, New Hampshire, a relative of Jeremiah Gilman's Newmarket branch of the large Gilman clan, was at Fort William Henry, at the southern tip of Lake George in New York, after its capitulation in August of 1757 to a French and Indian force under Montcalm. In "An Inventory of Cloaths &c taken by the Indians from Major John Gilman," he lists "my Negro boy's gun and Cloathing he being taken & carryd to Canada" (NHSP, vol. 11, pgs. 651–2). This slave's name was Ceaser Nero, who was a soldier in the company of Capt. Richard Emery at Fort William Henry. Maj. Gilman was later reimbursed for the loss of Ceaser Nero's possessions and "loss of time" (*ibid.*) for his service, but the fate of his slave is unknown.

Sources: PEN-S32729; PSR-MSS, vol. 6; PSR-NHRWR, vols. 1–3; PSR-NHSP, vol. 11, pgs. 651–52 — vol. 30, pgs. 499, 502, 508, 511, 514, 517, 520; OPS-Boatner, pg. 389; OPS-Wright, pg. 208.

GREEN, JOHN/JACK

John Green was a "negro" who lived in Henniker for "several years" who first served in the war for Massachusetts (Cogswell, pg. 351). Because the name John Green is a common one, it is difficult to sort out his Massachusetts service with any reasonable degree of certainty. He is likely the John Green who enlisted on May 30, 1775, in Col. Samuel Gerrish's Massachusetts regiment (later the 9th Massachusetts). Serving in the company of Capt. Timothy Corey, Green and others took the oath of service required by Massachusetts on June 10, and on June 13 were at camp in Cambridge. Gerrish's regiment was among the most controversial of those regiments that fought at the Battle of Bunker Hill. The regiment was not fully organized on June 17, the day of battle, and only a part of Gerrish's men took part. One Boston historian states that Gen. Israel Putnam tried to lead a portion of Col. Gerrish's men, who arrived with their leader exhausted in the interval between the first and second British attack on the hill. Putnam "endeavored to rally these troops ... but without much effect" (Frothingham, pg. 143). However, a portion of Gerrish's regiment was led by its adjutant, Christian Febiger, a native of Denmark, who "behaved with great gallantry in leading on a portion of this regiment in time to do efficient service" (*ibid.*, pg. 179).

Although Febiger gained further renown during the war, Col. Gerrish, perhaps unfairly, was cashiered from the service on August 19, 1775. What part John Green took part in the above activities is unknown, but he may have been a part of the men led by Febiger, since Capt. Corey was not among the many captains who were censored or cashiered for their lack of effort during the battle. It is unknown for certain which town John Green served for. Both Boston and Brookline, Massachusetts, are listed, though "Jack" Green, who enlisted on the same day for the same regiment and took the same oath is listed as being from Reading, Massachusetts (MSS, vol. 6, pg. 809). Whether John and Jack Green were one and the same man is unknown. The nickname "Jack" was a common one given to men named John, and several black soldiers went by both names as "John-Jack." Following the battle, Gerrish's Regiment, now commanded by Lt. Col. Loammi Baldwin, was stationed at Chelsea, Massachusetts. Both John and Jack Green appear on company rolls for August of 1775. John Green is listed as a deserter on September 15, 1775; Jack Green last appears on a company roll dated October 2, 1775. When John/Jack Green arrived in New Hampshire is unknown. John Green enlisted for service on July 1, 1777, in Capt. John Duncan's company in Col. Moses Kelly's regiment of militia. This regiment was raised to reinforce the garrison at Fort Ticonderoga, but only marched as far as Charlestown, Fort Number 4, before being ordered back. Green's service during this term lasted four days, the town he served from being unknown.

Green next saw service in July of 1779, when he enlisted in Continental service for one year and was stationed at West Point on garrison duty. Green served for the town of Westmoreland and was paid six pounds billeting money for the trip between Keene and Springfield, Massachusetts. When his service ended in July of 1780, Green enlisted again for militia service at West Point, this time in the company of Capt. John Eastman in Col. Thomas Bartlett's regiment. This term of service lasted from July 16 to October 24, 1780. Little else is known about John Green, though he was probably married and had at least one child. His son Holden Green was a servant "for many years" (Cogswell, pg. 351) in the family of Francis Borman.

Sources: PSR-MSS, vol. 6; TH-Cogswell, pg. 351; OPS-Frothingham, pgs. 143, 178–79; PSR-NHRWR, vols. 2–3; TR-Henniker, vol. 3, pgs. 386, 405, 439–440.

Griffin, Thomas

At the start of the Revolutionary War, Thomas Griffin was a resident of Sandown, where he was married to Anne (also Anna) Beck about April 15, 1775, by the Reverend Josiah Cotton. Less than two weeks later, on April 24, Thomas Griffin enlisted for Massachusetts service, his hometown listed as Chester, New Hampshire. He enrolled as a drummer and a fifer in Capt. Thomas Cogswell's company in Col. Samuel Gerrish's Regiment (later the 9th Massachusetts and 26th Continental Infantry) and appears on payroll records for this regiment through May of 1776. During his year with Gerrish's Regiment (later Baldwin's), Griffin took part in the Siege of Boston, and was likely part of Gerrish's men who fought honorably at Bunker Hill. See the record of John/Jack Green for complete details on Gerrish's Regiment at Bunker Hill.

Griffin was "honorably discharged" from his service in Gerrish's Regiment and returned to New Hampshire. Soon after, he enlisted on June 1, 1776, in Capt. James Sheppard's company in Col. Isaac Wyman's regiment raised to reinforce the Continental Army. Stationed at Fort Ticonderoga, Griffin served for five months. Griffin served the following year when he enlisted on July 20, 1777, as a fifer in Capt. Daniel Runnels's company in Col. Moses Nichols's regiment of militia in Gen. John Stark's Brigade. Serving for two months and nine days, Griffin fought at the Battle of Bennington and afterwards went to Saratoga, being discharged on September 28, 1777.

Following his two terms of New Hampshire militia service, Thomas Griffin enlisted for Massachusetts service again on June 12, 1778, serving for the town of Salisbury, Massachusetts. Enrolled in the company of Capt. John Blanchard in the 9th Massachusetts regiment, formerly his old regiment under Gerrish, Griffin served for nine months performing garrison duty in and around West Point, New York. While Thomas Griffin served in the war, his wife Anne lived in Sandown with a friend named Mary Bailey. After the war, the Griffins apparently lived in Chichester, though they are not listed for that town in the 1790 Census. The 1810 Census lists them as free, non-white residents of nearby Chester. Griffin was granted a pension for his military service in December of 1818, but died soon after, at the age of 65, on January 26, 1819. Thomas and Anne Griffin had at least two children, Nancy and one son, name unknown, whose birth dates are also unknown. Anne Griffin continued to live in Chester for some time after her husband's death, but is listed in the 1840 Census as a resident of Concord, with her daughter, Nancy Morrill. In 1838, Anne Griffin applied for a pension based on her husband's service. She was helped in her efforts by a lawyer named Franklin Pierce, who later became president, and her claim was allowed on September 25, 1838. Anne Griffin had at least two great grandchildren, including Mary Stenger, who was a resident of Aurora, Illinois, in 1920, and Oliver H. Griffin, who was a resident of Marion, Indiana, in 1922.

Sources: PSR-MSS, vol. 6; PSR-NHRWR, vols. 1–2; CEN-1810-NH; PEN-W14815.

HANSON, ROBIN

See the service record of "Robin" for details on this soldier.

HARVEY, JOHN

Harvey was a "Negro man" (RCR #A11910) from Portsmouth who first saw service in 1776 for New Hampshire. While living in Amesbury, Massachusetts, Harvey enlisted in Col. John Waldron's regiment of New Hampshire militia on February 4, 1776, whereupon he marched 30 miles to Winter Hill, near Boston, to help man the siege lines. Stationed at Temple's farm in Gen. John Sullivan's Brigade, Harvey and the rest of Waldron's men served for at least six weeks, agreeing to remain until April 1, 1776. John Harvey next saw service the following year when he enlisted from Portsmouth for Massachusetts service on January 19, 1777, in Capt. Stephen Buckland's company in Maj. Ebenezer Stevens's Provisional Artillery Battalion at Boston. As part of Stevens's Artillery regiment, Harvey saw action at Fort Ticonderoga and at Saratoga during 1777. Stevens's Artillery regiment remained in the north, near Albany, New York, until May 1778, when it was assigned to the Hudson Highlands area of New York. In mid-July 1778, Harvey and his regiment were assigned to the main army under Washington in New Jersey. Soon after, John Harvey may have become ill or otherwise unfit for regular duty, since he was assigned to the Corps of Invalids as a drummer for 26 days, from September 4 to October 1, 1778, being stationed at Boston. However, Harvey returned to his unit, staying with Steven's Provisional Artillery until December 22, 1778, when it was disbanded at Pluckemin, New Jersey. Following this, John Harvey was transferred to Maj. John Crane's Continental Artillery regiment (3rd Continental Artillery Regiment), where he served as a matross until he deserted on July 16, 1779. Nothing further regarding Harvey's military service is known. After the war, John Harvey appears in the records for 1791, when, on April 1, he was described as a "Negro man" (*ibid.*) and warned to depart the town of Exeter immediately, along with two other black individuals. Nothing further of John Harvey is known after this date.

Sources: PSR-NHSP, vol. 30, pg. 457; PSR-MSS, vol. 7, pg. 402; RCR #A11910; OPS-Wright, pgs. 338–39.

JACK, JOHN

John Jack was a slave of Jonathan Warner of Portsmouth. Jonathan Warner was both a wealthy merchant and held the office of commissary in Governor Wentworth's administration under the British Crown. Refusing to sign the Association Test, Warner was classified a Tory. His former slave, John Jack, went by the names John Jack and John Jack Warner, using both equally during his lifetime. While John Jack's war service is rather undistinguished he is better known for the lasting impression his family made on local residents. He is possibly the same John Jack who first served for Massachusetts in 1776. Enlisting on February 28, 1776, John Jack served as a private in Capt. William Lithgow's company in Col. Mitchell's regiment of militia, stationed at Falmouth, Maine, "for the defence of seacoast" (MSS, vol. 8, pg. 654). Jack continued in Lithgow's company until the end of his service on November 23, 1776. The following year, in July of 1777, Jack was once again stationed at Falmouth, this time as a matross in Capt. Abner Lowell's company of militia. Listed on a return dated July 31, 1777, it is unknown how long Jack served during this second term. John Jack saw limited service for New Hampshire when he enlisted as a six-month man from Greenland, but for the town of Hampton, on June 29, 1780, in the Continental Army at the age of 47. An order to the state treasurer of New Hampshire, dated July 4, 1780, asks that wages be paid to Lt. John Fogg "for a Negro Man named Jack, he being a slave of Jon. Warner Esqr. of Portsmouth" (National Archives-Record #0684) However, Jack was discharged after only one month and 16 days of service for reasons unknown. He may also be the same man as the John Jack who enlisted for three years for Continental service on September 21, 1781, for the town of Ipswich, Massachusetts.

Before the war, Jack married a free black woman of Greenland named Phillis, who was formerly the slave of Deacon James Brackett. They had three children, Nancy Jack (b. 1/28/1767), Phillis Jack (b. 1/12/1771), and Thomas Jack (b. 6/1/1775). The Jack children were treated by a local doctor, Ichabod Weeks, in the years 1769, 1776, and 1784. On May 3, 1792, Phillis Jack bought from John Cate of Allenstown one quarter of an acre of land at Bayside in Greenland. This land and the house upon it remained in the Jack family for over 50 years, and made a lasting impression on those who dropped in to visit. One account states that "A rude pathway led to a rustic bridge, spanning a running brook. Just on the other side was the hut, with the lovely flower garden, where ladies delights, sweet williams, canterbury bells, bachelors buttons, marigolds, hollyhocks, and other old fashioned flowers grew. There were also useful herbs of lavender, thyme, sweet marjoram, and sage. They had in summertime delicious fruit cake and either currant or raspberry shrub which they served to their guests" (*Exeter News-Letter*, January 5, 1917). Another account by a resident of Greenland, published in 1874, states how the writer, when a little girl, visited the Jack house,

The homestead of black soldier John Jack in Greenland, New Hampshire. The area of his home today has been reclaimed by the wilderness. All that remains are the remnants of the stone wall, seen at the left, and the stone fragments of his children's gravestones. From *Rambles About Greenland*, by M.O. Hall, 1900.

It was only a small cottage, and indeed not much more than a hut. It was blackened with time and age upon the outside, and within it contained but two rooms.... I enjoyed those visits, and how anxiously did I look forward to the time, when my mother having promised me, that on a certain day, she would "go down to Philis" with me. And when the day arrived, taking with us something for their comfort and pleasure, we found it a very pleasant walk across the fields and pastures; for those little rooms and indeed they were very small, contained many things which to me seemed very curious. And especially was the "front room" completely crowded with such things. There were quaint old dishes, with boxes, and shells, and books, and bottles innumerable. The walls, I think, were almost completely covered with pictures.... Miss Philis would go out and walk around the grounds with me, pointing out with her cane the different plants and flowers [*Exeter News-Letter*, December 18, 1874].

In 1803, the Jack household must have become a lively place with the arrival of a new resident. Ona (Oney) Judge was a personal slave of President George Washington's wife, Martha. Desirous of gaining her freedom, she ran away from Washington's executive mansion in Philadelphia in 1796, during the president's preparations to return to his home in Mount

Vernon for the summer. She took passage on a regular trading vessel to Portsmouth named the *Nancy*, under Capt. John Bowles, and after her arrival, "lodged at a Free Negroes" (Washington, pgs. 297–98) residence. Washington tried hard to get Ona Judge back, stating that his wife "is desirous of receiving her again" (*ibid.*), but without success. He wrote a letter to Joseph Whipple, the collector of customs at Portsmouth, in November of 1796, outlining how this might be done in a somewhat deceptive manner. Despite being a political appointee of Washington, Whipple politely refused, and Ona Judge stayed in New Hampshire the rest of her life. In 1797, she married John Staines, a "mulatto" (*ibid.*) sailor of Portsmouth, and they had two children. Eliza, born in Greenland in 1798, died on February 16, 1832. Nancy, perhaps named after the vessel that carried Ona to freedom, was born in 1802, and died September 11, 1833. John Staines and Ona lived in Portsmouth, and are listed there in the 1800 Census as a family of four, indicating they may have had a third child. However, John Staines, listed as "a man of colour" (Dow, pg. 273), died in May of 1803. Soon thereafter, Ona and her children moved in with the Jack family in Greenland, where she lived the rest of her life. She died in Greenland on February 25, 1848, at the approximate age of 80.

Advertisement for the sloop *Nancy*. This vessel traded between Portsmouth and Philadelphia and later, in 1796, carried George Washington's runaway slave Ona Judge to freedom in New Hampshire. Judge later lived with the family of veteran John Jack in Greenland. *Oracle of the Day*, July 28, 1791. Courtesy Robert Dishman.

John Jack's wife, Phillis, died on October 12, 1804. Advanced in years, John Jack found it hard to support himself, and his family often received support from the town, being regularly supplied with firewood between the years of 1810 and 1821. John Jack died at the age of 84 on October 19, 1817. On February 20, 1818, Samuel Whidden was paid $25 by the town for taking care of Jack when he was sick for 23 days during his final illness.

Jack's coffin was made by Joseph Clark for $2.75 and the town paid his funeral expenses amounting to $33.05. Both John Jack and his wife were buried in a small plot "but a few feet from their garden" (*ibid.*) on the westerly side of Dearborn Road in Greenland, about one hundred yards off the highway and 75 yards north of Brackett's Brook (formerly Martin's Brook). Barely recognizable today as a burial place, there are a few graves marked by rough fieldstones near the toppled remains of the stone wall that stood on the Jack homestead, now a small and lonely clearing on land that has reverted to wilderness. Only the gravestone of John Jack's daughter, Phillis, carved with her name and date of death, though fragmented, remains to identify who is buried there.

Following the death of their parents, Nancy and Phillis Jack continued to live on the Jack homestead as spinsters. It is recorded that "They were poor; and it was customary for the people not only of that town, but also those of Stratham and other neighboring towns, to visit them and carry to them such things as they needed from time to time" (*ibid.*). In 1845, Nancy sold the old homestead to Edwin and John Pickering for $12. Phillis died on December 8, 1845, at the age of 75, and Nancy was cared for by Benjamin Moulton in her last years. She received town support in 1848, and died on July 12 of that same year. Moulton was paid by the town of Greenland for supporting Nancy before she died, as well as for her funeral expenses. By 1874, the house had long since disappeared, "while scarcely a vestige remains to mark the spot where it once stood; and the garden itself is devastated, and is now used for a pasture by neighboring farmers" (*ibid.*).

Sources: PSR-MSS, vol. 8, pg. 654; PSR-NHRWR, vol. 3; NEW-*Exeter News-Letter*, December 18, 1874, and January 5, 1917; TH-Dow, pg. 273; TH-Brewster, vol. 1, pg. 273; TH-Hall, pg. 42; OPS-Washington, pg. 297–98; CEN-1800-NH; PEN-NA-Record #0684.

MCGREGOR, LONDON

London McGregor was probably the slave of Robert McGregor, a selectman of Goffstown, when he enlisted for Massachusetts service on July 23, 1778, for the town of Beverly, in Essex County, for a term of nine months. Although his regiment is not listed, he arrived in Fishkill, New York, near West Point, on July 23, 1778, but is reported as being not mustered. His residence was listed as Goffstown. McGregor's name appears on a return of men by Capt. Isaac Chapman, dated January 5, 1779, at Beverly, where he is listed as being aged 23 years old, five feet, two inches in height, and having "dark" (MSS, vol. 10, pg. 137) complexion, hair, and eyes. Following this term of service, London McGregor probably returned to Goffstown to live, though whether or not he was now a free man is unknown. He enlisted for New Hampshire service on July 13, 1782, serving under Capt. Ebenezer Frye in the 1st NH regiment for the town of Goffstown. McGregor's term of service was for three years, but his exact discharge date is unknown. He may have served until January 1784, when the 1st NH regiment was disbanded. After the war, the fate of London McGregor is unknown, as is his residence.

Sources: PSR-MSS, vol. 10, pg. 137; TH-Hadley, vol. 1, pg. 148; PSR-NHRWR, vol. 3, pgs. 287, 507.

NOKES, TIMOTHY

Timothy Nokes, his last name also spelled as Knokes, Nookes, Knox, and Noaks, is tentatively identified as a black soldier based on his name and several associations. Possibly of mixed ancestry, he was probably a relation, perhaps a son, of Cuffe Noaks, a free black of Stratham who practiced the trade of a tanner and sold a 10-acre parcel of land to William Pottle on February 13, 1753. Cuffe was a soldier in the French and Indian War. His last name spelled as "Noker" (Potter, vol. 2, pg. 168), he enlisted for service under Capt. John Hart on May 1, 1756, in the expedition against the French at Crown Point.

Little is known about Timothy Nokes. On July 12, 1774, he was warned to depart the town of Kensington along with another black named Ebenezer Mingo. Nokes first saw military service in 1775, when he enlisted prior to November 22, 1775, in Capt. Stephen Clark's company of militia from Epping and the surrounding area. Nokes was a private in Clark's company and appears on a list of his men, some of whom went to Winter Hill, near Boston, in December of 1775. It is unknown when, or for how long Nokes served in Clark's company. Nokes enlisted for Massachusetts service on March 1, 1777, in Col. Edward Wigglesworth's 6th Massachusetts regiment for Continental service in the company of Capt. Alexander. Though Nokes was from the town of Kensington, he served for Marshfield, Massachusetts. During Nokes's time with the 6th Massachusetts, he was stationed in the area of West Point, New York, but is reported as having died less than four months after his enlistment. Serving in the company of Maj. Joseph Thompson, Nokes died on June 18, 1777, from unspecified causes.

Sources: US-NH Province Deeds, vol. 44, pgs. 13–14; OPS-Potter, pg. 168); PSR-NHRWR, vols. 2–4; MSS, vol. 11, pg. 502; RCR #3061; TR-Stratham, vol. 1, pg. 584 — vol. 3, pg. 281; OPS-Potter.

Oxford, Derrick

Derrick Oxford was a slave of William Gallup of Hartford, Vermont. Oxford was born about 1753, possibly in Connecticut. His master came to Hartford, Vermont, in 1775 from Stonington, Connecticut, where seven of his ten children were born. Derrick Oxford enlisted for New Hampshire service on March 17, 1777, in Col. Joseph Cilley's 1st NH regiment in the company of Capt. John House. Military records indicate his residence as both Lebanon, a town close to the Vermont border, and Hartford. Oxford lived in Hartford with his master, but was probably credited to the town of Lebanon to help fill their quota of soldiers. One record, however, lists him as "Nego Darok," engaged for the town of "Hertford" (NHRWR, vol. 2, pg. 603). As part of the 1st NH, Derrick Oxford fought in the 1777 actions at Fort Ticonderoga and Saratoga. He appears on his regiment's absentee list, dated January 10, 1778, at Valley Forge, as being aged 25 and left sick at Albany, New York. It is unknown when Oxford returned to service, but it was likely not until the end of 1778 or early 1779. A "certificate relating to Derrick Oxford," dated September 20, 1781, at Hartford, Vermont, and signed by that town's selectmen, including William Gallop, reads as follows: "This may certify that Derrick Oxford a Negro slave to Mr. William Gallop of sd Hartford enlisted in ye three years service and continued til he obtained a furlow home to his master to Recruit his health and continued sick & chargeable to his sd master near one year and then returned to sd service" (NHRWR, vol. 4, pg. 422). It is unknown whether Derrick Oxford participated with the 1st NH regiment in Sullivan's campaign in 1779, but he continued his term of service until mid–1780. Historian Frederick Kidder lists his service as ending in December of 1780, but it was actually terminated at the end of July of 1780.

Following his New Hampshire service, Oxford immediately enlisted for militia service in the new state of Vermont. He served as a private in Capt. Jesse Safford's company of Rangers in Major Ebenezer Allen's Detachment "raised for the defense of the state of Vermont" (PSR-Fisher, pg. 292) from August 1, 1780. Oxford appears to have served in Vermont's state militia through November 27, 1781, without any interruption in service. In October of 1780 he appears in the militia company of Lt. Abisha Samson that did duty at Barnard, Vermont for eight days. He also appears on the "True List" (*ibid.*, pg. 386) of men in Capt. John Benjamin's company that served to June 30, 1781. Oxford was one of the highest paid soldiers on this list, except for some officers, being paid eight dollars for his 11 months of service. Oxford continued in Benjamin's company, in Col. Benjamin Wait's Battalion, for Vermont service until his discharge on November 27, 1781.

After the war, Derrick Oxford returned to live with his master, William Gallop, in Hartland (formerly Hartford), Vermont. In June of 1784 Gallup petitioned the New Hampshire government for depreciation money due him for Derrick Oxford's service, stating that Oxford "served out faithfully and applyd for a discharge but being ignorant of the rules of the army received one from a Sargent forged in the name of the Colonel, upon which the Said Soldier left the army and was returned a disarter by which means your Petitioner is deprived of the just demand he would otherwise have" (NH General Court Records-June 1784). Because Oxford's name appears on the depreciation pay lists for the 1st NH regiment in 1780, his last year of service, it seems likely that his master's demand was met. Little else about Derrick Oxford is known, but he is likely the one free, non-white individual listed in the 1790 Vermont Census for Hartland in the household of William Gallop.

Sources: US-Rogers-Gallup genealogy; PSR-NHRWR, vols. 2–4; PSR-Fisher, pgs. 292, 325, 386, 535, 829; OPS-Kidder, pg. 151; New Hampshire General Court Records; CEN-1790-Vermont.

PETERS, ROBINSON

Peters was a black man who was born in Newmarket in 1752, and was living with Col. Hilton there when the war began. It is unknown if Peters was a free black, or a slave. He first enlisted for service for New Hampshire at the age of 25 in 1777 when he joined the company of Capt. Robert Pike in Col. Joseph Senter's regiment of militia on July 8. Originally stationed at Portsmouth for the defense of Piscataqua Harbor, Senter's regiment marched to Rhode Island in September of 1778, arriving at Providence on the 12, and Warwick on the 14. Once at Warwick, Senter's men, including Peters, were put to work building a fort and collecting all the boats on shore from Greenwich to Pawtucket and repairing them. Once they were finished, on October 8 they crossed the Providence River to Warren, marched to Swanzey on the 10th, Tiverton on the 12th, and to Little Compton on October 14. Here, the troops were "badly armed" and had "but few Cartridges" (NHRWR, vol. 2, pg. 239). By the time needed supplies and ammunition were obtained from Boston, the Rhode Island campaign had taken a turn for the worse and the troops were withdrawn. Senter's men, Peters included, served until January 6, 1778, completing six months of service.

Nearly a year and a half later, in June of 1779, Robinson Peters enlisted for service in Massachusetts. His term of service listed as three months, Peters signed on as a sailor aboard the *Vengeance*, an 18-gun brig of the

Massachusetts State Navy, fitting out at Newburyport, Massachusetts, under a Capt. Thomas for the expedition against the British on the Penobscot River in Maine. The *Vengeance* sailed from Newburyport to Boston to join the invasion fleet, which contained ships from Massachusetts, New Hampshire, and the Continental Navy. The fleet, under Capt. Dudley Saltonstall, arrived in the Penobscot on July 25, 1779, but failed to take aggressive action and was bottled up in the river by a large British fleet on August 12. All of the vessels of the expedition were lost, many, like the *Vengeance*, were deliberately run ashore and blown up to prevent them from falling into British hands. While the Americans lost 474 men, including three or four aboard Peters's ship, the British lost only 13 men. Once the *Vengeance* was blown up on August 14, Peters and the rest of the crew "took to the woods, and with a small amount of provisions marched over to the Kennebec River and then to New Hampshire" (Pension #S11232).

His war service over, Robinson Peters returned to Newmarket. He was married in nearby Exeter on September 4, 1781, to a woman named Violet, and is listed in the 1790 Census for New Hampshire as a resident of Gilmanton. Listed as a non-white head of household, Peters had seven free non-white persons living with him, probably his wife and children. In August of 1832, at the age of 80, Peters, a resident of Meredith since 1792, applied for and received a government pension for his war service.

Sources: PSR-NHRWR, vol. 2, pgs. 238–39, 243, 245–46; PEN-S11232; TH-Bell; PSR-NHSP, vol. 30; TR-Meredith, vol. 1, pg. 474–75; OPS-Boatner, pg. 851–52; CEN-1790-NH.

Pharaoh, William

William Pharaoh, a "negro" (MSS, vol. 12, pg. 278) from York, Maine, first enlisted for the state of Massachusetts in 1775. Listed simply as "Pharaoh" (*ibid.*), he enlisted on May 3, 1775, in the company of Capt. Jonathan Norvell in Col. James Scamman's regiment of Massachusetts State troops in York County, Maine. Scamman's regiment helped man the siege lines around Boston, and was called on to do service during the Battle of Bunker Hill on June 17, 1775, but played no effective part. Scamman's men, including Pharaoh, were ordered to "go where the fighting was" (Frothingham, pg. 146), but went from Lechmere's Point to Cobble Hill, instead of Breed's Hill. Communication delays prevented Scamman's regiment "from reaching the field in season to do any good" (*ibid.*). Colonel Scamman was later court-martialed for his tardiness, but was not convicted of any misconduct. Pharaoh appears on a list of Scamman's men, dated

October 30, 1775, who received money for a regimental coat while at Cambridge. It is unknown how long Pharaoh served in Scamman's regiment, or when his service ended. Pharaoh is probably the same man as William Farrow, who served from August 8 to August 28, 1778, in the company of Capt. James Lewis in Col. Enoch Hale's "Regiment of Volunteers" (NHRWR, vol. 2, pg. 542) from New Hampshire who served in Rhode Island. Pharaoh was married in Portsmouth on September 14, 1809, to Phebe Williams, a "colored" (TR-Portsmouth) woman, by the Reverend Nathaniel Parker. Nothing further regarding his life is known.

Sources: PSR-MSS, vol. 12, pg. 278; PSR-NHRWR, vol. 2, pg. 542; OPS-Frothingham, pg. 146; TR-Portsmouth.

PICKERING, BOSTON

Pickering was a "molato" (NHRWR, vol. 3, pg. 61) of Newington who served briefly in the war. Nothing is known about his life other than his military service. Born about 1760, he likely was a slave at some point prior to the war, and may have had the same master as another black soldier, Tumbril Pickering. Boston first enlisted for service in Newbury, Massachusetts, in 1778 as part of that town's quota, but was rejected for an unspecified physical disability. He next enlisted for New Hampshire service on July 1, 1780, as a six-month man. Described as being "a molato" (*ibid.*), Boston was listed as age 20 and five feet, five inches in height, and served in the 3rd NH regiment in the company of Maj. Jason Wait. Pickering, along with another black soldier named Plato Coleman, was drafted for six months' service, or was subject to a fine of $500. He was to furnish his own clothing, blanket, and knapsack. On November 2, 1780, Boston is listed as being at camp Highlands in New York, at the age of 17. On December 4, 1780, he was discharged and paid after serving five months and twelve days.

Boston Pickering enlisted again for Massachusetts service, and was accepted, on April 14, 1781, for three years. Described as a "molatto" (Coffin, pg. 613), he served for the town of Newbury, Massachusetts, in the 10th Massachusetts regiment. Stationed at or near West Point, New York, Pickering's service this time was brief. He died from unspecified causes on March 4, 1782, after ten months and seventeen days of service.

Sources: TH-Coffin, pg. 613; PSR-NHRWR, vol. 3; PSR-MSS, vol. 12.

ROBERTS, REUBEN

Roberts was a free black from the town of Newmarket, where he lived just prior to the war. In 1774 he was a highway rate payer in the district of Lt. Winthrop Hilton, and on April 21, 1775, was among those townsmen who attended and voted at a town meeting to send 30 soldiers to defend the colonies after the battles at Lexington and Concord. Reuben Roberts himself must have been filled with patriotic spirit for within a month, on May 20, 1775, he enlisted under Capt. Jeremiah Gilman in Col. John Nixon's Regiment (later designated the 6th Massachusetts). Soon after, when New Hampshire began to form her own regiments, Reuben Roberts attempted to enlist in the company of Capt. Samuel Gilman in Poor's 2nd NH regiment. However, a roll of men enlisted for Gilman's company, dated June 6, 1775, lists a number of men "Not Accepted" for service (NHRWR, vol. 4, pg. 7). Among those on the list, designated as a "Negro" (*ibid.*), was Reuben Roberts. Although service closer to home in the 2nd NH, which was stationed on the Seacoast at Portsmouth, would probably have been more desirable to Roberts, he continued to serve in Nixon's regiment for Massachusetts. He was likely among Nixon's men who fought at Bunker Hill, and served in that regiment throughout 1775 and late into 1776, when his enlistment ran out. He appears on company returns for Gilman dated August 1 and September 30, 1775, and is on a list, dated December 25, 1775, of men who received a payment for coat money at Winter Hill, near Boston.

From April through November of 1776, Roberts fought in the 6th Massachusetts during the New York City campaign. As part of his regiment, Roberts fought at the Battle of White Plains on October 28, 1776, and on November 9, 1776, was listed as a private in Jeremiah Gilman's company at North Castle, New York, just north of White Plains. Several weeks later, Reuben Roberts's term of service with the 6th Massachusetts was over. However, he was not yet done serving. On November 24, 1776, he enlisted for further service in the war while in New York. No doubt feeling an affinity for his home state, he enlisted with the 1st NH regiment under Capt. Nathaniel Hutchins for three years. Since the 1st NH and the 6th Massachusetts regiments were in the same brigade in Washington's main army, and were stationed in the same location, the switch by Roberts to New Hampshire service, without any interruption, was easily made. Roberts served in Hutchins's company through at least 1778, and, as a soldier in the 1st NH regiment, took part in the retreat from Fort Ticonderoga, the heavy fighting at Saratoga in 1777, and the subsequent winter at Valley Forge. In 1778, Roberts fought with his regiment at Monmouth, but later in the year was listed as being sick at Princeton, New Jersey. Following the Battle of Monmouth, Roberts was sick at Princeton for the months of July, August, and September of 1778. This was likely due to the intensive heat exhaustion that affected many of the soldiers who fought in what turned out to be the war's longest and hottest battle. In October of 1778, Reuben Roberts returned to Hutchins's company on active duty, and is listed on company rolls through December of that year.

There is no doubt that Reuben Roberts was still in the army in 1779, but there is some mystery as to where he served. Although Roberts is not listed on the muster rolls for Hutchins's company in 1779, he does appear on Continental Army depreciation pay records as having served the entire year, and was paid as such. Since not all of the company rolls have been found for the 1st NH regiment for 1779, it is possible that Roberts, for reasons unknown, switched companies and served under a different captain. However, there is also some evidence that Roberts may have enlisted for another term of service for the state of Rhode Island. In July of 1779, a Reuben Roberts is listed in the company of Capt. Edward Slocum in Col. Christopher Greene's Battalion, also known as the 1st Rhode Island regiment, at East Greenwich, Rhode Island. When he enlisted is not specified, but his term of service was listed as "during war" (MSS, vol. 13, pg. 366). Because no other soldiers with the name Reuben Roberts have been found for either Massachusetts or Rhode Island, it is likely that the man in Rhode Island service was the same man who had previously served for Massachusetts and New Hampshire. The 1st RI regiment was originally formed in 1775, but was reorganized in early 1778 "with Negro enlisted personnel" (Wright, pg. 227). Most of the blacks who served at first were slaves who enlisted and were given their freedom by the state, which in turn compensated their masters. However, many free blacks joined soon after, and the predominantly black 1st RI regiment, led by white officers, fought valiantly at the Battle of Rhode Island in August of 1778. Given the composition of the 1st RI, and the good reputation they had achieved in the Continental Army, it is not surprising, though unusual in the Revolutionary War, that Roberts would have sought to join its ranks. During the Civil War, black men from all over the country were inspired and excited about the formation of black regiments and eagerly sought the opportunity to fight with such regiments as the famed 54th Massachusetts. For his service in the 1st RI regiment, the reputation of Reuben Roberts stands tall. He is the only black soldier from New Hampshire, and quite possibly the only soldier from the state, period, who served for three different states— in this case Massachusetts, New Hampshire, and Rhode Island—during the war. It is likely that Roberts only served for about a year in the 1st RI regiment. During this time, it was stationed in the army's Eastern Department and performed garrison duty in its home state, taking part in no battles.

Reuben Roberts returned to service for the state of New Hampshire in late 1779, or early 1780, when he enlisted again for three years in the 1st

NH regiment, this time under Capt. Isaac Frye. Records for the town of Newmarket, where the Roberts family lived in 1779, are interesting in that they show how much aid was given to his family while he was off to war. Totaling over £224 worth of goods and services from May to September, they include charges for beef, corn, potatoes, molasses, rum, lamb, salt, coffee, chocolate, pork, sugar, firewood, house rent, shoes for a woman and a child, and doctor's fees.

Roberts served garrison duty at and around West Point, New York, as well as taking part in skirmishes against Tory and Indian forces in 1781, being listed in company returns for his regiment in March of 1783. Though uncertain, his term of service probably expired between June and December of 1783, ending a remarkable record of service that, as far as is known, spanned a continuous eight years. If ever a soldier fit the term "battle-hardened veteran" it was Reuben Roberts.

Unfortunately, little is known about Roberts after the war. It was likely his wife and child, both named Persila Robards, that were warned to depart Brentwood, a town bordering Newmarket, on September 26, 1785, along with several other adults and their children. Where Reuben Roberts was at this time is unknown. He later returned to Newmarket, where he is listed in the 1790 Census as being a free black head of a household consisting of himself, a free white female, probably his wife, and one other free person, probably his daughter. Following this, no records regarding Roberts have been found. He should not be confused with another soldier by the same name who served with the 9th North Carolina regiment, and later moved to Jones County, Georgia.

Sources: TR-Newmarket; PSR-NHRWR, vols. 1–4; PSR-NHSP, vol. 30; PSR-MSS, vol. 13, pg. 366; OPS-Wright, pg. 227; CEN-1790-NH.

Robin

A black man named "Robin" (NHRWR, vol. 4, pgs. 7–8), with no last name given, first enlisted for military service on May 6, 1775, in Capt. Jeremiah Gilman's company in Col. John Nixon's 6th Massachusetts regiment (later designated the 4th Continental Infantry) from Sandown for an undetermined time, but probably for one year. However, he attempted to enlist for military service in New Hampshire on June 12, 1775, in Col. Enoch Poor's 2nd NH regiment under Capt. Samuel Gilman. Listed as a "husbandman" (farmer) from Sandown, aged 23, he had the consent of his master to do so. Enlisting with Robin were Sippio and Archelus, both "Negroes" (Ibid) from Plaistow. All of these men were not sworn into service and were rejected. Less than a week earlier, another black recruit,

Reuben Roberts of Newmarket, was also rejected for service in the 2nd NH regiment. Whether these men, including Robin, were rejected because of an old law, dating from 1719, on the books prohibiting blacks from serving, or less likely, because of their prior enlistment under Capt. Jeremiah Gilman, a distant relation to Capt. Samuel Gilman, for Massachusetts service is unknown. It is likely that Robin, as well as the others, sought to join the 2nd NH because it was stationed on the New Hampshire Seacoast at Portsmouth, closer to home than Nixon's regiment, which was stationed at Boston. As part of Nixon's regiment, Robin fought at the Battle of Bunker Hill, where Col. Nixon bravely led his men and was badly wounded. On December 25, 1775, Robin appears on a list of men stationed at aptly named Winter Hill, on the outskirts of Boston, who received payment for a regimental coat or its equivalent in money. Nothing further is known of Robin's Massachusetts service. His master was probably Thomas Rowell of Sandown, who was given a tax rebate in 1782 because "his nigger" (Holmes, pg. 143) was in the army for Sandown.

It is unknown if Robin is the same man as a "mulatto" (NHRWR, vol. 3, pg. 624) named Robin Hanson, who enlisted in the Continental Army for Dover on June 8, 1781. However, a list dated after November 20, 1781, states that Hanson never joined, and no further information regarding him is known.

Sources: PSR-NHRWR, vols. 2–4; PSR-MSS, vol. 13, pgs. 393, 420; TH-Holmes; OPS-Frothingham, pgs. 182–3.

ROGERS, CATO

Rogers was the slave of Capt. Daniel Rogers of Durham, New Hampshire, and later of Kittery, Maine. Cato was born in the colonies sometime between 1730 and 1737, and was advertised as a runaway slave twice in the 1760s while living in Durham. The first ad appeared in the *New Hampshire Gazette* on January 1, 1765, and described Rogers as "a middling size and a spry Fellow ... about 35 years old and has a scar a-cros his throat (lately done by a fall from a horse)..." The ad further offered an eight-dollar reward for his return, and cautioned others "against secreting or carrying off my said Negro." Two years later, on June 19, 1767, a similar ad appeared in the same paper, again describing Rogers, "who formerly went by the name of Mingo," as of "middling size" and a "well set spry fellow ... about 30 years of age." His master probably grew weary of Cato's attempts to run away, since he further describes him as "a great Lyer and very cunning," but offered to pay a five-dollar reward for his return, and "if he will return immediately he shall be forgiven this time."

Eight DOLLARS Reward.

RUN-AWAY from his Mafter Capt. *Daniel Rogers* of Durham, a Negro Man, named CATO, born in the Country, a midling Size, and a fpry Fellow ; had on when he went away a greyifh homefpun Coat, lin'd with ftrip'd homefpun, a light colour'd Jacket, Leather Breeches, white yarn Stockings ; he is about 35 Years old, and had a Scar a-crofs his Throat, (lately done by a fall from a Horfe)— WHOEVER will take up faid Negro, and bring him to his faid Mafter, or confine him fo that he may be had, fhall have EIGHT DOLLARS Reward and all neceffary Charges, paid by,
Daniel Rogers.

N. B. All Mafters of Veffels and others, are cautioned againft fecreting or tartving off faid Negro, on Penalty of the Law. *Durham,* in *New-Hampfhire, Jan.* 1, 1765.

RUNAWAY from his Mafter *Daniel Rogers,* Efq; of *Durham,* laft *Saturday,* a NEGRO MAN, named *Cato,* formerly went by the Name of *Mingo* —He was of a middling Size, well fet fpry Fellow, born in the Country ; about 30 Years of Age—Had on when he went away a blue Ratteen Coat; light colour'd Satge Jacket, Leather Breeches; and old Bever Hat—He's a great Lyer, and very Cunning ——— Whoever will take up faid *Negro,* and convey him to his faid Mafter, fhall have Five DOLLARS Reward, and neceffary charges paid by *Daniel Rogers.*—

N. B. All Matters of Veffels are forbid carrying off faid Servant, as they would avoid the Penalty of the Law.

Top: A typical ad of this type, this was the first time Cato Rogers was advertised as a runaway. *New Hampshire Gazette,* January 11, 1765. Courtesy Portsmouth Public Library. *Bottom:* Runaway slave ad for Cato Rogers. Cato ran away from his master twice before his service in the American Revolution. *New Hampshire Gazette,* June 12, 1767. Courtesy Portsmouth Public Library.

Cato Rogers first enlisted for service on January 1, 1776, in the company of Capt. Tobias Fernald in Col. Edmund Phinney's regiment of men raised from Cumberland County, District of Maine. Phinney's regiment (later designated the 18th Continental Infantry, subsequently the 12th Massachusetts regiment) was initially stationed in the Eastern Department, serving garrison duty at or around Boston. In August of 1776, Rogers and his regiment were sent to the Northern Department, in the Lake Champlain area of New York. Rogers appears on the company rolls for his regiment, dated December 8, 1776, at Fort George, but is reported as being sick in the general hospital. Rogers's term of service must have been for only one year in Phinney's regiment, as he re-enlisted for New Hampshire service on January 1, 1777. Stationed at Fort Sullivan, in Portsmouth Harbor, he served as a matross in the artillery company of Capt. Eliphalet Daniels in Col. Joshua Wingate's regiment of New Hampshire militia. On June 4, 1777, he was one of Daniels's men who signed a petition to New Hampshire's General Assembly in Exeter pleading for advance wages and support for their families. Rogers, who could not write, signed this petition with an X to make his mark. After his six months of service was up, Rogers again served for Massachusetts, enlisting in the company of Capt. Elisha Shapleigh on August 14, 1777, for service in Col. Joseph Storrs's regiment of Massachusetts militia raised to support the Continental Army at Saratoga during the campaign against Burgoyne. Rogers served until November 30, 1777, when he was discharged after 123 days of service at Bemis Heights, near Saratoga. Following this, nothing further of Cato Rogers is known.

Sources: NEW-*New Hampshire Gazette*; PSR-MSS, vol. 13, pg. 499; OPS-Remick, pg. 171; OPS-Wright, pg. 212; PSR-NHRWR, vol. 1; PENNA-M881-560.

SMALL, JONATHAN

Small was a resident of Dunstable, Massachusetts, on the New Hampshire border, when the war began on April 19, 1775, with the battles at Lexington and Concord. On that same day, Jonathan Small enlisted for service in Capt. Reuben Butterfield's company in Col. David Green's regiment of Massachusetts militia, which marched to Cambridge on the alarm. Here, Small served for six days, to April 25, 1775, in the early days of the Siege of Boston. Small then enlisted in the company of Capt. Josiah Crosbey in Col. James Reed's 3rd NH regiment, which was then forming. Small saw action at the Battle of Bunker Hill on June 17, 1775, as part of Reed's regiment, and appears on the payroll for Crosbey's company dated August 1, 1775, having served for three months and sixteen days. Small's term of enlistment is unknown, but he was likely still in the 3rd NH in August of 1776 when it was stationed at Fort Ticonderoga. Though the name is a common one, he is probably the same Jonathan Small "of Col. Reed's Regmt" who was tried on the charge of selling "liqour" against the order of the commanding officer (Neagles, pg. 244). Small pleaded guilty and was sentenced to receive 39 lashes on his bare back and return to duty.

Not surprisingly, this is the last record of military service for Small. Sometime thereafter, Jonathan Small moved to Goffstown, New Hampshire, where he resided in 1790. The 1790 Census lists him as a free, non-white inhabitant, the head of a household of seven free individuals and one free-white female. On December 13, 1790, "John" Small, and Aaron, Susannah, and Eunice Small, as well as a number of other individuals, were warned to depart the town of Goffstown (Hillsborough County Court Records-1790). Following this action, no further records regarding Jonathan Small in New Hampshire have been found. The Aaron Small who was warned to depart Goffstown with him was undoubtedly a close relative, possibly his brother, and also served in the war as a soldier for Massachusetts. His biography appears later under those soldiers who are associated with New Hampshire, but did not serve in New Hampshire forces during the war. The two Small women named in the order to depart Goffstown were probably the wives of Jonathan and Aaron Small.

Sources: PSR-MSS, vol. 14, pg. 315; PSR-NHRWR, vol. 1, pg. 103; OPS-Neagles; CEN-1790-NH; US-Hillsborough County Court Records.

SMITH, THOMAS

The 1790 Census for New Hampshire lists a man named Thomas Smith who was designated a free, non-white inhabitant, the head of a family of two individuals, in the town of Chesterfield. A check of this name against the military records for New Hampshire and Massachusetts reveals several possibilities for military service for this individual. However, due to the commonality of the name Thomas Smith, it is impossible to determine with any degree of certainty whether any of the records listed below actually pertains to the Thomas Smith who lived in Chesterfield in 1790. Whether Thomas Smith was a slave or freeborn is also unknown. Moses Smith was one of Chesterfield's original settlers when he came there from Leicester, Massachusetts, near Worcester, in 1761. However, it is unknown if Moses Smith was a slave owner.

It is very likely that Thomas Smith from Chesterfield served for a short time in 1777. Colonel Jonathan Chase raised a regiment of militia to reinforce the garrison at Ticonderoga on the alarms of June 27 and July 4, 1777, in the face of Burgoyne's advancing army. Chase's regiment, which marched from Cornish and towns nearby, has two men named Thomas Smith on its rolls. One of them was likely the white soldier who is listed in the 1790 Census as a resident of Surry, while the other was possibly Thomas Smith from Chesterfield. One of the men was paid travel money for 70 miles travel roundtrip to and from his home, a sum which was larger than that for most men in the regiment, and close to the distance between Chesterfield and Cornish. Thomas Smith may also be the same man who served in Capt. Samuel Cunningham's company in Col. Enoch Hale's regiment of New Hampshire militia raised for the defense of Rhode Island. The men in this regiment served for 21 days, August 10–28, 1778, plus time for travel home. Cunningham's company consisted of mostly men from Peterborough and the surrounding area. Since Chesterfield was only several towns away from Peterborough, the Thomas Smith who served in Rhode Island may have been the same man as the free black resident of Chesterfield.

In regards to sorting out potential service for Thomas Smith in Massachusetts, he may be the same man as the Thomas Smith who enlisted for the town of Richmond, at Lenox, Massachusetts, on February 17, 1781, for three years from Col. David Roseter's regiment of Berkshire County militia. Smith was described as "A Negro" (MSS, vol. 14, pg. 560), age 36 (approximate year of birth 1745), whose occupation was that of a laborer, and was paid the state bounty for enlisting. This man, possibly the same man as Thomas Smith of Chesterfield, is likely also the same man who moved to Grafton County, New Hampshire, in 1826, from Oxford County, Maine. This man received a pension for his service in the Massachusetts Line beginning in 1818, at the age of 74 (approximate year of birth 1744), and transferred his pension to New Hampshire on September 4, 1826. However, he died less than a year later, on June 2, 1827.

Sources: CEN-1790-NH; TH-Randall; PSR-NHRWR, vol. 2; PSR-MSS, vol. 14, pgs. 559–563; PSR-NHSP, vol. 30, pgs. 258–59.

Tash, Oxford

Oxford Tash was the slave of Col. Thomas Tash, a veteran of the French and Indian War, as well as the Revolution. Oxford Tash lived in Newmarket, and fought in the war for both New Hampshire and Massachusetts, though his name is not listed in any military records for New Hampshire. However, surviving pension records are more specific about when and where Tash served during the war. They indicate that Tash first enlisted in 1775 in the company of Capt. Winborn Adams in Poor's 2nd NH regiment for a term of one year. Since he does not appear on company rolls through October of 1775, and subsequent rolls for Adams's company for the rest of 1775, as well as 1776, are missing, it must be assumed that he enlisted in late 1775, or early January of 1776, probably at Winter Hill, near Boston. During his time in the 2nd NH regiment, Tash served in the Canadian campaign, and at Fort Ticonderoga. While at Whitehall, New York, Tash, like many other men, contracted smallpox, but survived. Another possibility for New Hampshire service, though also unrecorded, is that Oxford Tash served in the militia regiment of his master, Col. Thomas Tash, that reinforced the army in New York in September and October of 1776, and likely fought at the Battle of White Plains.

Following his New Hampshire service, Tash soon re-enlisted, this time for Massachusetts service, at Newburyport on March 22, 1777. He joined the company of Capt. Moses Greenleaf in Col. Benjamin Tupper's 11th Massachusetts regiment for a three year term. During his service, he fought with his regiment at Saratoga and Monmouth. Sometime during his military service, Tash was wounded "and carried the musket ball then received in his thigh until his death" (Pension #W16155). It is unknown, however, when or in what battle he was wounded. Oxford Tash's service in the 11th Massachusetts ended on March 22, 1780. He likely stayed in the Newburyport, Massachusetts, area where his future wife, Esther How Freeman, resided. Oxford Tash enlisted for a final term of service, again for Massachusetts, in an unknown regiment, on August 8, 1780. He served six months, mostly performing garrison duty at and around West Point, and was stationed at Tarrytown, New York, when the British spy, Maj. John Andre, was executed. He was discharged on February 25, 1781, and was paid for seven months' service, including thirteen days' travel time to his home.

After the war, Oxford Tash, now a free man, was married to Esther How Freeman at the First Presbyterian Church in Newburyport by the Reverend John Murray on November 18, 1781. After 1790, the Tashes lived in Exeter and were among the most prominent of the black families who lived in town. They lived in a house a few doors north of Josiah Batchelder and had a large family. Their children include Mary (b. 3/14/1784, d. 7/20/1819); Lucy (b. 4/6/1786, d. 11/23/1812); Susan (b. 7/3/1788); Robert (b. 9/3/1790, d. 3/26/1870); Catherine (b. 7/25/1792); Charles (b. 12/9/1794, d. 6/11/1864); William (b. 3/9/1797); and Matilda (b. 7/25/1799). Their son, Robert (Bob) was remembered as being good-natured and popular among his friends. He later became a preacher and returned to Exeter, where he died at the age of 79. Another son, William, married Sally, the daughter of Robert Duce, another black soldier living in Exeter. They published their marriage intentions on October 2, 1819. Sally died in Exeter on November 19, 1844, at the age of 50.

The most prominent of the Tash children was likely Charles Tash. He became quite successful in business and acquired a substantial amount of property. A newspaper advertisement dated April 5, 1847, describes nine properties for sale by Charles Tash, including four houses and several barns and outbuildings. Unfortunately, Charles Tash is better remembered for an affair he had with a white woman that ended badly when he tried, unsuccessfully, to take both her life and his own. One of Oxford Tash's sons, probably William, was a "domestic" in the house of Nathaniel Gilman of Exeter, having "lived many years in my family ... and is now (1818) in it" (Pension #W16155). Oxford Tash received an invalid pension for the wound he had received which commenced on June 1, 1807, amounting to $2.50 per month. Tash had earlier refused to apply for a pension, so long as he could work, but now was in need of support. He died several years later on October 15, 1810. His wife, Esther Tash, born at Cape Ann, Massachusetts, about 1759, applied for, and received, a widow's pension in 1838. This pension was renewed in 1843, but shortly thereafter, on March 28, 1844, Esther Tash died in Exeter at the age of 86, having survived her husband by more than 30 years. With the death of her son, Robert, in 1870, there were no members of the Tash family remaining in Exeter where they had lived for nearly one hundred years.

Sources: PEN-W16155; PSR-NHSP, vol. 30, pg. 226; TH-Bell; NEW-Exeter News-Letter, April 5, 1847, Dec. 11, 1841; Dec. 18, 1841.

TATTEN, ISAAC

Tatten was a "colored man" (TH: Bicentennial...) who served in the war from Lempster. He arrived in that town in 1767, sent there from East Haddam, Connecticut, by Joseph Spencer, one of Lempster's original grantees. He first saw military service for New Hampshire in 1777, when he enlisted in the company of Capt. Oliver Ashley in Col. Bejamin Bellows's regiment of militia. Tatten served for one month and two days, from September 21 to October 22, 1777, during which time his regiment was sent to Saratoga to reinforce the Continental Army during the campaign against Burgoyne. Isaac Tatten next saw service, still with New Hampshire, in 1779, when both he and his son, Isaac Tatten, Jr., enlisted in the company of Capt. Ephraim Stone in Col. Hercules Mooney's regiment of militia raised for the defense of Rhode Island. They served for five months and seventeen days, from July 19, 1778, to January 4, 1780, during this term and are the only known father and son team of black soldiers who served together during the war for New Hampshire. Later in 1780, Tatten served another term when he enlisted in the company of Capt. Peter Page in Col. Moses Nichol's regiment of New Hampshire militia raised to perform garrison duty at West Point, New York. Tatten enlisted on July 6, 1780, and served for three months and fifteen days during this final stint of New Hampshire service.

Isaac Tatten served one final term in 1781 when he enlisted on August 17, 1781, in the company of Capt. Peter Page in Lt. Col. Ebenezer Walbridge's regiment of Vermont militia. Tatten and his former commander, Capt. Peter Page, served together once again while in service for the state of Vermont. However, this was not unusual. Captain Page was from Charlestown, on the Vermont border, and Tatten's hometown of Lempster was only a short distance away. Tatten's war service was over when his term in the Vermont militia ended on November 18, 1781. After the war, Isaac Tatten returned to Lempster, where he was recorded as a resident in the 1790 Census for New Hampshire as a free, non-white head of a household of

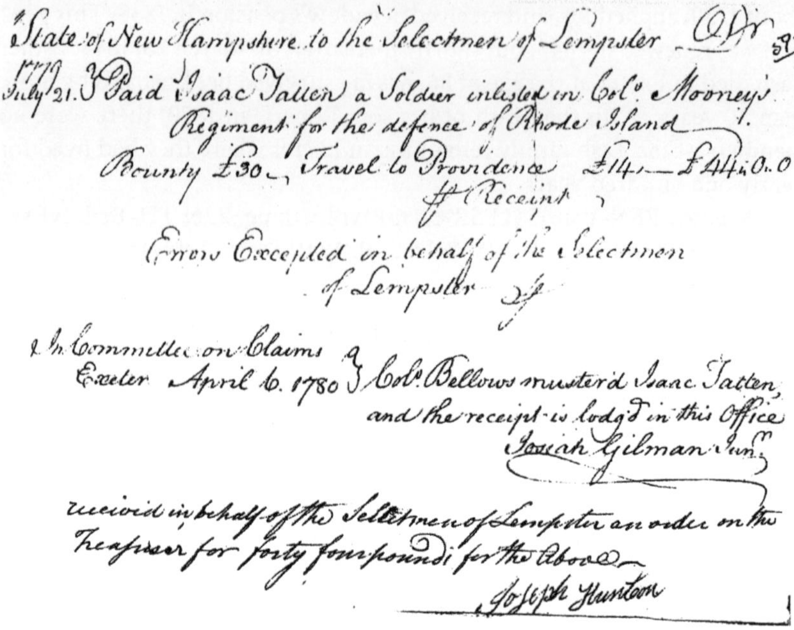
State of New Hampshire to the Selectmen of Lempster Dr 59
1779 July 21. To Paid Isaac Tatten a Soldier inlisted in Col. Mooney's Regiment for the defence of Rhode Island —
Bounty £30 — Travel to Providence £14 — £44..0..0
pr Receipt
Errors Excepted in behalf of the Selectmen of Lempster

In Committee on Claims Exeter April 6. 1780 } Col. Bellows muster'd Isaac Tatten, and the receipt is lodg'd in this Office
Josiah Gilman Junr

receivd in behalf of the Selectmen of Lempster an order on the Treasurer for forty four pounds for the Above
Joseph Huntoon

Bounty payment record for Isaac Tatten. This document records the £30 bounty, plus £14 travel expense, paid to soldier Isaac Tatten of Lempster for his service in Rhode Island in 1779. PSR-NHRWR, vol. 10, page 59. Courtesy New Hampshire Division of Records Management and Archives.

three free non-white individuals. Those who lived with him probably included his wife and his son, Isaac Tatten, Jr. While nothing further of Tatten is known, a local spot gained the name of Tatten's Spring, by which it is still known today.

Sources: TH-*Bicentennial History…*; PSR-NHRWR, vol. 2, pgs. 138, 371, 662, 669, 681; PSR-Fisher, pg. 529.

TAYLOR, PRINCE

Taylor first saw service for the state of New Hampshire in 1780, from June to November of 1780 in the company of Capt. Ephraim Stone in Col. Benjamin Whitcomb's Rangers for the defense of the western frontier. He is likely the same man who shortly thereafter was enlisted by the town of Lunenberg, Massachusetts, for Continental service on March 6, 1781. Taylor enlisted in the company of Capt. Daniel Pillsbury in Lt. Col. Calvin Smith's 6th Massachusetts regiment for three years and was described as being "black" (MSS, volume 15, pg. 449), aged 26, five feet, ten inches in height, and practiced the trade of a cooper. The 6th Massachusetts was stationed during this time in the Hudson Highlands area, performing garrison duty at and around West Point, New York. Nothing further about Prince Taylor is known.

Sources: PSR-NHRWR, vol. 3; PSR-MSS, vol. 15, pg. 449; OPS-Wright, pg. 208.

THOMPSON, THOMAS

Thompson was a "black man" (RCR #18299) who lived in Durham and was probably the slave of the prominent Thompson family in that town. His identification as a soldier in the Revolution for both New Hampshire and Massachusetts is tentative, based on the fact that several other men with the same name also served for Massachusetts. He first enlisted for military service on May 26, 1775, in the company of Capt. Winborn Adams in Poor's 2nd NH regiment. Thompson was listed as being a husbandman, aged 22, from Durham. It is unknown if Thompson was freed prior to his war service, or was given his freedom after serving. It is unknown how long Thomas Thompson served in Adams's company, but it was likely for one year. He last appears in company rolls dated August of 1775, when he was paid one pound and four shillings for a regimental coat. There is a slight chance that Thomas Thompson of Durham was the same man as the Thomas Thompson who served for one term of service eight years later, when he enlisted in the company of Capt. Isaac Frye in Col. Henry Jackson's Continental Regiment, also known as the 1st American Regiment. This regiment was organized in November of 1783, and consisted of nine companies of men, most of them veterans from Massachusetts regiments. However, some of these men were also from New Hampshire, including Capt. Frye, who was formerly a captain in the 1st NH regiment. Thompson served in the 1st American Regiment from January to April of 1784 and was stationed at West Point, New York. After the war, little is known about Thomas Thompson. He is not listed in any census records for New Hampshire in 1790, unless he is the same man from Durham named Thomas Thompson who is identified in the Census as a white head of household for a family of five individuals. Thomas Thompson was warned to depart the town of Rye on January 25, 1798, along with his wife Susana, having "lately come into this town to sojourn who are not inhabitants thereof" (*ibid.*). Later that same year, Thomas Thompson, described as a "Negro" (Osterlin, pg. 121), was a pauper for the town of Rye. Thomas Thompson of New Hampshire should not be confused with another soldier with the same name who served in the Maine militia during the war and later moved to New Hampshire.

Sources: PSR-NHRWR, vol. 1; PSR-NHSP, vol. 30, pg. 496; OPS-Wright, pg. 216; OPS-Heitman, pg. 315; RCR #18299; OPS-Osterlin.

TWILIGHT, ICHABOD

Twilight's service in the American Revolution was both brief and undistinguished. His connection with New Hampshire was somewhat fleeting, and he is better remembered as the father of a rather remarkable son who gained high levels of achievement. Ichabod Twilight was born in Boston about August of 1765 and is described in various records as a "molatto" (Lovejoy, pg. 1) or "a colored man" (Harriman, pg. 217). Little is known about his early life, but in 1781 he began to move westward as a young man, possibly with the idea of moving to the free state of Vermont. Although Twilight was likely freeborn, the Massachusetts coastal area was not always a safe place for free blacks or former slaves, since many were kidnapped and sold into slavery in the South. Ichabod Twilight appears in Massachusetts military records in 1781 when, on September 20, he was paid a bounty, for enlisting for three years in Continental service, by the town of Newbury. However, Twilight never served for Massachusetts and likely took the bounty money he received and moved north to New Hampshire. He continued his move to the northwest and settled for a short time in Warner, New Hampshire. On April 23, 1782, he enlisted for Continental service in the 2nd NH regiment under Capt. Jeremiah Fogg. Although Twilight lived in Warner, he was hired by the town of Sandown to help fill its quota of soldiers, his term of service being for one year. In his service record, Ichabod Twilight is described as a farmer, aged 16 years and 9 months, with a "yellow" (National Archives-M881, reel 519) complexion, and a height of five feet, three inches. He served through May of 1783, being stationed with the New Hampshire Brigade first in the Northern Department around Albany and Schenectady, New York, and later with the Main Army along the Hudson River.

Following his discharge, Twilight likely stayed in New York and never returned to Warner, New Hampshire. He was in the Lake Champlain area about 1789 when he was married to a woman named Mary (born ca. 1775). His first son, Aaron, was born on October 19, 1791, in Plattsburg, New York. However, shortly thereafter, he moved to Bradford, Vermont, in the eastern part of the state on the New Hampshire border, where his second son, Thomas, was born on July 29, 1792, and died less than a year later, on March 25, 1793. By 1795, Ichabod and his wife had moved about 10 miles to the west, to Corinth, Vermont, where they lived the rest of their lives. It was in Corinth, on September 23, 1795, that his son, Alexander Twilight, was born. Following Alexander were three more children, Polly (b. 6/25/1797), Asaph (b. 5/6/1802), and William (b. 3/11/1806). Ichabod Twilight and his family appear in both the 1800 and 1810 Census for Corinth, Vermont. Ichabod Twilight died sometime between 1810 and 1820, but his date of death is not known. His wife Mary lived with their son Aaron in nearby Orange, Vermont, and died in the 1820s.

The children of Ichabod Twilight and his wife Mary have been the focus of research by John Lovejoy, and their lives are well documented. Their oldest son, Aaron, was married twice, but had no children. He lived in Corinth until about 1819, when he moved to nearby Orange, Vermont, where he would live most of the rest of his life. His widowed mother, as well as his younger brothers, Asaph and William, lived with him in 1820. Aaron was a farmer and died from typhoid fever on March 24, 1861, while living on the farm of A.T. Borroughs in Orange.

The most notable of Ichabod Twilight's children was Alexander Lucius Twilight. At a young age he was indentured to a neighboring farmer. At the age of 20, he completed his term of indenture and attended Randolph Academy, followed by his entrance into Middlebury College in Vermont. Alexander graduated from college in 1823 and is claimed by Middlebury College to be the first black American college graduate. He soon after moved to Peru, New York, where he taught and was licensed to preach in 1827. About this same time, around 1826, Twilight married a white woman, Mercy Ladd Merrill, from Unity, New Hampshire. Alexander Twilight taught for a short time in Vergennes, Vermont, before coming to the village of Brownington, Vermont, in 1829. Here, he was pastor of the Congregational Church and principal of the Orleans County Grammar School. His time in Brownington was described as "eventful and even stormy" (Hayford, pg. 15) due to problems with competing schools. Because of budgetary problems, "Twilight decided to meet this threat head-on; he got himself elected to the State Legislature for a two-year term (1836–38), thus becoming, apparently, the first black American state legislator. His career was brief and unsuccessful" (*ibid.*). Continuing conflict caused Twilight to resign his school position in 1847, following which he spent five years in Quebec, Canada, teaching at Richmond and Hatley. He was invited back to Brownington, Vermont, in 1852, and given his old position back. However, in 1855 he suffered a stroke, and two years later, on June 18, 1857, he died at his home in Brownington.

He "was remembered by many students as a harsh disciplinarian, who always kept a long leather strap within reach. He was also remembered as a remarkable teacher with a strong sense of humor and a forceful, magnetic personality that set the tone for the entire institution" (*ibid.*).

Described as "short, heavy-set, and swarthy," Alexander Twilight "was a product of frontier Vermont" (Hayford, pg. 13). Without his guidance, the school he led for over 20 years failed and closed its doors in 1859. Twilight's widow, Mercy, lived in Brownington for a time, but later sold her land and moved to Derby, where she died of a fever on July 29, 1878. She is buried in the town cemetery in Brownington next to her husband. The couple had no children.

Ichabod Twilight's fourth child, Polly, was living with her brother, Aaron, in Orange in 1820, at the age of 23. Asaph, Ichabod Twilight's fifth child, lived in the area and was both a farmer and a blacksmith. He made his home in nearby Vershire, Vermont, and there married Patience Parker in 1829. He had six children, including his oldest son, Freeman Twilight, before his wife died in 1857. Asaph died on April 1, 1872.

Ichabod Twilight's youngest child, William, apparently acquired his father's taste for adventure. He moved eastward, settling for a time in Haverhill, Massachusetts, and by 1826 was in Meredith, New Hampshire, where he bought several acres of land. He was married in Gilford, New Hampshire, in May of 1834 to Sarah Crosby, and by 1840 the young couple had moved to Exeter, where William was a farmer. In 1850, he was an innkeeper in Hampton, but by 1860 had moved back to Exeter, where he was once again a farm laborer. By 1870, William and Sarah Twilight, and their youngest child, George, had moved to Raymond, where Sarah died on May 2, 1875. The oldest son of William Twilight, and second of his nine children, was William Henry Twilight. Born about 1838 in Gilford, he attended Exeter Academy briefly in 1859. No doubt inspired by his grandfather, Ichabod Twilight, he was an early volunteer in the Civil War, when he enlisted on June 8, 1861, in the 2nd NH regiment (ironically, the same regiment Ichabod served in during the Revolution) in Company K under Capt. William Sides. This regiment left for Washington, D.C., on June 20, 1861, and fought at the first Battle of Bull Run at Manassas, Virginia. William Henry Twilight was wounded during the battle and was discharged from service on July 31, 1861.

From the above, it is easy to understand the importance of Ichabod Twilight. Whether by luck, or design, he produced a son who, although now largely forgotten, gained a degree of eminence as America's first black college graduate, as well as the country's first black state legislator. In addition, his grandson, William Henry Twilight, carried on the family tradition of serving both New Hampshire, and his country.

Sources: US-Lovejoy; PSR-MSS, vol. 16; PSR-NHRWR, vol. 16; OPS-Hayford, pgs. 13–15; TH-Harriman, pg. 479; PEN-NA-M881-roll 519.

WEBB, JOHN

Webb was a resident of Stoneham, Massachusetts, near Boston, when he enlisted for Continental service on August 28, 1777, as a fifer in the company of Capt. Job Whipple in Col. Rufus Putnam's 5th Massachusetts regiment. He was described as "black" (MSS, vol. 16, pg. 746), aged 20, five feet, seven inches in height, and enlisted for his hometown, his term of service described as being "during war" (*ibid.*). The 5th Massachusetts regiment was stationed in the Hudson Highlands in New York during Webb's time with the regiment, and participated in the Saratoga campaign. However, on a list of deserters for the regiment, dated November 20, 1780, Webb's name appears. He deserted in late April of 1779, having been last seen at Boston. John Webb moved northward to New Hampshire after 1779, and appeared as a "Tranchant (transient) Person" (NHRWR, vol. 3, pg. 725) in Londonderry. He enlisted for that town on February 14, 1781, for three years in one of the New Hampshire regiments, and was described as aged 23, five feet, six inches in height, and was listed as "a molato" (*ibid.*, pg. 242). Paid the state bounty for enlisting, John Webb apparently served out his time, mostly performing garrison duty at and around West Point, New York. After the war, Webb resided for a time in Exeter, where he was married to Polly Carney. Nothing further about him is known.

Sources: PSR-MSS, vol. 16, pg. 746; PSR-NHRWR, vol. 3; OPS-Wright, pg. 207; TH-Bell.

WHITE, ARCHELAUS

Archelaus White, also known as Hercules White, was the "colored" (Pension #S43299) slave of James White of Plaistow. He was given his master's permission to enlist for military service and did so on May 4, 1775. He signed up for Massachusetts service in the company of Capt. Jeremiah Gilman in Col. John Nixon's Regiment (later designated the 4th Continental and subsequently the 6th Massachusetts regiment) for a term of about eight months on either April 23 or May 4, 1775. His birthplace was listed as New Ipswich, New Hampshire, his residence as Camden (now Washington), New Hampshire, and his occupation that of a farmer. He was described as being 21 years old, five feet, eight inches in height, with "black" eyes, but a "fair" complexion (MSS, vol. 17, pg. 45). It is not surprising that White would serve under Capt. Gilman, since he, too, was a resident of Plaistow, and was "near neighbors" (Pension #S43299) with his master, James White. Archelaus, described as a "Negro" (NHRWR, vol. 4, pgs. 7–8), also attempted to enlist in the 2nd NH regiment in the company of Capt. Samuel Gilman, but was not "Mustered, reviewed & sworn" (NHRWR, vol. 4, pg. 8) in, being one of "3 Negroes present effective able bodied men, but they are slaves" (*ibid.*). Archelaus subsequently fought with Nixon's Regiment at the Battle of Bunker Hill on June 17, 1775, and served for eight months during the Siege of Boston, being listed as serving under the main guard at Prospect Hill in July. On December 25, 1775, he was one of Gilman's company who received payment for a regimental coat while at Winter Hill. When his enlistment was up in December, White immediately re-enlisted in the same regiment for another year of service. In 1776, he went with his regiment to New York City, by way of Providence and New London in May, and took part in the disastrous New York City campaign through the summer and fall of 1776. White fought with his regiment at the Battle of White Plains, and was with Washington's main army during its retreat into New Jersey. It is also likely that White fought with the 6th Massachusetts regiment at the Battle of Trenton before his service expired "at the close of the year," when he was "verbally discharged" (Pension #S43299) at Bethlehem, Pennsylvania, in late December of 1776, or the early days of 1777.

After his Massachusetts service, Archelaus White returned to New Hampshire, probably to the Plaistow area. He served one final term in the war in 1777, when he enlisted in the company of Capt. Jesse Page in Col. Abraham Drake's regiment of New Hampshire militia raised to reinforce the Northern Army during the Saratoga campaign. White served from September 7 to December 15, 1777, in Page's company and was present at the capture of Burgoyne.

At the end of his military service, White returned to New Hampshire, where he lived the rest of his life. He lived in Exeter, and had a wife named Phillis, and at least one child, name unknown, that was born about April of 1818. For a time, Archelaus White lived with the family of Oliver Peabody of Exeter, but later lived on the Epping Road, making a living as a farmer. Archelaus White, "now very infirm and extremely poor" (*ibid.*), applied for a government pension for his military service in 1818. His claim for a pension was originally rejected due to a lack of proof and some confusion over the difference between the names Hercules and Archelaus White. His claim for a pension was finally allowed in 1820 after several men from Exeter testified that Hercules and Archelaus White were one and the same person, as well as stressing his dire need for a pension. Archelaus White died in Exeter on July 29, 1826; his wife died at Hampton in 1830.

Sources: PSR-MSS, vol. 1, pg. 286-vol. 17, pg. 45; PSR-NHRWR, vols. 2, 4; PEN-S43299; TH-Dow.

Soldiers from New Hampshire Who Served Other Colonies

While the larger part of this work is concerned with black soldiers who served for New Hampshire during the Revolutionary War, there is also another group to be considered: black soldiers who lived in New Hampshire, either before or after the war, but saw service in the war for another colony. Research thus far has identified 51 men, though there are undoubtedly more, who served for another colony during the war, but at some point lived in New Hampshire. One third of the men identified lived in New Hampshire prior to the war; the remainder lived in New Hampshire after the war. Of those soldiers who lived in New Hampshire before the war, 10 have been identified as slaves, including Pero Hall (Portsmouth), Caesar Hodgdon (Newington), Caesar Porter (Litchfield), Cocker Wiggin (Stratham), and Prince Walker (Concord). Once they received their freedom, many went to Massachusetts to serve in the war, never to return to New Hampshire as residents, perhaps understandably so. Hall was a slave for nearly 30 years before the war, but afterward took up residence in Newbury, Massachusetts. Both Caesar Porter and Prince Walker made Andover, Massachusetts, their home after the war, though Walker did return to Concord to visit from time to time. One slave, Cocker Wiggin, did not return because he was killed in action. However, some former slaves, such as Caesar Hodgdon and Pomp Peters, did return to live in New Hampshire after their service for other colonies ended. Hodgdon lived in the Newington-Portsmouth area for nearly 70 years, while Peters lived at various locations for 44 years. Several men, including Barzillai Lew (Hollis) and Prince Johonnot (Goffstown), lived in New Hampshire for only a brief time before the war, when they were warned to depart from the towns in which they resided. Johonnot, however, returned to New Hampshire after the war. One man, Silas Burdoo, despite his short stay in Jaffrey, is thought to have been the first free black to live in that town. He later moved to Vermont.

Those men who lived in New Hampshire after the war had varying connections with the state. Some men, such as Aaron Small (Goffstown), Joel Gill (Exeter), and Pomp Jackson (North Hampton), probably spent only a brief time in New Hampshire, having been warned to depart the towns in which they resided. Others, such as Cuff Chambers (Amherst), lived in New Hampshire only briefly before moving to another state. However, other men, such as Anthony Clark (Warner), Peleg Runnels (Alton), Barzillar Streeter (Swanzey), Pompey Woodward (Sullivan), Prince Johonnot (Goffstown), and Jack Driver (Portsmouth), moved to New Hampshire after the war and became long time residents. For example, Anthony Clark lived in Warner for over 50 years, and both Barzillar Streeter and Pompey Woodward lived in their communities for over 35 years. Peleg Runnels and his family lived in New Hampshire for nearly 40 years, living first at Somersworth, and then Rochester and Alton. Prince Johonnot lived in Goffstown for 35 years, and Jack Driver lived in Portsmouth for over 20 years.

The places these men came from to live in New Hampshire is also of interest. The prior residence, or area of origin, before their move to New Hampshire, is known for 33 of the men in question. As might be expected, nearly a third of them, nine men in all, came from Boston and the towns surrounding it. This is not surprising, since Boston and its environs had the largest black population in all of Massachusetts. Another 23 percent, eight men in all, came from towns located on or near the New Hampshire border, from Northfield, in western Massachusetts, to Newburyport, in the eastern part of the state. Due to that area's close social and commercial ties with New Hampshire, this, too, is not surprising. The remainder of the men who came from Massachusetts were spread throughout the state. An additional six men came from central Massachusetts, near Worcester to as far as Springfield. More unusual, five men came from points more distant in Massachusetts, including three from the far western part of the state, near New York, and two from the Cape Cod area. Finally, four men came from outside of Massachusetts to settle in New Hampshire, including two from Rhode Island, and one man each from Vermont and Virginia.

One may question why these men chose New Hampshire as their residence after the war. There are no statements from these veterans themselves detailing their reasons for moving to the state, but four possible explanations present themselves. First, those men that lived in New Hampshire for only a short time, and are listed in one Federal Census, but not subsequent ones, may have only been passing through the state on a journey to the west. They may have only stayed for a short time, perhaps to earn wages to pay for lodging and food, before continuing on. Their ultimate destination may have been the free state of Vermont, or possibly even farther to the Northwest Territory of Ohio. One black soldier, Robert Randall (Hanover), stated that he "went to the Westward to get the land granted to me as a Soldier" (Pension #S45165) and traveled to the area along the Ohio River near modern day West Virginia.

A second reason for moving to New Hampshire may have been the influence of friends and family members who also lived or settled there and encouraged them to do the same. This would be especially true for veterans who came from border towns, such as Newburyport and Andover, that had strong ties to New Hampshire. A third explanation may be one that is familiar to us today, namely that at the time they came to New Hampshire, they may have been persuaded to do so by the prospect of greater work opportunities, as well as the lower cost of land. Finally, some veterans and their families may have moved to New Hampshire to guard their freedom. The practice of kidnapping free blacks from Boston, and other seaport areas of New England, and selling them into slavery in the Southern states was not uncommon, but was much less of a danger in the more remote and less populated states of New Hampshire and Vermont.

Nearly all these men served for Massachusetts. Given the facts that it borders on New Hampshire, and that it raised 16 regiments for Continental Army service, due to higher troop quotas because of its larger population, as opposed to New Hampshire's three Continental regiments and several smaller ranger regiments, this is not surprising. Of the 51 men identified, 48 served for Massachusetts. The remaining three men, Barzillar Streeter, Peleg Runnells, and Robert Randall, all served for Rhode Island. Randall has the additional distinction of serving not only for Rhode Island, but also for Virginia, where he saw service in its navy. No black soldier from the colony of Connecticut, or any colony outside of New England, with the exception of Robert Randall from Virginia, has yet been identified as having been a resident of New Hampshire, either before or after the war.

The sources for these soldier biographies are presented in the same format as for those who served for New Hampshire, and are identified in the same manner, using the same abbreviations. All towns listed are in the state of New Hampshire, unless otherwise indicated, or obvious, such as Boston or New York.

BELL, BOSTON

Bell was the slave of Joseph Bell of Bedford, New Hampshire. He was born about 1746, place unknown, and was advertised as a runaway slave by his master on August 14, 1766, in the *New Hampshire Gazette*. Boston was described by his master as "about 20 yrs of age, a stout, lusty fellow," and "one who speaks broad Scotch." Joseph Bell offered a $3 reward for Boston's return, and stated further that "all masters of vessels are cautioned against carrying off said Negro, as they would avoid trouble." Whether Boston was captured, or returned voluntarily is unknown, but return he did. However, on December 30, 1777, he was sold to Robert Wilson of Londonderry for £84. Boston Bell enlisted for Massachusetts service on May 14, 1781, when he signed on for three years for Continental service, for the town of Ipswich. The regiment he served in is unknown,

RUNAWAY from the Subfcri-
ber, in the Night of the 14th Inft.—A Negro
Servant Man, Named BOSTON, about 20 Years of
Age, a ftout lufty Fellow; had on when he went away,
a brown homefpun Coat, lin'd with check'd Woifted,
and white Metal Buttons, likewife a diaper Jacket,
Faced with Chince, Worfted Stockings, a Felt Hatt,
Speaks broad Scotch.—Whoever fhall take up faid
NEGRO, and convey him to me in Londonderry
fhall have a Reward of three DOLLARS, and all
Charges paid by me,   JOSEPH BELL,
N. B. All Mafters of Veffels are cautioned againft
carrying off faid Negro, as they would avoid Trouble.
              Londonderry, Sept. 11. 1766.

Runaway slave ad for Boston Bell. This slave with a Scottish accent, indicative of his master's origin, later served in the war for Massachusetts. *New Hampshire Gazette*, October 10, 1766. Courtesy Portsmouth Public Library.

but was likely part of one of several Massachusetts brigades stationed at or around West Point, New York.

Several years after his service was ended, in January of 1786, Boston Bell, then a resident of Methuen, Massachusetts, brought suit against his former master, Robert Wilson, in the Rockingham County (NH) Court of Common Pleas, seeking damages of £200. He claimed that his master had assaulted and imprisoned him, and "restrained him of his liberty and sold him into the Continental Army for a Large sum of Money and Compelled him ... there in Servitude to continue & Remain for the space of three years ... against the Law of the land" (RCR #9549). Witnesses were called for Wilson's defense, however, who deposed that Boston Bell's former master, Joseph Bell, had given Boston "Leave to Choose another Master to be sold to, and he said he had Chosen Mr. Robert Wilson" (*ibid.*). Another witness stated that "the said Negro came to my Dwelling house and told me that Mr. Bell his then Master was About to Sell him and Wished or requested me (as I was a near Intimate neighbor to the said Wilson) to Use my influence to get the said Wilson to buy him as he preferred that for a home above any other" (*ibid.*). Boston Bell failed in his action against Robert Wilson, and was forced by another court action to pay Wilson for the costs he incurred in defending himself. It is unknown if this is a case where a slave was forced to enlist for military service in the war against his own free will, or whether Boston Bell had a personal enmity against his former master, perhaps because being Wilson's slave was not as pleasant as he thought it might be.

Sometime after 1790, Boston Bell married Florissa Taggart Sherburne, the widow of another black veteran, Pomp Sherburne. Bell last appears in the records when he was warned to depart the town of Londonderry in April of 1795, and subsequently moved back to Bedford.

Sources: NEW-*New Hampshire Gazette*; PSR-MSS, vol. 1, pg. 908; RCR #9549; TR-Bedford.

BENNET, BRISTER

Brister Bennet, also known as "Bristol" (MSS, vol. 1, pg. 946), was the "negro" (Pension #W24654) slave of Joseph Bennet of Cheshire, Massachusetts, a small town in Berkshire County, in the western part of the state. He enlisted for Continental service for three years on May 24, 1777, joining the company of Capt. Isaac Warren in Col. John Bailey's 2nd Massachusetts regiment. Bennet served with his regiment through the summer and fall of 1777, when it was part of the force under Gen. Benedict Arnold sent to aid in the defense of Fort Stanwick. This fort was located in western New York at the head of the Mohawk River and was manned by New York Continental troops under Col. Peter Gansevoort. Fort Stanwick was threatened by a British force of 2,000 men led by Lt. Col. Barry St. Leger, his operation being a "small diversionary effort" (Boatner, pg. 963) designed to aid Burgoyne in his main offensive against the main Continental Army further to the east. While St. Leger and his troops, many of whom were Indians, retreated before the arrival of Arnold's force, his arrival, nonetheless, helped ensure the safety of Fort Stanwick. Bennet and the men of the 2nd Massachusetts later returned to the Saratoga area, but played no significant part in the action there. As part of the main army, Bennet and his regiment spent the winter of 1777-78 at Valley Forge, Pennsylvania, and took an active part in the Battle of Monmouth on June 28, 1778. Bennet received his discharge at Fishkill, New York, in late 1779. He saw one final term of service, October 13–22, 1780, in the company of Capt. Samuel Low in Col. Benjamin Simonds's Berkshire County militia. This regiment was "marched to the Northward ... on an Alarm" (MSS, vol. 1, pg. 946), likely occasioned by the treason of Benedict Arnold at West Point, New York, in late September of 1780.

After the end of his military service, Bennet returned to Cheshire, Massachusetts. It is unknown if he was freed prior to the war, or after his military service was ended. He was married at Cheshire in 1786 or 1787 to a woman named Patience, a "black woman" (Pension #W24654) who was formerly the slave of a Mr. Lowe, by Reverend Peter Worden in the Baptist Church. Brister and Patience Bennet had four children, all of whom were likely born before the family moved to Vermont. Brister Jr. was born May 22, 1787, and James was born December 2, 1792. Two other children, names unknown, died in infancy. After their move to Vermont, about 1795, the Bennets lived on the farm of William Wolcott, of Shoreham. Their oldest son, Brister, was a "bound apprentice" (*ibid.*) for two years to Wolcott. In 1818, when he applied for a pension, Bennet lived in Benson, Vermont, and in 1820, when his pension was continued, lived in Clarendon, Vermont. About 1820, Brister Bennet left his wife in Benson and moved to New Hampshire, where he lived from 1821 to May of 1830. He moved back to Vermont, stating that his "only son resides in Vermont and I am expecting to live with him the rest of my life" (*ibid.*). This referred to his youngest son, James, since no further record of Brister Bennet, Jr., is found. However, after his return to Vermont, it seems that Brister Bennet did not live with his son, but with a white woman named Harriet, to whom he was not married. The two lived on the farm of Alanson Congdon in Clarendon, Vermont, for about a year, and then "in other houses in town ... until 1835 when he died" (*ibid.*). While he lived with Harriet, Brister "about once a year he would start for Benson (Vermont) to visit his wife, Patience" (*ibid.*).

Brister Bennet died on March 16, 1835, at Clarendon, Vermont. Soon after, Harriet Bennet testified that she was the lawful wife of Brister Bennet and applied for, and received, the arrears of his pension due at his death. Some years later, in 1839, Patience Bennet, the true widow of Brister, applied for, and also received, the arrears of her husband's pension. On January 6, 1851, James Bennet, the "only surviving child" (*ibid.*) of Patience and Brister Bennet, of Clarendon, Vermont, applied for the arrears of the pension due his mother, who died on July 14, 1844.

Sources: PSR-MSS, vol. 1, pg. 946; OPS-Boatner, pg. 963; OPS-Wright, pg. 204; PEN-W24654.

BLACK, EBENEZER

Ebenezer Black originally came from Sandwich, Massachusetts, on Cape Cod. He served briefly in the war, for an undetermined time, in 1776, in the company of Capt. Barachiah Basset during the Siege of Boston. He appears on the company payroll, dated January 13, 1776, and was paid a travel allowance to and from the company camp at Cambridge. In 1790, Black was a resident of Gilmanton, New Hampshire, where he is listed in the Federal Census as the head of household for a family of four free, non-white individuals. Nothing further regarding Black is known.

Sources: PSR-MSS, vol. 2, pg. 94; CEN-1790-NH.

BLACKMAN, POMPEY

Blackman, also known as Pompey Fortune and, late in life, Pomp Freeman, was born about 1755 and was likely a slave. When he gained his freedom is unknown, but he first enlisted for military service for Concord, Massachusetts, in 1775, serving for eight months in the regiment of Col. Samuel Gerrish (after Bunker Hill commanded by Col. Loammi Baldwin). He served first under Capt. John Wood, and subsequently in the companies of capts. John Baker and Joseph Pettengill. Following this term, Blackman served four days at Roxbury in March 1776 in the company of Capt. John Bridge, in Col. Eleazar Brooks's regiment of militia. Later in 1776, Blackman served for an unknown time in the company of Capt. Charles Miles in Col. Jonathan Reed's regiment of Massachusetts militia sent to reinforce the Northern Army at Fort Ticonderoga.

Already a seasoned veteran at the age of 21, Blackman was not yet done serving. On March 10, 1777, he signed up for a three year term in the 15th Massachusetts regiment commanded by Col. Timothy Bigelow, serving in the company of Capt. Edmund Munroe. On April 4, 1777, soon after his enlistment, Blackman granted his "Trusty Friend" (Quintal, pg. 61) Amos Fortune a power of attorney to act in his behalf on all financial matters. Fortune was a free black who was well known in the area and later lived in Jaffrey, New Hampshire. During his time in service, Blackman fought with his regiment at Saratoga and Monmouth, where his captain was killed, wintered at Valley Forge, and served for a short time in Providence, Rhode Island. He was formally discharged on March 10, 1780. Pompey Blackman served one last term when he enlisted in the company of Capt. William Green in Col. Cyprian How's regiment of militia in Rhode Island, being discharged on November 1, 1780.

After the war, Blackman was in Holliston, Massachusetts, where he filed an intent to marry Susanna Bay of that town in September 1781. Apparently, the marriage was forbidden and Pompey returned to Lexington. He was admitted to the First Congregational Church of Lexington on October 27, 1782, but was recorded as being sick. Lexington town records indicate that he died on January 1, 1783, but this is in error. By 1785 he had moved to Jaffrey, New Hampshire, where he worked in the tannery of his old friend, Amos Fortune. A surviving document dated November 25, 1785, details a loan Fortune made to Pomp Freeman in the sum of £20. This document was witnessed by another black veteran, Christopher Mann. As far as is known, Pompey Blackman, now known as Pompey Freeman, worked with Amos Fortune until his death on May 20, 1790. He is likely buried in Jaffrey near the plot occupied by Amos Fortune and his wife Violate.

Sources: PSR-MSS, vol. 2, pg. 110; TH-Annett; OPS-Quintal, pgs. 61–64.

BLANCHARD, CUFF

See the biography of Cuff Chambers.

BOSTON, CATO

Boston came from the town of Hardwick, in central Massachusetts, when he enlisted for Continental service for Massachusetts on February 19, 1781, for three years. He enlisted under Capt. Page, in Col. Rice's regiment, the designation of which is unknown. Boston was described as being aged 23, complexion "black" (MSS, vol. 2, pg. 293), and five feet, seven inches in height. His occupation was listed as that of a farmer. As part of the Massachusetts Line, he likely served garrison duty in one of the Massachusetts brigades stationed at or near West Point, New York. After the war, Cato Boston is listed in town records as a taxpayer for the town of Dublin in 1793. Nothing further is known of Cato Boston after 1793, since census and town records do not list him.

Sources: PSR-MSS, vol. 2, pg. 293; TH-Leonard, pg. 289.

BOSTON, PHILLIP

Phillip Boston is listed in the 1790 Census for New Hampshire as a free, non-white resident of a household of three individuals in Rabytown (now Brookline). Two men from Massachusetts with this name served in the war, one of whom later moved to New Hampshire. However, it is impossible to determine which one it was with any accuracy.

Boston Phillips, "alias Philip Boston" (MSS, vol. 12, pg. 311), enlisted for Continental service for Massachusetts, from the town of Holden, on October 31, 1777, in the company of Capt. John Peirce in Col. Timothy Bigelow's 15th Massachusetts regiment. His term of service was for three years, and he was discharged on December 31, 1779. During his time with the 15th Massachusetts, Boston fought at the Battle of Monmouth, and then was stationed with his regiment for a year in the Eastern Department at Providence, Rhode Island. During part of his time in Providence, Boston was in the company of Capt. William Gates. He was discharged from the service while on garrison duty in the Hudson Highlands area of New York. The second man named Phillip Boston came from the town of Carlisle, near Concord, Massachusetts. He enlisted on July 6, 1781, supposedly for three years, but his regiment was not specified. He was described as being 16 years old, five feet, three inches in height, with "black" (MSS, vol. 2, pg. 295) complexion, hair, and eyes. His occupation was listed as that of

a farmer or "labourer" (*ibid.*). Boston also appears on a list of men paid a bounty by the town of Concord for three months of service, having served in the company of Capt. John Hayward in Col. Webb's regiment of Massachusetts militia from August 15 to November 8, 1781.
Sources: CEN-1790-NH; PSR-MSS, vol. 12, pg. 311, vol. 2, pg. 295; OPS-Wright, pg. 214.

BRADLEY, THOMAS

Bradley is listed in military records as a crewmember on the ship *Lion*, commanded by Capt. Wingate Newman, in July of 1781 while in Boston. Bradley was described as being 21 years old, five feet, five inches in height, with a "dark" (MSS, vol. 2, pg. 420) complexion. It is unknown whether the *Lion* was a privateer, or a ship in the Massachusetts State Navy. This Thomas Bradley is likely the same man as the Thomas Bradley who lived in Portsmouth in 1800, where he is listed in the Federal Census for that city as a free, non-white head of a household of five free, non-white individuals.
Sources: PSR-MSS, vol. 2, pg. 420; CEN-1800-NH.

BURDOO, SILAS

The Burdoos were a family of free blacks in Massachusetts whose history has been well documented. Philip Burdoo, a man of "African descent" (Annett, pg. 114) was married in Medford on October 17, 1704, to one Ann Solomon. They soon moved to Lexington, where Philip Burdoo was admitted to the church there on December 26, 1708. The children of Philip and Ann Burdoo, all but one baptized at the church in Lexington, were Philip (b. April 10, 1709); Eunice (b. April 10, 1709, d. November 28, 1720); Moses (b. April 9, 1710, d. April 27, 1784); Aaron (b. July 27, 1712); Phineas (b. July 31, 1715, d. May 16, 1766); Lois, "A Negro" (*ibid.*) (b. March 12, 1720/21, admitted to the church at Bedford September 5, 1742).

Silas Burdoo was the third child of Philip and Mary Burdoo (d. June 19, 1785), and was born on February 14, 1748, a free black, in Lexington, Massachusetts. His brother Philip was born on March 2, 1738; his sister Mary was born on March 14, 1740 or 1741. A fourth child, name unknown, died in infancy on October 13, 1755.

Like several other black soldiers, military service was already a tradition in the family. Silas's uncle, Moses Burdoo, served in the French and Indian War and fought in Canada. While stationed at the Island of Orleans in 1759, Moses made out his will, stating, "I give my Body into the hands of Lt. Abijah Smith to be decently Buried if it shall please Almighty God to take me out of the World while I Remain under his Command" (Hudson, vol. 2, pg. 80n).

At the age of 25, Silas Burdoo moved north to New Hampshire, where he bought a plot of land on November 14, 1773, from Jonathan Parker, Jr. Identified as lot 13, range 10, it was located on the Rindge and Jaffrey town line. With this purchase, Silas Burdoo is said to be "probably the first Negro to live in Jaffrey" (Annett, pg. 115). How long Silas Burdoo lived in Jaffrey is unknown for certain, but his residence appears to have been of short duration. By the time the war began, he was a resident, again, of either Lexington or Cambridge.

Silas Burdoo first volunteered for military service on April 19, 1775, when he fought in "Capt. Boardman's company" (Pension #S21099) during the Battle of Lexington and Concord. His main action that day was not in the original fight on the Lexington town green in the early morning, but during the running battle that occurred when the British retreated from Lexington to Boston later that same day. Since there is no record of a Capt. Boardman in service for this day, it seems likely, though speculative, that Burdoo fought with Col. Loammi Baldwin's company of Woburn minutemen. These men were heavily involved in the action during the British retreat and Burdoo later enlisted in Baldwin's regiment for further service. No military records have been found for Silas Burdoo's service on this epic day, but there is no need to doubt his claim of service. The battle of Lexington and Concord was a running fight that lasted all day, with men trickling in all day to join in the fight any way they could. It is perhaps understandable that Burdoo could not remember the name of his commanding officer over 50 years later.

Following his service this day, Burdoo enlisted in the company of Capt. John Woods in Col. Samuel Gerrish's regiment of Massachusetts troops (later designated the 9th Massachusetts regiment) on May 28, 1775. The regiment's second in command was Lt. Col. Loammi Baldwin. Gerrish's regiment was one of the most controversial of those that took part in the Battle of Bunker Hill on June 17, 1775. Only part of his regiment, that led by Adj. Christian Febiger, the renowned Dane, took part in the fighting that day. The company of Capt. John Wood, with Silas Burdoo as a member, marched as far as Charlestown Common, "in plain sight of Bunker Hill ... where the celebrated Battle was then raging" (*ibid.*). While there, Wood's men "received several volleys of cannon & grape shot from the enemy" (*ibid.*), then returned to Cambridge. Afterwards, Burdoo and his company served guard duty on Prospect Hill and Inman's Point in Cambridge, later moving to Chelsea and Mystic (modern day Medford) and performing like duty. Burdoo also "stood guard at General Sullivan's quarters" (*ibid.*) while in Mystic. His name variously spelled as Bardoo, Birdoo, and Budoo, Silas Burdoo appears on company rolls for Capt. Wood, taken at Chelsea, Massachusetts, for the months of August, September, and October of 1775. Interestingly, the regiment was now commanded by Loammi Baldwin, Col. Gerrish having been cashiered for his cowardice at Bunker Hill. Burdoo continued to serve until December 22, 1775, declining to extend his service in January 1776.

Silas Burdoo served one final term six years later, when he enlisted in the company of Capt. John Hayward in Col. Webb's regiment of Massachusetts militia on September 15, 1781. He traveled to New York with one William Diamond, going by way of Springfield and "crossed the height of the green mountains at Mount Tom, near the west line" (*ibid.*) of Massachusetts. After eight days' travel he arrived at Gallows Hill, just south of West Point. Here,

> he was for a while employed on fatigue in making and repairing Roads, but ... subsequently volunteered with about ten or fifteen others, to go to Danbury in the state of Connecticut and receive one hundred and five head of Cattle designed to be driven to the American army ... then besieging Cornwallis. That the party took charge of said Cattle ... crossed the Hudson river at King's Ferry, landed the cattle on the Jersey shore, and proceeded with them to Morristown in the state of New Jersey, when he returned to Gallows Hill [*ibid.*].

Interestingly, while at King's Ferry, Burdoo saw an old acquaintance from his earlier service, Capt. John Callender. An artillery officer, Callender was cashiered from the service for his poor performance at Bunker Hill, but later won back his commission. Now stationed at Fishkill, Burdoo's term ended on December 4, 1781, having lasted two months and twenty-nine days.

Soon after the war, Silas Burdoo moved back to Rindge, New Hampshire. However, he soon removed to Reading, Vermont, where he is listed in town records in 1784. Both Silas and Aaron Burdoo, another cousin, are listed in the 1790 Census as the heads of household of a family of three free, non-white individuals of Reading. The Burdoos became well established in this area and were held in high standing. Silas had two wives, the first being Betsey, who died in Reading on August 7, 1816, at the age of 65. They may have had one child, but the records are silent in this regard. Silas's second wife was Rosannah. Silas Burdoo was granted a pension for his war service in March 1833. His wife Rosannah died on October 3, 1836, at the age of 73. Silas died soon after, on January 23, 1837, at the age of

The family plot of soldier Silas Burdoo. Burdoo and his two wives are buried in Bailey Mill's Cemetery in Reading, Vermont. Silas first saw service during the Battle of Lexington and Concord in 1775. After the war, he eventually moved to Reading where he resided until his death on January 23, 1837. The gravestone for Silas Burdoo is in the foreground, at far right. Photograph courtesy Tony Pickramenos.

89. Silas Burdoo and both his wives, as well as other relatives, are buried in Bailey's Mills Cemetery, where their gravestones can still be seen today.

One descendant of Silas Burdoo was his namesake second cousin and son to Aaron Burdoo, Silas Burdoo. Born on March 28, 1826, the younger Silas later lived in Woodstock, Vermont, and was said to have the largest personal library of anyone in the area. At the age of 37, Silas Burdoo continued his family's military tradition by enlisting for service in the Civil War. He mustered in with the 54th Massachusetts Regiment, the first Northern regiment to be formed with black enlisted personnel, on December 19, 1863, and served until September 1, 1865. Participating in the Southern campaign, Burdoo fought with his unit, in Company H, at Olustee and the Siege of Charleston. After the war, he returned to Woodstock and was a farmhand for the Ralph and Walker families in that town. At his death on November 18, 1900, due to a stroke, he had served the Walker family for 43 years. Described as "faithful, intelligent, industrious, a great reader, and a man very much liked by every one" (*Spirit of the Age*, 11/24/1900, pg. 4), this Civil War veteran is buried in the Walker Cemetery in South Woodstock, Vermont.

The Revolutionary War soldier Silas Burdoo had one brother, Philip Burdoo, who is listed as a free, non-white in the 1790 Census for Hampton (NH). Phillip Burdoo came to Hampton from Moultonborough and married Dinah Small on January 9, 1783. She was the widow of Caesar Small, a black soldier who died during the war. Phillip Burdoo worked in Dearborn's tavern in Hampton, and died on January 6, 1806. Dinah Small Burdoo was originally the slave of William Godfrey of North Hampton. After Phillip's death, she lived in a small house near the center schoolhouse, "where she spun and knit and lived contentedly" (Dow, pg. 287). In 1809, at an "advanced age," she was sent to live with the family of Josiah Dearborn, "where she can be taken proper care of till spring" (*ibid.*). The town paid Dearborn four shillings a week to board and care for Dinah, which was preferable to incurring "the expense of hauling her wood" (*ibid.*) to help heat her house.

The gravestone of Silas Burdoo (next generation). Buried in the Walker Cemetery in South Woodstock, Vermont, this Silas was the second cousin to Revolutionary War soldier Silas Burdoo. Living in Woodstock, he continued his family's tradition of military service by serving in the famed 54th Massachusetts Regiment during the Civil War. Photograph courtesy Tony Pickramenos.

Dinah continued in the care of the town and was living with Deacon John Lamprey when she died at the age of 92 on January 11, 1825.

Silas Burdoo only lived in Jaffrey for a short time, but other members of the Burdoo family lived in that community for nearly 70 years. Silas's cousin Moses (born in Lexington on July 20, 1755), perhaps following the lead of his older cousin, moved to Jaffrey after his marriage to Lois Ralf of Boston on December 3, 1778. On May 20, 1779, he bought 70 acres of land in town. On January 31, 1788, Moses sold his land to Amos Merritt of Lexington and later worked as a blacksmith. He died prior to August 1, 1790, leaving his wife and five children. In dire financial straits, Lois Burdoo was forced to send her children elsewhere to live. At least one child, Polly

(b. 1779), was sent to live with Amos and Violate Fortune, a prominent and well to do free black couple.

Amos Fortune was a former slave of Boston and Woburn, Massachusetts, who learned the trade of a tanner and purchased his freedom from his master, Ichabod Richardson, in 1770. In 1778, he purchased the freedom of a slave in Lexington named Lydia Somerset, and married her. When she died after several months, he bought and wed Violate Baldwin. Given his activities in the Lexington area, it is likely that Amos Fortune was well acquainted with the large Burdoo family. Perhaps at the behest of the Burdoos, Amos and Violate Fortune moved to Jaffrey in 1781. Amos set up a tannery and became a prominent citizen in town, joining the church and was a founding member of the Social Library. Amos Fortune died in Jaffrey on November 17, 1801, and Violate died the following year, on September 13, 1802.

Despite their wealth, the Fortunes helped out Lois Burdoo, taking in at least one child, and possibly another, to support. Polly Burdoo died at the Fortune residence in December 1793 at the age of 15. Her mother, Lois Burdoo, outlived all her children, dying "in the Poor House on June 3, 1847, aged 92, a long life but not a merry one" (Annett, pg. 116). While the elaborate gravestones of Amos and Violate Fortune can still be seen today, the same cannot be said of the Burdoo family. "The earth closed over them like the waters over one lost at sea and no mark remains of their place of burial to this day" (*ibid.*).

Sources: TH-Annett, pgs. 114–16; Dow, pg. 287; Hudson pgs. 80–81; TR-Rindge, Hampton, vol. 2, pg. 34, vol. 3, pgs. 1094, 1102; PSR-MSS, vol. 1, pg. 599, vol. 2, pgs. 69, 766, 828–29; CEN-1790-Vt, NH; OPS-French, pgs. 215, 220, 233, 242; OPS-Kaplan, pgs. 261–62; US-Griggs and Swain; OPS-Emilio, pg. 373; OPS-Urban, pg. 3; NEW-*Spirit of the Age* (Vermont), 11/24/1900; OPS-Quintal.

CHAMBERS, CUFF

Cuff Chambers was born about 1738 in Massachusetts. Only the last name of his parents is known. A resident of Andover, Massachusetts, he was married to Betty (last name unknown) on September 16, 1762. Both were listed as "Negro Servants" (Quintal, pg. 79). Prior to the war, Cuff was owned by Samuel Blanchard of Andover and was promised his freedom at war's end if he served.

Using his master's last name, Cuff Blanchard enlisted for military service on May 28, 1775, in the company of Capt. Charles Furbush in Col. Ebenezer Bridges's regiment of Massachusetts troops. Chambers was with

III. The Men

The gravestone of soldier Cuff Chambers. Laid to rest in the Dead River Cemetery in Leeds, Maine, he served under the name Cuff Blanchard and fought at the Battle of Bunker Hill in Furbush's company in Bridges's regiment of Massachusetts men. After the war, Chambers lived in Amherst, New Hampshire, for a short time before moving to Leeds. Photograph courtesy Ceceilia Knoblock.

his unit during the Battle of Bunker Hill and likely saw heavy action, since his captain was severely wounded. According to one historian, "Cuff was one of at least five men of color who served in Bridges's regiment" (Quintal, pg. 79). Following this action, Chambers served out the rest of his eight-month term. While at Cambridge on November 21, 1775, he received a bounty for coat money along with other members of his company. He was discharged in December 1775.

Though no proof exists, Cuff Blanchard was freed sometime after 1775, and then went by his original name of Cuff Chambers. In the years following, he moved from Andover to Amherst, New Hampshire, and from there to Leeds, Maine, by 1808, where he and his wife Betty lived the rest of their days. Betty, listed as "Elizabeth Chambers a black woman" (Quintal, pg. 80) joined the Leeds Baptist Church. Various government and town records indicate that Cuff and Betty had five children: two, whose names are unknown and were born before April 1775; Thaddeus (b. about 1782, d. before 1849); Mary (b. about 1785, d. prior to 1849); and Elizabeth (b. about 1787, d. after 1849).

While in Leeds, Cuff Chambers and his family experienced the financial difficulties common to many black veterans. They were town paupers from 1814 to 1816, living on the support of the town of Leeds, which in turn asked the town of Andover, Massachusetts, to contribute to their support. At about the age of 80, Cuff Chambers died in Leeds on June 8, 1818. His wife survived him for nearly 21 years, dying on January 26, 1839. Chambers's grave can still be seen today in the Dead River Cemetery in Leeds. Because of his limited service, Cuff Chambers never received a pension for his war service. However, his surviving daughter Elizabeth (Betty) Roberts applied for a pension based on his service on March 19, 1849. Much of what is known about Cuff Chambers comes from the affidavit she filed.

Sources: PSR-MSS, vol. 1, pg. 144; OPS-Quintal, pgs. 79–80; Pen-W23810.

CLARK, ANTHONY

Anthony Clark, a "black" (Pension #W9388) man, was born in Charlestown, Massachusetts, about 1752. It is unknown if he was a slave, or free born. In 1779 he was a resident of Dracut, Massachusetts, when he enlisted for that town on October 23, 1779, in the company of Capt. Solomon Pollard in Col. Samuel Denny's regiment of Massachusetts militia that was likely raised for the defense of Rhode Island. Clark served for one month and twelve days, receiving his discharge on December 4, 1779. Clark enlisted for service again, undoubtedly as a free man, in 1781, when he enlisted for Continental service on February 9 in the company of Capt. Joseph Bates in Lt. Col. John Brooks's 7th Massachusetts regiment. The 7th Massachusetts had previously served in the campaign against the Iroquois Indians in 1778-79, when its original commander, Ichabod Alden, was killed at Cherry Valley, New York. During Clark's service, the regiment was stationed mostly in the Hudson Highlands area of New York, near West Point, serving garrison duty as part of the 1st Massachusetts Brigade. Clark appears on muster rolls for his company at such locations as Camp Peekskill and at York Huts through February of 1782, and at one time was listed as "on command at the lines" (MSS, vol. 3, pg. 582).

Clark was described in company records as having "black" (*ibid.*) hair, eyes, and complexion, was five feet, three inches in height, and was aged 19 when he enlisted. Company records also state his occupation at various times as a farmer, laborer, or cordwainer (a skilled leather worker). Anthony Clark, also known as "Toney" (*ibid.*), was furloughed from service on June 12, 1783, and received his final discharge on November 15, 1783, when his regiment was disbanded after the peace treaty was signed.

After the war, at an unknown time between 1790 and 1798, Clark moved to New Hampshire. He first lived in Dunbarton, where his house was destroyed by fire about 1798. Clark later moved to Warner, where he was married to Lucinda (Lucy) Moore, who was also described as "black" (Pension #W9388), on January 12, 1804, by Reverend William Kelly.

The Clarks had seven children that are known, including Lucy (b. ca. 1804); Anna (b. ca. 1805); Simon (b. ca. 1806); Mary (b. ca. 1808); Lucy (b. ca. 1813); Timothy (b. ca. 1816); and Bula (b. ca. 7/1819). Tony Clark was well known in Warner, and certainly well liked. He was known for playing the fiddle and acting as "inspector-general" on the traditional Muster Day festivities, as well as being a "dancing-master" (Worthen, pgs. 504–5). The town historian of Sutton paid Clark a great compliment when he wrote that Clark "probably did more towards instructing the young people in the arts and graces of politeness and good manners than any other man of his day and generation" (*ibid.*). In April of 1818, Anthony Clark, now aged 66, applied for a government pension for his military service. Despite the fact that his original discharge papers were destroyed when his house in Dunbarton burned down, his claim for a pension was granted in 1819. Among those who helped him get his pension was retired Brig. Gen. John Brooks of Medford, Massachusetts, his old regimental commander 36 years earlier.

Anthony Clark lived the rest of his life in Warner, until his death, according to pension records, on January 4, 1854. However, his gravestone at Pine Hill Cemetery in Warner lists his date of death as January 8, 1856, at the age of 100 years. It is doubtful whether Clark's true age was known, since other sources say that he died at age 107. The military funeral that he was given in honor of his war service

The gravestone of soldier Anthony Clark in Pine Hill Cemetery, Warner, New Hampshire. Records vary as to the date of Clark's death and his age, but one fact is indisputable: He achieved a level of respect in his community seldom accorded to most free black veterans in the state. Photograph by Glenn Knoblock.

was called a "splendid affair" (*ibid.*). Shortly after her husband's death, Lucinda Clark, now aged 64, filed a claim as a veteran's widow, and the following year applied for a grant of bounty land based on her husband's service. Her application was granted, and on July 12, 1856, she was granted 60 acres of land, followed by another grant for an additional 100 acres on February 14, 1857. It is not known whether Lucinda Clark subsequently sold this land to speculators, as was often the case. Lucinda Clark outlived her husband for six years, dying on May 26, 1862, at the age of 70.

Sources: PSR-MSS, vol. 3, pg. 582; OPS-Wright-pg. 209; OPS-Heitman, pg. 123; TH-Worthen, pgs. 504–05; PEN-W9388.

COBURN, TITUS

Titus Coburn has been identified as a black soldier by historian George Quintal, Jr., on the basis of his first name. The name "Titus" was one that was commonly given to slaves during the Colonial era. The first known record of Titus Coburn is dated November 12, 1771, when he filed marriage intentions at Harvard, Massachusetts. His wife to be was named Peggy Whittemore, and Coburn's place of residence is listed as Camden, New Hampshire. The town of Camden, renamed Washington in 1776, was first settled by families from Massachusetts in 1768. It may be that Titus was a slave of one of these families. In any case, his residence there in 1771 makes him one of the town's early settlers, maybe even the first black man to reside there. However, his stay there was short, since the census for that town conducted in 1773 lists no persons of color.

Coburn first saw service during the Lexington Alarm on April 19, 1775. He marched from Shirley as a minuteman in the company of Capt. Henry Haskell, in Col. James Prescott's regiment. The Shirley men did not participate in the running battle of that day, but Coburn continued on duty for 17 days during the opening phase of the Siege of Boston. Coburn, his name spelled variously as Coburn, Colbrn, and Colburn, soon signed up for an eight-month term of service in the company of Capt. Ephraim Corey in Col. William Prescott's regiment on May 6, 1775. As part of Prescott's regiment, Titus Coburn saw heavy action during the Battle of Bunker Hill on June 17, 1775, being stationed in the redoubt where his company lost several men killed. The following day, his name appears on a list of men who needed cartridge boxes while at camp in Cambridge. This was likely because he had expended all his ammunition during the previous day's battle. Following this, Coburn is listed as serving in the main guard under the command of Lt. Col. Loammi Baldwin on June 22, 1775. Coburn continued in the service in Prescott's regiment under Capt. Corey and Lt. Nathaniel Sartell. On October 31, 1775, his name appears on an order for a bounty coat. He was discharged at an unknown date, probably in December 1775.

Titus Coburn served another term in 1776, when he joined the company of Capt. Fortunatus Eager in Col. Josiah Whitney's regiment of Massachusetts militia. This regiment marched to New Jersey to reinforce Washington's army on December 17, 1776, and may have taken part in the Battle of Trenton. Coburn was discharged on March 27, 1777, having served 3½ months.

However, within two weeks, on April 14, 1777, Coburn again enlisted for service, joining the company of Capt. Joshua Brown in Col. Timothy Bigelow's 15th Massachusetts regiment. Coburn and his regiment took part in the Battle of Saratoga, and afterward moved south to join Washington's Main Army in Pennsylvania. While at Valley Forge, Titus Coburn died on April 14, 1778, likely due to an illness.

Sources: OPS-Quintal, pg. 87; PSR-MSS, vol. 3, pgs. 687, 695, 736, 744; OPS-Heitman, pg. 171; OPS-*Memorial of the American Patriots*, pg. 116.

CROCKER, JEREMIAH

Jeremiah Crocker, his last name also spelled as "Croker," is designated as a "Negro" (MSS, vol. 4, pgs. 120–1) in Massachusetts military records. There were probably two men named Jeremiah Crocker who served for Massachusetts during the war, but records would seem to indicate that the man covered in this biography served several terms of service from 1777 to 1780. The man who served from Dedham during the Siege of Boston is likely not the same man, but the possibility exists that all the records for Massachusetts pertain to just one individual.

Crocker is believed to have been born in Natick, Massachusetts, the slave of Thaddeus Gibson, of Bellingham, Massachusetts, in whose family he lived after the war when they moved to the town of Henniker in late 1780 or early 1781.

Crocker is believed to have first seen service on April 21, 1777, when he enlisted in the company of Capt. Samuel Fisher, of Wrentham, Massachusetts, in Col. Ephraim Wheelock's regiment of militia. This regiment marched to Rhode Island on the alarm of April 21, 1777, and served for 12 days. It was drafted for an additional two months' service, from May 3, 1777, in the regiment of Col. Jonathan Titcomb. Since Wrentham is a neighboring town of Bellingham, the Jeremiah Crocker who served under Capt. Fisher is believed to be the same man associated with Thaddeus Gibson. Jeremiah "Croker" (*ibid.*) entered another term of service when he enlisted for another 25 days in Rhode Island in the Wrentham company of Lt. Hezekiah Ware in Col. Nathaniel Wade's regiment of Massachusetts militia, from June 20 to July 14, 1778. Crocker saw one final term of service in 1780, when he enlisted for six months of Continental service on July 9, 1780. He is listed as serving for Medway, Massachusetts, a town close to both Wrentham and Bellingham, and is described as having the complexion of a "Negro" (*ibid.*), aged 29, with a height of five feet, eight inches. He was marched to camp at Springfield, Massachusetts, by an artillery officer, Lt. Jackson, and was received there by Brig. Gen. John Glover. Crocker likely saw duty during his six months of service at or around the vicinity of West Point, New York, performing garrison duty.

After his service ended in late 1780, or early 1781, Crocker soon after, according to tradition, came to Henniker, New Hampshire, to live with the family of Thaddeus Gibson. However, although Gibson is listed in the 1790 Census for Henniker, there are no non-whites or slaves listed as residing with him. Jeremiah Crocker does not appear in the census records until 1800, when he is listed as the head of a household of six free, non-white individuals in Henniker. Local tradition further states that Crocker was a drummer in the war, and that he often went by the title of Maj. Crocker. This was probably in deference to his military service, and he, like Anthony Clark, may have been prominent at local Muster Day festivities, perhaps playing the drum as he did during the war. Crocker died on June 11, 1836, at the age of "about 100" years, according to his gravestone. He is buried in Center Cemetery in Henniker, a short distance from Thadeus Gibson.

Sources: PSR-MSS, vol.

The gravestone of Jeremiah Crocker. Buried in Center Cemetery in Henniker, New Hampshire, Crocker was a soldier of the Revolution who served for Massachusetts and later moved to Henniker with his master, Thaddeus Gibson. Crocker died in 1836, "about 100 years" old. Photograph by Glenn A. Knoblock.

4, pgs. 120–21, 135; CEN-1790, 1800-NH; TH-Cogswell; TR-Henniker, vol. 3, pgs. 10, 194, 198.

DODGE, HAMPSHIRE

Dodge's connection with New Hampshire is based solely on his name. Though he is not identified specifically as a black man, the name Hampshire was commonly given to slaves who at one time resided in that colony. Dodge served aboard the Continental Navy frigate *Boston*, being listed as a member of Capt. Hector McNeill's crew on a list dated July 16, 1777. Described as being in the larboard watch, Dodge manned gun #10 on the 32-gun warship. Other blacks who served aboard the *Boston*, most from Massachusetts, were Scippio Brown, Cuff Wood, Cato Wood, Nero Freeman, Cuff Freeman, Caesar Fairweather, Caesar Lee, and Prince Gilbert. *Sources:* NHGR, vol. 4, pgs. 30–32.

DRIVER, JOHN/JACK

John, also known as "Jack" (MSS, vol. 2, pg. 979), Driver was a sailor during the Revolution. He served aboard the privateer *Jason*, commanded by Capt. John Manly, of Boston, and experienced firsthand the war at sea. The story of the activities of the *Jason* are fascinating, and give some idea of the dangers faced by Driver, but it is unfortunate that there is no record of the role that he played during her several cruises. He may originally have come from Salem, Massachusetts, from which several other soldiers and sailors with the same last name came.

Captain Manly had previously been commander of the Continental Navy 32-gun frigate *Hancock*, built at Boston. The *Hancock* was captured by the HMS *Rainbow* in June of 1777. After being released from captivity, Manly returned to Boston, where he took command of the 16-gun privateer *Cumberland* early in 1779. However, bad luck followed Manly and he was captured during his first cruise by the HMS *Pomona* and carried to the Barbados as a prisoner. Undaunted, Manly soon escaped and returned to Boston, where he was given command of the privateer *Jason*, a ship of 20 guns manned by 100 men. The *Jason* sailed from Boston on or about June 25, 1779, and headed for Portsmouth, where her second officer was busy recruiting crew members. Though John Driver may have come from Boston and been recruited there, it is most likely that he was recruited in Portsmouth. Driver was engaged as the quartermaster on the *Jason*.

After securing a full crew, the *Jason* departed Portsmouth Harbor and within several days encountered two ships under full sail. Thought at first to be friendly, they soon gave chase to the *Jason*, and by the time she reached the Isle of Shoals, off Portsmouth Harbor, were close to gunshot range. However, at this time a sudden squall struck the *Jason*, dismasting the ship and turning her deck into a shambles. One man was caught under a sail and drowned. The crew soon got to work, setting up a jury rig and stood off the entrance to Portsmouth Harbor. While Capt. Manly went into Portsmouth to secure the needed masts and rigging, he did not allow his ship to make port for fear his sailors would desert him. When Manly returned to his ship, he found the crew in a mutinous state, refusing to work until the ship made port. Manly boldly confronted the ringleaders of the mutiny, two of whom he struck with his cutlass. Once this happened, the rest of the crew soon went back to work, getting the *Jason* repaired in 36 hours. Just as he was ready to depart the Portsmouth area, Manly sighted the American privateer *Hazard*, of Boston, and was informed that he was to "repair to the Penobscot without fail" (Maclay, pg. 196). However, Manly did not obey orders, and thus avoided the loss of his ship in that ill-fated expedition. Instead, he set sail for New York, arriving off Sandy Hook in late July. On the 25th, Manly's crew caught sight of several sails, and the chase was on. The fast sailing *Jason* soon caught up with two vessels, which immediately hoisted the English flag and fired upon her. Manly responded by sailing his ship alongside the enemy and "opened fire with every gun that would bear," which "caused great havoc aboard the stranger, killing many men and wounding more" (Maclay, pg. 197). Once Manly had subdued this vessel, he set off in pursuit of its companion. When the *Jason* was within gunshot, a few well-placed shots from her bow guns forced the English vessel to heave to, and she was ordered to send a boat aboard the *Jason* to complete her surrender. The English vessel delayed, and refused to send her boat until Manly finally called out "You shall come on board or I will fire into you" (*ibid.*). The English vessel took heed of Manly's warning and sent her boat aboard to effect her surrender. The vessels both turned out to be privateer brigs of 18 guns, one, the *Hazard*, hailing from Liverpool, and the other, the *Adventurer*, hailing from Glasgow. Captain Manly secured his prizes, put his prisoners in irons, and took them to Boston.

After only a few days in port, Manly set sail again in the *Jason*, this time in pursuit of a large convoy of English merchantmen bound for home. Off Nantucket Shoals he caught up with the convoy and made his way among them. However, he was soon detected and was nearly captured by a faster sailing escort before the fog crept in and allowed him to escape. A few days later, Manly and the *Jason* fell in with the Continental frigates

Deane and *Boston*, sailing in company with them for nearly two weeks before parting company. Nearly two weeks later, the *Jason* saw action again when she captured a 16-gun English privateer with a cargo of foodstuffs heading for the Barbados. The prize was secured, manned, and sent safely to Boston. Several days later, on September 30, 1779, another sail was sighted in the distance. Captain Manly recognized the stranger as "a ship of force" (Maclay, pg. 201), and piled on sail in an attempt to outrun her. However, by 11 P.M. the stranger had caught up with the *Jason*, and identified herself as the British frigate *Surprise*. When the British frigate demanded to know what ship she was dealing with, Capt. Manly replied that he was the "United States 32-gun frigate *Deane*" (*ibid.*). The British responded by telling Manly to "Heave to or we will fire into you." Manly shot back with the words "Fire away and be damned. We have got as many guns as you," and the battle ensued with the *Surprise* firing the first broadside (*ibid.*). Manly delayed his firing until he came to close range, then let go with a broadside that knocked out two of the enemy's forward guns. The battle raged until 1 A.M., when the *Jason*'s forward guns were silenced and her crew refused to fight further. Captain Manly, realizing he had no chance, called for quarter and surrendered the *Jason*, which had 18 killed and 12 wounded during the fight. The *Surprise* suffered seven killed, and a similar number wounded. The crew of the *Jason*, John Driver included, were carried to the British base at St. John's, Nova Scotia, and held there. Manly himself was sent to notorious Mill Prison in England, where he was exchanged in 1782. Driver is listed as being captured, "but not committed" (MSS, vol. 2, pg. 979). This likely meant that he was held in Nova Scotia, rather than being sent to prison in England, or to one of the notorious prison ships in New York. John Driver was released after two years, on October 15, 1781.

Whether Driver was originally from Portsmouth is unknown, but he returned there to live. In January of 1793 he married Dinah Dearborn in Portsmouth and, five years later, was married yet again to June (Jenney) Tarleton by the Reverend Joseph Buckminster. The following year, on July 21, 1799, John Driver's wife, Jenney, and his daughter, Katherine, were baptized in Portsmouth. Driver continued in Portsmouth for some years. He is listed in the 1800 Census as a free, non-white with his wife and daughter, and in 1812 brought suit against one Anthony Pedro in the Rockingham County Common Pleas Court. In 1821, Driver is listed in the Portsmouth city directory as a resident on Pickering Lane.

Sources: PSR-MSS, vol. 2, pg. 979; OPS-Maclay, pgs. 192–204; OPS-Boatner, pg. 672; CEN-1800-NH; TR-Portsmouth, vol. 4, pg. 418, vol. 11, pg. 224; RCR #A24721; OPS-Portsmouth City Directory, pg. 76.

FOGG, FORTUNE

Fortunatus, also known as Fortune, was a "Negro boy" (Dow, pg. 288) baptized in Hampton in 1741, the slave of Abner Fogg. Nothing is known of his early years, but in May of 1777 he enlisted for Massachusetts Continental service in the company of Capt. Isaac Warren in Col. John Bailey's 2nd Massachusetts regiment. Fortune Fogg signed up for three years, for and from the town of Great Barrington, Massachusetts, in Berkshire County. While with his regiment, Fogg served in the Saratoga campaign, and spent the winter at Valley Forge, where his name appears on the company muster roll dated January 24, 1778. Fogg fought with his regiment at Monmouth, and served afterward while it was stationed in the Hudson Highlands area of New York. Fogg was discharged from the army on May 15, 1780, having served his three years. After the war, he returned to New Hampshire, residing in Exeter, a town adjacent to Hampton, where he was previously baptized. Fortune Fogg is listed in the 1790 Census for Exeter as a free, non-white head of a household of six other free, non-white individuals. He also appears again in the 1800 Census for Exeter, listed simply as "Fortune," with no last name, this time the head of household for three other free, non-white individuals. Nothing further is known of Fortune Fogg after 1800.

Sources: TH-Dow, pg. 288; PSR-MSS, vol. 5, pg. 823; CEN-1790, 1800-NH.

FREEMAN, POMP/POMPEY

See the biography of Pompey Blackman.

GILL, JOEL

Little is known about Joel Gill, either before the war, or after. He enlisted as a private in the company of Capt. James Tisdale, of Medfield, Massachusetts, in Col. Michael Jackson's 3rd Massachusetts regiment for Continental service. Though it is uncertain, Joel Gill may have previously been the slave of Benjamin Gill, of Stoughton, Massachusetts, a town close to Medfield. Benjamin Gill was first a lieutenant colonel, and subsequently a colonel, commanding his own regiment of militia in Massachusetts during the war. Joel Gill enlisted for three years of service in January of 1783 while his regiment was stationed at the Hudson Highlands, around West Point, New York. It is not known when Gill was discharged, but he appears on company rolls for August and September of 1783. He was likely discharged at West Point on November 3, 1783, when the 3rd Massachusetts regiment was officially disbanded at the war's official end.

After the war, Joel Gill is listed in the 1790 Census as a resident of Exeter, the head of a household of three, free, non-white individuals, likely his wife and child. On April 21, 1790, Joel Gill, a "Negro Man" (RCR #11910), and his wife and children were warned from the town of Exeter. His activities following this are unknown.

Sources: PSR-MSS, vol. 6, pgs. 437–38; OPS-Wright, pg. 205; CEN-1790-NH; RCR #11910.

HAFFORD, PRINCE

Virtually nothing is known about this black soldier, and his inclusion in this work is somewhat doubtful. On April 20, 1778, he enlisted for Salem, Massachusetts, in the Continental Army for nine months' service, the regiment he served in being unspecified. He was described as having a "dark" complexion, and "black" (MSS, vol. 7, pg. 22) hair and eyes. He was aged 22, with a height of five feet, six inches. He arrived at Fishkill, New York, near West Point, on June 23, 1778. Though nothing further is known about Hafford's service, his residence was listed as Chester. However, the records do not state whether this was Chester, New Hampshire, or Chester, Massachusetts, thereby giving rise to some uncertainty. Chester, New Hampshire, is much closer to Salem, the town for which Prince Hafford enlisted, but Chester, Massachusetts, is in the western part of the state, close to New York, where Hafford traveled to perform his nine months of service. It was not unusual for towns throughout New England, like Salem, to recruit men from other towns, both in and out of the colony, near and far, to help them fill their quota of soldiers for the army.

Sources: PSR-MSS, vol. 7, pg. 22.

HALE, AESOP/ESOP

Little is known about Aesop Hale, who served early in the war in one of the Continental Army's most distinguished and important regiments. He enlisted for Continental service on February 1, 1776, in the company of Capt. Moses Brown in Col. John Glover's 14th Continental Regiment. This regiment was composed mostly of Marblehead, Massachusetts, fishermen and was renowned in its exploits for transporting Washington's army to safety under difficult situations. They accomplished this feat both after the Battle of Long Island, and during the famous crossing of the Delaware River on the evening of December 24-25, 1776, en route to the surprise attack, and subsequent victory, on the Hessian outpost at Trenton, New Jersey. Hale appears on pay abstracts for Glover's regiment through August of 1776, but likely served until the regiment was disbanded in Pennsylvania on December 31, 1776.

Soon after the war, "Esop" Hale came to Exeter, where he married Lucy Sinegall, who was designated as a "Negro" (Bell, pg. 54), on April 3, 1777. Since this marriage occurred within months from the end of Hale's war service, it is probable that he was previously acquainted with the area, and may have even resided in Exeter before the war. It is also likely that his new wife, Lucy, was an ex-slave who probably was transported from the area of the West African coast known as Senegal, a location much frequented by slave traders. Aesop Hale may have been a mariner, since he is not listed in the 1790 Census for Exeter, but appears in the 1800 Census for the town as a free, non-white individual. Unfortunately, further details regarding Hale and his family are lacking.

Sources: PSR-MSS, vol. 7, pg. 44; TH-Bell, pg. 54; CEN-1800-NH; OPS-Wright, pg. 218.

HALL, PERO

Hall was a freeborn "Mollatto or Negro man" (NH Superior Court Records, vol. 31, pg. 463) who was born about 1720. His first name is likely a derivative of the name "Pharaoh," one that was common for slaves in Colonial times. His origin and early life details are unknown, but on August 14, 1746, he was married to Catherine Small of Ipswich in Newbury, Massachusetts. In 1747 he was living in Portsmouth when he was indicted for the theft of £25 6s. from Charles Gorwood. Hall requested a jury trial and was found guilty of the charge on December 7, 1747, being forced to pay Gorwood triple the value of the money he stole, plus an additional £3 6s. for court costs. One of those who testified for Hall was George Massey, "the master of said Pero" (NH General Sessions Records, Dec. 1, 1747). Hall must have paid what he owed, since it was also ordered by the court that he would receive "ten stripes on his naked back at the post" (*ibid.*) if he failed to follow the court's ruling.

In 1748, Hall was in the courts yet again when he filed an "Action of Trespass" (NH Common Pleas Court, March 10, 1748, pg. 315) against George Massey. Hall claimed that he was "a Free Man born and as such had a Right to his Liberty," but claimed that Massey had "Restrained him of his Liberty" and "Detained him ... as a Servant for Life for the Term of Two years" (*ibid.*). The Common Pleas Court ruled, with the mutual consent of both sides, that, while "the Negro Pero Hall was free born," he "should faithfully serve the said George Massey ... for the term of six years from this day" (*ibid.*). It was further stipulated that Hall "should behave himself as a true, honest & faithfull servant," and that Massey "shall provide ... sufficient meat, drink, washing & lodging and apparrell" (*ibid.*). Later in 1748, Pero Hall's indenture was sold to William Blair, an innkeeper in Londonderry.

Pero Hall was involved in the court system in New Hampshire yet another time in 1749, the third time in as many years. This time he was ordered on July 29, 1749, to be questioned regarding the case of his master, William Blair, and one John Mitchell, against Jotham Odiorne. Blair and Mitchell, among others, were accused of sending two anonymous, "menacing" letters to Odiorne, "demanding the sum of 500 pounds lawful money" (NHSP, vol. 5, pg. 128), on July 14. If this money was not left "on the long bridge between Kingstown & Chester," they threatened "to destroy his person & estate" (*ibid.*). These letters were given to one Robert Elliot Gerrish at Newbury, Massachusetts, by Pero Hall, who "said his Master sent it" (*ibid.*). Hall was detained for a time "in ye Custody of ye Sheriff" (NHSP, vol. 5, pg. 129), but was "dismissed out of the Sherriffs Custody" (*ibid.*) in August of 1749, because the court's business was finished for the term.

Following this court business, Hall disappears from the records for a time, but comes to light again in 1761, when his name appears on a list of soldiers who served during the French and Indian War. Pero Hall is listed in the company of Capt. Samuel Gerrish in Col. John Goffe's New Hampshire regiment that were supplied by the sutlers Porter and Caldwell for sundry items during that year. It is unknown how long Hall served under Capt. Gerrish, but he probably saw service during the 1760 campaign against the French in upstate New York. Pero Hall's military service was over by 1763, when he was a resident of Newmarket. He was warned from that town on May 9, 1763, along with his wife Jean and their child Ann. Stating that they had "come from Exeter to dwell in Newmarket," they were warned to leave within 14 days, to return "into Exeter again," or to "secure Sufficient Security to the Select men for the time being to Indemnify the said town against Cost or Charge that may hereafter arise" (RCR-1763). Whether Hall and his family returned to Exeter is unknown. However, by the time of the Revolution, Pero Hall was a resident of Newbury, Massachusetts, a town with which he was already familiar.

When the American Revolution began in 1775, Pero Hall was approximately 55 years old. Despite his age, he enlisted early in the contest to fight the British, joining the company of Capt. Jonathan Evans in Col. James Frye's Regiment of men raised from Essex County, Massachusetts.

Hall's exact date of enlistment is unknown, but his name appears on a return of men at camp in Cambridge, dated May 17, 1775. Hall was likely one of the 450 men in Frye's regiment who started to build fortifications at Cambridge on May 4, 1775, at the start of the Siege of Boston. As part of Frye's regiment, Pero Hall saw heavy action at the Battle of Bunker Hill on June 17, 1775. Colonel James Frye lost 16 men killed and 31 wounded during the battle, a figure higher than that of any other regiment engaged, except for that under Col. William Prescott, stationed in the redoubt, and that of New Hampshire's Col. James Reed at the rail fence. Pero Hall's name appears on a subsequent list, titled "Return of Articles lost at Bunker Hill" (MSS, vol. 7, pg. 104), and he was reimbursed for his losses there nearly a year later, on June 13, 1776. After the Battle of Bunker Hill, Hall continued in Frye's regiment. He is listed on company returns dated October 6, 1775, and received money for a regimental coat at Cambridge on November 13, 1775. It is unknown when Hall's service under Frye ceased, but it was likely sometime between December of 1775 and May of 1776. Pero Hall did not remain idle for long. In December of 1776 he enlisted in the company of Capt. Paul Moodey in Col. Timothy Pickering's regiment of Massachusetts militia, which was stationed at Winter Hill near Boston, and early in 1777 marched to Danbury, Connecticut. Though his discharge date is unknown, Hall was paid for four months and twenty days of service in 1777, making it likely he served through May of that year during this second term.

Pero Hall enlisted for a third term of service on August 24, 1777, in the company of Capt. John Noyes in Col. Samuel Johnson's regiment of Massachusetts militia. This regiment was raised to reinforce the Continental Army during the Saratoga campaign. Hall served until November 30, 1777, for three months and eighteen days. The following year, on June 1, 1778, Hall enlisted for a fourth term of service, this time he enlisted in the company of Capt. Stephen Jenkins in Col. Thomas Poor's regiment of Massachusetts militia, and performed garrison duty in New York at North River, Fort Clinton, and King's Ferry. Hall was discharged on February 16, 1779, having served eight months and twenty-nine days.

Pero Hall signed on for a fifth term during the war on July 22, 1779, when he was one of many men from Essex County who enlisted for Continental service. He was described as being 59 years of age, five feet, four inches in height, with a "black" (*ibid.*) complexion. Hall was "delivered to" (*ibid.*) Lt. William Storey of the 8th Massachusetts regiment in the Hudson Highlands area of New York, where most of the state's regiments were stationed at the time, and also served under Capt. Abraham Hunt of the 1st Massachusetts regiment. Hall served nine months, receiving his discharge on April 22, 1780. He enlisted for a sixth, and final, term of service at the approximate age of 60 on January 30, 1781, for the town of Newbury, Massachusetts. His term was for three years, but the regiment he served in is unknown. It is not known if Hall served out this entire term, which likely ended sometime between June of 1783, when some regiments were placed on furlough, and November of that same year, when all of the Massachusetts Continental regiments were disbanded and their men sent home. However, there is no indication that Pero Hall finished his service prior to this time. With the end of his term in 1783, Hall had seen military service, though not continuous, in every year of the war from 1775 to 1783. This is all the more incredible when his advanced age is taken into account.

What happened to Pero Hall after the war is unknown. He is not listed in Census records for Massachusetts or New Hampshire, nor has his death been recorded. However, due to his age, and the fact that he served at some length during the war, it is probable that Hall died before 1800.

Sources: PSR-NHSP, vol. 5, pgs. 128–30, vol. 6, pgs. 866–67; UPS-NHSCR, vol. 31, pgs. 129, 463; UPS-NHGSR, Dec. 1, 1747; UPS-NHCPC, Mar. 10, 1748, pg. 315; TR-Portsmouth, #21245, #24355, #25018; PSR-MSS, vol. 7, pg. 104; OPS-*Memorial*, pgs. 8,1 94; TH-Coffin; OPS-Quintal, pg. 120; RCR #1763.

HIBBERY, ABNER

Hibbery was a resident of Brookfield, Massachusetts, when he enlisted for military service for that town on June 30, 1780. He enlisted as a six-month man for Massachusetts in the Continental Army, with his last name spelled several different ways, "Hebery" and "Hibray" (MSS, vol. 7, pgs. 687, 815). He was "marched" (*ibid.*) to camp on June 30 and received by Maj. Peter Harwood of the 6th Massachusetts regiment at Springfield, Massachusetts, on July 1st. Hibbery was subsequently marched to camp under the command of Ensign Joseph Miller. Enlistment records describe Hibbery as being aged 31, five feet, six inches in height, with a "black" (*ibid.*) complexion. After serving for five months and twenty-eight days at West Point, New York, and the surrounding area, Hibbery was discharged from duty on December 20, 1780. After the war, Hibbery moved north to Swanzey, where he is listed in the 1790 Census for that town as a free, non-white head of a household of six free, non-white individuals. Nothing further is known about Hibbery.

Sources: PSR-MSS, vol. 7, pgs. 687, 815; CEN-1790-NH.

HILL, TOWER

Hill was a resident of Wilbraham, Massachusetts, when he enlisted for that town on July 5, 1781. On July 12, 1781, he was paid a bounty, "on behalf of a class of the town of Wilbraham" (MSS, vol. 7, pg. 907), by one Silas Bliss, to serve in the Continental Army for three years. Hill was described as being aged 22, five feet, nine inches in height, with "black" (*ibid.*) complexion and hair. He was a farmer. Tower Hill never served out his term. His name appears on a list of recruits sent by the state to fill her quota who were reported "unfit for duty" (*ibid.*). Hill was rejected because he was "lame in both legs" (*ibid.*). After the war, Hill appears in the 1790 Census for Charlestown, New Hampshire, as a free, non-white individual, living by himself. Later that year, on September 5, 1790, Hill married Rose Tuttle, a "Negro" (TR-Charlestown, NH, vol. 2, pg. 573) of Littleton. Nothing further is known about Tower Hill or his family.

Sources: PSR-MSS, vol. 7, pg. 907; CEN-1790-NH; TR-Charlestown, NH, vol. 2, pgs. 573, 652.

HODGDON, CAESAR

Caesar Hodgdon was the slave of John Hodgdon of Newington. Listed as a "Negro boy" (GSP-NH Genealogical Record, vol. 4, pg. 61), he was baptized on September 4, 1749. It is unknown if this is the same man named Caesar Hodgon who served on board the Continental Navy ship *Ranger*, which was built and manned in Portsmouth in 1776-77, and first commanded by John Paul Jones. The logbook for the "United States Ship of War *Ranger*" (Quarles, pg. 85n), dated February 25, 1780, records that "at ten this night a Negro called Caesar Hodgdon died" (*ibid.*) while the ship was in harbor at Charleston, South Carolina. It is not inconceivable that Hodgdon did, indeed, serve aboard the *Ranger*, since the ship was heavily manned with local sailors, including some who were black. If our man in question is, however, the same Caesar Hodgdon who served on the *Ranger*, then the logbook of that vessel is wrong about his death.

In any event, whether our Caesar Hodgdon served aboard the *Ranger*, he was still a slave to John Hodgdon in 1781. In June of that year, however, Caesar, described as "a Negroman" (RCR #13200) was purchased by a Mr. March for 250 "Spanish Milled Dollars" (*ibid.*) and agreed, upon being promised a silver watch, "and his freedom from the said March when the war was over" (*ibid.*) to enter the army. Hodgdon, who was later said to be "free and Willing to go" (*ibid.*), enlisted for Massachusetts Continental service on June 9, 1781, for three years for the town of Newbury and was paid the town bounty for so doing. It is unknown what regiment Caesar Hodgdon served in, but he likely served out his term on garrison duty at and around the vicinity of West Point, New York. After his discharge in 1784, Hodgdon returned to his old master in Newington, John

Ran Away

FROM the Alms-Houfe, on the night of the 4th inft. a black pauper, by the name of CÆSAR HODGDON. This is to forbid all perfons from harboring or trufting, or entering into any contract with him, as the Overfeers of the Poor will not be accountable for any debts or charges of his contracting.

By order of the Board of Overfeers.

JOHN DAVENPORT,

Portfmouth, Mar. 10   *Chairman.*

Runaway pauper ad for Caesar Hodgdon. Different from runaway slave ads, this type of ad was placed for both black and white individuals who ran away from alms houses (poor houses) and were liable to incur debts that the town might later be forced to pay. *New Hampshire Gazette*, March 10, 1818. Courtesy Portsmouth Public Library.

Hodgdon, where he lived and worked from May to July of that year. What arrangements he made with John Hodgdon are unknown, but Caesar later brought suit against him, on February 23, 1791, claiming that Hodgdon owed him £78 3s. Of the amount that Caesar claimed was due him, £76 was for "Cash 250 dollars Pd of Mr. Huntress" (*ibid.*) in 1781. This likely referred to the price of 250 "Spanish Milled Dollars" that Mr. March paid for him prior to his enlistment, and which Caesar now believed should have been paid to him instead. The remainder of the balance Caesar claimed John Hodgdon owed him, all dated 1784, included amounts for "one thousand boards," three days of work in the month of April, four days of work in June, and five days of work, plus "mowing and making hay," in July (*ibid.*). The case between Caesar and John Hodgdon continued in the courts for two years, with John Hodgdon originally ordered to pay his former slave the damages he sought. However, he appealed and a subsequent jury trial reversed the earlier decision, with Caesar's claim denied. Following this decision, Caesar appealed and a jury trial was held yet again. On May 6, 1793, a judgment was again issued in favor of John Hodgdon, with Caesar Hodgdon charged court costs of £12 4s. Thus, the lengthy suit between a master and his former slave was ended.

Caesar Hodgdon was a resident of Portsmouth, and is found listed for that town in both the 1790 and 1800 Federal Census as a free, non-white head of a household of two free, non-white individuals. On March 4, 1818, he was a pauper who ran away from the almshouse (poor house). The overseers of the poor warned that the town would not be responsible for any debts Hodgdon might incur. There is no further record of Caesar Hodgdon after this time to shed light on his subsequent fate.

Sources: GSP-NHGR, vol. 4, pg. 61; OPS-Quarles-pg. 85; PSR-MSS, vol. 8, pgs. 28 and 32; RCR #13200; CEN-1790 and 1800-NH; NEW-*New Hampshire Gazette*, 3/10/1818, pg. 3.

HUZZEY, JAMES

Huzzey was a slave before the war who may have originally lived on Cape Cod, Massachusetts. Born about 1747, his wife later stated that he served two terms of service as a substitute for his master's sons, "being at that time a slave" (Quintal, pg. 137). Huzzey, his name spelled variously as Hussy, Hussey, Husza, and Huzzi, was paid a bounty for enlisting by the selectman of Conway on April 19, 1775. He officially enlisted for service on June 8, 1775, in the company of Capt. Moses Harvey in Col. Jonathan Brewer's Regiment of Massachusetts State Troops. He served with his regiment and fought at Bunker Hill on June 17, 1775. Subsequently, on June 24 his name appears on an order for cartridge boxes (ammunition) while at Cambridge, probably to replace that which he had expended in battle. He is further listed on company rolls for August and October 1775 and his name appears on an order for a bounty coat or money on October 26, 1775. His term of service likely ended in December 1775. Soon after, on January 20, 1776, James Huzzey married Susannah Tobey, probably at the town of Upton, near Worcester. James and Susannah Huzzey had one child, name unknown, who died at the age of 10 months during the war. Huzzey served for a second term during the war when, on March 30, 1781, he enlisted for three years in the company of Capt. Jeremiah Miller in Col. Joseph Vose's 1st Massachusetts regiment. At this time, Huzzey is described as being aged 34, five feet, seven inches in height, with "black" hair and complexion (MSS, vol. 8, pg. 595). Stationed with his regiment in and around West Point, New York, on garrison duty, Huzzey is listed as serving on foraging teams, as well as being "on command at New Windsor" (*ibid.*, pg. 571). At war's end in late 1783, he was discharged from duty.

After the war, Huzzey and his wife resided in the Worcester area, living in the towns of Upton, Northbridge, Leicester, and Warwick. They then removed to Westmoreland, New Hampshire, where they stayed "for a number of years" (Quintal, pg. 138) before moving to Townshend, Vermont. At the age of 80 years or more, and "wholly destitute of property" (*ibid.*),

James Huzzey applied for a pension for his service on April 9, 1818. When he applied for a continuance of his pension in 1820, his occupation was listed as that of a laborer and he stated that he was "dependant on the town and private charity for support" (*ibid.*), and that his wife was in poor health. Huzzey died in Townshend, Vermont, on March 11, 1822. His wife, Susannah, continued to receive a widow's pension and, in 1855, was a resident of Shaftsbury, Vermont, when she received a grant of land for her husband's service at the age of 104.

Sources: PSR-MSS, vol. 8, pgs. 571, 594–95; OPS-Quintal, pgs. 137–38.

JACKSON, POMP

Pomp Jackson was formerly the slave of Jonathan Jackson of Newburyport, Massachusetts, when he enlisted for Continental service on June 15, 1776. He was originally from Africa before being brought to the colonies as a slave. Though it is uncertain, he was likely freed by his master prior to his enlistment, with his residence listed as the town of Newbury, Massachusetts. Jackson first joined the company of Capt. Jeremiah Hill in Col. Edmund Phinney's Regiment (later the 18th Continental regiment, subsequently reorganized as the 12th Massachusetts regiment) as a private, but was promoted to fifer on August 1, 1776, while on duty with his regiment in the Northern Department around Lake Champlain. This first term of service lasted about six months, but Pomp Jackson enlisted in the same company and the same regiment, without an interruption of service, on November 14, 1776. He continued in the same regiment, which was organized several times, being designated as Col. John Patterson's regiment, then Col. Joseph Vose's regiment, and finally the 1st Massachusetts regiment, without an interruption in service through February of 1782, a period of nearly seven years. He appears on company rolls dated at Fort George, New York, on December 8, 1776, at Valley Forge, Pennsylvania, in December of 1777, at Providence, Rhode Island, in December of 1778, and at West Point, New York, on February 4, 1781. On this last roll, Pomp Jackson was described as being 25 years old, five feet, six inches in height, complexion "black," and hair "wool" (MSS, vol. 8, pg. 685). His birthplace was listed as Africa. Pomp Jackson served first in the company of Captain Hill, then that of Capt. Belcher Hancock, Capt. Robert Davis, Capt. Timothy Remick, and finally, Capt. Jeremiah Miller. During his time with the 1st Massachusetts regiment, he fought in such places as Trenton and Princeton, the Battle of Saratoga, the Battle of Monmouth, and the Battle of Rhode Island. In a list of men at "York Hutts" (*ibid.*), near West Point, New York, dated February of 1782, Jackson was reported as being "absent with leave" (*ibid.*). It is unknown if he returned from leave to continue his service, or when his service ended. The 1st Massachusetts regiment was disbanded on November 3, 1783, at West Point, New York.

After the war, Pomp Jackson likely returned to his home in Newbury, Massachusetts, near the New Hampshire border. In 1794 he was living in North Hampton, when he was warned to depart that town "as a poor man" immediately and return to his "legal residence" (RCR #14018) on January 29. He evidently complied with the town of North Hampton's demand and went to Exeter, from which he was warned to depart immediately on February 3, 1794. Jackson seems to have ignored Exeter's demand, since he was married in that town two months later, on April 5, 1794, to Susanna Dimond, who was listed as a "Negro" (Bell, pg. 55). Susanna was likely the widow of another black soldier, John-Jack Diamond. Subsequent details of Pomp Jackson's life are unknown.

Sources: TH-Coffin, pg. 71, 97, 99; PSR-MSS, vol. 8, pg. 685; RCR #14018; TH-Bell; OPS-Wright, pgs. 203–04, 212; TH-Bell.

JOHONNOT, PRINCE

Born in Boston on July 6, 1749, Prince Johonnot was probably the slave of Andrew Johonnot of that town. He was likely the unnamed "negro man" (NEHGR, vol. 6, pg. 360) listed in an inventory of Andrew Johonnot's estate on June 11, 1760, valued at £53. A "negro woman" was also listed, being valued at only £16. When Prince Johonnot gained his freedom is unknown, but it was likely prior to 1774, when, at the age of 25, he moved to Methuen, Massachusetts. In 1773 he married Mehitable Emerson and two of their six children were born there, Peter (born December 25, 1773), and Titus (born August 16, 1775). Peter later married Bathsheba Camp and moved to Vermont, where he died on November 22, 1806. Titus married Rebecca Ditson and later moved to Palmyra, Maine, where he died in 1854.

Listed as Prince "Johnnot" (MSS, vol. 8, pg. 811), Prince was a resident of Methuen when he joined the minuteman company of nearby Andover, Massachusetts, under Capt. John Davis in December of 1774. According to Johonnot, Davis's "company was kept organized and drilled two half days in each week, when the weather would permit" (Pension #S18057). He appears in the rolls for that company again in 1775, when he re-enlisted on February 14, 1775. When war broke out at Lexington and Concord, on April 19, 1775, Davis's company of Andover minutemen gathered and went to the scene of action, reporting to Col. William Heath (later major-general in the Continental Army), at about 8 P.M. that evening just after the British regulars crossed Charlestown Neck back into Boston. Due to their late arrival, they did not take part in any action on that momentous day, but immediately joined with the minuteman companies of other towns during the early stage of what was later known as the Siege of Boston. Capt. John Davis and his company of Andover men later joined the regiment of Col. James Frye, with Prince Johonnot's enlistment date recorded as May 14, 1775. As part of Frye's regiment, Johonnot was stationed in the "Centre College Building" (MSS, vol. 8, pg. 811) in Cambridge and was probably employed, like most of Frye's regiment, building fortifications. However, on the night of June 16, 1775, Johonnot and the rest of Frye's men were marched to Bunker Hill to help build a breastwork and fort that was being constructed at a breakneck pace that evening in anticipation of a British attack on their position the following day. The next day, June 17, 1775, the Battle of Bunker Hill took place, with Frye's men, including Prince Johonnot, in the thick of battle. When the battle was over, Col. James Frye's regiment had sustained heavy casualties, including two men killed in Capt. John Davis's company. Following this, Prince Johonnot continued in the service of Frye's regiment until December of 1775, when he was "verbally discharged" (Pension #S18057) after nine months of service.

Prince Johonnot lived in Methuen during most of the war years, but he was in Goffstown, New Hampshire, in 1776, when he was warned to depart there, being listed as a "malatto" (Hadley, vol. 1, pg. 405). Where Johonnot went to live after his warning from Goffstown is unknown, but he returned to that town by 1789, when he was chosen to act as a highway surveyor on the north side of the Piscataquog River. Prince and Mehitable Johonnot's other children, four in number, were all born in Goffstown. They were Moses (birthdate unknown), Mehitable (birthdate unknown, married Jacob Kidder), William (birthdate unknown, married Sarah Emerson), and James (born February 7, 1782, died in Goffstown July 16, 1846).

Prince Johonnot is listed in the 1790 Census for Goffstown as the head of household for a family of nine free blacks and in 1792 was a member of the First Baptist Society organized in Goffstown. The 1800 Census for Goffstown also lists Prince Johonnot. A long-term resident of Goffstown, Johonnot moved from there about 1830 to New Boston, where he is listed in the 1830 Census. In 1832, now nearly 84 years old, he applied for a government pension for his military service. Prince Johonnot's claim for a pension was approved and a certificate for such was issued on April 2, 1833. New Hampshire pension records indicate that Johonnot saw New Hampshire militia service during the war. However, this is likely an error, since nowhere in his pension application does Johonnot claim any service for the state of New Hampshire. Prince Johonnot died in Goffstown on May 25, 1836.

Sources: PEN-S18057; OPS-*Memorial*, pg. 94; PSR-MSS, vol. 8, pg. 811; TH-Hadley, vol. 1, pg. 405, vol. 2, pg. 239; PSR-NHSP, vol. 30, pg. 338; OPS-Quintal, pgs. 142–43; NEHGR, vol. 6, p. 360.

LEW, BARZILLAI

Lew was a "Negro" (MSS, vol. 9, pg. 725) from Dracut, Massachusetts. Barzillai, listed as "Zelah" (Quintal, pg. 150n), was born in Groton, Massachusetts, on November 5, 1743, the son of Primus and Margaret Lew (married 1742). Primus was a servant to Capt. Boyden of Groton, while his mother, described as a "mulatto" (*ibid.*), was a former servant to Samuel Scripture. In 1745 the Lew family moved to Dracut. The first record of Barzillai Lew as an adult is his service in the French and Indian War. In 1760 he enlisted for nearly 10 months of service in the company of Dracut men commanded by Capt. Thomas Farrington. In 1763, with the death of his stepmother, Lew, now a resident of Groton, selected Francis Blood of Concord, Massachusetts, as his guardian. In 1767, Barzillai Lew purchased the freedom of a "mulatto" (Quintal, pg. 151) girl named Dinah Bowman from Maj. Abraham Blood for $400 and married her. By February 1768 he came to Hollis, New Hampshire, to live with his wife, Dinah, and their child, Zadock, who had previously come to that town on January 19, 1768. The following year, on March 21, 1769, Lew and his family were warned in the name of the king to depart Hollis within 14 days. Whether they left within this time frame or not is unknown, but by 1775 he had returned to Massachusetts, living in Chelmsford, a town near his previous residence of Dracut. He lived on a farm in a part of town called Pawtucketville, on what is now Totman Street.

Barzillai Lew first saw military service in the Revolutionary War when, on May 6, 1775, he enlisted from and for Chelmsford in the company of Capt. John Ford in Col. Ebenezer Bridges's regiment of Massachusetts State Troops. Holding the rank of a fifer and drummer, Lew, whose last name is also given as "Low," was described as being aged 30, with a height of six feet, and was reported a "Negro" (*ibid.*). His occupation was listed as that of a cooper. As part of Bridges's regiment, Lew fought at the Battle of Bunker Hill on June 17, 1775. One authority on the battle states that Lew's company under Capt. John Ford "reached the field just before the action began" (Frothingham, pg. 176). Records for Bridges's regimental losses are incomplete, but estimates of his losses, which were nearly equal to those of Frye, and exceeded only by those of Prescott and Reed, show that his men were

III. The Men   279

in the thick of battle. Following this battle, Lew remained with Bridges's regiment during the summer and fall months of the Siege of Boston. He appears on company rolls dated August 1 and September 2, 1775.

Though his length of service is unknown, Lew likely continued in Bridges's regiment until it was disbanded on December 31, 1775. Following this, he continued in the company of Capt. John Ford, but now served in Col. John Robinson's regiment of Massachusetts Militia. Lew appears on the payroll for Robinson's regiment starting on February 5, 1776, perhaps indicating he took a month off after his service in Bridges's regiment ended. Robinson's regiment was stationed in the Boston area during the first half of 1776, but on July 25, 1776, Ford's company, including Barzillai Lew, marched from Chelmsford to Fort Ticonderoga, probably to help augment the Continental Army after its disastrous retreat from Canada. Lew served the rest of his time in the Northern Department under Capt. Ford before receiving his discharge at Albany, New York, on January 1, 1777. Barzillai "Lue" (MSS, vol. 10, pg. 24) served one last term during the war as a fifer in Capt. Joseph Bradley Varnum's company of Dracut volunteers in the militia regiment of Col. Jonathan Reed. Raised to reinforce the Northern Army during the campaign against Burgoyne, Varnum's men marched from Dracut on November 4, 1777, and returned on November 17, having marched 40 miles before it was decided that, with Burgoyne's surrender, their services were not needed. This is the last official service recorded for Lew during the war, but one historian states that "he organized for guerilla warfare at a later period of the struggle a band of Negro men, all in one family, known as Lew's men" (Kaplan, pg. 22). Whether such a partisan group was really organized, or where it may have operated, is unknown.

After the war, Barzillai Lew returned to Chelmsford, Massachusetts, to live, where he is listed in that town for the 1790 Federal Census as a free, non-white head of a household of 14 free, non-white individuals. Local tradition states that the 13 children of Barzillai and Dinah Lew were natural-born musicians. They formed a band and played at many gatherings throughout the area, and were in demand in Boston, and even played in far-off Portland, Maine. Barzillai Lew died in Dracut on January 18, 1822, at the age of 78. He is buried in Clay Pit Cemetery in Lowell. His wife Dinah continued to collect a widow's pension for her husband's service until her death in Andover, Massachusetts, on January 1, 1837. The offspring of Barzillai and Dinah Lew, listed below, were notable for their success. Incredibly, one grandson and one great-grandson of Barzillai Lew served in the Civil War, continuing a family tradition of military service dating back to 1760.

The children of Barzillai and Dinah Lew were as follows: Zadock, born in Dracut April 29, 1768, married Sarah Brister 1794, died in Dracut May 5, 1826; Amy, born December 8, 1771, in Chelmsford, married Peleg Gardner in December 1792, died March 1796; Zirviah, born June 26, 1773, in Chelmsford, married Frances Davis in August 1796, died May 8, 1826, in Lancaster, Massachusetts; Euebra, born April 26, 1775, in Chelmsford, died March 3, 1826; Barzillai Jr., born February 4, 1777, in Dracut, married first Dorcas Brister in September 1801 in Dracut, married second Sarah, married third Nancy Riley in September 1823 in Andover, married fourth Eliza, died February 22, 1861. Barzillai Jr. was "well educated" and "a man of some property and consequence ... owned the largest library in town ... was tall and dignified in appearance ... was remarkably intelligent, refined and pleasing in his address.... Had it not been for the social degradation to which the race to which he belonged had been reduced, he would have been chosen to the first offices in his town, if not the State" (Quintal, pg. 151n); Peter, born January 28, 1779, in Dracut, wife Mary, died July 22, 1817, in Boston; Reophas, born August 21, 1780, in Dracut. In 1808, presumably in Boston, he was impressed for duty on a British warship and never seen again by his family; Eri, born March 21, 1782, in Dracut, settled in Boston, where he appeared in the city directory for 1816 as a resident of May Street. He held office in the Prince Hall Masonic Lodge in Boston at the same time as his brother Peter, and died on January 6, 1818; Dinah, born January 25, 1784, in Dracut, married Moses Freeman in October 1808, died about 1870; Zimri, born November 27, 1785, in Dracut, married Mahala Freeman in August 1811, died April 9, 1847, in Dracut due to a train accident. His son Zimri Jr. enlisted for service in the Civil War in late 1864. He joined the famed 54th Massachusetts Regiment, but on January 11, 1865, was transferred to the 55th Massachusetts. Serving in Company F, he died during his service; Phebe, born April 20, 1788, in Dracut, married Frederic Hoyt November 1812, died December 7, 1853; Lucy, born May 7, 1790, in Dracut, married Thomas Dalton, died April 12, 1865, in Charlestown, Massachusetts. Lucy's grandson, Cornelius Henson, served in the 54th Massachusetts Regiment during the Civil War. Born about 1841, he enlisted on February 28, 1863, from New Bedford, Massachusetts. During the famed assault on Fort Wagner on July 11, 1863, Henson was captured. Held prisoner for nearly two years, he was exchanged on March 4, 1865, at Goldsboro, North Carolina; Adrastus, born December 23, 1793, in Dracut, married Hannah, died September 6, 1819.

Sources: TR-Hollis; OPS-Quintal, pgs. 150–52; OPS-Frothingham, pg. 176; PSR-MSS, vol. 9, pg. 725; vol. 10, p. 24; OPS-Wright, pg. 221; OPS-Kaplan, pgs. 21–22; CEN-1790-MA, pg. 146; OPS-Emilio, pgs. 351, 388.

LOVEJOY, PETER

Peter Lovejoy was the "Negro" (MSS, vol. 9, pg. 994) slave of Joshua Lovejoy of Andover, Massachusetts. Nothing is known about Peter Lovejoy's life before the war, though his master, too, served in the early stage of the war as a sergeant in Col. James Frye's regiment. Listed as "Pompe" (MSS, vol. 9, pg. 996) Lovejoy, Peter served early in the war as a private in the Andover company of Capt. Henry Abbott, which marched on the Lexington and Concord Alarm of April 19, 1775. Pompe, who was likely only a young boy aged 12 or 13 at the time, served for one and a half days before returning home to Andover. Peter Lovejoy remained as a slave to Joshua Lovejoy when he enlisted as a six-month man for Massachusetts in 1780. He was sent to Springfield, Massachusetts, where he was received by Maj. Peter Harwood of the 6th Massachusetts regiment on July 1, 1780, and "marched to camp" (MSS, vol. 9, pg. 994) under the command of Capt. Phineas Parker, of Baldwin's Artillery Artificer Corp. Lovejoy was described as being a "Negro" (*ibid.*), aged 17, and five feet, seven inches in height. His name is on a list of men at Camp Totoway, dated October 25, 1780, but his discharge date is not recorded. He was probably discharged in early December of 1780. During this term of service, Lovejoy may have accompanied his master, or his master's son. Joshua Lovejoy of Andover also served as a six-month man in 1780, when he was marched to camp on June 26, and discharged on December 6, 1780. There is no record of what regiment either Peter or Joshua Lovejoy served in, but it was undoubtedly one of the Massachusetts brigades stationed at or near West Point, New York, for garrison duty.

Peter Lovejoy was still a slave when, on March 1, 1782, he enlisted for three years in Col. Benjamin Tupper's 10th Massachusetts regiment for Continental service. The following month, on April 9, 1782, Joshua Lovejoy was paid the town bounty for "the service of said Peter-his servant" by Capt. Henry Abbott, "chairman of Class No. 5 of the town of Andover" (*ibid.*). This was the same Capt. Abbott who had in his company Pompe Lovejoy in 1775. Peter Lovejoy is listed on the rolls for the 10th Massachusetts regiment on January 1, 1783, when the regiment was disbanded in New York at Verplanck's Point, near West Point.

After the war was over, it is likely that Peter Lovejoy then became a free man. Soon after, he married a woman named Lydia Greenleaf on October 3, 1786. Peter and Lydia moved to Amherst, New Hampshire, after 1787, where they had six children, Lydia (b. 8/2/1788); Martha (b. 1/7/1791); Lucy (b. 6/12/1792); Betsey (b. 11/15/1794); Diadamia (b. 5/26/1797); and Leafjoy Ingalls (b. 2/14/1800). The 1800 Census for New Hampshire lists

Peter Lovejoy as a resident of Amherst, the head of a household of seven free black individuals in its First Parish. His former master, Joshua Lovejoy, had previously moved to Amherst, where he was listed as a resident in the 1790 Census. After 1800, nothing further of Peter Lovejoy and is family is known. He should not be confused with another soldier of the same name who was white and served for New Hampshire during the war and was later a resident of Westminster, Vermont.

Sources: PSR-MSS, vol. 9, pgs. 994–96; OPS-Wright, pg. 211; CEN-1790-1800-NH; TR-Amherst; PSR-NHSP, vol. 30, pg. 220; OPS-Hatcher, vol. 3, pg. 34.

MANN, CHRISTOPHER

Mann was formerly the slave of James Mann. It is unknown if he belonged to the James Mann who lived in Pembroke, and was a signer of the Association Test there, or the James Mann who lived in Canterbury in 1790. According to the Mason, New Hampshire, town history, Christopher Mann lived in Mason. In 1773 he was given freedom to "pass on lawful business" (Hill, pg. 93) in Mason, and in 1774 is said to have lived at James Mann's orchard. In July of 1776 he is listed in town records as a former slave who paid taxes for the first time. However, on February 4, 1778, the town voted to abate his tax rate for the following year. This may have been because he enlisted for Massachusetts service on August 13, 1779, for the town of Lexington, Massachusetts. Christopher Mann enlisted in the company of Capt. Thomas Hovey in Col. Nathan Tyler's regiment of militia raised for service in Rhode Island. He served for four months and seventeen days at Rhode Island before receiving his discharge on December 25, 1779. Christopher Mann, his last name spelled "Man" (MSS, vol. 10, pg. 162), saw one final term of service for Massachusetts when he enlisted on August 26, 1781, in the company of Capt. John Hayward in Col. Webb's regiment of militia raised to reinforce the Continental Army at New York. Mann served for three months and fourteen days, receiving his discharge on November 30, 1781. After the war, little is known about Christopher Mann. He witnessed a loan agreement between two free blacks of Jaffrey, the well known Amos Fortune and black veteran Pomp Freeman (Blackman) in November 1785. He is said to have "removed to New Ipswich" (Hill, pg. 218) and died there at an unknown time.

Sources: TH-Hill, pgs. 93, 218; TR-Mason; PSR-MSS, vol. 10, pgs. 162, 180; OPS-Quintal, pg. 64.

MCGAW, TITUS

While little is known about Titus McGaw, he is included in this work both on the basis of his name, as well as the town in New Hampshire from which he came. The name Titus was a name commonly given to slaves during this period, a name, like Caesar, derived from ancient Roman times. When Titus McGaw enlisted into John Nixon's 6th Massachusetts regiment in 1776, he was listed as coming from New Hampshire's 5th Regiment of Militia, with his residence listed as Merrimac, New Hampshire. Titus was likely the slave of Jacob McGaw of that town. Jacob McGaw arrived in Merrimac from Ireland prior to 1770 and was a prominent man in town, operating a tavern and a store in the northern part of town, near the ferry landing along the Merrimac River. The number of slaves in Merrimac increased from just three in 1767 to thirteen in 1773, and it is likely that Titus McGaw was one of them.

Titus McGaw enlisted in Nixon's 6th Massachusetts regiment, in the company of Capt. Micajah Gleason sometime in 1776. He appears on company rolls from September to December of 1776, and was listed as a private in Gleason's company on November 9, 1776, at North Castle, New York, near White Plains. As part of Nixon's regiment during this time, McGaw took part in the heavy fighting during the New York City campaign, including the Battle of White Plains, and subsequently took part in the historic battles at Trenton and Princeton in December of 1776. It is unknown when Titus McGaw received his discharge and, as a result, how long he served. Nothing further is known about him after his service in 1776.

Sources: PSR-NHRWR, vol. 1, pg. 573; TH-*Hist. of Merrimac*, pgs. 60, 165; PSR-MSS, vol. 10, pg. 489; OPS-Wright, pg. 208.

MINGO, WILLIAM

William Mingo is another man about whom little is known, thus making his inclusion in this work doubtful. South Hampton, New Hampshire, town records indicate that he was a "colored soldier who died on the frontier" (S. Hampton Town Records, vol. 1, pg. 256), but do not state when he died, or in what unit he served. The record further states that the woman to whom William Mingo was "betrothed," Phyllis Parsons, later, after his death, "was engaged to his brother Ebenezer Mingo, but refused to be married until she should be free, for she declared that she would never bring a slave into the world" (*ibid.*). Ebenezer "Mingoe" (RCR #3061) was previously warned to depart the town of Kensington, near South Hampton, on July 12, 1774, with no family listed. However, on February 4, 1780, he was warned to depart the town of Northwood, along with "Philis his wife and his children" (RCR #4331). This indicates that Ebenezer Mingo married Phyllis Parsons sometime between 1774 and 1780.

Whether Ebenezer's brother William served in the Revolutionary War or the French and Indian War before that is unknown. Two William Mingos served for Massachusetts during the Revolution; none is listed for New Hampshire. It is unknown if either of these men is the William Mingo in question who was to marry Phyllis Parsons of South Hampton. Neither of the Massachusetts men is recorded as having died in the service on the frontier. William Mingo of Dartmouth, Massachusetts, enlisted May 6, 1775, in the company of Capt. Daniel Egery in Col. Timothy Danielson's regiment of Massachusetts State Troops. Stationed at camp at Roxbury, Massachusetts, during the Siege of Boston, Mingo appears on company rolls for August and October of 1775, and received money for a regimental coat on November 6, 1775. The other William Mingo, whose residence and date of service are not listed, served as a seaman aboard the Continental Navy sloop of war *Providence*, commanded by Capt. Hoysted Hacker. Mingo's name is on a list of officers and men of the sloop who were entitled to prize shares in the captured vessels *Mellish* and *Active*. One final reference appears regarding the Mingo family when, on February 13, 1800, Eli Mingo and Violet Whittier, both "Negroes" (NHGR, vol. 53, pg. 165), were married in South Hampton. Eli was likely the son of Ebenezer Mingo and his wife Phyllis.

Sources: TR-South Hampton, vol. 1, pg. 256; RCR #3061, #4331; PSR-MSS, vol. 10, pg. 814; GSP-NHGR, vol. 53, pg. 165.

MINOR, DROVER

Minor was a "colored" (Cogswell, pg. 351) man who was a resident of Falmouth, Massachusetts, when he enlisted for three years in Capt. John Russell's company in Col. Gamaliel Bradford's regiment (later designated as the 14th Massachusetts regiment). Minor was mustered into Continental service on March 4, 1777, having been raised from Col. Nathaniel Freeman's 1st Barnstable company of militia. During his time in Bradford's regiment, Minor saw action during the campaign at Saratoga, spent the winter of 1777-78 at Valley Forge, and fought at the Battle of Monmouth. Following this, the newly designated 14th Massachusetts regiment spent the rest of its service performing garrison duty in the Hudson Highlands area of New York. When Drover Minor received his discharge is unknown, but it likely occurred in June of 1780, six months before the 14th Massachusetts regiment was disbanded at West Point. Soon after his service for

Massachusetts ended, Drover Minor moved to New Hampshire. In 1781 he was a resident of Londonderry when he billed Rockingham County for two days at the Court of Common Pleas, and three days for the court's general session for his service as a bell-ringer. Minor later moved to Henniker, where he lived with his wife, name unknown, and several children.

Sources: PSR-MSS, vol. 10, pg. 816; RCR #4402; TH-Cogswell, pg. 351; OPS-Wright, pg. 214.

PETERS, POMP

Little is known about Pomp, short for Pompey, Peters prior to the war. He resided in Exeter, New Hampshire, at least for a time, when in 1776 he was employed as a bell ringer by the town. The meetinghouse bell was "duly rung by Pompey Peter at 1 and 9pm as according to ancient custom" (Bell, pg. 13) in Exeter. Whether Pomp was a slave, most likely, or free born, is unknown, as is his place of origin. When he moved to Massachusetts is also unknown.

Pomp Peters was a resident of Charlton, Massachusetts, when he enlisted for Continental service in May 1778 from the regiment of Massachusetts militia commanded by Col. Jonathan Holman. Peters enlisted for nine months for the town of Charlton and was mustered into service on May 15, 1778. A list dated May 26, 1778, describes Peters as being 26 years old, five feet, six inches in height, with a "black" (MSS, vol. 12, pg. 245) complexion.

Pomp Peters arrived in Fishkill, New York, on June 7, 1778, and appears again on the muster roll taken at Fishkill on August 1, 1778. Peters was later assigned to the company of Capt. Josiah Smith in Col. Thomas Marshall's 10th Massachusetts regiment, and likely performed garrison duty at and around West Point, New York, where he appears on muster rolls for January of 1779. At the end of his nine months of service, Pomp Peters likely returned home for several months, but enlisted again in July 1779 from the company of Capt. Josiah Cutler in the militia regiment of Col. Rice. This time, Peters served for the town of Western, Massachusetts, of which he was also a resident. In a list of men raised for the town of Western, Peters is described as being aged 36, a 10-year discrepancy from the previous year, five feet, four inches in height, with a "black" (*ibid.*) complexion. Peters was marched to Springfield, Massachusetts, on July 8, 1779, and was "reported delivered" to Col. Marshall's 10th Massachusetts regiment, where he was listed as a "negro" (*ibid.*). During this time, Pomp Peters's term of service was not specified, but was likely for three years or the duration of the war.

Peters continued his service with the 10th Massachusetts regiment from July, 1779, to January 1, 1783, when the regiment was disbanded at Verplanck's Point, New York, Peters having served in the companies of both capts. Josiah Smith and Othniel Taylor. During this time, Pomp Peters fought with his regiment at the Battle of Monmouth, and took part in the action at Kingsbridge, New York, on July 3, 1781, when a force of Hessian troops attacked a force of Continental light infantry under Gen. Benjamin Lincoln. Pomp Peters later remembered that he had "fought the enemy on our retreat nearly the whole of the forenoon" during this "skirmish" (Pension #S45062). Peters was also among those New England Continental troops assigned to the light infantry that fought at Yorktown, Virginia, and was at the subsequent "taking of Corn Wallace" (*ibid.*) on October 17, 1781. Peters later returned to the 10th Massachusetts regiment, on garrison duty at and around West Point, where he served with that unit until it was disbanded. He subsequently was transferred to the 6th Massachusetts regiment of Lt. Col. Calvin Smith, serving under Capt. Daniel Pillsbury. Peters served with the 6th Massachusetts until June 12, 1783, when his regiment was furloughed at West Point, New York. At an unspecified time in 1783, according to Massachusetts records, Peters was among those soldiers paid an $80 gratuity for serving during the war.

Following his military service, a few facts about Pomp Peters and his activities in New Hampshire are known. He was married, with a wife and daughter, both named Sarah, when he was warned to depart the town of Loudon on August 18, 1790. The following year, on December 15, 1791, he was warned to depart the nearby town of Chester, along with his wife and daughter. Pomp Peters was warned again on April 10, 1794, along with his two children (but not his wife), from the town of Brentwood. Since Brentwood is a neighboring town of Exeter, where Peters had worked, and probably resided, in 1776, it is likely that he returned to this area because it was a place he was familiar with, and may have even known people still living in the area. It is certainly evident from the many warnings out that Peters and his family received that he, like many other free blacks during this time, was having a hard time making a living. This is probably what prompted Pomp Peters to assign, or sell, his bounty certificate for land in the west (100 acres) to William Smith Thom, a merchant of Philadelphia, for $20 on October 28, 1796. At this time, Peters was a resident of Meredith. The sale of land bounty certificates during this time was common, since many soldiers never planned to move to the land they were granted. Instead, these certificates were often sold to merchants and other speculators who bought them at discounted prices in hopes of reselling them at a large profit. The certificate that Thom bought from Pomp Peters was later sold to one J. Cass on June 1, 1803.

Pomp Peters, described as a "man of color" (Pension #S45062), applied for a pension for his service on April 6, 1818, when he was a resident of New Boston. This request was approved, and his pension was issued on June 9, 1819. The following year, on July 4, 1820, Peters, aged 70, was a resident of Newmarket when his pension was up for renewal. He testified that he had a wife, aged 41 (b. ca. 1779), a son, aged 19 (b. ca. 1801), and a daughter, aged 15 (b. ca. 1805). However, since he does not give their names, this causes some confusion. In the warnings out issued to Pomp Peters from 1790 to 1794, his children are also included, indicating their birth prior to 1801. When Peters was warned from Brentwood in 1794, his children were mentioned, but not his wife. This may indicate that he had a first wife, Sarah, who died between 1791 and 1794, and that Pomp later remarried and had children, born after 1800, by a second wife whose name is unknown. What became of Pomp Peters and his family after 1820 is unknown.

Sources: TH-Bell, pg. 13; PSR-MSS, vol. 12, pg. 245; OPS-Heitman, pg. 297; OPS-Wright, pg. 211; RCR #14339; PEN-S45062; PSR-NHSP, vol. 30, pg. 270.

PORTER, CAESAR

Caesar Porter, also known as Caesar Parker, was a slave who was born in Boston and was, at an early age, brought to Litchfield, New Hampshire. He is thought to have lived there with Jonathan Parker and, at least for a time, adopted his last name as his own. He was later reported as living in Amherst, New Hampshire, but it is unknown if this occurred before or after his Massachusetts military service. Caesar Porter was a resident of Andover, Massachusetts, when he enlisted for military service on May 30, 1775, in the company of Capt. Charles Furbush in Col. Ebenezer Bridge's Regiment of Massachusetts State troops. It is unknown if Caesar Porter saw any action at the Battle of Bunker Hill, on June 17, 1775, since Bridges's Regiment was not wholly engaged in the battle. Of the nine companies in Bridges's Regiment, four fought in the battle and suffered numerous casualties. Of the remainder, three companies did not go into battle, and two were on their way to the hill under Maj. John Brooks when the Americans began their retreat. Furbush's company, including Caesar Porter, was in one of these last two groups, but which one is unknown. Porter continued in Bridges's Regiment through at least November 21, 1775, when his name appears on a list of men who received a regimental coat or its equivalent in money. He appears on company rolls before that, having received advance pay at Cambridge on June 30, 1775, and was mustered in Furbush's company on August 1.

It is unknown where Caesar Porter lived after his service in 1775, but by 1786 he was back in Litchfield, from which he was warned to depart on January 27, 1786, along with his wife Phillis and family (no names specified). At some unknown time, Caesar Porter, "in his old age" (Hurd, pg. 492), was said to have moved to Newport, Rhode Island, where he is reported to have died in 1858 at the age of 105. Nothing further regarding Caesar Porter is known.

Sources: CH-Hurd, *Merrimack*, pg. 492; OPS-Frothingham, pgs. 176–77; PSR-MSS, vol. 12, pg. 584.

POWERS, THOMAS

The inclusion of Powers in this work is somewhat doubtful, since there is no evidence to link the man who served in the American Revolution with the man who later committed a "hideous crime" (Whitcher, pg. 361) in New Hampshire. However, the story is such an interesting one, and the possibility that both the soldier and the criminal are one and the same, that it merits further attention. No black soldiers named Thomas Powers (or Powars) served for either New Hampshire or Massachusetts during the war, though one white soldier with that name served for New Hampshire. However, there is record of a possible black sailor who "belonged to Massachusetts" (MSS, vol. 12, pg. 658) who served as a seaman aboard the ship *General Mifflin*, commanded by Capt. George Babcock. Powers, who was aged 23, and described as having a "dark" (*ibid.*) complexion, enlisted on September 9, 1780, for an unknown period of time. Fifteen years later, in 1795, a Thomas Powers was in Lebanon, New Hampshire. Described as either a "negro" (Whitcher, pg. 361) or a "mulatto" (Bittinger, pg. 395), he committed the crime of rape on December 7, 1795. Details are few, but Powers was soon arrested. He was tried in the Superior Court held at Plymouth, New Hampshire, and, on May 4, 1796, was pronounced guilty and sentenced to "be hanged by the neck until he be dead" (NH Superior Court Records-1796). The execution was set for July 8, but was postponed until July 28, when the court's judgment was carried out. The hanging took place at Haverhill, New Hampshire, where the crime was committed. Prior to the event, Powers is said to have sold his body for future dissection to two physicians, Dr. Daniel Peterson, of Boscawen, and Dr. Lacy, of Hopkinton. Both men were present at the execution, and Dr. Lacy was later reported as having skinned the body of Powers and having it tanned and made into a pair of boots. Powers rode to Powder House Hill, sitting on his coffin in the back of a wagon, as was the custom of the time, and was said to have chewed tobacco during the sermon delivered by the Reverend Noah Worcester of Thornton. After Worcester's sermon, which was directed both at Thomas Powers, for his crime, and to the large audience, "in which the great increase in crime was dwelt upon" (Whitcher, pg. 361), the execution was carried out by Sheriff David Webster. It was later reported that the gallows were left standing upon the spot, perhaps as a warning, until they "fell to the ground by decay" (*Portsmouth Journal*, 1/16/1836). Were Thomas Powers the sailor and Thomas Powers the criminal one and the same man? There is no evidence in hand to prove it, or disprove it for that matter.

Sources: PSR-MSS, vol. 12, pg. 658; TH-Whitcher, pgs. 361–62, 395; NEWS-*The Portsmouth Journal*, Jan. 16, 1836; US-Grafton County Court Records; TH-Bittinger, UPS-NHSCR, 1796.

RAND, JACK

Jack Rand, also known as Jack Austin, was a resident of Charlestown, Massachusetts, when he enlisted for Continental service on March 10, 1778, as a private in Capt. Elijah Danforth's company in Col. Thomas Nixon's 6th Massachusetts regiment. His term of service was for three years, during which time he fought with his regiment during the Saratoga campaign, wintered at Valley Forge in 1777-78, and spent the remainder of his time on garrison duty in the Hudson Highlands area of New York, near West Point. Rand's name appears on a list of men, dated December 5, 1779, at Peekskill, New York, who received clothing for the year. Prior to his discharge on March 29, 1780, Rand served in the companies of Capt. Danforth, Lt. Col. Calvin Smith, and Lt. Col. Daniel Whiting. Following this, Rand returned home for several months, but enlisted again, on July 7, 1780, as a six month man in the company of Capt. Job Sumner in Col. John Greaton's 3rd Massachusetts regiment. Jack Rand was described as being aged 27, five feet, nine inches in height, and was reported as a "negro" (MSS, vol. 12, pg. 929). Though a resident of nearby Charlestown, he was engaged by the town of Woburn, Massachusetts. Rand was marched to camp at Springfield, Massachusetts, by Capt. Abner Howard on July 17, 1780, and was received there by Brig. Gen. John Glover. After serving for six months and eight days, mostly on garrison duty at or around West Point, New York, Rand was discharged on January 9, 1781. Once again, though Rand returned home, it was only for a short time. He enlisted for a final term of service on April 27, 1781, in the company of Capt. Abraham Watson in the 3rd Massachusetts regiment, the unit he had served in just several months before. This time, Rand enlisted for three years, and was engaged by the town of Medford. Now Rand was described as being aged 28, five feet, ten inches in height, with "black" (MSS, vol. 12, pg. 930) hair and eyes. His occupation was listed as that of a farmer, but later as that of a hatter. Prior to his discharge on June 15, 1783, when the entire 3rd Massachusetts was furloughed, Rand was stationed in the West Point, New York, area at a variety of locations. In August of 1781, he was in camp at Peekskill, and in the following month he was at Continental Village and was reported as being on duty at the lines. In October and November of 1781, Rand was at the Highlands, and from December 1781 to January of 1782 was at the Hutts, New Boston. Beginning in June of 1782, Rand served in the company of Capt. Simon Jackson, and from December of 1782 until his discharge served in the company of Capt. William Watson. During the winter of 1782-83, the 3rd Massachusetts was stationed at the New Windsor cantonment, near Newburgh, New York, where Washington's headquarters was located. Jack Rand, like many other soldiers during this rough time, received various articles of clothing between December 14, 1782, and June 15, 1783.

Just as little is known about Jack Rand before the war, the same holds true afterward. By 1790, Rand had moved north to New Hampshire, where he is listed as a resident in the town of Litchfield in both the 1790 and 1800 Census for New Hampshire. Because he is listed as the head of a household of two free, non-white individuals, it is likely that he had a wife, but this is not known for certain. Nothing further is known about Jack Rand after 1800.

Sources: PSR-MSS, vol. 12, pgs. 929-30; CEN-1790, 1800-NH; OPS-Wright, pg. 208.

RANDALL, ROBERT

The story of Robert Randall's service in the Revolution is both a fascinating and confusing one. His military record, described here, is based entirely on his own description of his service in his pension application, and is difficult to reconcile with any particular state regiment with any degree of certainty. However, this is not to suggest that Randall did not serve, as he states, during the war. Indeed, since Randall's pension application was approved, without any apparent hesitation, there can be no doubt that he served just as he stated. Pension applications are usually considered a reliable source of a veteran's service, since the government usually needed some kind of proof of service to accept a soldier's pension claim. Randall's description of his service is described here in his own words, with some attempt afterwards to analyze what unit he served in, the officers he served under, and the time frame in which he served.

Randall deposed on May 2, 1818, that he "enlisted in Fairfax County, Virginia, under Lieutenant Rogers, who brought me to Rhode Island, where I joined the Regiment under Colonel Patterson, under the command of General Gandlebuss and served two years, in which time I marched to Fort Stanwix, by order of General Clinton; was confined six months in the hospital by reason of a wound I received in my arm from a musket shot, after which (having served out my time), I had a discharge from Colonel Patterson at Albany, and went home to Virginia" (Pension #S45165).

In examining the facts that Randall presents, it is unclear if he was a slave before his military service, or freeborn. It is unclear who the Lt. Rogers is to whom he refers. Possibilities include 2nd Lt. Robert Rogers, of Tallman's Rhode Island State Regiment; Andrew Rogers, of the 14th Virginia regiment; or 2nd Lt. William Rogers, of the 4th Virginia regiment. Once in Rhode Island, probably in late 1775 or early 1776, Randall likely served in Col. John Patterson's Massachusetts regiment of state troops, or its successor, the 15th Continental Infantry regiment. Paterson commanded both units in succession from April of 1775 to January of 1777, when he was promoted to Brig. Gen. It is unknown who "General Gandlebuss" (*ibid.*) was, but it may have been a nickname for one of the generals in the northern theatre of the war. The fact that Randall saw action at Fort Stanwix, now Rome, New York, indicates that he saw service during the Saratoga campaign in 1777. Only three Continental regiments saw action at Fort Stanwix, other than local militia units. They were the 3rd New York, under Col. Peter Gansevoort, the 1st Canadian regiment under Col. James Livingston, and the 9th Massachusetts, under Col. James Wesson. Given Randall's possible prior service under Paterson, it seems likely that Randall served in Wesson's 9th Massachusetts. However, it is also possible that Randall served with the 3rd New York under Col. Gansevoort, whose unusual name Randall may not have remembered accurately over 40 years after the event occurred.

By his account, it seems likely that Robert Randall was wounded at Fort Stanwix during the action that took place there between August 2 and August 24, 1777, and was hospitalized at Albany for six months after, placing his discharge around February of 1778. To continue with Randall's narrative, he further states that he "enlisted under Captain Richardson, and with a great number of other soldiers was put on board of a seventy-gun Frigate, commanded by Captain Monk at Williamsburg, Virginia; We were the next day taken by the British and taken to the Isle of Wight and there detained six months; we were then brought to the forks of the James River, where I ran away from them, intending to go home" (*ibid.*). Just who Capt. Richardson was is unknown, but, given the fact that he led "a great number of soldiers" on board a frigate, one is inclined to believe that he was a captain of a marine company, either for Maryland or Virginia. The frigate that Robert Randall served on was likely the *Virginia*, a 28-gun vessel in the Continental Navy built at Baltimore and commanded by the Navy's most senior man, Capt. James Nicholson. The *Virginia* was ready to sail from Baltimore as early as January 24, 1777, but her captain "seemed a better politician than a seaman" (Miller, pg. 316) and refused to set sail, due in part to a lack of men and supplies. There was also the British blockade of Chesapeake Bay to contend with. A braver or more daring captain might have tried earlier to run the British blockade, but Capt. Nicholson was not such a man, and he had to be "urged and cajoled" (*ibid.*) into action.

Finally, on the early evening of March 31, 1778, the *Virginia* set sail, planning to sneak past the British ships patrolling the mouth of Chesapeake Bay under the cover of darkness. Things were going as planned until about midnight, when the brig piloting the *Virginia* down the bay ran her aground on a shoal at the mouth of the bay. She bumped along the shoals before passing into deep water, where it was soon learned that the *Virginia*'s rudder had been torn off, leaving the frigate helpless. When day broke on April 1, 1778, several British ships were in sight. Nicholson, seeing the ships, had himself rowed ashore to safety, along with nine other officers. Left in charge was 18-year-old 1st Lt. Joshua Barney. He attempted to cut the anchor cables so the *Virginia* might drift ashore, allowing her crew to escape and enable the frigate to be scuttled so as not to fall into British hands. However, the remaining officers and men refused to cooperate and, waiting for the British to send a boarding party, "broke into the spirit room and got reeling drunk" (Miller, pg. 318) . The *Virginia* was captured that day "without ever having fired a shot at the enemy" (*ibid.*). It seems likely that the *Virginia* was the frigate Robert Randall served on. The Continental Navy had no operational 70-gun frigate, as described by Randall, and the *Virginia* was the only Navy vessel captured the day after setting sail from the Chesapeake Bay area during the war. The other possibility is that Randall was mistaken over the type of vessel he served on, and may instead have served on a privateer that was captured. Given his description of the vessel he served on as a "frigate" (Pension #S45165), this possibility seems less plausible. Randall further states that, after six months detention, he was brought by the British back to Yorktown, Virginia, when he ran away. It is unclear if Randall was brought back with the other men as prisoners to be exchanged or paroled.

Following his return to Virginia, probably in early 1779, Randall further states that he "met Captain Sharpe and enlisted under him, and went again into the service, and remained about two months, when we were dismissed by Colonel Lyme" (*ibid.*). Neither the name of Capt. Sharpe nor Col. Lyme can be positively reconciled with any known Continental Army officers in Virginia at the time, so it seems likely that Randall served in a local militia regiment. After his last term of service, Randall's wages were small, and "would not hardly bring anything" (*ibid.*). He then "went to the Westward to get the land granted to me as a soldier, when I was taken up by the Indians between Limestone and Fort Wheeling on the Ohio, who kept me a prisoner eighteen months. I then ran away from them, and by way of Detroit went to Montreal, and from there to New Hampshire about twenty-five years since; and whilst with the Indians I lost my discharge" (*ibid.*).

When Randall made his original pension application on May 2, 1818, he had already been in New Hampshire about 25 years, placing his time of arrival in the state about 1793. Since he had previously been held by the "Indians" for nearly two years, and making time allowances for his other travels, it seems likely that Randall made his westward trek in the late 1780s, after the war was officially over. In 1818, Randall was a resident of Hanover, and in 1820, he gives his residence as Lebanon. He further states in 1820 that he has two children, James, aged 15 (b. ca. 1805), and Edward, 12 years old (b. ca. 1808). He also lists that he has "two children from home" (*ibid.*), but it is not clear if this means that they, like him, came from Virginia. One of these children may have been Jenny Randall, who died in Hanover in 1828 at the age of 33. Randall also restates his service under Col. Patterson, but claims it was under a Capt. J. Gurty in the Rhode Island Line. Once again, things are confused, since Patterson was an officer from Massachusetts, not Rhode Island, and there is no known Continental Army officer from Rhode Island matching the name of Gurty.

Robert Randall lived the rest of his life in either Hanover or Lebanon. His age and date of birth are unknown; he describes his age as 60 in 1818, and 84 in 1820. Randall's pension application was approved, and he died several years later, on May 24, 1823, at Hanover. His wife, Hannah, left Hanover soon after Randall's death, but returned and, in a letter from her attorney dated December 27, 1832, asked to collect the "arrears of pension due her husband" (*ibid.*). These arrears were paid, and nothing further regarding Hannah Randall, or her children, is known. Unfortunately, nothing further about Robert Randall is known either, but the brief account of his wartime exploits in his pension application certainly outlines the many difficulties he went through, and is one, of undoubtedly many, lost stories in the Revolution that has come to light through the examination of these records.

Sources: PEN-S45165; OPS-Heitman; OPS-Wright, pgs. 211, 249, 317;

OPS-Peckham, pgs. 36, 38–39; OPS-Miller, pgs. 316–18; TH-J.K. Lord, pg. 301.

RUNNELS, PELEG

Runnels is one of several black soldiers who served for Rhode Island during the war and later moved to New Hampshire. Like Robert Randall, much of his service record is based on the information he provides in his pension application. He enlisted into Col. Christopher Greene's 1st Rhode Island regiment under Capt. Alexander Hopkins for a term of two years. Although Runnels later states in his pension application that he enlisted in the spring of 1777, this is likely incorrect. Since he further states that he served most of his time in Rhode Island, he probably enlisted in the 1st Rhode Island regiment in the spring of 1778. It was precisely at that time that the 1st Rhode Island regiment made history when it became the first military unit in America organized with "Negro personnel" (Wright, pg. 227). The 1st Rhode Island had already made a name for itself in 1777 when it defeated a force of 2,000 Hessian troops at Fort Mercer, near Red Bank, New Jersey, on October 21. Col. Greene, a cousin to Rhode Island's Gen. Nathaniel Greene, had also distinguished himself as a military leader during the campaign early in the war against Quebec. Because Peleg Runnels does not mention the battle at Fort Mercer, it is likely he did not join that regiment until it was re-organized with black soldiers in early 1778.

When he enlisted, Peleg Runnels was a slave, and states that he "was placed by his master under ... Col. Christopher Green, on condition that if he would serve two years he should then have his freedom; that the regiment was composed mostly of blacks" (Pension #W15295). The law passed by the Rhode Island Legislature on February 21, 1778, declared that "Liberty is given to every effective slave to enter the service during the war; and upon passing muster, he is absolutely made free, and entitled to all the wages, bounties and encouragements given by Congress to any soldier enlisting into their service. The masters are compensated, allowed at the rate of £120 for the most valuable slave, and in proportion for those of less value" (Greene, pg. 156). A later law was passed by the same legislature that prohibited all slave enlistment after June 10, 1778. Runnels likely enlisted sometime between February and June of 1778, but it is also possible that he enlisted later, since a number of black soldiers were enlisted after the June deadline. There are no enlistment records for Runnels, but he later states that he served for two years, making it most likely that he served until the spring of 1780. During this time, the 1st Rhode Island regiment was stationed in the Continental Army's Eastern Department, serving all its time in Rhode Island. Runnels, with the rest of his regiment, took part in the Battle of Rhode Island on August 29, 1778. The American attempt in this campaign to gain total control of Rhode Island from the British was unsuccessful, but the black 1st Rhode Island regiment played a major role when it showed "desperate valor" (Greene, pg. 162) in repulsing several assaults made on the American positions by Hessian troops.

Following his service, Runnels soon moved northward. He married Martha (also known as Patty) Hall in Salem, Massachusetts, when she was "about fifteen years of age" (Pension #W15295). Martha, who later gave her birth date as July 31, 1763, was the daughter of one Tom Hall of Newington, New Hampshire. It is unknown if she was black or white. Following their marriage in the Baptist church by Elder Trefford, of which there is no record, the couple moved north to New Hampshire. Though the exact date is unknown, they first lived in Somersworth, at a place called Quampegan, and subsequently moved farther north, first to Rochester, for two years, and finally to Alton.

The Runnels had seven children, including James, who was the oldest and was born within the first year of their marriage. They also had three children born between 1799 and 1806, including two daughters, whose names are unknown (b. ca. 1799 and 1806), and Peleg Jr. (b. ca. 1804 in Rochester). The four remaining children, whose names and dates of birth are unknown, were born at Alton. Peleg Runnels first applied for a pension for his service in April of 1818, but his claim was denied "for lack of sufficient evidence of his service" (*ibid.*). However, he applied again in January of 1824 and his claim was subsequently allowed. Eight years later, Runnels died at his home in Alton between September 11 and November 7, 1832, according to pension records.

Five years after Peleg Runnels's death, in October of 1837, his widow Martha applied for a pension based on her husband's service. Among those individuals who testified for her was another black veteran, Dan Woodman, of Durham. Woodman, who was now 88 years old, testified that he knew Martha and her family "from her childhood" (*ibid.*), and that he had heard of her marriage to Runnels. He also, erroneously, states that he served with Runnels in 1777 under Col. Winborn Adams "in the retreat from Ticonderoga" (*ibid.*). Woodman likely knew Martha Hall, Runnels's future wife, but there is no evidence to support his statement that he served with Peleg Runnels during his term in the 2nd NH regiment. Runnels himself never claimed New Hampshire service, stating only that he served under Col. Greene in Rhode Island in a regiment that "was composed mostly of blacks" (*ibid.*). Martha Runnels's claim for a pension was approved

on November 20, 1838, retroactive to November 12, 1832, and was set at $80 per year.
Sources: PEN-W15295; OPS-Greene, pgs. 156, 162; OPS-Ward, pgs. 373-74, 374; OPS-Wright, pg. 227.

SANDS, EDWARD

Little is known about Edward Sands's service as a soldier in the Revolution, except for the information he provides in his pension application in 1818. Sands, described in his application as a "black man" (Pension #W16148), enlisted at some time in either 1780 or 1781, in the company of Capt. Jeremiah Miller in Col. Joseph Vose's 1st Massachusetts regiment for Continental service. Sands later claimed that he served in Capt. Miller's "Company of Blacks" (*ibid.*) for three years, and served until the war ended. He received his discharge at West Point, New York, likely on or about November 3, 1783, when the regiment was formally disbanded. During his time in service, Sands served with his regiment mostly on garrison duty at and around West Point, but also saw action in "several skirmishes" (*ibid.*), and was in the battle at Kingsbridge, New York. This action took place on July 2, 1781, and it seems likely that Sands was one of 400 men who served in the light infantry regiment under Col. Alexander Scammell in a force commanded by Gen. Benjamin Lincoln. A fellow soldier of Sands, who served in the same regiment at the same time, testified that Sands also served as a waiter to Col. Vose "for a month or more" (*ibid.*). It is unknown when Sands enlisted, since several soldiers who served with him and testified on his behalf for a pension give conflicting information regarding the year he enlisted. As a result, Sands's pension application in 1818 was denied "for lack of proof of service" (*ibid.*). However, despite this conflicting information, as well as a lack of documentation for his service in Massachusetts records, his pension application was later approved in 1821.

Following the war, Edward Sands moved to New Hampshire. His pension application does not state specifically when he came to New Hampshire, but he was in the state by 1793. In October of that year Sands was married to Dinah (Dianna) Heart at the house of Nathaniel Bachelder in Chichester by Reverend Josiah Carpenter, pastor of the town's Congregational Church. In 1800 Edward Sands was living in Loudon, and is recorded as a black head of household there in the 1800 Census for New Hampshire. He was still a resident of Loudon in 1818-1821, when he made his pension application. After nearly 31 years of marriage to Dinah, Edward Sands died on August 19, 1824, probably at Loudon. Fourteen years later, on September

10, 1838, Dinah Sands, 80 years of age and a resident of Gilmanton, deposed that she was Sands's widow, and applied for a pension based on her husband's service. Her claim was approved in 1839, as was the claim she made in 1843, while still a resident of Gilmanton, that allowed her an $80 annual pension. No mention is made for any children for Edward and Dinah Sands, and nothing further about Dinah is known.

Sources: PEN-W16148; OPS-Peckham, pg. 87; OPS-Wright, pg. 204.

SAVAGE, JUBE

Little is known about Savage, other than his militia service during the war. A resident of Lincoln, Massachusetts, Savage first saw service in 1776, when he enlisted on March 4 under Capt. John Hartwell in Col. Eleazer Brooks's regiment of militia "called out" (MSS, vol. 13, pg. 840) to fortify Dorchester Heights during the Siege of Boston. Savage served for only five days and was likely employed using a pickaxe or shovel to help dig trenches or other fortifications. He re-enlisted in Capt. Hartwell's company on December 23, 1776, and saw service in Col. Dike's regiment of militia until March 1, 1777. During this term, Savage also served in the company of Capt. John Minot, but it is unknown where he served. Savage may have been a part of those Massachusetts militia regiments that guarded Boston, or may have served garrison duty at Fort Ticonderoga, New York. He served one final term from July to September 1778 when he enlisted in the company of Capt. Francis Brown in Gen. Solomon Lovell's Brigade raised for the expedition to Rhode Island. It is unknown what action, if any, Savage saw during the Battle of Rhode Island on August 29, 1778.

After the war, Jube Savage lived in New Hampshire, at least for a time, in 1790. He is listed as a free, non-white head of a household of three free, non-white individuals for the town of Temple in the 1790 Federal Census. Nothing further is known about Savage after 1790.

Sources: PSR-MSS, vol. 13, pg. 840; CEN-1790-NH.

SEPEO/SIPPIO

This man, his name properly spelled as "Scippio," was a slave living in Plaistow when war broke out in 1775. His master's name is unknown. Sepeo enlisted for Massachusetts service on May 2, 1775, in the company of Capt. Jeremiah Gilman in Col. John Nixon's regiment of Massachusetts State Troops. Though no details are known, Sepeo likely enlisted with his master's consent under Capt. Gilman, who was also a resident of Plaistow. It is not surprising that both Sepeo and Capt. Gilman served for Massachusetts. Not only is Plaistow located right on the state border, but Massachusetts regiments were also organized earlier than those from New Hampshire. Although Sepeo enlisted in May, on June 12, 1775, just days before the Battle of Bunker Hill, "Sippio" attempted to enlist in the 2nd New Hampshire regiment, based on the New Hampshire Seacoast, under Capt. Samuel Gilman. Sippio enlisted along with two other slaves, Archelaus White and Robin, also of Plaistow, and was described as a 27-year-old "husbandman" (NHRWR, vol. 4, pg. 8) who enlisted with the consent of his master. However, all three men were "not sworn," and did not serve due to the fact that "they are slaves" (*ibid.*). Apparently undaunted, Sepeo continued to serve in Nixon's regiment, and likely fought under Gilman at the Battle of Bunker Hill on June 17, 1775. Sepeo is subsequently listed in Capt. Jeremiah Gilman's roster of men, dated September 30, 1775, and appears on a list of men who received a payment of coat money at Winter Hill, near Boston, on December 25, 1775. It is unknown when Sepeo's term of service ended, or what became of him after December of 1775.

Sources: PSR-MSS, vol. 13, pg. 986; PSR-NHRWR, vol. 4, p.8, vol. 15, pg. 742, vol. 17, pg. 8; PSR-NHSP, vol. 30, pg. 193.

SMALL, AARON

Aaron Small was a relative of Jonathan Small, a black soldier who served for both New Hampshire and Massachusetts during the war. Like Jonathan Small, Aaron Small came from Dunstable, Massachusetts, along the border with New Hampshire. Though his date of enlistment is unknown, he probably first saw service in 1776, when he enlisted in the company of Capt. Zaccheus Wright in Col. Paul Dudley Sargent's 16th Continental infantry regiment. This regiment was later re-designated as the 8th Massachusetts regiment and was commanded by Lt. Col. John Brooks, from November of 1776 to January 1, 1777, after Sargent was promoted to brigadier general. Aaron Small saw action with his regiment during the New York City campaign and fought at the Battle of White Plains. His name appears on a company return, dated October 31, 1776, while in camp at White Plains, New York, and he was reported as being "fit for duty" (MSS, vol. 14, pg. 309). It is unknown when Small's term of service ended, but it was likely in late December 1776 or early January of 1777. It is highly likely that Small also fought with his regiment at the historic battles of Trenton and Princeton. Small served for a second time during the war, from September 27 to November 8, 1777, when he enlisted in the company of Capt. John Ford in Col. Jonathan Reed's regiment of Massachusetts militia raised to reinforce the Northern Army during Burgoyne's campaign. After serving for 43 days, Aaron Small was discharged from service.

After the war, Small moved to Goffstown, New Hampshire, where he is listed as the head of a household of four free, non-white individuals in the 1790 Census for New Hampshire. However, like so many other blacks, Small was warned to depart from his new residence on December 13, 1790, along with John Small, Eunice Small, and Susannah Small. It seems likely that the two women mentioned were the wives of Aaron and Jonathan (John) Small. Nothing further is known about Aaron Small or his family after 1790.

Sources: PSR-MSS, vol. 14, pg. 309; OPS-Wright, pgs. 209–10; OPS-Heitman, pg. 123; TH-Hadley, vol. 1, pg. 183.

SNELL, GEORGE

Little is known about George Snell and his military service. As early as December of 1775, he was a private in Capt. Moses McFarland's company in Col. John Nixon's regiment (re-designated in 1776 as the 4th Continental Infantry, and subsequently as the 6th Massachusetts regiment). His name appears on a list of men, dated September 26, 1776, at camp, Mt. Washington, New York, who were due wages and billeting money for the month of December 1775. It is unknown when Snell's service in the 4th Continental regiment ended, but he likely served through December of 1776. From April through August of that year, the 4th Continental, of which Snell was a part, belonged to the brigade of Gen. William Alexander (Lord Sterling) and saw action during the New York City campaign. Snell's regiment later joined Washington's main army, and fought at White Plains and the battles of Trenton and Princeton.

Following his service, George Snell resided in Portsmouth in 1779. Described as a "black fellow" (RCR #4331), he was warned to depart from there on August 4, 1779. Snell later moved to Newmarket and then Nottingham. Referred to as a "negro man" (RCR #10397), he was warned, along with his son Benjamin, to depart the latter town on March 11, 1788. However, Snell either did not heed this warning, or returned soon after. In the 1790 Census for New Hampshire, Snell is listed as the head of a household of three free, non-white individuals in Nottingham. Snell's wife may have been Lucy Snell, who was warned to depart the town of Stratham on November 14, 1794. Since George Snell is not listed in this warning, it may be an indication that he had died by this time, leaving Lucy as a widow struggling to survive on her own. Nothing further is known of Snell and his family after 1794.

Sources: PSR-MSS, vol. 14, pg. 591; CEN-1790-NH; RCR #4331, #10397, #14648.

STREETER, BARZILLAR

Streeter was a black soldier who served for Rhode Island during the war, and afterwards moved to New Hampshire, where he lived from 1796 until his death in 1839. It is unknown whether or not Streeter was a slave prior to the war. He was born at Cumberland, Rhode Island, in May of 1760, and was a resident there when he first saw service. At the age of 16, he enlisted in November of 1776 under Capt. John Carr in the 2nd Rhode Island State Militia regiment (later known as Lippitt's Regiment). During this term of service, which lasted for 15 months, Streeter served first as a boatman, employed in "bringing provisions for the army" (Pension #W16076), and later served as an "Adjutant" (*ibid.*) under Lt. Daniel Dexter. He was discharged at Bristol, Rhode Island, about February of 1778. Streeter subsequently served a second term in Rhode Island's State Militia, either in 1778 or 1779, which lasted nine months. He enlisted under Capt. Abimeleck Riggs in Tallman's Rhode Island State regiment, but "was soon taken out of the company as a waiter to Adjutant Simeon Martin, where he also served as Clerk" (*ibid.*). Following his service, Streeter was once again discharged at Bristol. Following his second term of militia service, which probably ended in 1779, Streeter was married to Nancy Brown. The ceremony took place about October of 1779 at Cumberland, officiated by Justice of the Peace Nathaniel Shepardson. Nearly nine months later, less than three weeks before he began his third tour of duty, a daughter named Laura was born to Barzillar and Nancy Streeter on May 24, 1780, at Cumberland. Before entering the service again, Barzillar worked for the Streeter family, either as a slave or as a former slave. Hannah Streeter of Smithfield, Rhode Island, testified in 1839 that Barzillar "worked for my father in the spring of 1780 and was planting on the dark day, May 19, 1780" (*ibid.*). With a wife and a newborn child at home, Streeter, likely enticed by the bounty money then being offered, enlisted on June 8, 1780, under Capt. Phillip Trafton in Col. Christopher Greene's 1st Rhode Island regiment for Continental service. Streeter served for six months "and was a waggoner for the regiment the whole time" (*ibid.*). During this time, Streeter's regiment was stationed in Rhode Island, and he was "honorably discharged" (*ibid.*) December 6, 1780, at Providence, Rhode Island.

III. The Men   301

After the war, Barzillar Streeter and his family moved to New Hampshire about 1796. They first lived in the town of Chesterfield, but in 1797 moved to the neighboring town of Swanzey, where Streeter lived the last 42 years of his life. In 1832, Streeter applied for a government pension for his war service. Among those individuals who testified on his behalf was his brother, Joel Streeter, who was 72 years old at the time and a resident of Acton, Vermont. Barzillar Streeter's pension application was subsequently approved. During their years together, Barzillar and Nancy Streeter had 11 children, including Laura (later Laura Peck, widowed by 1839), the oldest, and a son, Rufus. The names of their other children are unknown. Barzillar Streeter died at Swanzey on April 6, 1839, just shy of his 79th birthday, and is buried in Mount Caesar Cemetery.

Shortly after her husband's death, Nancy Streeter, now aged 82, applied for a widow's pension. Among those who testified on her behalf were Nathan Streeter, another brother of Barzillar, and a resident of Woodstock, Vermont, and Hannah Streeter, the daughter of his former employer (or master) in 1780. Also testifying were Rufus Streeter and Laura Peck, the children of Nancy and Barzillar. Nancy Streeter's pension application was subsequently approved, being retroactive to the date her husband died.

Sources: PEN-W16076; CEN-1800-1810-1820-N.H.

SWETT, CICERO

Swett was a resident of Marblehead, Massachusetts, when he enlisted for Continental service on November 9, 1779, from the 5th Essex County regiment of militia commanded by Col. Jonathan Glover. Swett, who was likely a slave at the time, enlisted in the company of Capt. Elijah Danforth in Col. Thomas Nixon's 6th Massachusetts regiment. He later was transferred from the company he was first in to one called "the black company, commanded by Capt. Matthew Chambers" (Pension #S43189), and then saw final service in the companies of Lt. Col. Daniel Whiting and Capt. Daniel Pillsbury. At the time of his enlistment, Swett was described as being five feet, six inches in height, with "black" (MSS, vol. 15, pg. 308) hair and eyes. During his entire time with the 6th Massachusetts, Cicero Swett saw little or no fighting, and took part in no military campaigns. His regiment was based in the Hudson Highlands department from 1779 to the end of the war, primarily performing garrison duty at and around West Point, New York. The 6th Massachusetts was furloughed from active service on June 12, 1783, at West Point, and was disbanded on November 15, 1783, thus ending Cicero Swett's term of service. His name appears on a list, dated about 1783, of men entitled to an $80 gratuity for their service during the war.

After the war, it is not known for certain if Swett remained a slave. It seems likely, however, that he did. On November 11, 1783, just days before his regiment was disbanded, an order signed at Boston directed that Swett's wages "for service as a Private" (MSS, vol. 15, pg. 286) from 1781 to 1783 were payable to one Joshua Reed. Five years later, on November 12, 1788, Swett signed for wages that were due him "for services in said regiment" (*ibid.*) that were paid to Thomas Curtice, dated at Merrimac, New Hampshire. It may be that Cicero Swett was originally a slave to Joshua Reed, and may have been sold to Thomas Curtice, a resident of Merrimac. Curtice then may have accepted a portion of Swett's wages as a soldier in return for granting him his freedom. Whether this was the case, Cicero Swett came to Merrimac to live at some point, possibly as early as 1788. He was still a resident there in 1818 when, at the age of 62, he applied for and received a government pension for his service. He was still a resident of Merrimac in 1820, when he testified to knowledge of service for one Edward Pollack, who served with Swett in the same regiment and company. Nothing further is known about Cicero Swett.

Sources: PSR-MSS, vol. 15, pgs. 285–6, 308; PEN-S43189, W22002; OPS-Wright, pg. 208.

TUFTS, CATO

There is only a small amount of information about Cato Tufts in the records, but he has the dubious distinction of being one of only two black soldiers associated with New Hampshire who were subject to disciplinarian action while in the army. Jonathan Small was court-martialed for selling liquor to his fellow soldiers and later returned to duty; Tufts is the only black soldier associated with New Hampshire, as far as is known, who was dishonorably discharged from the army.

Cato Tufts began his military service at an unknown time in 1775, when he enlisted in the company of Capt. Ephraim Corey in Col. William Prescott's regiment of Massachusetts State Troops. His name appears on a list of men, dated October 31, 1775, at camp in Cambridge, who had on order a bounty (regimental) coat. Nothing further is known about Tufts's service in Prescott's regiment. If he had enlisted in May, or early June of 1775, Tufts may have fought at the Battle of Bunker Hill on June 17, 1775. If so, then he took part in the fierce hand-to-hand fighting that took place in the redoubt at the top of Breed's Hill when the British finally overran the American position. Prescott's regiment suffered the most casualties of any American unit that day, including two men who were killed in Capt. Corey's company. The following year, on August 1, 1776, Tufts enlisted in the company of Capt. James Swan in Col. Thomas Craft's Artillery regiment. Serving as a matross, Tufts was listed as coming from Medford, Massachusetts. His term of service is unknown, but lasted only three months before he was "drummed out of service" (MSS, vol. 16, pg. 132) on November 1, 1776. The reason for this action is not given, but it was not an uncommon occurrence. Men who were drummed out of service were usually those who did not get along with either their fellow soldiers or the officers in charge. Perhaps Tufts was not given to following orders, or performing the many mundane and, at times, arduous tasks assigned to the enlisted men. Being a black man, he was probably assigned to perform the least desirable tasks, such as digging latrines or gathering firewood, and may have rebelled. It may also be that Cato Tufts simply did not like being a soldier, and behaved in a less than exemplary fashion. In any event, it is unlikely that he committed any particular crime, otherwise he probably would have been court-martialed and received some kind of corporal punishment. Following his service, Cato Tufts later moved from Medford to Woburn, Massachusetts. He went from Woburn to Londonderry, New Hampshire, from which he was warned to depart on September 20, 1788. Evidently he did not heed this warning, since he was warned again from that town on May 3, 1789. Regrettably, no more is known about Cato Tufts. He was likely a slave prior to the war and, given the fact that he came from Medford, may have been owned by the prominent Tufts family there. This family later founded Tufts University and its companion institute, the well-known Tufts Medical Center.

Sources: PSR-MSS, vol. 16, pg. 132; OPS-*Memorial*, pg. 116.

TURNER, ISHMAEL

Turner was a "negro" (MSS, vol. 16, pg. 168) from Northfield, Massachusetts, when he first enlisted for military service on December 16, 1776. He joined the company of Capt. Reuben Petty in Col. Samuel Williams's regiment of Massachusetts Militia, raised to support the Continental Army at Fort Ticonderoga, New York, during the winter of 1776-77. Turner served for three months and fifteen days before receiving his discharge on March 19, 1777. It is unknown whether Turner returned home after his discharge, since he re-enlisted two weeks later, on April 2, 1777, in Col. Rufus Putnam's 5th Massachusetts regiment for Continental service, which was on station in the Northern Department at Fort Ticonderoga and the surrounding area. Reported as a "negro" (*ibid.*), Turner served under Capt.

Samuel Sheldon, and then Capt. Joshua Benson. During his time in the 5th Massachusetts, Turner took part in the fighting during the Saratoga campaign, and spent the remainder of his time with the regiment on garrison duty, first in the Northern Department, where he appears on a list of men at Albany, New York, dated February 1, 1778, and later in the Hudson Highlands area of New York, near West Point. Ismael Turner was discharged on April 1, 1780, after serving out his three-year term of enlistment.

After the war, little is known about Turner and his family. Undoubtedly a free man, Turner moved to the northwest, perhaps with Vermont in mind as his final destination. His movements are well tracked by the fact that he is recorded in the 1790 Census in two different states. He first appears in the list for Winchester, New Hampshire, as the head of a household of three free, non-white individuals. Since Winchester is on the Massachusetts border, and only about 10 miles away from Turner's hometown of Northfield, Massachusetts, this is not surprising. Turner also appears in the 1790 Census as a resident of Chester, Vermont, about 60 miles away from Winchester to the north, following the Connecticut River and its tributary, the Williams River. The fact that Turner appears in the 1790 Census for both states, although unusual, is easily explained. Not only is Chester, Vermont, relatively close to Winchester, but not all communities completed their census taking at the same time. The 1790 Census was supposed to reflect an individual's usual place of residence on the first Monday in August of that year, but there were many "difficulties which confronted the census taker" (Census-1790-NH, pg. 5), including poor or impassable roads, as well as remote areas where roads were nonexistent. It was simply impossible for all communities to complete their census taking at the same time. It is unknown if Vermont was Turner's final destination, but this seems likely, given his northward movement. Like many other free blacks, Turner may have been attracted by the state's guarantee of freedom as embodied in its constitution. Nothing further is known about Turner and his family at this time.

Sources: PSR-MSS, vol. 16, pg. 168; OPS-Wright, pgs. 207–08; CEN-1790-VT, NH, pgs. 5–7.

WALKER, PRINCE

Prince Walker was born in Londonderry, New Hampshire, about 1758 and was the slave of the Reverend Timothy Walker, the prominent first minister of Penacook Plantation, later known as Concord, New Hampshire. Timothy Walker was a graduate of Harvard College and a native of

Woburn, Massachusetts. He was ordained at Penacook on November 18, 1730, and preached there until his death on September 1, 1782, at the age of 78. Referred to as "a man of native good sense, sound judgment, of agreeable manners and exemplary life" (Lawrence, pg. 367), his ownership of slaves, while seemingly strange for someone in his position, was not unusual. Clergymen throughout New England, New Hampshire included, often owned slaves, and, until the Revolution, had no qualms about doing so. Other examples of New Hampshire clergymen who owned slaves that later served in the war include the Reverend Josiah Stearns (Epping), and the Reverend Arthur Browne (Portsmouth).

It is unknown how long Prince Walker served as a slave, but tradition states that, with the adoption of New Hampshire's first state constitution on January 5, 1776, he was granted his freedom by the Reverend Walker. After gaining his freedom, Prince Walker moved to Andover, Massachusetts, where many of Concord's first inhabitants originated. Walker lived there with Dr. Thomas Kittredge and was subsequently married at an unknown date.

Prince, also referred to as Primus and Prentice, Walker first saw service on March 9, 1781, when he enlisted for Continental service for the town of Amesbury, Massachusetts. He joined the company of Capt. Joseph Bates in Lt. Col. John Brooks's 7th Massachusetts regiment, with his term specified as for the war. During most of his time in service in 1781, Walker was stationed at West Point, New York, and the surrounding area, performing garrison duty. He appears on company muster rolls for April and May, and is reported as being "on command" (MSS, vol. 16, pg. 474) at West Point during June and July. In August he was mustered at Camp Peekskill, and from September to December of 1781 he is reported as being among the "sick at New Windsor" (*ibid.*) in the hospital from the 1st Massachusetts Brigade. Walker continued to be sick at New Windsor in January and February of 1782, and appears on a descriptive list of men in Brooks's 7th Massachusetts regiment dated February 20, 1782. Listed as being aged 26, and his birthplace as Londonderry, New Hampshire, Walker was described as five feet, five and a half inches tall, with "dark" (MSS, vol. 16, pg. 475) hair and complexion. Prince Walker evidently continued to be sick "on account of a chronic complaint" (*ibid.*) since his name appears on a list of men mustered out by the inspector general, dated at West Point on May 26, 1782. However, it appears that Prince Walker continued to serve, despite his illness. His name appears on another list, dated June 23, 1782, at West Point, of men from the 7th Massachusetts regiment who were "transferred to the regiment of invalids, or assigned to other duties, or to be discharged" (*ibid.*). Prince Walker apparently could perform some duties, since he was transferred to the Corps of Invalids. This regiment, organized in 1777 and approved by Congress, was mainly used to perform guard duty in and around the West Point area. It is unknown when Prince Walker's term of service ended, but was probably sometime between April of 1783 and December of 1784, when the Corps of Invalids was disbanded at West Point.

After the war, Prince Walker seems to have returned to either Andover or Woburn, Massachusetts. Local tradition states that he came back to Concord at one time dressed in a red coat which he displayed with much pride, saying, "I rides in the troop, I do" (Bouton, pg. 253). No doubt proud of his military service, his reference to riding in the troop likely refers to his participation as a war veteran in the traditional Muster Day festivities that were commonplace throughout New England at that time. Little is known about Prince Walker after the war, but the chronic complaint he experienced during his enlistment seems to have continued. He is last reported as having become very "infirm" (*ibid.*) and relied on the town of Woburn for his support until his death at an unknown time.

Sources: OPS-Lawrence, pgs. 366–67; OPS-Upton, pg. 178; TH-Bouton, pgs. 252–53; MSS, vol. 16, pgs. 474–75; OPS-Boatner, pg. 289; OPS-Wright, pg. 330.

WARD, JACOB

Ward was a resident of Springfield, Massachusetts, when he enlisted for military service on April 28, 1775. He joined the company of Capt. Gideon Burt in Col. Timothy Danielson's regiment of Massachusetts State Troops and served throughout 1775 during the Siege of Boston. Ward appears on muster rolls for his company dated August 1 and October 6, 1775, at Roxbury camp. His name appears on a list of men, dated December 22, 1775, who received a payment of money in lieu of a regimental coat. It is unknown when Ward was discharged from service, but this probably occurred at the end of 1775, or early 1776. Jacob Ward enlisted for a second time on April 25, 1777, when he marched from Pittsfield, Massachusetts, to Fort Ticonderoga in the militia company under the command of Lt. Stephen Crofoot. Ward only served about a month until his discharge on May 22, 1777. Ward served for one final term in 1777 when he enlisted on July 8, 1777, in the company of Capt. William Francis in Maj. Caleb Hyde's detachment of militia. This unit marched from Pittsfield to Fort Edward, New York, during the campaign against Burgoyne. Ward's term ended on August 26, 1777, but it is unknown what type of action, if any, Ward may have experienced.

After the war, little is known about Jacob Ward. He moved north to

New Hampshire, where he was a resident of Hanover in 1800. He is listed as a resident of that town in the 1800 Census, the non-white head of a family of five free, non-white individuals. The other people listed, whose names are unknown, are likely his family members. Ward further appears in Massachusetts military records, his name on a list, dated February 18, 1804, of men who "furnished evidence of their service" (MSS, vol. 16, pg. 531) and, as such, was entitled to a gratuity. By this time, Ward had moved to Vermont, since he is "reported as belonging to Vermont" (*ibid.*) on the list aforementioned. Nothing is known about Jacob Ward after 1804.
Sources: PSR-MSS, vol. 16, pg. 531; CEN-NH-1800.

WHITE, LEVI

White is listed in the 1790 Census for New Hampshire as a free, non-white, the head of a household of five free, non-white individuals residing in the town of Londonderry. Several men by the same name served for Massachusetts during the war, but the man who lived in Lancaster, in Worcester County, is most likely the man who later moved to New Hampshire. Levi White from Lancaster served two terms of service during the war. He first enlisted for service on July 28, 1780, in the company of Capt. Bezaleel Taft in Col. Nathan Tyler's regiment of Worcester County militia. This regiment was sent to Rhode Island during the Tiverton alarm and served for 14 days, including travel to and from Rhode Island. Levi White was not paid for this service until 1781, when his name appears on a list of men, dated April 25, 1781, at Uxbridge, Massachusetts, paid for a part of the wages due them by Capt. Edward Seagrave, constable, on behalf of Capt. Bezaleel Taft. Later in 1781, White served for a second time when he enlisted in the company of Capt. Nathaniel Wright in Col. Luke Drury's regiment of Massachusetts militia. White began his march to camp on October 2, 1781, and arrived at West Point on October 11. Here, White and his regiment performed garrison duty. White was discharged in December of 1781 and was paid for the 400 miles he had to travel from camp to his home. White enlisted for a third time in 1782 for Continental service. He joined Col. Benjamin Tupper's 10th Massachusetts regiment for a term of three years, and was paid the bounty for his enlistment on April 16, 1782. It is unknown when White was discharged, but this probably occurred on January 1, 1783, when the 10th Massachusetts was formally disbanded at Verplanck's Point, New York.

Nothing further is known about Levi White, other than his New Hampshire residency, as listed in the 1790 Census.
Sources: PSR-MSS, vol. 16, pgs. 106–07; OPS-Wright, pg. 211.

WIGGIN, COCKER

Little is known about Wiggin, also known as "Cooker" (NHRWR, vol. 19, pg. 597) Wiggin. A resident of Stratham, he was undoubtedly a slave of one of the members of that prominent family in town. He may be the same individual, listed as "my negro boy Loeses' second child" (NHSP, vol. 34, pg. 441), bequeathed by Andrew Wiggin to his grandson Jonathan Wiggin on July 20, 1753. After the death of Andrew Wiggin, an inventory of his estate dated February 27, 1756, lists a "negro man" named "filander," and an unnamed "neggrow boy" valued at £90 (NH Provincial Probate Records, vol. 20, pg. 339). This was likely Cocker Wiggin.

Cocker Wiggin first saw service in 1775, when he enlisted at an unknown time in the company of Capt. Moses McFarland in Col. John Nixon's regiment of Massachusetts State Troops. This regiment was reformed and reorganized in 1776 as the 4th Continental Infantry regiment. Wiggin's name appears on a list of men, dated September 26, 1776, at Camp Mount Washington, New York, of wages and billeting money due for December of 1775. Though his enlistment and discharge dates are unknown, it is likely that Wiggin served with the 4th Continental regiment during the New York City campaign and fought at the Battle of White Plains. Following this, Wiggin probably was still in the service when his regiment retreated across New Jersey to Valley Forge, Pennsylvania, and later took part in the pivotal battles at Trenton and Princeton. After this, nothing positive is known about Cocker Wiggin. His name appears in New Hampshire records, in a list dated February 1779, of men who enlisted for Continental service, but no details about his service are listed. However, Stratham's town historian states that "Coker" Wiggin was "killed by the enemy at sea" (Nelson, pg. 169) in 1781. It is unknown if this was due to service aboard a Continental Navy vessel, or a privateer, since neither the vessel he served on, nor its state of origin, is cited.

Sources: PSR-MSS, vol. 17, pg. 301; PSR-NHRWR, vol. 15, pg. 487; TH-Nelson; PSR-NHSP, vol. 34, pg. 441; US, NH Provincial Probate Records, vol. 20, pg. 339.

WOODWARD, POMPEY

Much of what is known about Pompey Woodward comes from the pension application he filed with the government in 1832, when he was about 70 years old. He was born in June 1762, probably in Massachusetts. That he was a slave is fairly certain, though nothing is known about his early activities. He was living in Bradford, Vermont, in 1776 when he began his term of military service at the age of 14. His name is not listed in any Massachusetts military records, so it is probable that he did not formally enlist. However, he joined the army at Crown Point in June 1776, after its retreat from Canada. He immediately contracted smallpox and was placed in the hospital. After his recovery, he was "taken for a waiter" (Pension #W4867) by Capt. Edward Raymond. Raymond was an officer in the Massachusetts Militia and, on September 8, 1776, was appointed Wagon-Master to the division stationed on Lake Champlain opposite Point Independence. Pompey Woodward was stationed at Fort Ticonderoga and the area for over a year, and was first employed in repairing the fort, as well as the fortifications at Mount Independence. When Gen. Burgoyne's advancing British force threatened Fort Ticonderoga in July 1777, Woodward was still stationed there, and took part in the retreat through Hubbardton toward Bennington, Vermont. Pompey Woodward did not participate in the Battle of Hubbardton, since he states that he was "in the ambulance at the time" (*ibid.*). Woodward then went with a portion of the American troops to Castleton, Vermont, and later to Bennington. At Bennington, Pompey Woodward witnessed the prisoners who were taken by Stark's Brigade, and recalled an incident when they were "put into the meeting house" (*ibid.*). A "disturbance" (*ibid.*) occurred among the prisoners that night, and they were subsequently fired upon by the sentries, who killed several men.

Woodward stayed at Bennington until at least October 1777, after Burgoyne's surrender. He then went with Capt. Raymond to Castleton, where he was left while Raymond went back to the Fort Ticonderoga area "to look after some property he owned there" (*ibid.*). It must have been while Capt. Raymond was on this personal business that he was captured by the British. This is not surprising, since Ticonderoga was still under British control, despite the defeat of Burgoyne. Raymond was taken as prisoner to Halifax, Nova Scotia, where he was held for nearly a year before being sent to Boston as part of a prisoner exchange on October 8, 1778, on the cartel (ship) *Silver Eel*. Once Raymond was taken prisoner about November 1777, Pompey Woodward went home, stating that he "did no further duty" (*ibid.*).

After the war, Woodward, described as "a Colored man" (Seward, vol. 2, pg. 237), moved to Sterling, Massachusetts. Little is known about his activities in Sterling, but he is known to have married twice. Woodward first married Rosanna Hendly, of Sterling, on April 15, 1788. He was married again on February 16, 1800, at Worcester, to Mary (Polly) Harry of that town. The couple lived in Sterling before moving to Sullivan, New Hampshire, about the year 1807. Described as a "professor of religion for a great number of years ... always maintaining a character for strict integrity, and was highly respected by his neighbors" (Seward, vol. 2, pg. 238), Pompey Woodward lived in Sullivan for the rest of his life. He applied for, and received, a government pension for his military service in August 1832. He died there on January 13, 1843, at the approximate age of 81 (also given as 77) and is buried in the Four Corners Cemetery (range 16, lot 1).

In March 1853, Pompey Woodward's widow Mary applied for, and received, a widow's pension. Two years later, on March 27, 1855, Mary Woodward, aged 77 and now residing in Worcester, Massachusetts, applied for a grant of bounty land. This application was approved and, on May 22, 1856, Mary Woodward, described as a "the widow of Pompey Woodward a negro" (Pension #W4867), was granted 160 acres of land. Born in nearby Southboro, Massachusetts, Mary (Polly) Woodward died in Worcester on July 28, 1856. Pension records and town records make no mention of any children, so it seems likely that Pompey Woodward had no sons to carry on his name.

Sources: PEN-W4867, pgs. 173–77; PSR-MSS, vol. 12, pg. 1003; PSR-NHSP, vol. 30, pg. 316; TH-Seward, vol. 2, pgs. 237–38.

Appendix 1: Black Soldiers Who Died During the War

Name	Town	Regiment	Date/Place of Death
Richard Black	Kittery, Me.	11th Mass.	2/1/1778 — Valley Forge
*Peter Brewer	Amherst	1st NH	10/7/1777 — Bemis Heights
*Primas Chandler	Amherst	Rangers	May 1776 — The Cedars
Prince Clements	Dover	2nd NH	11/20/1781 — unknown
Titus Coburn	Shirley, Mass.	15th Mass.	April 14, 1778 — Valley Forge
Ezra Fuller	Mason	3rd NH	7/1/1778 — Valley Forge
Jesse Knott	Walpole	1st NH	7/18/1778 — unknown
Prince Liberty	Somersworth	2nd NH	6/18/1777 — Fort Ticonderoga
Nimshi Locke	Rye	Tash's Militia	1776-77 — unknown
Cato Marcy	Walpole	1st NH	1778? — unknown
Sidon Martin	Lee	3rd NH	11/12/1777 — New York
William Mingo	S. Hampton	Militia?	Unknown
Timothy Nokes	Kensington	6th Mass.	06/18/1777 — New York
*Aaron Oliver	Temple	3rd NH	4/30/1778 — unknown, released as prisoner
Asa Perham	New Ipswich	2nd NH	1778? — unknown
Boston Pickering	Newbury, Mass.	10th Mass.	3/4/1782 — New York
Peter Pomp	Epsom	3rd NH	3/15/1778 — Valley Forge
*Peter Poor	Hollis	Prescott's Mass.	June 17, 1775 — Bunker Hill
*Thomas Rhymes	Portsmouth	Privateer	After 1777 — England
Caesar Small	Hampton	Wingate's Militia	1777? — Fort Ticonderoga
Cocker Wiggin	Stratham	Naval service	1781? — unknown
*Titus Wilson	Peterborough	1st NH	7/7/1777 — Mt. Independence

Total Known Deaths = 22
*Indicates a soldier known to have died as a result of battle.

Appendix 2: Breakdown by Regiment of Black Soldiers Who Served for New Hampshire

1st NH Regiment 12
2nd NH Regiment 27
3rd NH Regiment 9
Ranger Service 11
Unspecified Regimental Service 7
Combination of two or more of above 5
Militia service only 28
Combination of Militia and 1st, 2nd,
  or 3rd Regimental Service 29
Naval Service 11
Privateer Service 1
Combination of Militia and Naval or Privateer Service 1
Total 141

Particularly noteworthy is the number of blacks who served in the 2nd NH regiment, more than double that of the 1st NH, and triple that of the 3rd NH. This is explained by the fact that the majority of New Hampshire's slave population lived in Rockingham and Strafford counties, from which areas the 2nd NH was heavily recruited. Also of note is the relatively high number of men, 29 in all, who served several times during the war, both in Continental service, as well as state or local militia regiments. As previously stated, due to a lack of surviving records the number of black sailors and privateersmen listed here represents only a small fraction of the actual number thought to have served.

Appendix 3: Black Soldiers Before the Revolution

During the Revolutionary War was not the first time that black soldiers served for New Hampshire. They also saw limited service in the French and Indian War (1754–1763) and in King George's War (1744–45). They may have even served earlier, during Queen Anne's War (1702–1713).

The two men listed below are thought to be black soldiers who served for New Hampshire during Queen Anne's War, though their race is not designated as such in state records. Following each name is the year of service, the regiment or company in which the soldier served, and where he saw service.

William (no last name)   July 21–Nov. 8, 1710; Col. Shadrach Walton; expedition against Port Royal, Canada.

Hut Blackman   Died February 23, 1711; Capt. John Robertson; Annapolis Royal, Canada.

The following dozen men, known black soldiers, served in King George's War and the French and Indian War for New Hampshire.

+Seser (Caesar) Deckson (Dickinson)   1757–59; Capt. Thomas Bell; garrison duty at Fort William and Mary, Portsmouth Harbor.

Cesar Durham   "by the consent of his master Nathl Randel" (PSR-NHRWR, vol. 1, pg. 21), aged 45; 1758; Capt. Thomas Tash, Hart's Regmt.; expedition against Crown Point.

John Gloster, Slave to Theodore Atkinson   1745; Capt. Mason's company; Siege of Louisburg, Canada; his gun "was Shot to pieces with a Cannon ball" (OPS-Gilmore, pg. 35).

+Pero Hall   1760; Capt. Samuel Gerrish, Goffe's Regmt.; Crown Point.

313

Appendix 3: Black Soldiers Before the Revolution

Cuff Manis September–October, 1745; Col. Moulton's Regiment; a laborer "Imployed on the Repairs of his majestis garrison at Luisbourg," Canada (OPS-Potter, pg. 95).

+Sippo (Martin), Negro Servant to Doctor Joseph Atkinson 1758; Capt. Thomas Tash, Hart's Regmt.; expedition against Crown Point. Also, 1760; Capt. Ephraim Berry, Goffe's Regmt; road built.

*Robert Miller, Sr. 1745; Capt. Edward Williams, Pepperell's Regmt.; Siege of Louisburg; lost his arm in battle.

=Caesar Nero (slave of Major John Gilman) 1757; Capt. Richard Emery; expedition to Lake George against Fort William Henry; captured and taken to Canada, fate unknown.

Cuffe Noker (Noaks) 1756; Capt. John Hart, Meserve's Regmt.; expedition against French at Crown Point.

*Samuel Perham 1755; Capt. Power's company, Blanchard's Regmt.; fought at Lake George.

Peter, "Majr Greenleafs Negro" 1748; Capt. Job Clement; "a gard for Rochester and Barrenton" (OPS-Potter, pg. 110).

Solomon Sipio April to October, 1761; Capt. Joseph Wait's company of Rangers.

*Indicates a soldier whose son served as a soldier in the Revolution.

= See the biography of Anthony Gilman for full details, in section for Soldiers with Service to New Hampshire and Other Colonies.

+Indicates a soldier who also served in the Revolution.

Sources: NHRWR-vol. 14, pp. 1, 3, 7, 18, 20–21; NHSP, vol. 18, pp. 68, 279, 906. OPS-Boatner, pp. 252–55; see individual soldier biographies for additional sources.

Appendix 4: Black Place Names and Locales in New Hampshire

The list below, which is by no means complete, itemizes places associated with New Hampshire's black soldiers mentioned in this book. These include natural features, such as rivers or ponds, named after black soldiers, as well as named areas where black soldiers or their descendants resided. Not included are individually owned homesteads or farms.

Enfield— George Knox has left his imprint on this town. Within its environs, to the southeast, are Knox River and George Pond, as well as George Hill Road.

Exeter— Jude's Pond, in the southern part of this town, the state's Revolutionary War capital, is named after Jude Hall, who lived in its vicinity.

Lancaster— The Israel River runs from the neighboring town of Jefferson to its end point in Lancaster at the Connecticut River. It is named after Israel Glines of Moultonborough, a man who hunted and trapped all along its course before any settlements were established.

Lempster— A natural spring in town is still known as Tatten's Spring, named after Isaac Tatten, a soldier in the war and one of the town's first settlers.

Newport— The area around Coit Mountain, in the northeast part of town, is described as the location of a black settlement. Among those who lived here were the veterans Salem Colby, formerly of Rumford, and Jesse Sherburne, the son of soldier Pomp Sherburne of Londonderry. The black settlement on the eastern slope of Coit Mountain was established early in the history of the town, probably in the late 1760s. The mountain was named after a free black named Vance Coit whose home was near the summit. The remains of the cellar wall were still visible, as was a rosebush, as late as 1879. Vance Coit was married to a white woman and was once whipped at the post for the theft of a bag of meal in Claremont. His wife, who tried to stop the punishment, may have instigated the theft. In another incident showing Coit's colorful character, a neighbor asked his help in taking in hay on the Sabbath, offering him a pound of sugar as payment. Coit replied, "Do you think I would have my soul fry in hell to all eternity for a pound of sugar? No!... Give me two pounds and I will risk it" (TH-Wheeler, pg. 252-53). Coit Mountain remained a haven for free blacks well into the 19th century. About the time of the Civil War, Charles Hall was another resident in the area. He had been a slave in Florida, but was smuggled aboard a vessel to Boston, hidden in a sugar hogshead. From Boston, Hall made it to Coit Mountain with the help of Deacon Jonathan Cushing.

Sandwich—Mount Israel, a 2,630-foot high peak in the Sandwich Range, is also named for Israel Glines, an early pioneer and soldier who settled in neighboring Moultonborough.

Stratham—The area where Guinea Road now lies is said to be the locale where blacks in that town lived. This road is likely named after the African country of the same name where many slaves were captured. It is likely that the town's black soldiers, or their descendants, lived in this area.

Swanzey—The area of the town known as Mount Caesar is named after a freed slave, Caezer Freeman, who was an original proprietor of that town. Mount Caesar Cemetery is the final resting place of Barzillar Streeter, a black soldier who came to the state from Rhode Island.

Bibliography

Published State Records

Fisher, Carleton Edward, and Sue Gray. *Soldiers, Sailors, and Patriots of the Revolutionary War, Vermont.* Camden, ME: Picton Press, 1992.
Maine. *Maine Wills 1640–1760.* Edited by William Sargent. Portland, ME: Brown and Thurston, 1887.
_____. *York County Deeds.* 10 volumes. Portland, ME: Brown and Thurston, 1887–1910.
Massachusetts. *Massachusetts Soldiers and Sailors of the Revolutionary War.* 17 volumes. Boston: Wright and Potter, 1896–1908.
New Hampshire. *New Hampshire State Papers.* 40 vols. Concord, NH, 1867–1943.
_____. *New Hampshire State Papers: Revolutionary Rolls.* 4 vols. Edited by Isaac Hammond. Concord and Manchester, 1885–1889. These volumes comprise volumes 14–17 in the *New Hampshire State Papers* series, as listed above.

Pension Records and Service Records

Pension numbers referred to in the text are officially numbered groups of original documents for soldiers found in the records of the National Archives. For those outside New Hampshire without easy access to Draper's useful work, these record numbers are the most reliable and useful when viewing original documents on microfilm at the National Archives.

Draper, Belle Merrill. *Pension Papers of New Hampshire Soldiers in the Revolutionary War.* 71 volumes. Washington, D.C., 1917–1922. An alphabetical abstract of pension papers copied from National Archive records, in the collection of Tuck Library at the New Hampshire Historical Society Museum.
National Archives. *Records of the Veterans Administration, Record Group 15.* Microfilm: Series M-804. Washington, D.C. This series reproduces Revolutionary War pension and bounty–land warrant application files.

317

National Archives. *War Department Collection of Revolutionary War Records, Record Group 93.* Microfilm: Series M-246, M-879, M-880, M-881. Washington, D.C.

Census Records

Jackson, Ronald Vernon (ed.). *New Hampshire 1800.* North Salt Lake, UT: Accelerated Indexing, 1974.
Jackson, Ronald Vernon, and Gary Ronald Teeples (eds.). *New Hampshire 1830 Census Index.* Bountiful, UT: Accelerated Indexing, 1977.
_____. *New Hampshire 1840 Census Index.* Bountiful, UT: Accelerated Indexing, 1978.
_____. *New Hampshire 1850 Census Index.* Bountiful, UT: Accelerated Indexing, 1978.
Jackson, Ronald Vernon, Gary Ronald Teeples, and David Schaefermeyer (eds.). *New Hampshire 1810 Census Index.* Bountiful, UT: Accelerated Indexing, 1976.
_____. *New Hampshire 1820 Census Index.* Bountiful, UT: Accelerated Indexing, 1976.
Maine. *Heads of Families at the First Census of the United States Taken in the Year 1790: Maine.* Washington, D.C.: Government Printing Office, 1908.
Massachusetts. *Heads of Families at the First Census of the United States Taken in the Year 1790: Massachusetts.* Washington, D.C.: Government Printing Office, 1908.
New Hampshire. *Heads of Families at the First Census of the United States Taken in the Year 1790: New Hampshire.* Washington, D.C.: Government Printing Office, 1908.
Vermont. *Heads of Families at the First Census of the United States Taken in the Year 1790: Vermont.* Washington, D.C.: Government Printing Office, 1908.

Town Histories

Aldrich, George. *Walpole as It Was and as It Is.* Claremont, NH: Claremont Mfg. Co., 1880.
Annett, Albert, and Alice E. Lehtinen. *History of Jaffrey New Hampshire,* vol. 1. Jaffrey: Town of Jaffrey, 1937.
_____. *The History of Jaffrey, NH; The Generations of Jaffrey,* vol. 2. Jaffrey: Town of Jaffrey, 1937.
Barnum, Louise Noyes. *Atkinson Then and Now.* Atkinson: Atkinson Historical Society, 1975.
Bedford. *History of Bedford, NH from 1737.* Concord, NH: Rumford Printing, 1903.
Bell, Charles H. *History of the Town of Exeter.* Boston: J.E. Farwell, 1888.
A Bicentennial History of the Town of Lempster 1767–1776. Lempster: Bicentennial Commission, 1976. Unpaginated pamphlet.
Bittinger, the Rev. J.O. *History of Haverhill, NH.* Haverhill: Cohos Steam Press, 1888.
Bixby, Roland. *History of Warren.* Crawfordsville, IN: Donnelley's and Sons, 1986.

Bibliography 319

Blood, Henry Ames. *History of Temple, NH*. Boston: George Rand, 1860.
Bouton, Nathaniel. *History of Concord*. Concord: Benning Sanborn, 1856.
Brewster, Charles W. *Rambles About Portsmouth: First Series*. Portsmouth: Lewis Brewster, 1859.
Brown, Warren. *History of the Town of Hampton Falls*, vol. 1. Manchester, NH: J.B. Clarke, 1900.
Chase, Frederick. *A History of Dartmouth College and the Town of Hanover New Hampshire*, vol. 1. Cambridge, MA: University Press, 1891.
Coffin, Joshua. *A Sketch of the History of Newbury, Newburyport, and West Newbury from 1635 to 1845*. Boston: Samuel Drake, 1845.
Cogswell, Leander. *History of the Town of Henniker*. Concord: Republican Press Assoc., 1880.
Dow, Joseph. *History of the Town of Hampton, NH*. Salem, MA: Salem Press, 1893.
Fox, Charles J. *History of the Old Township of Dunstable, including Nashua, Nashville, Hollis, Hudson, Litchfield, and Merrimac, NH*. Nashua: Charles Gill, 1846.
French, John C. *Manchester Historical Society Collections*, vol. 4. Manchester: John Clarke, 1910.
George, Nellie Palmer. *Old Newmarket, New Hampshire Historical Sketches*. Exeter, NH: News-Letter Press, 1932.
Griffin, S.G. *A History of the Town of Keene*. Keene: Sentinel Publishing, 1904.
Hadley, George Plummer. *History of the Town of Goffstown*, vol. 1. Concord: Rumsford Press, 1922.
Hall, M.O. *Rambles About Greenland in Rhyme*. Boston: Alfred Mudge and Sons, 1900.
Hanaford, Mary Neal. *Meredith NH Annals and Genealogies*. Meredith: privately printed, n.d.
Harriman, Walter. *The History of Warner, New Hampshire*. Concord: Republican Press Assoc., 1879.
Hill, John B. *History of the Town of Mason NH*. Boston: Lucius Elliot, 1858.
The History of Merrimac, New Hampshire. Merrimac: Merrimac Hist. Soc., 1976.
Holmes, Richard. *A View from Meeting House Hill: A History of Sandown, New Hampshire*. Portsmouth: Peter Randall, 1988.
Hudson, Charles. *History of the Town of Lexington, Middlesex County, Massachusetts*, vol. 2. Boston: Houghton-Mifflin, 1913.
Kidder, Frederic, and Augustus A. Gould. *The History of New Ipswich*. Boston: Gould and Lincoln, 1852.
Kingsbury, Frank B. *History of the Town of Surry*. Concord: Concord Press, 1925.
Leonard, the Rev. Levi and the Rev. Josiah Seward. *The History of Dublin, NH*. Cambridge, MA: University Press, 1919.
Little, William. *The History of Warren: A Mountain Hamlet*. Manchester, NH: William Moore, 1870.
Livermore, Abiel Abbot, and Sewall Putnam. *History of the Town of Wilton*. Lowell, MA: Marden and Rowell, 1888.
Lord, C.C. *Life and Times in Hopkinton, NH*. Concord: Republican Press Assoc., 1890.
Lord, John King. *A History of the Town of Hanover, NH*. Hanover: Dartmouth Press, 1928.

Lyford, James Otis. *History of Concord, NH*. Concord: Rumford Press, 1903.
———. *History of the Town of Canterbury, NH 1727–1912*. Concord: Rumford Press, 1912.
McDuffee, Franklin. *History of Rochester New Hampshire*, vol. 1. Manchester, NH: John Clarke, 1892.
Nelson, Charles B. *History of Stratham New Hampshire 1631–1900*. Somersworth, NH: New Hampshire Publishing, 1965.
Parsons, Langdon B. *History of the Town of Rye New Hampshire*, vol. 1. Bowie, MD: Heritage Press, 1992.
Ramsdell, George. *The History of Milford, 1738–1901*. Concord: Rumford Press, 1901.
Randall, Oran E. *History of Chesterfield*. Brattleboro, VT: D. Leonard, 1882.
Read, Benjamin. *History of Swanzey, New Hampshire, from 1734 to 1890*. Salem, MA: Salem Press, 1892.
Rowe, John Frink. *Newington, New Hampshire: A Heritage of Independence Since 1630*. Canaan, NH: Phoenix Publishing, 1987.
Sanborn, Richard. *A Bicentennial History of Epping, New Hampshire*. Seabrook, NH: Withey Press, 1976.
Sawyer, the Rev. Roland D. *The History of Kensington, New Hampshire, 1663 to 1945*. Farmington, ME: Knowlton and McLeary, 1946.
Scales, John. *History of Dover, New Hampshire*, vol. 1. Manchester, NH: John Clarke, 1923.
Secomb, Daniel F. *History of the Town of Amherst*. Concord: Evans, Sleeper and Woodbury, 1883.
Seward, Rev. Josiah. *A History of the Town of Sullivan, New Hampshire*, vol. 1. Cambridge, MA: University Press, 1921.
Smith, Albert. *History of the Town of Peterborough*. Boston: George Ellis, 1876.
Stackpole, Everett S. *Old Kittery and Her Families*. Lewiston, ME: Lewiston Journal Press, 1903.
———, Lucien Thompson, and Winthrop Meserve. *History of the Town of Durham, New Hampshire*. Somersworth, NH: New Hampshire Publishing, 1973.
Stearns, Ezra. *History of the Town of Rindge, New Hampshire*. Boston: George Ellis, 1875.
Topalian, Naomi. *People, Places, and Moultonborough*. Watertown, MD: Baikar Publishing, 1989.
Wadleigh, George. *Notable Events in the History of Dover, New Hampshire*. Medford, MA: Tufts College Press, 1913.
Wheeler, Edmund. *The History of Newport, New Hampshire from 1766 to 1878*. Concord: Republican Press Assoc., 1879.
Whitcher, William. *History of the Town of Haverhill, New Hampshire*. Concord: Rumford Press, 1919.
Wiggin, Morton. *A History of Barrington, NH*. South Berwick, ME: Chronic Print Shop, 1983.
Willis, John. *Old Elliot*, 3 vols. Somersworth, NH: New England History Press, 1985.
Worcester, Samuel T. *History of the Town of Hollis, New Hampshire*. Boston: A. Williams, 1879.

Worthen, Augusta Harvey and Evastus Wadleigh. *The History of Sutton, New Hampshire*. Concord: Republican Press Assoc., 1890.

New Hampshire County Histories

Hurd, D. Hamilton. *History of Cheshire and Sullivan Counties, New Hampshire*. Philadelphia: J.W. Lewis, 1886.
_____. *History of Hillsborough County, New Hampshire*. Philadelphia: J.W. Lewis, 1885.
_____. *History of Merrimack and Belknap Counties, New Hampshire*. Philadelphia: J.W. Lewis, 1885.
_____. *History of Rockingham and Strafford Counties, New Hampshire*. Philadelphia: J.W. Lewis, 1882.

Genealogical and Societal Publications

National Society, Daughters of the American Revolution (NSDAR). *Minority Military Service, Massachusetts, 1775–1783*. Washington, D.C., 1989.
_____. *Minority Military Service, New Hampshire–Vermont, 1775–1783*. Washington, D.C., 1991.
_____. *Minority Military Service, Rhode Island, 1775–1783*. Washington, D.C., 1988.
New England Genealogical Society. *New England Historical and Genealogical Record*. Boston.
The New Hampshire Genealogical Record. Edited by Charles W. Tibbets. Vols. 2–5. Dover, NH: 1904–1908.
Newmarket, New Hampshire. *Newmarket Club of Boston*. Boston: Undated collection of the Historical Committee of the Newmarket Club, on file at the Newmarket Historical Society.
Noyes, Sybil, Charles Thornton Libby, and Walter Goodwin Davis. *Genealogical Dictionary of Maine and New Hampshire*. Baltimore: Genealogical Publishing Co., 1996.
Proceedings of the American Antiquarian Society. Worcester, MA: 1925.
Society of Friends. *A Bill of Mortality for the Society of Friends, in Dover N.H. from 1708 to 1791*. Dover: James K. Remich, 1803.

Other Published Sources

Aptheker, Herbert. *American Negro Slave Revolts*. New York: International Publishers, 1970.
_____. *The Negro in the American Revolution*. New York: International Publishers, 1940.
Ayling, Augustus. *Revised Register of the Soldiers and Sailors of New Hampshire in the War of the Rebellion, 1861–1866*. Concord: Ira Evans, 1895.

Bartlett, Josiah. *Papers of Josiah Bartlett.* Edited by Frank D. Mevers. Hanover, NH: University Press of New England, 1979.
Belknap, Jane. *Life of Jeremy Belknap, D.D.* New York: Harper, 1847.
Bird, Harrison. *Attack on Quebec: The American Invasion of Canada, 1775–1776.* New York: Oxford University Press, 1968.
Boardman, Fon, Jr. *W. Against the Iroquois: The Sullivan Campaign of 1779 in New York State.* New York: David McKay, 1978.
Boatner, Mark M. *Encyclopedia of the American Revolution.* Mechanicsburg, PA: Stackpole Books, 1994.
Brighton, Raymond A. *They Came to Fish: A Brief Look at Portsmouth's 350 Years of History.* Portsmouth, NH: Portsmouth 350, Inc., 1973.
Canney, Robert S. *The Early Marriages of Strafford County, New Hampshire, 1630–1850.* Bowie, MD: Heritage, 1991.
Clark, Charles E. *The Eastern Frontier: The Settlement of Northern New England, 1610–1763.* New York: Knopf, 1970.
Crawford, Lucy. *Lucy Crawford's History of the White Mountains.* Edited by Stearns Morse. Boston: Appalachian Mountain Club, 1978.
Cunningham, Valerie, and Mark W. Sammons. *Portsmouth Black Heritage Trail.* Portsmouth: Portsmouth Black Heritage Trail, 1998.
Emilio, Luis F. *A Brave Black Regiment: The History of the 54th Massachusetts, 1863–1865.* New York: Da Capo Press, 1995.
Fisk, Moses. *Tyrannical Libertymen: A Discourse Upon Negro-Slavery in the United States.* Hanover, NH: Eagle Office, 1795.
Free Baptist Cyclopaedia. Chicago: Free Baptist Cyclopaedia Co., 1889.
Free Will Baptists. *Free Will Baptist Registry.* Dover, NH: 1844.
French, Allen. *The Day of Concord and Lexington.* Boston: Little, Brown, 1925.
Frothingham, Richard. *History of the Siege of Boston.* Boston: Little, Brown, 1903.
Gilmore, George C. *Roll of New Hampshire Soldiers at the Battle of Bennington, August 16, 1777.* Manchester, NH: John Clarke, 1891.
———. *Roll of New Hampshire Men at Louisburg, Cape Breton, 1745.* Concord, NH: 1896.
Greene, Lorenzo Johnston. *The Negro in Colonial New England, 1620–1776.* Port Washington, NY: Kennikat Press, 1966.
Hatcher, Patricia Law. *Abstract of Graves of Revolutionary Patriots.* 4 vols. Dallas: Pioneer Heritage Press, 1987.
Hayford, James. *Old Stone House Museum.* Brownington, VT: Orleans County Historical Society, 1985.
Heitman, Francis B. *Historical Register of Officers of the Continental Army During the War of the Revolution.* Baltimore: Genealogical Publishing Company, 1982.
Historical Data Systems (HDS). www.civilwardata.com
Jaffe, Irma B. *John Trumbull, Patriot-Artist of the American Revolution.* Boston: New York Graphic Society, 1975.
Kaplan, Sidney, and Emma Nogrady Kaplan. *The Black Presence in the Era of the American Revolution.* Amherst, MA: University of Massachusetts Press, 1989.
Ketchum, Richard M. *Saratoga: Turning Point of America's Revolutionary War.* New York: Henry Holt, 1997.

Kidder, Frederic. *History of the First New Hampshire Regiment in the War of the Revolution.* Hampton, NH: Peter E. Randall, 1975.
Knoblock, Glenn A. *Historic Burial Grounds of the New Hampshire Seacoast.* Charleston, SC: Arcadia Publishing, 1999.
Lawrence, Robert F. *The New Hampshire Churches: Comprising Histories of the Congregational and Presbyterian Churches in the State.* Claremont, NH: Claremont Power Press, 1856.
Lewis, John W., Eld. *The Life, Labors, and Travels of Elder Charles Bowles, of the Free Will Baptist Denomination.* Watertown: Ingalls and Stowell, 1852.
Maclay, Edgar Stanton. *A History of American Privateers.* New York: D. Appleton, 1899.
Martin, James Kirby. *Benedict Arnold, Revolutionary Hero: An American Warrior Reconsidered.* New York: New York University Press, 1997.
A Memorial of the American Patriots Who Fell at the Battle of Bunker Hill, June 17, 1775. Boston: City of Boston, 1889.
Miller, Nathan. *Sea of Glory: The Continental Navy Fights for Independence, 1775–1783.* New York: Donald McKay, 1974.
Morison, Samuel Eliot. *John Paul Jones: A Sailor's Biography.* Boston: Little, Brown, 1959.
Neagles, James C. *Summer Soldiers: A Survey & Index of Revolutionary War Courts-Martial.* Salt Lake City, UT: Ancestry Incorporated, 1986.
Nell, William C. *The Colored Patriots of the American Revolution.* Salem, NH: Ayer Publishers, 1986.
The New Hampshire Atlas. Freeport, ME: DeLorme Mapping, 1988.
Oesterlin, Pauline Johnson. *Rockingham County, New Hampshire, Paupers.* Bowie, MD: Heritage Books, 1992.
Peckham, Howard H. *The Toll of Independence: Engagements & Battle Casualties of the American Revolution.* Chicago: University of Chicago Press, 1974.
Portsmouth, NH. *City Directory, 1821.* Portsmouth, 1821.
_____. *City Directory, 1827.* Portsmouth, 1827.
Potter, Chandler E. *Military History of New Hampshire, 1623–1861.* Concord: McFarland and Jenks, 1869. A bound volume of Potter's work that first appeared in Adjutant General Reports for the State of New Hampshire in 1866 in two volumes.
Quarles, Benjamin. *The Negro in the American Revolution.* New York: W.W. Norton, 1973.
Quinlan, Maurice J. "George Knox, a Black Soldier in the American Revolution." *Dartmouth College Library Bulletin* XX, Number 2 (April 1980): 54–62.
Quintal, George, Jr. *Patriots of Color: "A Peculiar Beauty and Merit": African Americans and Native Americans at Battle Road & Bunker Hill.* Boston: National Park Service, 2002.
Rainville, Lynn. "Hanover Deathscapes: Attitudes Toward Death and Community as Reflected in Cemeteries and Gravestones: An Archaeological Investigation of Mortuary Variability in Hanover Township, 1770–1920." Senior honors thesis, Dartmouth College, 1993.
Remick, Oliver P. *A Record of the Services of the Commissioned Officers and Enlisted Men of Kittery and Eliot, Maine Who Served in the American Revolution.* Somersworth, NH: New Hampshire History Press, 1986.

Roberts, James A. *New York in the Revolution*. Albany: Brandow Printing, 1898.
Seaver, Frederick J. *Historical Sketches of Franklin County*. Malone, NY: Franklin County Historical and Museum Society, 1918.
Shipton, Clifford K. *Sibley's Harvard Graduates*. Volumes 7–12 Boston: Massachusetts Historical Society, 1945–1962.
Smith, Jonathan. *Peterborough New Hampshire in the American Revolution*. Peterborough: Peterborough Historical Society, 1913.
Smith, Page. *A New Age Now Begins: A People's History of the American Revolution*. 2 vols. New York: McGraw-Hill, 1976.
Sprague, William B. *Annals of the American Pulpit*, vol. 1. New York: Robert Carter, 1857.
Stark, Caleb. *Memoir and Official Correspondence of General John Stark*. Concord: Edson Eastman, 1877.
Upton, Richard F. *Revolutionary New Hampshire*. Hanover, NH: Dartmouth College Publications, 1936.
Urban, Cori. "Woodstock Parish Celebrates Black History Month." *The Vermont Catholic Tribune* (February 23, 2001): 1–3.
Ward, Christopher. *The War of the Revolution*. 2 vols. New York: Macmillan, 1952.
Washington, George. *The Writings of George Washington from the Original Manuscript Sources, 1745–1799*, vol. 35. Edited by John Fitzpatrick. Washington, D.C.: Government Printing Office, 1941.
Wentworth, William E. *Vital Records 1829 from Dover, New Hampshire's First Newspaper*. Camden, ME: Picton Press, 1995.
White, Anna, and Leila S. Taylor. *Shakerism: Its Meaning and Message*. Columbus, OH: Fred J. Heer, 1905.
White, David O. *Connecticut's Black Soldiers, 1775–1783*. Chester, CT: Pequot Press, 1973.
Williams, John. *The Battle of Hubbardton: The American Rebels Stem the Tide*. N.P.: Vermont Division for Historic Preservation, 1988.
Winslow, Richard E. *"Wealth and Honour": Portsmouth During the Golden Age of Privateering, 1775–1815*. Portsmouth, NH: Portsmouth Marine Society, 1988.
Wolkomir, Richard. "In Vermont, a Valiant Stand for Freedom." *Smithsonian* 29 (July 1998): 54–65.
Wright, Robert K. *The Continental Army*. Washington, D.C.: Center of Military History, 1989.

Period Newspapers

The Boston News-Letter
The Exeter News-Letter
The Exeter Watchman
The New Hampshire Gazette— Published with the dual title of *The Freeman's Journal* from 1775 to 1781.
The Portsmouth Journal.
Spirit of the Age, Vermont

Unpublished Sources

Maine State Provincial Records (Maine State Archives, Augusta)
North Church Records and South Church Records, Portsmouth, NH
From the New Hampshire Office of Records Management (state archives), Concord, New Hampshire:
Grafton County Court Records
Hillsborough County Court Records
New Hampshire Common Pleas Court Records
New Hampshire General Sessions Records
New Hampshire Provincial Deed Records
New Hampshire Provincial Probate Records
New Hampshire Superior Court Records
Papers of Governor Meshach Weare
Rockingham County Court Records
Rockingham County Probate Records
Strafford County Probate Records

Document numbers or individual volumes used from the above sources have been cited within the main body of this work.

The following unpublished genealogical compilations have been used:
Griggs, Laura, and Marjorie Swain. Burdoo Family notes. On file at the Reading, Vermont, Historical Society.
Lovejoy, John. "Ichabod Twilight Genealogy," 1995 (Wilbraham, MA). On file at Orleans County Historical Society, Brownington, VT.
McRoberts, George. "Revolutionary War Soldiers of Enfield New Hampshire." N.d. (Enfield, NH). On file at Town of Enfield Historical records.
Rogers, May. Gallup Genealogy, 1963 (Hartland, VT). On file at Hartland Historical Society.

Town Records

Records for the following towns have been consulted. All are in New Hampshire. Individual volumes and page numbers have been cited within the main body of this work. The locations of these records vary by town. Most can be found at the town's public library, though in smaller communities they may be located at the town hall, or the local historical society.

Amherst	E. Kingston
Andover	Exeter
Bedford	Fremont
Candia	Gilmanton
Charlestown	Greenland
Chichester	Hampstead
Croydon	Hampton

Hampton Falls
Henniker
Hollis
Hudson
Kensington
Kingston
Kittery, ME
Mason
Meredith
Milford
Moultonborough
Nelson

New Castle
New Ipswich
Newmarket
Newport
Portsmouth
Raymond
Rindge
S. Hampton
Somersworth
Stoddard
Stratham
Temple

Index

Abbott, Henry (Capt.) 281
Abbott, Joshua (Capt.) 150, 152
Abbott, Peter 19, 48, 58, 64, 74
Abbott, Samuel 74
Active (ship) 284
Acton (VT) 301
Acworth (NH) 167, 180
Adam 116
Adams, Benjamin 158
Adams, John 11
Adams, Joseph (the Rev.) 89
Adams, Neptune 173
Adams, Peter 24, 30, 45, 56, 74, 75
Adams, Winborn (Lt. Col.) 50, 233, 237, 295
Adventurer (ship) 264
Africanus, Scippio 53, 75, 88
Aide de Camp, black soldiers as 185
Albany (NY) 12, 87, 101, 114, 154, 157, 176, 189, 202, 222, 238, 279, 304
Alden, Ichabod (Col.) 258
Aldrich, George (Capt.) 172
Alexander, William (Gen., Lord Stirling) 199, 212, 299
Alfred (ship) 136
Allen, Ebenezer (Maj.) 222
Allen, Ethan 47
Allen, John 24
Allenstown (NH) 217
Alton (NH) 244, 295
Amabou, Africa 184
Amesbury (MA) 78, 216, 305
Amherst (NH) 120, 129, 257, 281, 282, 287

Amphitrite (ship) 23
Anderson, Elizabeth 118
Andover (MA) 162, 243, 244, 256, 257, 258, 276, 279, 280, 280, 281, 287, 305, 306
Andre, John (Maj.) 60, 137, 234
Annapolis-Royal (Can.) 212, 213
Aptheker, Herbert 82, 193, 209
Ariadne, HMS (ship) 136
Arnold, Benedict (Col.-Gen.) 43, 44, 47, 50, 59, 115, 170, 171, 179, 209
Arnold, James (Capt.) 163, 177, 188
Ashburnham (MA) 201
Ashley, Oliver (Capt.) 235
Ashley, Samuel (Col.) 161
The Association Test 13, 82, 83, 85, 93, 138, 191, 217, 282
Atkinson (NH) 119, 170
Atkinson, Joseph (Dr.) 145, 314
Atkinson, Theodore 313
Aurora (IL) 215
Aurora (ship) 88
Austin, Benjamin 116
Austin, Jack 289

Babcock, George (Capt.) 288
Badge of Merit 65, 102, 109
Badger, Joseph (Capt.) 135, 146
Bailey, John (Col.) 247, 266
Bailey, Mary 215
Bailey's Mills Cemetery (VT) 254
Baker, Cato 14, 16, 17, 20, 30, 50, 55, 56, 75–78
Baker, John (Capt.) 249

327

Baker, Otis (Col.) 16, 55, 75, 77, 78
Baker, Samuel 101
Balch, Joseph (Capt.) 207
Baldwin, John 55
Baldwin, Loammi (Col.) 214, 249, 252, 253, 260
Baldwin, Violate 256
Baldwin's Artillery Artificers 210, 281
Baltimore (MD) 184, 292
Bancroft, James (Capt.) 206
Barbadoes (BWI) 263, 265
Barber, John 25, 194–95
Barhew, Nancy 102
Barnard (VT) 222
Barnard, Joseph 78
Barnard, Seco 16, 25, 78
Barnes, Caesar 51, 55, 78, 87
Barnes, Fanny 79
Barnes, John 79
Barnes, Pamelia 79
Barnes, Sally 143
Barnes, Thomas 78, 79
Barney, Joshua (Lt.) 292
Barrington (NH) 109, 127, 182, 314
Barron, William (Capt.) 99, 156
Bartlett, Elisha 153, 154
Bartlett, Josiah 19, 79, 101, 115
Bartlett, Peter 19, 60, 79, 113
Bartlett, Thomas (Col.) 204, 214
Basset, Barachiah (Capt.) 248
Batchelder, Josiah 79, 80, 234
Batchelder, Nathaniel 296
Batchelder, Prince 79–80
Bates, Joseph (Capt.) 258, 305
Battis, John 153
Battis, Sampson 80, 152, 153
Baum, Friedrich (Lt. Col.) 48, 49
Bay, Susanna 249
Beal, Zachariah (Capt.) 74, 128
Beck, Anne 214
Beck, Henry 92
Bedel's Rangers 44, 82, 89, 111, 112, 114, 141, 172, 183, 197, 209
Bedford (MA) 251
Bedford (NH) 181, 245, 246
Belfast (ME) 122
Belinder 116
Belknap, Jeremy (the Rev.) 14–17, 30, 55, 75, 76, 77, 78, 90, 108, 127, 182
Bell, Boston 26, 63, 72, 167, 245–46
Bell, Flora 89

Bell, Frederic (Capt.) 100, 118, 156
Bell, Joseph 245, 246
Bell, Thomas (Capt.) 106, 314
Bellingham (MA) 261, 262
Bellows, Thomas 142
Bemis Heights (NY) 22, 49, 51, 84
Benjamin, John (Capt.) 222
Bennet, Brister, Jr. 247, 248
Bennett, Brister 52, 247–48
Bennett, Harriet 248
Bennett, James 247, 248
Bennett, Joseph 247
Bennett, Patience 247, 248
Bennington, Battle of 48–50, 83, 85, 161, 162, 171, 200, 215, 309
Benson (VT) 248
Benson, Joshua (Capt.) 304
Berkshire County (MA) 211, 233
Berry, Benjamin 143
Berry, Ephraim (Capt.) 145, 314
Berry, Marifield 140, 141
Berwick (ME) 163
Bethlehem (PA) 242
Betsey (ship) 23
Beverly (MA) 220
Bigelow, Timothy (Col.) 249, 250, 261
Bird, William (Capt.) 206
Black, Amanda 196
Black, Benjamin 196
Black, Caesar 55, 58, 70, 80, 170
Black, Catharine 196
Black, Cicero 70, 80–81
Black, Ebenezer 248
Black, George 70, 81, 125
Black, Henry 196
Black, Jonathan 196
Black, Joshua 195, 196
Black, Margarey 196
Black, Mary 196
Black, Primas 44, 81–82
Black, Richard 30, 52, 90, 92, 195–97, 311
Black, Sarah 196
Black, Thomas 196
Black, William 195–96
Blackman, Benajah 44, 70, 82
Blackman, Hut 313
Blackman, John 44, 70, 82
Blackman, Pompey 248, 249, 266, 282
Blair, William 269
Blaisdell, John 122

Index 329

Blake, Nathan 139
Blake, Philemon 119
Blanchard, Anna 83
Blanchard, Betty 83
Blanchard, Cuff 250, 256–257
Blanchard, Elisabeth 83
Blanchard, George 13, 14, 16, 82–83
Blanchard, George Washington 83
Blanchard, Hannah 83
Blanchard, Hepsibah 83
Blanchard, James 83
Blanchard, John 83
Blanchard, John (Capt.) 215
Blanchard, Joseph (Col.) 157
Blanchard, Jotham 83
Blanchard, Molly 83
Blanchard, Peter 46, 49, 83–84
Blanchard, Ruth 83
Blanchard, Sally 83
Blanchard, Samuel 256
Blanchard, Timothy 83
Bliss, Silas 272
Blood, Abraham (Maj.) 278
Blood, Francis 278
Boardman (Capt.) 252
bodyguards, black soldiers as 185
Bonhomme Richard (ship) 75, 88
Borman, Francis 214
Borroughs, A.T. 239
Boscawen (NH) 166, 197, 288
Boston (MA) 197, 198, 201, 210, 214, 223, 224, 225, 229, 230, 233, 238, 240, 244, 245, 255, 256, 263, 264, 265, 270, 275, 279, 280, 287, 309, 316
Boston (ship) 263, 265
Boston, Anthony 14, 197–98
Boston, Cato 63, 250
Boston, Phillip 52, 63, 69, 250, 251
Boston, Siege of 11, 12, 13, 80, 144, 152, 175, 207, 211, 215, 231, 242, 248, 260, 261, 279, 284, 297, 306
Bowes, Hannah 98
Bowles, Charles 25, 26, 29, 31, 33, 45, 49, 198, 200–203
Bowles, Charles, Jr. 200, 201, 202
Bowles, Elenor 200
Bowles, Euna 200
Bowles, Hannah 200
Bowles, James 200
Bowles, Jesse 200
Bowles, John (Capt.) 219

Bowles, Jonathan 200, 201
Bowles, Molly 200, 201
Bowles, Samuel 202
Bowles, Sarah 200
Bowles, William 202
Bowman, Dinah 278
Brackett, James (Dea.) 217
Brada 116
Bradford (VT) 238, 308
Bradford, Gamaliel (Col.) 284
Bradley, Thomas 251
Bradstreet, Lyonel 103
Brant, Joseph 57
Brentwood (NH) 110, 168, 182, 228, 286, 287
Brewer, Jonathan (Col.) 42, 274
Brewer, Peter 51, 84, 311
Brewer, Samuel (Col.) 208
Brewster, Charles 37
Brewster, John (Capt.) 173
Bridge, John (Capt.) 249
Bridges, Ebenezer (Col.) 206, 256, 257, 278, 279, 287
Bridgewater (NH) 202
Brister, Dorcas 280
Brister, Sarah 280
Bristol (RI) 300
Brookfield (MA) 271
Brookline (MA) 214
Brooks, Eleazor (Col.) 249, 297
Brooks, Elizabeth 195
Brooks, John (Col.-Gen.) 208, 258, 259, 287, 298, 305
Brown, Francis (Capt.) 297
Brown, Jesse 49, 84–85
Brown, John (Maj.) 81, 82, 106
Brown, Joseph (Capt.) 171
Brown, Joshua (Capt.) 261
Brown, Josiah (Capt.) 183
Brown, Michael 24
Brown, Moses (Capt.) 267
Brown, Nancy 300
Brown, Nathan (Capt.) 148, 207
Brown, Nathaniel 86
Brown, Peter 16, 43, 56, 85–86
Brown, Peter, Jr. 86
Brown, Scipio 16, 27, 86–87, 263
Brown, Sybil 86
Browne, Arthur (the Rev.) 84, 105, 305
Browne, Elizabeth 105
Browne, Marmaduke 105

Brownington (VT) 239, 240
Brunswick (NJ) 95
Bryan, Katharine 150, 151
Buckland, Stephen (Capt.) 216
Buckminster, Joseph (the Rev.) 186, 265
Buell, Augustus 75
Bull Run, Battle of 240
Bunker Hill, Battle of 11, 13, 34, 36, 42–43, 85, 119, 126, 129, 130, 159, 160, 161, 170, 178, 183, 198, 205, 210, 213, 215, 224, 226, 229, 242, 252, 253, 260, 270, 274, 277, 278, 287, 298, 302
Burbeck, Edward (Capt.) 210
Burdoo, Aaron 251, 253
Burdoo, Betsey 253
Burdoo, Eunice 251
Burdoo, Lois 251, 255, 256
Burdoo, Mary 251
Burdoo, Moses 251, 255
Burdoo, Phillip 168, 251, 255
Burdoo, Phineas 251
Burdoo, Polly 255, 256
Burdoo, Rosannah 253
Burdoo, Silas 29, 30, 33, 42, 63, 168, 243, 251-56
Burgoyne, John (Gen.) 51, 73, 161, 184, 200, 235, 242, 279, 299, 299, 309
Burley, James 101
Burns, Caesar 87
Burt, Gideon (Capt.) 306
Buss, John 163
Buss, Tobey 163
Butler, Benjamin 88
Butler, Henry 87, 88
Butler, John (Maj.) 57
Butler, Negro 87
Butler, Walter (Capt.) 63
Butler, Zepariah 88
Butterfield, Isaac (Maj.) 44
Butterfield, Reuben (Capt.) 231

Calfe, John (Capt.) 74, 78, 86, 118, 177, 196
Calhoun, John C. 134
Callendar, John (Capt.) 253
Cambridge (MA) 12, 13, 185, 205, 206, 213, 225, 231, 248, 252, 257, 260, 270, 274, 277, 287, 302
Camden (NH) 29, 241, 260
Camp, Bathsheba 276

Campton (NH) 116
Canterbury (NH) 115, 152, 153, 162, 166, 176, 282
Cape Ann (MA) 234
Cape Breton Island (Can.) 150
Cape Cod (MA) 244, 248, 274
Carleton, Kimball (Capt.) 85, 161
Carlisle (MA) 251
Carlisle, Cato 53, 75, 88
Carlisle, Daniel (Capt.) 88
Carlisle, John 88
Carlisle, William 88
Carney, Polly 241
Carpenter, Josiah (the Rev.) 296
Carr, James (Capt.) 47, 95, 136, 158, 166, 173, 177, 178, 181, 191, 204
Carr, John (Capt.) 300
Carter, John 88-89
Casco (ME) 170
Castleton (VT) 47, 309
Cate, Clement 92
Cate, Jane 92
Cate, John 92, 217
Cate, Samuel White 188
Cato 127
The Cedars 44, 89, 209
Center Cemetery (Henniker) 32
Center Cemetery (Warner) 262
Center Harbor (NH) 115
Ceres, HMS (ship) 136
Cesar, Prince 181
Chadwick, John (Capt.) 208
Chamberlain, Samuel 102
Chambers, Betty 256, 257
Chambers, Cuff 31, 243, 250, 256-58
Chambers, Elizabeth 257
Chambers, Mary 257
Chambers, Matthew (Capt.) 5, 301
Chambers, Thadeus 257
Chandler, Eri 89
Chandler, Hannah 89
Chandler, Primas 19, 44, 82, 89, 311
Chandler, Primas, Jr. 89
Chandler, Zachariah 89
Chapman, Isaac (Capt.) 220
Charleston (SC) 53, 124
Charleston, Siege of (Civil War) 254
Charlestown (MA) 162, 252, 258, 277, 280, 289
Charlestown (NH) 188, 199, 212, 235, 272

Charlton (MA) 285
Charming Polly (ship) 163
Chase, Dinah 186
Chase, Jonathan (Col.) 112, 132, 232
Chase, Stephen (the Rev.) 186
Chelmsford (MA) 278, 279, 280
Chelsea (MA) 214, 252, 253
Chemung (NY) 57
Cherry, Samuel (Capt.) 158
Cherry Valley (NY) 258
Cheshire (MA) 247
Chesley, Corydon 16, 17, 20, 30, 55, 58, 89–90, 127
Chesley, James 89
Chesley, Lydia 90
Chester (MA) 267
Chester (NH) 139, 214, 215, 267, 269, 286
Chester (VT) 304
Chesterfield (NH) 161, 232, 233, 301
Cheswill, Abagail 94
Cheswill, Elizabeth 94
Cheswill, Hopestill 92, 93
Cheswill, Martha 94
Cheswill, Mary 94
Cheswill, Mehitable 94
Cheswill, Nancy 94
Cheswill, Paul 94
Cheswill, Richard 91–92
Cheswill, Samuel 94
Cheswill, Sarah 94
Cheswill, Thomas 94
Cheswill, Wentworth 13, 16, 32, 49, 68, 71, 90–94
Cheswill, William 94
Chichester (NH) 215, 296
Chimney Point (NY) 125, 156, 162, 207
Church, Job 94–5
Cilley, Diana 101
Cilley, Joseph (Col.) 50, 51, 53, 54, 55, 57, 161, 176, 189, 212, 222
Cisco, Francis 198
Civil War 33, 34, 35, 123, 124, 179, 202, 227, 240, 254, 255, 279, 286, 316
Clapp, Daniel (Capt.) 98
Claremont (NH) 315
Clarendon (VT) 248
Clark, Anna 259
Clark, Anthony 25, 32, 73, 243, 244, 258–59, 262
Clark, Bula 259

Clark, Elijah (Capt.) 120
Clark, Jonathan 174
Clark, Joseph 220
Clark, Lucy 259, 260
Clark, Mary 259
Clark, Phillis 89, 135
Clark, Simon 259
Clark, Stephen (Capt.) 111, 144, 146, 147, 221
Clark, Timothy 259
Clay Pit Cemetery (Lowell, MA) 279
Cleaveland, Ebenezer (Capt.) 206
Clement, Job (Capt.) 314
Clements, Prince 62, 95, 311
Clogstone, Fan 105
Clogstone, John 105
Clough, Caesar 95–6
Clough, Cill 96
Clough, Jeremiah (Capt.) 197
Clough, Zaccheus 96
Coburn, Dinena 84
Coburn, Titus 26, 260–61, 311
Cochrane, Robert (Capt.) 106
Coffin, Eliphalet (Capt.) 96
Coffin, Enoch 96
Coffin, Peter (the Rev.) 96
Coffin, Primas 8, 55, 96–98, 135
Coffin, Prince 96
Coffin, William 153
Coggswell, Thomas (Capt.) 215
Coit, Vance 315–16
Colburn, Andrew (Lt. Col.) 50
Colby, Lot 98
Colby, Salem 17, 25, 69–70, 98, 315
Cold Harbor, Battle of 202
Cole, Amos 203
Cole, Elizabeth 205
Cole, Judith 90
Cole, Margaret 205
Cole, Sarah 205
Cole, Tobias 60, 95, 203–5
Coleman, James 99
Coleman, Plato 99, 225
Collins, Dodge 193, 205
Committee of Safety 13
Concord (MA) 249, 250, 251, 252, 272, 278
Concord (NH) 153, 176, 215, 304, 305, 306
Congdon, Alanson 248
Connecticut Regiments: 3rd 36; 4th 5

Connor, Benjamin 144
Connor, Elizabeth 144
Constable (NY) 202, 203
Constitution Island (NY) 179
Continental Congress 11, 12, 14, 27, 52, 79, 165, 174
Continental Navy 23–25, 45, 53, 136, 224, 263, 292, 308
Continental Regiments: 1st Canadian 291; 3rd Artilley 216; 4th Inf. 199, 211, 228, 241, 299, 308; 7th Inf. 205; 14th Inf. 267; 15th Inf. 291; 16th Inf. 298; 18th Inf. 230, 275; 26th Inf. 215
Conway (MA) 274
Cook, John 20, 50, 62, 99–100
Cook, Rhoda 122
Coos (NH) 59, 60, 64
Corey, Ephraim (Capt.) 260, 302, 303
Corey, Timothy (Capt.) 213
Corinth (VT) 238, 239
Corliss, Molly 200
Cornish (NH) 113, 232
Cornwallis, (Lord-Gen.) 36, 37, 45, 54, 61, 62, 100, 286
Corps of Invalids 216, 306
Cotton, Eleazor 100
Cotton, James 100
Cotton, Joseph 100
Cotton, Joseph, Jr. 100, 101
Cotton, Josiah (the Rev.) 214
Cotton, Nancy 100
Cotton, William 100
Craft, Thomas (Col.) 203, 207
Craft's Artillery Regiment 303
Crane, John (Maj.) 216
Crane's Artillery Regiment 216
Crocker, Jeremiah 32, 261–62
Crofoot, Stephen (Lt.) 306
Crosbey, Josiah (Capt.) 231
Crosby, Sarah 240
Crown Point (NY) 47, 145, 157, 207, 221, 309, 314
Croydon (NH) 162
Cumberland (RI) 300
Cumberland (ship) 263
Cumberland County (ME) 230
Cunningham, Samuel (Capt.) 232
Currier, Ephraim 86
Currier, Ezra (Capt.) 80
Currier, Lydia 177
Currier, Phillis 137

Curtice, Thomas 302
Curtis, Jonathan (the Rev.) 32
Cushing, Jonathan (Dea.) 316
Cutler, Josiah (Capt.) 285
Cutler, Mary 101
Cutler, Robert (the Rev.) 173
Cutler, Rufus 101, 103
Cutler, Tobias 16, 70, 101, 122
Cyane, USS (ship) 179

Dailey, Abraham 102, 103
Dailey, Jack 102
Dailey, Jerry 102
Dailey, London 26, 65, 69, 70, 96, 101–3, 107, 138, 179
Dailey, Margaret 102, 107
Dailey, Nancy 103
Dailey, Robert 102, 103
Dalton, Thomas 280
Danbury (CT) 55, 58, 59, 78, 85, 153, 179, 181, 212, 270
Danforth, Elijah (Capt.) 289, 301
Danforth, Jacob 43, 161, 194, 205–6
Danforth, Jacob, Jr. 206
Daniels, Eliphalet (Capt.) 230
Danielson, Timothy (Col.) 284, 306
Dartmouth (MA) 284
Dartmouth College (NH) 106, 131, 132
Davenport, John 273
Davidson, David 25, 45, 103–4, 111
Davis, Frances 280
Davis, John (Capt.) 276, 277
Davis, Mary 93
Davis, Robert (Capt.) 275
Davison, William 19, 194, 207
Dead River Cemetery (Leeds, ME) 257, 258
Dean, Clark 107
Deane (ship) 265
Dearborn, Dinah 265
Dearborn, Samuel (Capt.) 87
Dearborn, Henry (Capt.-Maj.-Col.) 42, 49, 50, 51, 54, 57, 58, 89
Dearborn, Josiah 255
Dearing, Cato 8, 9, 104
Dearing, Ebenezer (Capt.) 104
Declaration of Independence 19, 79, 116, 184
Dedham (MA) 261
Deerfield (NH) 110, 129, 135
Dego, Peter 207–9

Index   333

Delaware River, crossing of 36, 39, 46, 175, 184, 199, 267
Derby (VT) 240
Derry (NH) 147
deserters, black soldiers as 15, 21, 109, 111, 166, 173, 179, 130, 146, 148, 153, 165, 188, 200, 208, 214, 216, 223, 241
Detroit (MI) 293
Dexter, Daniel (Lt.) 300
Diamond, John (Jack) 19, 55, 104–5, 276
Diamond, Susanna 105, 276
Diamond, William 253
Dibbel, Charles (Capt.) 208
Dickey, James (Capt.) 167
Dickinson (NY) 202
Dickinson, Caesar (Castor) 16, 105–6, 314
Dinah 181
Ditson, Rebecca 276
Dodge, Hampshire 263
Doolittle, James (Col.) 42
Dorchester Heights (MA) 42, 297
Dover (NH) 15, 16, 17, 164, 172, 173, 182, 229
Dow, London 19, 31, 44, 106
Dow, Peggy 106
Dow, Reuben (Capt.) 43, 160, 161, 205, 206
Downing, Richard 107
Downing, Simon 107
Dracut (MA) 258, 278, 279, 280
Drake, Abraham (Col.) 80, 188, 242
Drake, HMS (ship) 53, 75, 164
Drew, John (Capt.) 20, 75, 78, 90, 125, 127, 128, 182, 194
Driver, Jenney 265
Driver, John (Jack) 25, 243, 244, 263, 265
Driver, Katherine 265
Drowne, Peter (Capt.) 74, 204
Druid, HMS (ship) 135
Drury, Luke (Col.) 307
Dublin (NH) 250
Duce, Cato 107–8
Duce, Katy 179
Duce, Robert (Bob) 107–8, 234
Duce, Sally 234
Dudley, Samuel 93
Dudley, Susannah 93
Dummer Academy (MA) 93

Dunbarton (NH) 152, 259
Duncan, John (Capt.) 214
Dunkin, John 19, 108
Dunkin, Thomas 19, 51, 108
Dunstable (MA) 298
Durham (NH) 114, 142, 143, 174, 176, 185, 229, 230, 237, 295
Durham, Cesar 314
Duxbury (VT) 201

Eager, Fortunatus (Capt.) 261
East Greenwich (RI) 227
East Haddam (CT) 29, 235
Eastman, John (Capt.) 214
Easton (PA) 57, 58
Egery, Daniel (Capt.) 284
Eighty-Eight Battalion Resolve 14
Elizabeth (ship) 116
Elkins, Henry (Capt.) 207
Elmira (NY) 57
Emerson, Amos (Capt.) 86, 165, 200
Emerson, Edward (Capt.) 80
Emerson, Mary 145
Emerson, Mehitable 276
Emerson, Sarah 277
Emerson, Smith (Capt.) 111, 146
Emerson, Solomon 108
Emerson, Timothy 145
Emerson, Timothy (Capt.) 204
Emery, Richard (Capt.) 213, 314
Enfield (NH) 108, 131, 132, 315
Enos, Roger (Col.) 171
Enosburg (VT) 201
Epping (NH) 34, 109, 113, 123, 124, 144, 168, 173, 174, 221
Epsom (NH) 32, 110, 159
Estabrook, Prince 42
Evans, Benjamin 108
Evans, George 22, 70, 108–9, 127
Evans, Jonathan (Capt.) 269
Evans, Stephen (Col.) 125, 127, 133, 173, 204
Exeter (NH) 35, 101, 102, 107, 110, 121, 122, 123, 124, 128, 137, 144, 164, 179, 182, 213, 216, 224, 234, 235, 240, 241, 242, 266, 267, 268, 269, 276, 285, 286, 315

Fair Oaks, Battle of (Civil War) 202
Fairweather, Caesar 263
Falkenham, John 212

Falmouth (MA) 284
Falmouth (ME) 217
Farrar, Stephen (the Rev.) 126
Farrington, Thomas (Capt.) 278
Farrow, William 225
Febiger, Christian (Adj.) 213, 252
Fellows, John (Gen.) 210
Ferguson, Alexander 196
Fernald, Tobias (Capt.) 230
filander 308
First Baptist Society (Goffstown, NH) 277
First Barnstable Militia (MA) 284
First Congregational Church (Lexington, MA) 249
First Presbyterian Church (Newburyport, MA) 234
Fisher, Samuel (Capt.) 261
Fishkill (NY) 161, 194, 197, 204, 220, 247, 253, 267, 285
Fisk, Cato 16, 19, 21, 25, 27, 28, 30, 32, 51, 65, 109–10
Fisk, Ebenezer 110
Fisk, Ebenezer (Dr.) 109
Fisk, James 110
Fisk, Nancy 110
Fogg, Abner 266
Fogg, Ann-Marie 207
Fogg, Fortune 52, 266
Fogg, Jeremiah (Capt.) 100, 238
Fogg, Jockey 110
Fogg, John (Lt.) 217
Follett, Robert (Capt.) 80, 81, 118
Follett, William 25, 45, 111
Folsom, Ephraim 92
Ford, John (Capt.) 152, 278, 279, 299
Fort #4 Charlestown (NH) 140, 146, 152, 153, 157, 189, 200, 214
Fort Ann (NY) 48, 155, 159
Fort Clinton (NY) 270
Fort Edward (NY) 48, 152, 306
Fort George (NY) 230, 275
Fort Mercer (NJ) 294
Fort Stanwix (NY) 247, 291
Fort Sullivan (NH) 230
Fort Ticonderoga (NY) 12, 21, 47, 78, 83, 84, 95, 96, 99, 100, 104, 109, 110, 112, 113, 114, 118, 125, 130, 131, 136, 139, 140, 143, 151, 155, 156, 158, 159, 161, 162, 164, 168, 171, 173, 177, 178, 183, 189, 190, 196, 208, 211, 212, 214,
215, 216, 222, 226, 231, 232, 233, 249, 279, 295, 297, 303, 306, 309
Fort Wagner (SC-CW) 124, 280
Fort Washington (NH) 207
Fort Washington (NY) 208
Fort Wheeling (VA) 293
Fort William and Mary (NH) 106, 314
Fort William Henry (NY) 213, 314
Fortune 44, 82, 111, 179
Fortune, Amos 249, 256, 282
Fortune, Pompey 248
Fortune, Violate 249, 256
Four Corners Cemetery (Sullivan, NH) 310
Fox, Benjamin 111–12
Francis, Ebenezer (Col.) 47, 48, 196
Francis, William (Capt.) 306
Freeman, Anthony 195
Freeman, Caezar 29, 316
Freeman, Cuff 263
Freeman, Dan 142
Freeman, Esther How 234
Freeman, John 112
Freeman, Jonathan (Lt.) 113
Freeman, Mahala 280
Freeman, Moody 112–13
Freeman, Moses 250
Freeman, Nathaniel (Col.) 284
Freeman, Nero 263
Freeman, Peter 113
Freeman, Pomp 248–49, 266, 282
Freeman, Titus 44, 209–10
Free-Will Baptists 25, 26, 30, 31, 33, 166, 201, 202, 203
French, Abraham (Capt.) 86
French, Daniel-Chester 123
French, Gould 113
French, Henry (Judge) 123
French, Oliver 50, 113–14
French, William 123
French and Indian War 33, 47, 105, 106, 145, 157, 196, 212, 213, 221, 233, 251, 269, 278, 313
Friends Adventurer (ship) 180
Frost, Charles 195
Frost, William 84
Frye, Daniel (Lt.) 209
Frye, Ebenezer (Capt.) 85, 119, 146, 161, 164, 176, 221
Frye, Isaac (Capt.) 140, 148, 149, 156, 172, 211, 228, 237

Frye, James (Col.) 269, 270, 277, 278, 281
Fryman, Isaac (Col.) 215
Fuller, Amos 211
Fuller, David 211
Fuller, Ezra 13, 16, 17, 43, 52, 210–11, 311
Furbush, Charles (Capt.) 256, 257, 287

Gabriel 193–94
Gale, Jacob (Col.) 56
Gallows Hill (NY) 253
Gallup, William 222, 223
Gamby 90
Gansevoort, Peter (Col.) 247, 291
Gardner, Lydia 165
Gardner, Peleg 280
Gates, Horatio (Gen.) 11, 51, 171, 176
Gates, William (Capt.) 250
General Sullivan (ship) 23, 24, 116, 117, 288
Geneva (NY) 58
Gerrish, Benjamin 24
Gerrish, Robert Elliot 269
Gerrish, Samuel (Capt.-Col.) 213, 214, 215, 249, 252, 253, 269, 314
Gibson, Thadeus 261, 262
Gilbert, Prince 263
Giles, Ezekiel (Capt.) 87
Gilford (NH) 128, 240
Gill, Benjamin 266
Gill, Joel 64, 243, 266–67
Gilman, Anthony 45, 61, 211–12, 314
Gilman, David (Col.) 83, 140, 148, 158, 161, 164, 131, 155
Gilman, Jeremiah (Capt.) 172, 211, 212, 213, 226, 228, 229, 297, 298
Gilman, John (Maj.) 213, 314
Gilman, Nathaniel 234
Gilman, Nicholas (Col.) 137
Gilman, Samuel (Capt.) 226, 228, 229, 242, 298
Gilman, Zebulon (Capt.) 137
Gilmanton (NH) 135, 179, 180, 182, 224, 248, 297
Glasgo, Priscilla 96
Gleason, Micajah (Capt.) 198, 199, 283
Glidden, Asa 172
Glidden, Catherine 172, 173
Glines, Abraham 114
Glines, Affa 115

Glines, Amos 115
Glines, Burnham 115
Glines, Dustin 115
Glines, Hannah 115
Glines, Israel 22, 25, 29, 114–16, 315, 316
Glines, Lydia 115
Glines, Robert 22, 29, 60, 115–16
Glines, William 114
Gloster, John 313
Gloucester (RI) 201
Glover, John (Col.-Gen.) 11, 39, 45, 50, 56, 184, 255, 262, 267, 268, 289, 301
Godfrey, William 168, 225
Goffe, John (Col.) 139, 145, 269
Goffstown (NH) 79, 220, 221, 231, 232, 244, 277, 278, 299
Goldsboro (NC) 280
Goodrich, William (Capt.) 208
Gookin, Daniel 98
Gorwood, Charles 267
Goss, John (Capt.) 162
Grafton County (NH) 233
Grantham (NH) 108
Granville (ship) 165
Gray, Harrison 116
Gray, Scipio 24, 116–17
Graydon, Alexander (Col.) 11
Great Barrington (MA) 266
Greaton, John (Col.) 289
Greele, Enoch 117–18
Green, David (Col.) 231
Green, Ebenezer (Capt.) 114
Green, Holden 214
Green, John-Jack (John) 213–15, 300
Green, Joseph 149
Green, William (Capt.) 249
Green Mountain Boys 106
Greene, Betsey 122
Greene, Christopher (Col.) 56, 227, 294, 295
Greene, Nathaniel (Gen.) 46, 294
Greenland (NH) 92, 143, 158, 159, 217, 218, 219, 220
Greenleaf, Lydia 281
Greenleaf, Moses (Capt.) 233
Greenwich (RI) 223
Gridley, Richard (Col.) 207, 210
Griffin, Ann 215
Griffin, Nancy 215
Griffin, Oliver 215
Griffin, Thomas 194, 214–15

Griffith, William 48, 118
Grosvenor, Thomas (Lt.) 36
Groton (MA) 278
Gurty, J. (Capt.) 293

Hackensack Ridge (NJ) 115
Hacker, Hoysted (Capt.) 284
Hafford, Prince 267
Hale, Aesop 39, 45, 267–68
Hale, Cato 95, 119
Hale, Enoch (Col.) 56, 85, 101, 171, 183, 225, 232
Hale, Lucy 268
Hale, Nathan (Col.) 47, 48, 75, 118, 120, 142, 158, 177, 178, 190
Halifax (NS, Can.) 35, 116, 117, 309
Hall, Aaron 34, 121–24
Hall, Ann 269
Hall, Betsey 121, 122
Hall, Charles 316
Hall, Clarissa 121
Hall, Dolly 121
Hall, Eliza 124
Hall, George 121–22
Hall, James 121
Hall, Jean 269
Hall, Jude 1, 15, 27, 34, 43, 50, 55, 70, 119–24, 131, 315
Hall, Martha 295
Hall, Moses 34, 122–24
Hall, Nathaniel 121
Hall, Pero 43, 63, 243, 268–71, 314
Hall, Rhoda 121, 122
Hall, Seneca 10
Hall, Stacy 123
Hall, Tom 295
Hall, William 121, 122
Ham, Jonathan (Capt.) 190, 191
Hamilton, Alexander (Lt. Col.) 62
Hampstead (NH) 119, 147
Hampton (NH) 139, 149, 153, 168, 186, 217, 240, 242, 255, 266
Hampton Falls (NH) 147, 148, 149, 150, 151
Hancock (ship) 263
Hancock, Belcher (Capt.) 275
Hancock, John 12
Hannibal (ship) 121
Hanover (MA) 198
Hanover (NH) 31, 112, 113, 131, 132, 293, 307

Hanscom, Alice 195
Hanson, Elizabeth 204
Hanson, Robin 193, 216, 229
Haraden, Jonathan (Capt.) 194
Hardwick (MA) 250
Harlem Heights, Battle of 44, 199, 212
Harper, William (Capt.) 137, 148
Harpswell (ME) 196
Harry, Mary 309
Hart, Bridget 173
Hart, John 145
Hart, John (Capt.) 221, 314
Hartford (VT) 108, 222
Hartland (VT) 222
Hartwell, John (Capt.) 297
Hartwood (MA) 208
Harvard (MA) 166, 260
Harvard College (MA) 304
Harvey, John 216
Harvey, Moses (Capt.) 274
Harwood, Peter (Maj.) 209, 271, 281
Haskell, Henry (Capt.) 260
Hastings, Libbeus 195
Hatch, John 143
Hatley (Quebec, Can.) 239
Haverhill (MA) 123, 124, 240
Haverhill (NH) 194, 288
Hayes, Abigail 125
Hayes, George 47, 56, 125
Hayes, Reuben 125
Hayward, John (Capt.) 251, 253, 282
Hayward, Joshua 131
Hazard (ship) 264
Head, Nathaniel (Capt.) 83, 152
Healey, Nathaniel 119
Heart, Dinah 296
Heath, William (Col.-Gen.) 63, 276
Hebron (CT) 106
Hendly, Rosanna 309
Henniker (NH) 32, 213, 261, 262, 285
Henson, Cornelius 280
Herkimer, Battle of 178
Hessian troops 21, 46, 56, 62, 63, 199, 268, 286, 294
Hibbery, Abner 271
Hill, David 125
Hill, Jeremiah (Capt.) 275
Hill, John 125
Hill, Tower 271–72
Hillsboro (NH) 129
Hilton, Joseph 91, 92

Index 337

Hilton, Winthrop (Lt.) 226
Hind, Jacob (Capt.) 119
Hinesburg (VT) 201
hired substitutes, black soldiers as 14, 149, 175, 197, 274
Hobart, David (Col.) 200
Hodgdon, Alexander (Capt.) 210
Hodgdon, Caesar 243, 272–74
Hodgdon, Caleb (Capt.) 163
Hodgdon, John 272, 273
Hoit, Jeremiah 56, 126
Holden (MA) 250
Hollis (NH) 157, 160, 205, 206, 278
Holliston (MA) 249
Holman, Jonathan (Col.) 285
Hopkins, Alexander (Capt.) 294
Hopkins, Mark (Col.) 211
Hopkinton (NY) 201, 288
hospital attendants, black soldiers as 20
House, John (Capt.) 108, 131, 151, 222
housebuilders, blacks as 92
Hovey, Thomas (Capt.) 282
How, Bezekiel (Capt.) 84
How, Cyprian (Col.) 249
How, Israel 83
Howard, Abner (Capt.) 289
Howard, Joseph 24
Hoyt, Frederic 280
Hubbard, Elisha 16, 20, 43, 126
Hubbard, Ephraim 126
Hubbardton, Battle of 27, 47–48, 50, 109, 118, 126, 143, 156, 158, 178, 181, 182, 190, 197, 309
Hughes, Samuel 143
Hunking, Mark (Capt.) 127
Hunking, Richard 16, 20, 30, 55, 127
Hunt, Abraham (Capt.) 270
Huntington (VT) 201
Husow, Elsa 110
Husow, Sara 110
Hutchins, Hezekiah (Capt.) 129
Hutchins, Nathaniel (Capt.) 98, 226, 227
Huzzey, James 274–75
Huzzey, Susannah 274, 275
Hyde, Caleb (Maj.) 306

indentured servants, blacks as 6, 131, 132, 269
Inman's Point (MA) 252
Ipswich (MA) 217, 245, 267

Island of Orleans (Can.) 251
Isle Au Noix (Can.) 44, 111, 114
Isle of Shoals (NH) 74, 264
Israel River (NH) 114, 315

Jack, John 60, 216–20
Jack, Nancy 217, 219–20
Jack, Phillis 217, 218–20
Jack, Thomas 217
Jackson, Hall (Dr.) 104
Jackson, Henry (Col.) 65, 237
Jackson, Jonathan 275
Jackson, Michael (Col.) 206, 266
Jackson, Pomp 52, 243, 275–76
Jackson, Simon (Capt.) 290
Jacksonville (FL) 123
Jaffrey (NH) 29, 189, 243, 249, 252, 256, 282
James River (VA) 100, 291
Jason (ship) 25, 263–65
Jefferson (NH) 315
Jenkins, James 143
Jenkins, Stephen (Capt.) 270
Jenness, Job 17, 128, 140
Jenness, Paul 17, 127, 140
Jenness, Prince 17, 127–28, 136, 140
Jerseyfield (NY) 63
Johnson, Phillip (Capt.) 145
Johnson, Samuel (Col.) 270
Johnstown (NY) 63
Johonnot, Andrew 276
Johonnot, James 279
Johonnot, Mehitable 279
Johonnot, Moses 279
Johonnot, Peter 276
Johonnot, Prince 31, 43, 243, 244, 276–78
Johonnot, Titus 276
Johonnot, William 279
Jones, Cato 75
Jones, John 89
Jones, John Paul (Capt.) 23, 53, 75, 88, 164
Juba 144
Judge, Ona (Oney) 218–19
Julie 127

Keene (NH) 180, 214
Kelly, Moses (Col.) 56, 214
Kelly, William (the Rev.) 259
Kelsey, "Yellow Beck" 128

Kelsey, Josh 128
Kelsey, Rachel 128
Kelsey, Zack 20, 55, 127–28
Keniston, Catherine 93
Kennebec River (ME) 224
Kensington (NH) 13, 119, 120, 149, 221, 283
Kent, Peter 27, 43
Kidder, Frederick 222
Kidder, Jacob 279
Kidder, Reuben 158
kidnapping, practice of 121, 128, 245, 280
Kimball, John 138
Kimball, Peter (Capt.) 83
Kimball, Sally 206
Kimball, Thomas 55, 58, 129
King George's War 313
Kings Bridge (NY) 286, 296
King's Ferry (NY) 253, 270
Kingston (NH) 79, 86, 115, 117, 137, 269
Kips Bay, Battle of 44
Kitcath, Widow 116
Kittery (ME) 80, 81, 177, 195, 196, 229
Kittredge, Thomas (Dr.) 305
Knight, Bone 22, 129–30
Knight, Joseph 22, 129
Knott, Jesse 129, 130–31
Knowles, James (Dea.) 146
Knox, Catherine 134, 135
Knox, Ermanda 133
Knox, George 26, 29, 46, 55, 58, 108, 131–35, 315
Knox, George, Jr. 134
Knox, Harriet 133, 134
Knox, Harvey 133
Knox, Jemima 133

Ladies Charitable African School 35, 187
Lafayette, Marquis de 12, 54, 56, 61
Lafayette's Light Infantry Regiment 100
Laighton, John 135
Lake Champlain 208, 230, 238, 275, 309
Lake City (FL) 123
Lake George (NY) 157, 213, 314
Lake Mascoma (NH) 133
Lake Tarleton (NH) 199
Lamprey, John (Dea.) 255
Lancaster (MA) 280, 307, 315

landowners, blacks as 28, 34, 86, 87, 91, 92, 196, 234, 255
Lane, Primus 97–98, 135
Lane, Prince 64, 96
Langdon, John (Col.) 49, 93, 188
Lankton, Noah (Capt.) 211
Laurens, Henry 12
Laurens, John (Lt. Col.) 62
Lawrence, David 90
Lear, Caesar 14, 24, 135–36
Lear, Tobias (Capt.) 14, 135
Lear, Tobias, Jr. 135, 136
Lebanon (NH) 222, 288, 293
Lechmere's Point (MA) 224
Lee (NH) 146, 166, 174
Lee, Caesar 263
Lee, Charles (Gen.) 53, 54
Leeds (ME) 257, 258
Leicester (MA) 232, 274
Lempster (NH) 29, 175, 235, 236, 315
Lenox (MA) 233
Leutze, Emanuel 36, 39, 184
Lew, Adrastus 280
Lew, Amy 280
Lew, Barzillai 19, 35, 243, 278–80
Lew, Barzillai, Jr. 280
Lew, Dinah 279, 280
Lew, Eri 280
Lew, Euebra 280
Lew, Hannah 280
Lew, Lucy 280
Lew, Margaret 278
Lew, Mary 280
Lew, Peter 280
Lew, Phebe 280
Lew, Primus 278
Lew, Reophas 280
Lew, Zadock 278, 279, 280
Lew, Zimri 280
Lew, Zimri, Jr. 280
Lew, Zirviah 280
Lewis, James (Capt.) 85, 225
Lewis, John (Eld.) 201
Lexington (MA) 29, 249, 251, 252, 255, 256, 282
Lexington and Concord, Battle of 13, 41–42, 85, 152, 155, 160, 205, 210, 226, 231, 252, 254, 260, 276, 281
Libby, James (Capt.) 22, 173, 203, 204
Libby, Joseph 182
Liberty, Prince 47, 128, 136, 311

Light, John 137
Light, Prince 59, 102, 137-38
Light, Robert (Capt.) 137
Lincoln (MA) 297
Lincoln, Benjamin (Gen.) 60, 61, 286, 296
Lion (ship) 251
Litchfield (NH) 141, 287, 288, 290
Lithgow, William (Capt.) 217
Little Beards Town (NY) 58
Little Compton (RI) 223
Littleton (NH) 272
Livermore, Daniel (Capt.) 98, 101, 115
Livingston, James (Col.) 291
Lock, Jeremiah 138
Lock, Joseph (Capt.) 138
Lock, Nimshi 47, 138-39, 311
Loeses 308
London (Eng) 122
Londonderry (NH) 167, 241, 245, 246, 269, 285, 303, 304, 305, 307, 315
Long, Benjamin 139
Long, Caesar 139-40
Long, Joshua 139
Long, Paul 46, 127, 140
Long, Peter 8, 140-41
Long, Pierce (Col.) 47, 48, 74, 78, 86, 104, 112, 118, 163, 173, 177, 196
Long Island, Battle of 44-45, 175, 204, 212, 267
Loudon (NH) 152, 286, 296
Louisburg, Siege of (FIW) 149-50, 313
Lovejoy, Betsey 281
Lovejoy, Diadamia 281
Lovejoy, John 239
Lovejoy, Joshua 281, 282
Lovejoy, Leafjoy Ingalls 281
Lovejoy, Lucy 281
Lovejoy, Lydia 281
Lovejoy, Martha 281
Lovejoy, Peter 281-82
Lovejoy, Pomp 281
Lovell, Solomon (Gen.) 297
Lovewell, Noah (Col.) 129, 141
Lovewell, Stephen 19, 44, 141
Low, Samuel (Capt.) 247
Lowell (MA) 279
Lowell, Abner (Capt.) 217
Lunenburg (MA) 198, 236
Lyford, John 168

Lyman (NH) 195
Lynn (MA) 210

MacGregor, London 64, 220-21
Malone (NY) 33, 202, 203
Manassas (VA) 240
Manchester (MA) 212
Manchester (VT) 152
Manly, John (Capt.) 263-65
Mann, Christopher 249, 282
Mann, James 148, 149, 282
Manning, Thomas (Capt.) 116
Mansfield, John (Col.) 207
Marblehead (MA) 156, 267, 301
March, Clement 92
March, George (Capt.) 19
March, Israel 92
March, Paul 92
Marcy, Cato 21, 52, 141-42, 311
Marcy, John (Capt.) 130, 142
Marion (IN) 215
Mars (ship) 206
Marshall, Thomas (Col.) 43, 193
Marshfield (MA) 221
Marston, Jeremiah (Capt.) 139
Marston, Simon (Capt.) 80, 88
Martin, Archelaus 143
Martin, Dan 16, 25, 55, 58, 142-43
Martin, Jubal 144, 147
Martin, Mary 144
Martin, Scipio 16, 47, 145-46, 314
Martin, Sidon 51, 144, 146-47
Martin, Simeon 300
Mary (ship) 117
Mason (NH) 210, 282
Massachusetts Regiments 1st Brigade, 258, 305; 1st Inf. 194, 208, 270, 274, 275, 276, 296; 2nd Inf. 247, 266; 3rd Inf. 289, 290; 5th Inf. 197, 204, 207, 241, 303, 304; 6th Inf. 5, 199, 209, 210, 211, 212, 221, 226, 228, 236, 241, 242, 271, 281, 283, 286, 289, 299, 301; 7th Inf. 258, 305; 8th Inf. 206, 208, 270, 298; 9th Inf. 178, 215, 252, 291; 10th Inf. 225, 281, 285, 286, 307; 11th Inf. 47, 196, 197, 233, 234; 12th Inf. 208, 230, 275; 14th Inf. 284; 15th Inf. 249, 250, 261; 54th Inf. 33, 34, 124, 227, 254, 255, 280; 55th Inf. 280
Massachusetts State Navy 194, 224, 251
Massey, George 268, 269

McClary, Andrew (Maj.) 159, 160
McClary, Michael (Capt.-Gen.) 110, 146, 152, 159
McCobb, Samuel (Capt.) 170, 171
McDaniel, Andrew 22, 24, 146–47, 160
McDuffee, Daniel (Capt.) 125
McFarland, Moses (Capt.) 299, 308
McGaw, Jacob 283
McGaw, Titus 45, 283
McGregor, Robert 220
McIntyer, Neal 147
McIntyer, Primus 45, 147
McIntyre, Cato 147
McIntyre, Mecum 147
McLain, Caesar 144, 147
McMillan, Andrew 80
McNeill, Hector (Capt.) 263
Means, James (Capt.) 208
Medfield (MA) 266
Medford (MA) 107, 120, 125, 126, 129, 150, 183, 251, 252, 259, 289, 303
medical orderlies, black soldiers as 100
Medway (MA) 262
Mellish (ship) 284
Merchant, William 89
Meredith (NH) 179, 180, 240, 286
Merrill, Jonathan 201
Merrill, Mercy Ladd 239
Merrimack (NH) 79, 283, 302
Merritt, Amos 255
Methuen (MA) 226
Middlebury College (VT) 33, 239
Middlesex (VT) 201
Miles, Charles (Capt.) 249
Miles, Mary 196
Miller, Jeremiah (Capt.) 274, 296
Miller, Jonathan 14, 16, 22, 55, 147–49
Miller, Joseph (Ens) 271
Miller, Neb 149
Miller, Robert 13, 16, 22, 47, 55, 108, 147–50
Miller, Robert, Sr. 148, 149, 150, 151, 313
Minerva (ship) 84
Mingo, Ebenezer 221, 283, 284
Mingo, Eli 284
Mingo, Phyllis 284
Mingo, William 283–84, 311
Minor, Drover 24, 52, 284–85
Minot, Catherine 133
Minot, John (Capt.) 297
Mitchell, John 269

Mohawk River (NY) 247
Mohawk Valley (NY) 62
Monk, (Capt.) 291
Monmouth, Battle of 34, 41, 53–56, 90, 96, 100, 110, 120, 131, 142, 143, 148, 151, 152, 155, 162, 178, 181, 182, 200, 208, 212, 226, 233, 247, 249, 250, 266, 275, 284, 286
Monroe, James (Gov.) 194
Montreal (Can.) 43, 44, 82, 111, 114, 209, 293
Montserrat (BWI) 116
Moody, Paul (Capt.) 270
Mooney, Hercules (Col.) 22, 59, 169, 170, 175, 235
Moor, Thomas 152
Moore, Archelaus (Col.) 17, 152
Moore, Daniel (Col.) 99
Moore, Fortain 51
Moore, Fortune 152
Moore, Lucinda 259
Moore, Lucy 153
Moore, Sampson 17, 152–53
Morgan, Daniel (Col.) 49, 50, 51, 198
Morison, Hiram 174
Morison, Samuel Eliot 75, 88
Morrill, Amos (Capt.) 78, 84, 129
Morrill, Nancy 215
Morrisania (NY) 61, 212
Morristown (NJ) 99, 253
Moulton, Benjamin 220
Moulton, Cato 8, 19, 47, 153–55
Moulton, Jonathan (Col.) 153, 154
Moultonborough (NH) 29, 114, 115, 116, 165, 255, 315, 316
Mount Caesar Cemetery (Swanzey) 301, 316
Mount Independence (NY) 114, 130, 151, 190, 309
Mount Israel (NH) 114
Mount Tom (MA) 253
Mount Vernon (VA) 219
Mount Washington (NY) 299, 308
Mullinaux, Anna 187
Mullinaux, Esther 187
Mullinaux, William 187
Mullinaux, William Prince 187
Munroe, Edmund (Capt.) 249
Murray, John (the Rev.) 234
musicians, blacks as 19, 25, 109
Mystic (MA) 252

Index 341

Nan 153
Nancy (ship) 219
Natick (MA) 209, 261
Nay, Samuel (Capt.) 140, 168
Neal, Walter 139
Nealley, Edward 174
Negro, Fortune 152
Negro Burying Ground (Hanover) 31, 32
Nell, William 6, 36, 37, 184
Nelly (ship) 103
Nelson, Charles (Capt.) 81, 82
Nero, Caesar 213, 314
Nesmith, John (Capt.) 177
New Bedford (MA) 280
New Boston (NH) 277, 287
New Cape Newagen Island (ME) 196
New Castle (NH) 86, 112, 118, 139, 163, 173, 177, 186, 196
New Hampshire Battalion 64, 107, 120, 149, 162, 168, 172, 177, 190, 191, 192, 238
New Hampshire General Assembly 87
New Hampshire Grants 106
New Hampshire Regiments: 1st Infantry 19, 41, 42, 50, 51, 53, 54, 55, 60, 64, 78, 80, 84, 86, 98, 108, 111, 119, 129, 130, 131, 132, 133, 142, 146, 150, 151, 161, 162, 164, 165, 172, 176, 189, 190, 200, 212, 221, 221, 222, 223, 226, 227, 228, 312; 2nd Infantry 16, 19, 20, 22, 42, 47, 48, 50, 51, 58, 60, 64, 75, 77, 90, 95, 96, 98, 99, 100, 101, 102, 104, 107, 109, 113, 117, 118, 120, 125, 127, 128, 129, 136, 142, 148, 150, 156, 158, 162, 166, 167, 172, 173, 177, 178, 180, 181, 182, 190, 191, 197, 204, 208, 226, 228, 229, 233, 237, 238, 241, 295, 298, 312; 2nd Infantry (Civil War) 240; 3rd Infantry 42, 50, 51, 54, 58, 74, 85, 95, 115, 119, 126, 128, 129, 130, 140, 142, 146, 148, 152, 155, 156, 159, 166, 169, 170, 176, 183, 210, 211, 225, 231, 312
New Ipswich (NH) 13, 126, 156, 157, 158, 170, 171, 183, 241, 282
New Light Baptists 30–31, 166
New London (CT) 212, 242
New Milford (CT) 55
New Orleans (LA) 121
New Windsor (NY) 64, 274, 290, 305

New York Regiments: 3rd Inf. 291; 98th Inf. (Civil War) 202
Newburgh (NY) 99, 128, 149, 290
Newbury (MA) 178, 225, 238, 243, 267, 269, 271, 272, 274, 276
Newburyport (MA) 121, 185, 197, 224, 225, 233, 234, 244, 275
Newcastle-upon-Tyne (Eng.) 122
Newington (NH) 225, 243, 272, 295
Newman, Wingate (Capt.) 251
Newmarket (NH) 32, 92, 93, 94, 213, 223, 224, 225, 228, 229, 233, 269, 287, 299
Newport (NH) 71, 98, 130, 131, 167, 315
Newport (RI) 75, 288
Newton (NH) 178
Newtown (NY) 57, 58
Nichols, Moses (Col.) 56, 85, 156, 161, 162, 171, 215, 235
Nicholson, James (Capt.) 292
Nivens, James (Capt.) 206
Nixon, John (Col.) 42, 170, 198, 199, 211, 226, 228, 229, 241, 242, 283, 289, 297, 298, 299, 308
Nixon, Thomas (Col.) 301
Noaks, Cuffe 221, 314
Noice, George 132
Nokes, Timothy 46, 144, 221, 311
Norris, James (Capt.) 96, 113, 146, 169, 178
North Castle (NY) 45, 95, 104, 199, 208, 226, 283
North Cemetery (Portsmouth) 31
North Church (Portsmouth) 35, 151, 177, 187, 188
North Hampton (NH) 129, 140, 168, 255, 276
North River (NY) 270
Northbridge (MA) 274
Northfield (MA) 244, 303, 304
Northwood (NH) 173, 174, 284
Norvell, Jonathan (Capt.) 224
Nott, Robert 130
Nottingham (NH) 88, 174, 299
Noyes, John (Capt.) 270

Odiorne, Jotham 269
Ohio, USS (ship) 179
Ohio Territory 29, 244
Old Dunstable (NH) 105, 141
Old Mill Prison (Eng) 117, 163, 265

342   Index

Oliver, Aaron 13, 16, 27, 43, 48, 155–56, 311
Oliver, Aaron, Jr. 27, 156
Oliver, Abigail 27, 156
Olustee (FL) 124
Orange (NJ) 115
Orange (VT) 239, 240
Orford (NH) 111, 114, 154, 200
Oriskany, Battle of 178
Orleans County Grammar School (VT) 239
Osborne, George (Capt.) 100, 101
Osgood, James (Capt 82, 209
Oxford, Derrick 21, 25, 108, 222–23
Oxford County (ME) 233

Packersfield (NH) 163
Page 153
Page, Jesse (Capt.) 242
Page, John 180
Page, Peter (Capt.) 235
Paine, Amos 115
Paine, Margaret 115
Palmyra (ME) 276
Parke, Joseph (Capt.) 156
Parker, Caesar 287
Parker, John (Capt.) 141, 183
Parker, Jonathan 287
Parker, Jonathan, Jr. 252
Parker, Nathaniel (the Rev.) 225
Parker, Patience 240
Parker, Phineas (Capt.) 281
Parker, Steven (Capt.) 171
Parker, William (Capt.) 180
Parsons, Joseph (Capt.) 139, 140
Parsons, Phyllis 283, 284
Parsons, Samuel 156
Patterson, John (Col.) 208, 275, 291, 293
Paul, Benjamin Jacob 122
Paul, Caesar 101
Paul, Mary Ann 122
Paul, Parker 122
Paul, Rhoda 120
paupers, black soldiers as 27, 110, 126, 129, 135, 137, 237, 255, 273, 274
Pawtucket (RI) 223
Peabody, Oliver 242
Peabody, Stephen (Col.) 56, 74, 87, 95
Peck, Laura 301
Pedro, Anthony 265

Peekskill (NY) 258, 289, 290, 305
Peirce, John (Capt.) 250
Pembroke (NH) 99, 282
Penacook Plantation (NH) 304, 305
Pendexter, Thomas 144
Penobscot Expedition 24, 224
Pension system 27–28
Pepperell, William 150
Perham, Amos 158
Perham, Asa 16, 46, 48, 157–58, 311
Perham, Elizabeth 157
Perham, Lemuel 157
Perham, Lydia 157
Perham, Mary 157
Perham, Samuel 157, 158, 314
Perham, Sarah 157
Perkins, Abraham (Capt.) 163
Peru (NY) 239
Peter 137, 314
Peterborough (NH) 189, 232
Peters, Pomp 25, 61–62, 79, 243, 285–87
Peters, Robinson 25, 223–24
Peters, Sarah 286, 287
Peters, Violet 224
Petersburg, Siege of (Civil War) 202
Peterson, Daniel (Dr.) 288
Pettengill, Joseph (Capt.) 249
Petty, Reuben (Capt.) 303
Pharaoh, William 56
Philadelphia (PA) 52, 53, 218, 219, 286
Phillips, Boston 250
Phillips Exeter Academy (NH) 102, 240
Phillis 108, 109, 181
Phinney, Edmund (Col.) 230, 275
Pickering, Boston 60, 225, 311
Pickering, Edwin 220
Pickering, John 220
Pickering, Nicholas 159
Pickering, Timothy (Col.) 270
Pickering, Tumbril 95, 158–59, 225
Pierce, Benjamin (Dea.) 90
Pierce, Franklin 215
Pike, Benjamin (Lt.) 209
Pike, Robert (Capt.) 223, 259
Pillsbury, Daniel (Capt.) 236, 286, 301
Pine Hill Cemetery (Warner) 32
Pinkham, Polly 167
pioneer settlers, blacks as 29
Piper, Samuel (Lt.) 173
Piscataqua River (NH) 117, 118

Pittsfield (MA) 208
Pittsfield (MA) 306
Pittsfield (NH) 143
Place, David (Capt.) 135
Plaistow (NH) 170, 211, 212, 228, 241, 242, 297, 298
Plattsburg (NY) 238
Pluckemin (NJ) 216
Plumer, George 173
Plumer, John 173, 224–25
Plumer, Samuel 173
Plymouth (NH) 288
Pollack, Edward 302
Pollard, Solomon (Capt.) 258
Pomfret (VT) 165
Pomona, HMS (ship) 263
Pomp 105
Pomp, Peter 52, 159–60, 311
Poor, Enoch (Col.-Gen.) 42, 55, 57, 107, 125, 148, 150, 156, 162, 197, 208, 226, 228, 233, 237
Poor, Peter 43, 160–61, 311
Poor, Thomas (Col.) 270
Poplin (NH) 110
Port Royal (Can.) 313
Porter, Asa 8, 9
Porter, Caesar 26, 243, 287–88
Porter, David (Capt.) 88
Porter, Phillis 288
Portland (ME) 279
Portsmouth (NH) 7, 9, 10, 23, 31, 35, 59, 60, 64, 116, 135, 146, 165, 173, 175, 177, 182, 184, 185, 186, 188, 194, 205, 206, 207, 216, 219, 223, 225, 226, 230, 243, 244, 251, 263, 264, 265, 268, 272, 273, 299, 314
Post, Jeremiah (Capt.) 200
Pottle, William 221
Poughkeepsie (NY) 109, 182
Powers, Peter (Capt.) 157
Powers, Thomas 288–89
Prescott, James (Col.) 260
Prescott, William (Col.) 42, 155, 160, 205, 206, 260, 270, 278, 302
Prince Hall Masonic Lodge (Boston) 280
Princeton, Battle of 41, 131, 136, 140, 155, 158, 161, 164, 199, 275, 283, 298, 299, 308
prisoners of war, black soldiers as 156
privateering 23–24, 116, 117, 163

Prospect Hill (MA) 242, 252
Providence (RI) 56, 121, 223, 242, 249, 250, 275, 300
Providence (ship) 284
Putnam, Rufus (Col.) 204, 241, 303

Quarles, Benjamin 5
Quebec (Can.) 43, 82, 106, 171, 208, 239, 294
Queen Anne's War 313
Queen's Chapel Church (Portsmouth) 84
Quincy, Edmund 9–10
Quintal, George, Jr. 260

Rabytown (NH) 250
Rainbow, HMS (ship) 263
Raleigh (ship) 23–25, 45, 53, 74–75, 100, 103, 111, 136, 147, 165, 170, 175, 205
Ralf, Lois 255
Ramsey, Peter (Capt.) 116
Rand, Jack 289–90
Randall, Benjamin (Eld.) 166
Randall, Edward 293
Randall, Hannah 293
Randall, James 293
Randall, Jenney 293
Randall, Robert 1, 25, 29, 31, 244, 245, 290–94
Randel, Nathaniel 314
Randolph Academy (VT) 239
Ranger (ship) 23, 53, 75, 88, 164, 272
Rawling, Nicholas (Capt.) 188, 189
Rawlins, Eliphalet 148
Rawlins, Elizabeth 92
Rawlins, Samuel 92
Rawson, Edmund 86
Raymond (NH) 86, 87, 110, 112, 139, 240
Raymond, Edward (Capt.) 309
Reading (MA) 183
Reading (VT) 33, 214, 253, 254
Red Bank (NJ) 294
Reed, James (Col.) 42, 85, 119, 120, 126, 129, 130, 142, 155, 170, 183, 210, 231, 270, 278
Reed, John 47, 161–62
Reed, Jonathan (Col.) 249, 279, 299
Reed, Joseph 134
Reed, Joshua 302

Reid, George (Col.) 51, 57, 58, 104, 105, 167, 172
Remick, Oliver 88
Remick, Timothy (Capt.) 275
Reynolds, Daniel (Capt.-Col.) 83, 87, 90, 169
Rhode Island Regiments: 1st Infantry 5, 56, 227, 294–95, 300
Rhode Island State Regiments: Lippitts Militia 300; Tallman's 291, 300
Rhode Island, Battle of 22, 56, 59, 74, 126, 175, 210, 223, 227, 235, 275, 295, 297
Rhymes, Samuel 163
Rhymes, Thomas 163, 311
Richardson (Capt.) 291
Richardson, Ichabod 256
Richmond (MA) 233
Richmond 181
Richmond (Quebec, Can.) 239
Richmond (VA) 193, 202
Richmond (VT) 201
Riggs, Abimelech (Capt.) 300
Riley, Nancy 280
Rindge (NH) 101, 171, 183, 252, 253
Robards, Persila 228
Roberts, Elizabeth 258
Roberts, Reuben 15–16, 46, 193, 225–29
Robertson, James (Lt.) 161
Robertson, John (Capt.) 313
Robin 43, 216, 228–29
Robinson, Caleb (Capt.) 80, 95, 102, 104, 178
Robinson, Ephraim 137
Robinson, Jack 162
Robinson, John (Col.) 279
Robinson, Jonathan (Capt.) 139
Robinson, Mark 138
Robinson, Mary 137
Robinson, Phillis 138
Robinson, Prince 137
Robinson, Samuel 137
Robinson, Zack 128
Rochester (NH) 125, 129, 166, 190, 191, 244, 295, 314
Rodney, Caesar 69
Rogers, Andrew 291
Rogers, Cato 229–31
Rogers, Daniel (Capt.) 229, 230
Rogers, Robert (Capt.) 105, 106
Rogers, Robert (Lt.) 291

Rogers, William (Lt.) 291
Rollins, Dorothy 101
Rollins, Lovely 101
Roseter, David (Col.) 233
Ross, John (Maj.) 63
Rowe, Enoch 120
Rowe, John 116
Rowe, Winthrop (Capt.) 13, 22, 107, 148, 150
Rowell, Thomas 229
Rowell, William (Capt.) 109, 120, 129, 143
Roxbury (MA) 121, 249, 284, 306
Rumney (NH) 117, 166
Rundlett, James 92
Runnells, Daniel (Capt.) 214
Runnels, James 295
Runnels, Martha 295
Runnels, Peleg 56, 243, 244, 245, 294–95
Runnels, Peleg, Jr. 295
Russell, John (Capt.) 284
Russell, Pomp 25, 162–63
Rutland (VT) 171, 183
Rutledge, Edward 12
Rye (NH) 128, 138, 139, 140, 177, 178, 179, 180, 207, 237

Safford, Jesse (Capt.) 222
sailors, blacks as 23–25
St. Clair, Arthur (Gen.) 48
St. John (Can.) 183, 265
St. Leger, Barry (Col.) 247
Salem (MA) 180, 185, 198, 200, 207, 263, 267, 295
Salem, Peter 36
Salisbury Fort (NH) 157
Saltonstall, Dudley (Capt.) 224
Sampson, John 47, 163–64
Samson, Abisha (Lt.) 222
Sandown (NH) 215, 228, 229, 238
Sands, Dinah 297
Sands, Edward 30, 61, 63, 296–97
Sandwich (MA) 248
Sandwich (NH) 316
Sanford (ME) 204
Sankey, Caesar 31, 46, 164–65
Sankey, Sarah 165
Sankey, Simon 164
Sanno, Peter 165
Saratoga, Battle of 21, 41, 49–51, 63, 83,

84, 85, 95, 96, 100, 110, 112, 114, 125, 130, 137, 140, 142, 143, 146, 148, 151, 152, 155, 159, 161, 176, 181, 182, 184, 188, 189, 197, 204, 207, 208, 211, 212, 215, 216, 222, 226, 231, 233, 235, 241, 242, 247, 249, 261, 266, 270, 275, 284, 304
Sargent, Paul Dudley (Col.) 298
Sartell, Nathaniel (Lt.) 261
Savage, Jube 56, 297
Scammans, James (Col.) 224, 225
Scammell, Alexander (Col.) 50, 51, 60, 61, 74, 85, 128, 132, 140, 146, 148, 152, 155, 156, 159, 176, 211, 296
Schenectady (NY) 63, 95, 102, 238
Scippio 43
Scott, William (Maj.) 107, 189
Scribner, Edward 86
Scripture, Samuel 278
Seabrook (NH) 148
Seagrave, Edward (Capt.) 307
Seavey, Caesar 180
Seavey, Phyllis 180
Seavey's Island (NH) 111
Senter, Joseph (Col.) 88, 223
Shackford, William 89
Shaftsbury (VT) 275
The Shakers 30–31, 166
Shapleigh, Elisha (Capt.) 231
Shapleigh, John 195
Shapleigh, Nicholas (Maj.) 195
Sharp, Sarah 164
Sharpe, (Capt.) 292, 293
Sharper, William 22, 165–66
Shedd, Peter 83
Shelburn (VT) 201
Sheldon, Samuel (Capt.) 304
Shepard, John 31, 166
Shepardson, Nathaniel 300
Sheppard, James (Capt.) 215
Sherburne, Daniel 84
Sherburne, Florissa 246
Sherburne, Henry (Maj.) 44
Sherburne, Jesse 167, 315
Sherburne, Pomp 167, 246, 315
Sherburne, Samuel 84
Shirley (MA) 260
Shoreham (VT) 247
Shortridge, Richard (Capt.) 94, 95, 125
Sias, Benjamin (Capt.) 83, 152, 155
Sides, William (Capt.) 240

Silpha 175
Silver Eel (ship) 309
Simonds, Benjamin (Col.) 247
Simpson, Thomas (Capt.) 53
Simsbury (CT) 55
Sinegall, Lucy 268
Sipio, Solomon 314
Sippio 228, 297–98
Sippo 145
slave petitions for freedom 10, 186, 230
slave uprisings 11–12, 192, 194
slaves, as runaways 8, 72, 79, 96, 97, 104, 113, 130, 147, 154, 229, 230, 245, 246; manumission of 30, 90, 195; naming of 69–70; sale of 89, 98, 116–17, 138
Slocum, Edward (Capt.) 227
Small, Aaron 26, 231–32, 243, 298–99
Small, Caesar 47, 168, 255, 311
Small, Catherine 268
Small, Dinah 168, 255
Small, Eunice 231, 299
Small, John 299
Small, Jonathan 43, 231–32, 298–99, 302
Small, Patience 29
Small, Susannah 231, 299
Small, William 29
Small, William, Jr. 19
Smart, John 93
Smith, Abijah (Lt.) 252
Smith, Anna 115
Smith, Calvin (Lt. Col.) 236, 286, 289
Smith, Cato 25, 64, 168
Smith, Elizabeth 187
Smith, John 93
Smith, Josiah (Capt.) 285, 286
Smith, Moses 232
Smith, Peter 58
Smith, Sylvanus (Capt.) 197
Smith, Thomas 232–33
Smithfield (RI) 300
Snell, Benjamin 299
Snell, George 45, 298–300
Snell, Lucy 299
Society of Friends (Quakers) 30–31, 90
Solomon, Ann 251
Somerset, Lydia 256
Somersworth (NH) 17, 136, 181, 203, 204, 208, 244, 295
Soper, Amasa (Capt.) 197

Sopers, Joseph (Lt.) 166
South Hampton (NH) 283, 284
South Woodstock (VT) 254, 255
Southboro (MA) 310
Sparhawk, Nathaniel (Col.) 81
Spencer, Joseph 235
Springfield (MA) 153, 180, 209, 214, 244, 253, 262, 271, 281, 285, 289, 306
Staines, Eliza 219
Staines, John 219
Stark, John (Col.-Gen.) 42, 43, 46, 48–9, 60, 63, 150, 152, 161, 162, 171, 200, 215, 309
Stearns, John 59, 169, 170
Stearns, Josiah (the Rev.) 16, 59, 168, 169, 170, 305
Stearns, Peter 16–17, 30, 59, 168–70
Stenger, Mary 215
Stephenson, Cato 170
Sterling (MA) 309
Stevens, Benjamin (the Rev.) 177
Stevens, Caesar 170
Stevens, Ebenezer 80
Stevens, Ebenezer (Maj.) 216
Stevens, Edward 168
Stevens, Ephraim 43, 170–71
Stevens, Jerusha 171
Stevenstown (NH) 157
Stewart, Primus 64, 172
Stickney, Jonathan (Capt.) 206
Stickney, Thomas (Col.) 83, 166
Stillwater (NY) 171, 200
Stockbridge (MA) 208
Stockbridge, John 172
Stone, Benjamin (Capt.) 166
Stone, Ephraim (Capt.) 175, 235, 236
Stone, Isaac (Capt.) 121
Stoneham (MA) 241
Stonington (CT) 222
Stoodley, James (Capt.) 8
Storey, William (Lt.) 270
Storrs, Joseph (Col.) 231
Stoughton (MA) 266
Stowe (VT) 201
Stratham (NH) 191, 192, 220, 221, 299, 308, 316
Streeter, Barzillar 56, 243–45, 300, 301, 316
Streeter, Hannah 300, 301
Streeter, Joel 301

Streeter, Laura 300, 301
Streeter, Nancy 300, 301
Streeter, Nathan 301
Streeter, Rufus 301
Sturtevant, Hosea 115
Sturtevant, Joanna 115
Sudrick, Bridget 174
Sudrick, Catharine 173
Sudrick, Joseph 22, 25, 172–73
Sudrick, Michael 22, 60, 71, 95, 172–74
Sullivan (NH) 309, 310
Sullivan, George 174
Sullivan, John (Gen.) 36, 39, 46, 56, 57, 58, 77, 78, 90, 96, 120, 161, 174, 175, 180, 181, 182, 185, 205, 212, 216, 222, 253
Sullivan, Noble 36, 39, 174–75, 185
Sully, Thomas 36, 39, 175, 184
Sumner, Job (Capt.) 289
Surprise, HMS (ship) 265
Surry (NH) 232
Sutton (NH) 259
Swan, James (Capt.) 303
Swanzey (NH) 29, 271, 301, 316
Swanzey (RI) 223
Sweat, John 175
Sweat, Pomp 175
Swett, Cicero 301–2
Sylvia 105

Taft, Bezaleel (Capt.) 307
Taggert, Florissa 167
Tallahasee (FL) 123
Tappan (NY) 59, 60
Tappin, James 86
Tarleton, June 265
Tarleton, William (Capt.) 197
Tarleton's Legion 61
Tarrytown (NY) 234
Tash, Catherine 234
Tash, Charles 33, 34, 234
Tash, Esther 235
Tash, Lucy 234
Tash, Mary 234
Tash, Matilda 234
Tash, Oxford 17, 31, 33, 34, 45, 233–34
Tash, Robert 234, 235
Tash, Susan 234
Tash, Thomas (Capt.-Col.) 17, 139, 145, 155, 233, 314
Tash, William 234

Index 347

Tatten, Isaac 16, 22, 29, 59, 175, 235–36, 315
Tatten, Isaac, Jr. 16, 22, 59, 175–76, 235, 236
Taunton (MA) 198
Taylor, Benjamin (Capt.) 83
Taylor, Joseph (Capt.) 172
Taylor, Othniel (Capt.) 286
Taylor, Prince 60, 236–37
Temple (NH) 27, 85, 155, 156, 211, 297
Thayer, Ebenezer (Col.) 210
Thayer, Ebenezer (the Rev.) 186
Thetford (VT) 133, 134
Thom, William Smith 286
Thompson, Caesar 50, 176
Thompson, Joseph (Maj.) 221
Thompson, Prince 176
Thompson, Robert 153, 176
Thompson, Samuel 146
Thompson, Sarah 176
Thompson, Susana 237
Thompson, Thomas 65, 237
Thompson, Thomas (Capt.) 75, 111, 136
Thornton (NH) 289
Thorp, Edward 24
Tilton, Joseph (Dr.) 97
Tilton, Phillip (Capt.) 117, 162
Tioga (NY) 57, 58
Tisdale, James (Capt.) 266
Titcomb, Benjamin (Maj.) 48
Titcomb, Jonathan (Col.) 261
Tiverton (RI) 223, 307
Tobey, Susannah 274
Tom 8–10
Toppan, Christopher (Col.) 149
torture, black soldiers killed by 44
Towne, Ezra (Capt.) 13, 126, 155, 170, 183, 210
Towne, Francis (Capt.) 158, 161
Townshend (VT) 274, 275
Trafton, Phillip (Capt.) 300
Trask, Nathaniel (the Rev.) 110
Trenton, Battle of 41, 45–46, 110, 131, 136, 140, 155, 158, 161, 164, 175, 184, 199, 242, 261, 267, 275, 283, 298, 299, 308
Trevett, Samuel (Capt.) 207
Trois Rivers (Can.) 44
Troy (PA) 205

Trumbull, John 36
Tufts, Cato 19, 302–03
Tufts University (MA) 303
Tupper, Benjamin (Col.) 233, 281, 307
Turner, George (Capt.) 104
Turner, Ishmael 303–4
Tuttle, Rose 272
Twilight, Aaron 238–40
Twilight, Alexander 31, 33, 238–40
Twilight, Asaph 239, 240
Twilight, Freeman 240
Twilight, George 240
Twilight, Ichabod 16, 31, 33, 63, 71, 238, 240
Twilight, Mary 238, 239
Twilight, Polly 239, 240
Twilight, Sarah 240
Twilight, Thomas 238
Twilight, William 239, 240
Twilight, William Henry 240
Tyler, Nathan (Col.) 282, 307
Tyrannicide (ship) 25, 194

Underwood, Boston 30, 177
Underwood, John (Capt.) 177
Union (ship) 117
United States Regiments: 1st American 237; 3rd Colored Inf. (Civil War) 34, 123; 127th Colored Inf. (Civil War) 179
Unity (NH) 172, 239
Upton (MA) 274
Uxbridge (MA) 307

Valley Forge (PA) 20, 51–52, 56, 76, 78, 100, 120, 128, 159, 160, 166, 176, 182, 189, 190, 197, 208, 211, 212, 222, 226, 247, 249, 261, 266, 275, 289, 308
Varnum, James (Gen.) 56
Varnum, Joseph Bradley (Capt.) 279
Varrell, William 177
Vengeance (ship) 25, 223–24
Ventrum, Nicholas 48, 177–78
Vergennes (VT) 239
Vermont Continentals 49
Verplanck's Point (NY) 281, 286, 307
Virgin, Joel 174
Virginia (ship) 292
Virginia Continental Regiments 291
von Steuben, Baron (Gen.) 52
Vose, Joseph (Col.) 194, 274, 275, 295

Wade, Nathaniel (Col.) 262
Wadleigh, John 122
Wait, Benjamin (Col.) 222
Wait, Jason (Capt.) 129, 142, 225
Waite, Nathan 99
Walbridge, Ebenezer (Lt. Col.) 235
Waldron, John (Col.) 80, 216
Walker, Prince 30, 64, 243, 304–06
Walker, Timothy (the Rev.) 304, 305
Wallace, Caesar 28, 35, 55, 65, 71, 129, 178–80
Wallace, Freeman 179
Wallace, James 179
Wallace, Katy 179, 180
Wallace, Lucy 179
Walley, Prince 180–81
Wallingford, Cato 17, 26, 55, 179, 181–82
Wallingford, Elizabeth 17, 181
Wallingford, Pegg 182
Wallingford, Samuel (Capt.) 164
Wallingford, Thomas (Col.) 181
Wallis, Samuel (Lt.) 178, 180
Walpole (NH) 21, 141, 142, 189
Walton, John (Capt.) 208
Walton, Shadrach (Col.) 313
Ward, Henry 75
Ward, Jacob 306–7
Ware, Hezekiah (Lt.) 262
Warner (NH) 32, 238, 244, 259
Warner, John-Jack 217
Warner, Jonathan (Gen.) 194, 195
Warner, Jonathan 216
Warner, Seth (Col.) 49
Warren (NH) 29, 199, 200, 201
Warren (RI) 223
Warren, Isaac (Capt.) 266
Warwick (RI) 223, 274
Washington (NH) 79
Washington, George (Gen.-Pres.) 136, 179, 218, 219, 247, 266
Washington, Martha 218
Waterbury (VT) 201
Watertown (NY) 201
Watson, Abraham (Capt.) 289
Watson, Dudley 182
Watson, Gloster 14, 15, 16, 17, 20, 30, 51, 69, 127, 182
Watson, Thomas 182
Watson, William (Capt.) 290
Weare, Meshach 150

Weare, Richard (Capt.) 140, 148, 155
Weare, Samuel 189
Weatherbee, Samuel (Capt.) 130
Webb, John 160, 241
Webster, David 289
Webster, Ebenezer (Capt.) 74, 126
Wedgewood, David 121
Wells (ME) 163
Wendell, John 9, 10
Wentworth, Exeter 69
Wentworth, Jonathan (Capt.) 208
Wentworth, Samuel 69
Wesson, James (Col.) 178, 291
West Bangor (NY) 202
West Fairlee (VT) 98
West Indies 99, 103, 121, 127
West Point (NY) 59, 60, 74, 85–6, 96, 99, 102, 115, 120, 137, 152, 156, 162, 165, 167, 172, 173, 177, 178, 179, 180, 182, 191, 192, 197, 200, 204, 206, 208, 210, 212, 214, 215, 220, 221, 225, 228, 234, 235, 237, 241, 246, 251, 253, 258, 262, 266, 267, 271, 272, 275, 276, 281, 284, 285, 286, 289, 290, 296, 301, 304, 305, 306, 307
Western (MA) 285
Westfield (CT) 131
Westminster (VT) 282
Westmoreland (NH) 129, 214, 274
Weston, Hannah 183
Weston, James 183
Weston, Nathan 20, 43, 183
Wheeler, Prime 19, 44, 82, 183
Wheeler, Seth (Lt.) 183, 184
Wheelock, Eleazor 131
Wheelock, Ephraim (Col.) 261
Wheelock, Ithamar 48
Wheelock, James 132, 133
Wheelwright, Daniel (Capt.) 196
Whidden, Samuel 219
Whipple, Catherine 186, 187
Whipple, Cuffee 35, 184, 186, 187
Whipple, Dinah 35, 188
Whipple, Elizabeth 186
Whipple, Esther 35, 186
Whipple, Hannah 186
Whipple, Jeremiah 186
Whipple, Job (Capt.) 241
Whipple, Joseph 219
Whipple, Prince 8, 10, 20, 31, 35–36, 37, 39, 184–87

Whipple, Rebecca 35, 187
Whipple, Robert 186
Whipple, Susannah 186
Whipple, William (Gen.) 20, 36, 37, 56, 126, 184, 185, 186, 188
Whitcomb, Benjamin (Maj.-Col.) 60, 236
White, Archelaus 28, 43, 45, 193, 228, 241–42
White, James 241
White, Levi 64, 307
White, Phillis 242
White, Pomp 188–89
White, Samuel 188–89
White Mountains (NH) 114
White Plains (NY) 55, 131, 299
White Plains, Battle of 45, 199, 204, 208, 212, 226, 233, 242, 283, 298, 308
Whitehall (NY) 233
Whiting, Daniel (Lt. Col.) 289, 301
Whitney, Josiah (Col.) 261
Whittemore, Peggy 260
Whittier, Violet 284
Wier, Samuel 189
Wiggin, Andrew 308
Wiggin, Cocker 243, 308, 311
Wiggin, Jonathan 308
Wiggin, Mark (Capt.) 112
Wigglesworth, Edward (Col.) 221
Wilbraham (MA) 271, 272
Wilkins, Daniel (Capt.) 89
Will, Black 195–96
Will, Black, Jr. 196
Willett, Marinus (Col.) 63
William 313
Williams, Edward (Capt.) 149, 313
Williams, Phebe 225
Williams, Samuel (Col.) 303
Williams River (VT) 304
Williamsburg (VA) 291
Williamstown (VT) 201
Willoughby, Benjamin Burnham 115
Willoughby, Charles Henry 115
Willoughby, Daniel 115
Willoughby, John 115
Willoughby, Luther 115
Willoughby, Luther Perry 115

Wilmington (MA) 206
Wilna (NY) 86
Wilson, Robert 72, 245, 246
Wilson, Titus 48, 189–90. 311
Wilton (NH) 162
Winchester (NH) 304
Windham (NH) 177
Windsor (NY) 41
Wingate, Caesar 25, 63, 95, 190–91
Wingate, Daniel (Judge) 191
Wingate, Joshua (Col.) 56, 80, 86, 111, 118, 125, 135, 139, 140, 146, 163, 168, 177, 188, 230
Winter Hill (MA) 83, 111, 139, 146, 147, 216, 221, 226, 229, 233, 242, 270, 298
Woburn (MA) 256, 289, 303, 305, 306
Wolcott, William 247, 248
Wood, Caesar 19, 31, 63, 95, 191–92
Wood, Cato 263
Wood, Cuff 263
Wood, John (Capt.) 249, 252, 253
Woodman, Dan 142–43, 193, 295
Woodman, John 142
Woodman, Jonathan 142
Woodman, Joshua (Capt.) 90
Woodstock (VT) 33, 254, 301
Woodward, Mary 310
Woodward, Moses 118
Woodward, Peg 133
Woodward, Pompey 243, 244, 308–10
Worcester (MA) 137, 205, 232, 244, 274, 309, 310
Worcester, Noah (the Rev.) 289
Worden, Peter (the Rev.) 247
Worthen, Ezekiel (Capt.) 95
Wrentham (MA) 261, 262
Wright, Nathaniel (Capt.) 307
Wright, Zaccheus (Capt.) 298
Wyman, Isaac (Col.) 125, 130, 135, 137, 148, 156, 194

York Huts 258, 275, 290
York (ME) 175, 196, 224
Yorktown (VA) 36, 61, 153, 292
Yorktown, Battle of 37, 62, 95, 100, 286
Young, Samuel (Capt.) 82, 111

www.ingramcontent.com/pod-product-compliance
Ingram Content Group UK Ltd.
Pitfield, Milton Keynes, MK11 3LW, UK
UKHW031827070125
453106UK00011B/147